SHIP DECORATION

SHIP DECORATION

1630–1780

ANDREW PETERS

Seaforth
PUBLISHING

To my father
For his love and patience

FRONTISPIECE:
The 70-gun ship *Royal Oak*, launched from Plymouth Dockyard in 1741.
(National Maritime Museum L5774-004)

First published in Great Britain in 2013 by
Seaforth Publishing
An imprint of Pen & Sword Books Ltd
47 Church Street, Barnsley
S Yorkshire S70 2AS

www.seaforthpublishing.com
Email info@seaforthpublishing.com

British Library Cataloguing in Publication Data
A CIP data record for this book is available from the British Library

ISBN 978-1-84832-176-2

Typeset and designed by Mousemat Design Limited
Printed and bound in China

Contents

Acknowledgements   6

Foreword by Richard Hunter   7

Glossary   8

Introduction   11

PART I: A Brief History of the East India Companies   13

PART II: Ship Decoration   37

1.   France   38

2.   The Netherlands   65

3.   Great Britain   95

4.   Denmark   143

5.   Sweden   169

PART III: The *Götheborg* Project   211

Bibliography   230

Index   234

⟨⟩ Acknowledgements ⟨⟩

The writing of this book has taken some twelve years, during which time I have been blessed with the unwavering support of faithful friends. It is to them that acknowledgement must first be given; in particular to my long-standing partner Lily, who, with rarely a complaint, has been dragged around practically every maritime museum in Scandinavia, England, France and the Netherlands. For a person who likes her feet placed firmly on dry, unmoving, preferably warm land, she has undertaken countless sea voyages and walked the streets of many frozen cities, taking copious notes and holding camera lenses whilst I photograph yet another interesting ornamental detail. Thanks also go to Mike and Gordon who on our return from foreign lands have endured my endless ramblings with support, encouragement and good English ale.

My involvement in historical ship projects has provided not only a focus for research, but also the ability to work as a professional ship-carver. For this I am eternally grateful to all who have had enough confidence in my ability to offer employment, particularly those of the *Hermione* project in France, and especially the *Götheborg* project in Sweden, where thanks must also go to the woodcarver Ingemar Johansson without whom I may never have been introduced to this most wonderful of countries and the many friends I have made there.

Then there are all those who in the course of their daily work have given their time with a generosity of spirit, allowing the information held deep within their archives to see the light of day. My thanks to all whose names I do not know or have failed to mention, but in particular to the following:

The late Peter Fitzgerald and library staff of the Science Museum London.
Bernard Bryant, store manager of the National Maritime Museum's Kidbrooke store, Blackheath, London.
Mrs Geven and Mr Ab Hoving of the Rijksmuseum Amsterdam.
The staff of the Stadsarchief, Amsterdam.
Mrs Spits and Mr Schokkenbroek of the Scheepvaartmuseum, Amsterdam.
Mr Marcel Croon of the Maritiem Museum, Rotterdam.
The staff of the maritime museums of Brest and Rochefort.
Mr Jacob Seerun of the Orlogsmuseet, Copenhagen.
The staff of the Krigsarkivet, Stockholm.
Mrs Eva Karlsson and Mr W Nittnaus of the Nationalmuseum, Stockholm.
Mr Michael Brandt and Mr Gunvor Vretblad of the Sjöhistoriskmuseet, Stockholm.
The staff of the Stadsmuseum, Göteborg.
Mrs Christina Lönnqvist and staff of the Sjöfartsmuseet, Göteborg.

Foreword

When Andy first set up his woodcarving business in 1990 it was always his intention to learn as much as possible about the traditional art of the ship-carver. Ship-carving offered the craftsman a number of exacting problems, unrelated to other carving trades, such as architectural or domestic, and the physical rigours of a working life at sea held their own unique challenges in design, construction and ultimately execution. In many ways this relationship with the elements would become fundamental in how the art of the ship-carver, unlike any other, became such a specialist field.

During the early 1990s a project began in Sweden to build a full size replica of a Swedish East India Company ship of 1738 to be called the *Götheborg*, authenticity in both materials and construction was seen as paramount. Andy was fortunately commissioned by the building committee to research what the ornamentation of a Swedish East Indiaman from the first half of the eighteenth century would have been like. Once this was established he would have the daunting task of producing single-handed from within the Terra Nova shipyard in Gothenburg the entire carved decoration scheme for this impressive vessel, from its 15-foot high lion figurehead to the intricate stern and gallery carvings, each area meticulously researched in museums and collections throughout Northern Europe. It is this initial research work that forms the foundation of this book, looking as it does into the development of styles of decorative carved work in France, The Netherlands, England, Denmark and Sweden and how this applied to the overall ornamentation of vessels both merchant and naval during a period of just over one hundred and fifty years. This detailed and original research enabled Andy to create a series of outstanding works of art befitting a vessel and project of this kind.

This is the first comprehensive insight by a professional woodcarver into how artist styles and attitudes in Northern Europe applied to the ornamentation of ships. On a more technical basis, Andy describes in detail this fascinating journey from the preliminary design concept, to the final fixing, with all the procedures in between. The techniques and skills of a true craftsman remain the same whether the workshop is in modern-day Oxfordshire, or eighteenth-century France or Sweden: technology holds no substitute for skill and expertise with the chisel and mallet.

Over the past 100 years many traditional trades and skills have been lost, or are in serious decline, replaced by modern materials and techniques. Sadly, modernity has no place or regard for superficial decoration or sentiment, what at one time was seen as commonplace is now looked upon as rare and fascinating. Unfortunately, in this rush for simplicity and minimalism so much has been lost. Looking over old photographs of previous ship-carvers' workshops we see a world that was strong and confident in its future, unaware of the relentless pace of change and how this would effectively transform the working lives of so many master craftsmen.

In this book Andy shows us that, armed with the benefits and advantages of modern technology, plus an in depth knowledge of styles and techniques, it is still possible to create figureheads and other decorative carved work, comparable with what has gone before. The legacy of these craftsmen is still very much alive and working in a workshop in rural Oxfordshire.

Richard Hunter
Figurehead Historian,
Yorkshire 2013
www.figureheads.co.uk

Glossary

with page numbers for definition

Abacus 126
Anthemion 135
Arc soutenant le bossoir 64
Arcading 95, 123
Baluster 126
Bossoir 45, 64
Bouteilles 49
Bowsprit 123
Basket weave 52
Beakhead 123
Brackets 120
Breast rail 10
Bumpkin 123
Cagouille 61, 62
Cat head 9
Cheeks 9
Clew 123
Cove line 122, 129, 138
Cul de lamp 48, 51
Deck transom 10
Diaper pattern 52
Double vase baluster 126
Espagnolette 48, 50
Fashion piece 10
Figures de poupe 51
Fluyt 69
Foot rail 10
Fore mast 179
Frontispiece 109
Girdled 180
Gadrooning 51
Great board 68, 75, 109
Hakkebord 75, 113
Hansings 99
Hackebrädet 174
Hair bracket 120
Hawse piece 99
Head brackets 99
Head rails 120
Head timbers 120
Herm 45
Herpes 64
Hoekman (Quarter piece) 79
Hörnposten (Quarter piece) 199
Jambettes 45
Jottereaux 48
Knight heads 102

Lambrequin 48
Lower cheek 120
Lower counter 10
Lower counter rail 10
Lower deck 10
Lower finishing 10
Lower rail 10
Lunette 75
Main channel 10
Main mast 10
Main rail 10, 120
Margent drop 10
Médaillon aveugle 51
Médaillon du vaisseau 48
Middle rail 10
Mizzen mast 10
Mullions 10, 130
Patera rosette 48
Palmette 52
Pilaster 10
Poop deck 10
Poop drift rail 10
Poop fife rail 10
Projecting walkway 10
Quarter deck 10
Quarterdeck drift rail 10
Quarterdeck fife rail 10
Quarter gallery 10, 69
Roerkoppen 70
Scotia mould 126
Sheer rail 10
slijngerlist 69
Strongmen (*Hoekman*) 69
Tableau de poupe 51, 52
Tafferel 10, 69
Torus mould 126
Trailboard 120
Upper cheek 120
Upper counter 10
Upper counter rail 10
Upper deck 10
Upper head rail 9
Upper finishing 10
Upper tafferel 75
Vase baluster 149, 151
Waist rail 10

An example of how the design of French
ships began to differ from Dutch and English
can be seen in the layout of the head rails,
as illustrated in this sketch.

Cat head

Main rail terminating before the cat head

Upper head rail rises under the cat head

Head timbers (x 3)

Lower rail terminates against bow; similarly
middle rail when used

Upper cheek rising to form hair bracket

Lower cheek

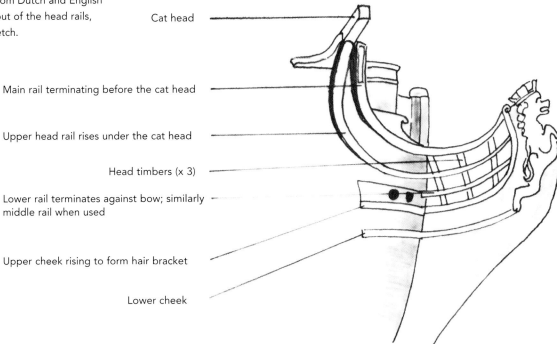

TYPICAL ARRANGEMENT OF HEAD RAILS ON ENGLISH AND DUTCH SHIPS

DEVELOPMENT OF HEAD RAILS ON FRENCH SHIPS

All rails terminate behind the cat head,
with substantial decorative motifs

The head timbers are often depicted as
balusters, with ornate brackets below,
connecting the lower rail back to the
upper cheek

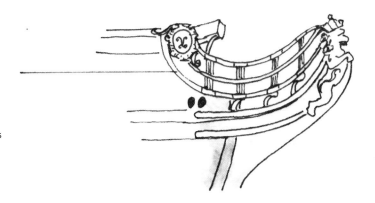

Later French variant, where the lower rail
terminates against the bow

Stern of the East Indiaman *Somerset* of 1738, as depicted
by a model in the National Maritime Museum, Greenwich,
ref no SLR 0452.

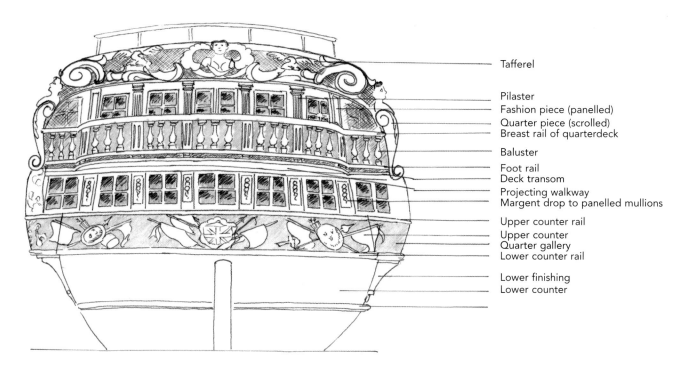

Tafferel

Pilaster
Fashion piece (panelled)
Quarter piece (scrolled)
Breast rail of quarterdeck

Baluster

Foot rail
Deck transom
Projecting walkway
Margent drop to panelled mullions

Upper counter rail
Upper counter
Quarter gallery
Lower counter rail

Lower finishing
Lower counter

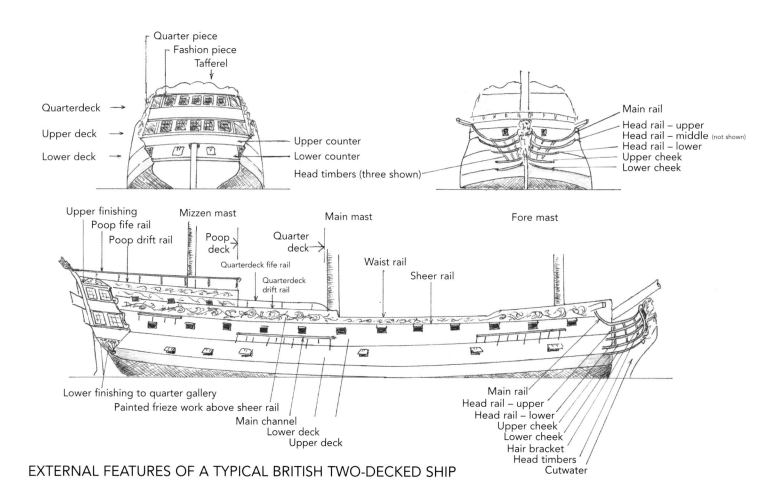

Quarter piece
Fashion piece
Tafferel

Quarterdeck →

Upper deck →

Lower deck →

Upper counter
Lower counter
Head timbers (three shown)

Main rail
Head rail – upper
Head rail – middle (not shown)
Head rail – lower
Upper cheek
Lower cheek

Upper finishing
Poop fife rail
Poop drift rail

Mizzen mast

Main mast

Fore mast

Poop
deck

Quarter
deck →

Quarterdeck fife rail

Quarterdeck
drift rail

Waist rail

Sheer rail

Lower finishing to quarter gallery
Painted frieze work above sheer rail
Main channel
Lower deck
Upper deck

Main rail
Head rail – upper
Head rail – lower
Upper cheek
Lower cheek
Hair bracket
Head timbers
Cutwater

EXTERNAL FEATURES OF A TYPICAL BRITISH TWO-DECKED SHIP

Introduction

Ships

I cannot tell their wonder nor make known
magic that once thrilled me to the bone,
But all men praise some beauty, tell some tale,
vent a high mood which makes the rest seem pale,
Pour their hearts blood to flourish one green leaf,
Follow some Helen for her gift of grief,
And fail in what they mean, what'er they do;
You should have seen, man cannot tell to you
The beauty of the ships of that my city.
That beauty now is spoiled by the sea's pity:

For one may haunt the pier a score of times
Hearing St Nicholas' bells ring out the chimes,
Yet never see those proud ones swaying home,
With mainyards backed and bows a cream of foam,
Those bows so lovely-curving, cut so fine
Those coulters of the many-bubbled brine,
As once, long since, when all the docks were filled
With that sea beauty man has ceased to build.

So wrote John Masefield in one of his many poems reflecting on a way of life which, although harsh in some respects, also provided a sense of well being and contentment – imagine producing in your daily work an object that not only serves its economic and practical function, but fills hearts and minds with awe and wonder. Masefield reflects upon a time when beauty of form went hand in hand with function, a time when machinery did not have the power to plough an obstinate path through sea or land, but relied on human skill, giving each and every one purpose and pride in mastering their trade. We live in a world of increased specialisation, where the end-user is so divorced from the initial concept, and the complexity in design and construction of our tools so far beyond the understanding of the user, that often we are left numbed in a cocoon of separation.

When Masefield looked into the empty docks, we can be sure it was not the sight of the ships alone that he missed, but the magic of a life that once thrilled him to the bone, a magic that is only experienced through knowing the wind, and knowing the waves and mastering whatever skill is required to become part of them.

He may be heartened to know that the docks are not totally empty of tall ships, nor have we totally stopped building them. Fortunately in the last days of commercial sail sufficient men held on to the belief that it was important to preserve the traditions of building and sailing such ships before generations of knowledge were lost.

It was to this purpose that I set up Maritima Woodcarving in 1990 in an effort to keep alive the art of the ship-carver, gathering together any information still available and turning this into true understanding, through the practical experience of producing work for ships that actually put to sea, and by sailing on them to note how they stand the test of time in the most punishing of environments. It is from this practical viewpoint that the book is written, rather than from a purely academic study of the subject.

By far the greatest insight into understanding period styles and how to replicate them comes from restoring original works of art. Through this physical touch with history, one learns how individual craftsmen created the shapes that defined the character of their work. In replicating their depth of cut and sharpness of detail, the body learns to adopt the same sense of movement, appreciating their quality of touch and efficiency of action, bringing to life the qualities inherent in an original piece of work, allowing the new and old to become one.

The naval architect Fredrik af Chapman wrote in 1799 of 'the need for ornament to express its purpose in a manner that retains the beautiful contours of the ships lines.' To achieve this, ship-carvers worked alongside shipwrights, who often prepared the carving blocks. The need also arises to create art forms that are not vulnerable to damage through the manoeuvres of anchoring, sailing, berthing, and so forth, or that hinder the practicalities of carrying out such operations.

From the 1600s through to the mid-1800s every naval dockyard and major merchant shipyard would have employed carvers to carry out the wealth of ornamentation that adorned their ships. So why did the world's navies and merchant companies spend so much of a ship's building cost on decoration?

There is a natural desire among all craftsmen in mastering their craft to produce objects that perform the practical aspect of their given function. This process of refinement naturally creates objects that rise above a utilitarian existence, to become works of art in their own right. Such beauty of form sings out to be further adorned with artistic embellishment, as an act of pride in one's work and an appreciation of the importance of aesthetics – values that hold the key to restoring a little of the magic that once thrilled Masefield to the bone.

The period covered by this book looks back to a time when the worth of aesthetics was appreciated on a national level, when decorative form and function were inseparable. Empire-building was of course a high priority for established nations, bringing with it the expansion of their navies to quell resistance or defend their exploits. The primary function for a ship of war is to present military power, and through continued development it takes the most efficient form to achieve this. When decoration was applied to such a vessel, it was for the purpose of presenting an overwhelming sense of indomitable strength. Imagery taken from biblical texts or ancient myths and legends provided heroic figures that not only emphasised their power, but through the context of the composition established the political and theological ideology that each nation wished to uphold (or impose). Such imagery is immediate and can be understood even by those who speak a different tongue!

The standard of craftsmanship and degree of artistic mastery was also important, as it served to display the cultural development if its people, and it is this aspect that was of prime importance in the decoration of its merchant ships, where the picture it wished to portray to its trading partners was one of wealth, dependability and a sense of social conduct that would be mutually conducive to trade.

The discovery of new lands and cultures allowed a joyous explosion of artistic endeavour to take place, embracing images inspired by foreign travel. The inclusion of elephants, palms, exotic fruits, and the like in the decorative composition of merchant ships returning to their trading partners would show visibly the impact of such trade, and highlights the role that the East India companies played in the development of the decorative arts, not only through the goods that were imported to the countries of their home ports, but in the wealth that was created to provide patrons who subsequently allowed artists to set the course for the evolution of the decorative arts.

In focusing on the five principal countries that engaged in trade with the East Indies this book attempts to chart the developing styles of ornamentation that evolved in their naval and merchant ships. A brief look into the establishment of their merchant ventures provides a useful insight into the creation of wealth that allowed such artistic endeavours to take place.

PART I

A Brief History of the East India Companies

Consider for a moment the colossal impact that international trade has made in every aspect of life: how the simple exchange of material goods can open the hearts and minds of one society to the ideas, culture and artistic achievements of another. Art and trade have therefore always been inextricably linked.

Since the earliest of times man has decorated even the most utilitarian of objects. The ability to express and therefore share the emotional uplift that such expressions of beauty and harmony bring would seem to be a basic need, and since every civilisation has endeavoured to formulate these uniting principles, this need is universal. When a society struggles to maintain the basic necessities of food and shelter, the mind has little encouragement or energy to pursue the advancement of higher ideals, but fair trade creates the wealth to free society from such bondage.

The spare time enabled by such wealth can of course be filled in a variety of ways, not all of which hold the benefit of mankind as its guiding principle, with the greed of one inevitably leading to the deprivation of another. The ancient trade route known as the Silk Road, extending from China out into central Asia initially existed to aid military expansion, but by the first century BC it had become an established highway of commerce.

Cities of incredible wealth sprang from harsh desert landscapes along a road that linked the peoples and traditions of the East with those of Europe, allowing not only the movement of goods but the exchange of cultures and knowledge. Eventually the societies that rose to create these amazing places would dwindle and die as sea routes replaced them, leaving the cities to crumble back into sand.

The Tang dynasty, which ruled China from 618 AD, established internal stability and an economic climate in which the road reached its golden age, by which time silk accounted for 30 per cent of the merchants' goods. Silk reached Rome as early as 1 AD, becoming so popular that it was literally worth its weight in gold. The year 632 in the Christian calendar marked the death of the prophet Mohammed and the rapid expansion of Islam, which by 712 AD stretched from parts of India and Afghanistan in the east to North Africa and Spain in the west. Traditional trade routes between the Christian and Muslim worlds were then disrupted, to the detriment of western European economies.

It is interesting to consider at this point what was happening in Scandinavia, the eighth century seeing a massive expansion within the Viking world as they embarked on their voyages of exploration. The Belgian historian Henri Pirenne contends that these voyages were not just acts of pillage, but that archaeological finds in Denmark and Sweden show they were trading with Constantinople (which the Vikings called Miklagård) and Muslim lands on the Black and Caspian Seas. Hoards of Arabic coins have been found in Sweden with dates from this period to the mid-eleventh century. However, a greater mystery than the origin of the Viking expansion is its abrupt demise, which came to a halt in the eleventh century.

The Abbasid rulers of the Muslim world had allowed the passage of Christian pilgrims, but in 1040 they were displaced by the Seljuk Turks, invaders from central Asia. All roads across Asia Minor were then closed to Western Christians attempting to reach the Holy Land. This gave rise

The Silk Road

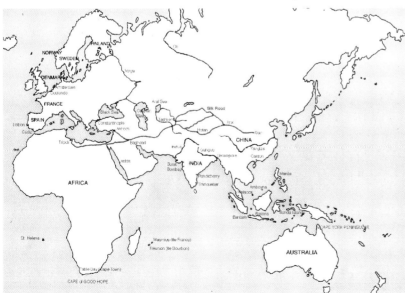

to the first crusade when Pope Urban II called upon Christians to help liberate the Holy Lands from the Muslim Turks, who had already overrun most of the Byzantine Empire and were within striking distance of its capital Constantinople. The first crusade, which set out in 1095, was successful in the recapture of Jerusalem and allowed the trade routes to flow once more. This effectively undermined the Vikings' position and coincides with the period of their rapid decline.

Throughout the Middle Ages demand for Asian goods grew, especially for the spices that made the diet of better-off Europeans palatable. That eventually inspired the search for sea routes free from the political turmoil, dangers and high costs of overland transport, sowing the seeds for a new era where dominion of the seas would give a nation the power and stability to develop trade. The formation of the East India companies transformed the wealth of those that bore the enterprise and hardships to establish them. Not surprisingly, once established they fought hard to maintain their positions. Their merchant ships were heavily armed, their sea charts and business dealings surrounded in secrecy, and their diplomatic powers immense.

In the 1500s Spain and Portugal had command of the seas, and the Catholic world endorsed their control by a Papal decree issued in 1493, in effect giving Spain dominion of the New World and trade with the East to Portugal. Their advances in navigation, mapmaking and ship design ensured their monopoly of the trade routes and their riches. To this end, the Portuguese king controlled the sale of spices by issuing licences to merchants who could then secure cargoes, but had to deliver them to Lisbon where they were purchased by the crown at a fixed price. Authorised merchants could then buy from the crown and sell them on to the open market.

By capturing Spanish ships laden with gold and silver exploited from the New World, Francis Drake and his fellow 'privateers' found a more expedient method of obtaining cargoes, but it also began to undermine the Spanish position as masters of the seas. At the same time the Dutch sought to free themselves from the Spanish empire and the Catholic Church. Fuelled by stories of sailors captured and subjected to the tortures of the Spanish Inquisition, thousands of volunteers crossed the Channel to aid the Dutch and Dutch privateers found shelter in English ports in their resolve to break Spanish hegemony. In 1592 the Dutch cartographer Lucas Janszoon Waghenaer published his second sea atlas, which included information obtained by Dutch sailors who had crewed on Portuguese ships, which also gave them a valuable insight into the procedures of conducting trade with Asia. The Dutch already had an established trade with the Baltic, and this

An oil painting by Andries van Eertvelt depicts the excitement surrounding the arrival of the second Dutch expedition to the East Indies at Amsterdam on 19 July 1599. This was the first commercially successful voyage and led to the establishment of the VOC. The painting shows the *Overijssel*, *Vriesland*, *Mauritius* and *Hollandia* in the middle distance with numerous smaller vessels surrounding them. (National Maritime Museum BHC0748)

gave their merchants the funding to embark on their own expedition to the East.

When the first Dutch merchant fleet set out in 1595, the voyage was fraught with difficulties: of the 240 crew that set out, only 87 survived and one of the ships had to be abandoned through lack of manpower. When the remaining ships finally returned in 1597, the cost of the undertaking left little profit for its investors, but it had been successful in showing that the Portuguese monopoly could be broken and it provided the confidence for further investment. When the next fleet returned [...] became appar[...] there were eig[...] the lucrative t[...]

In Englan[d ...] granted Fran[cis ...] circumnavig[...] completed du[...] down to the [...] by the disru[...] securing of [...] capture of [...] powers' mor[...] made some [...] was success[...] gain any re[...] voyage did [...] English ship[s ...] of gold, sil[ver ...] half a milli[on ...]

The ou[tcome ...] already su[...] refusal of h[...] arrest, but [...] made him [...] Elizabeth [...] return wit[h ...] presented [...] her crow[n ...] burgeoned [...] by Ralph [...] gathering [...] geared up [...] had doub[...] the Atlant[ic ...] with an u[...] defiance [...] and his a[...]

The r[...] to set sai[l ...] fleet and [...]

set sail. His attack on three ports with fireships completed what he termed his 'singeing of the King of Spain's beard'. During the attack on Cadiz in 1587 he captured the Portuguese carrack *San Felipe*. She had recently returned from the East Indies and, as luck would have it, on board were not only the charts of her voyage but the even more valuable accounts of her trade with the East.

When Fitch returned in 1590 he found no shortage of merchants willing to fund a further expedition and in 1591 three ships led by James Lancaster set out on what proved to be a disastrous voyage. By the time they reached Table Bay at the Cape of Good Hope, scurvy had depleted the crew to such an extent that insufficient remained alive to man the three ships. The *Merchant Royal* was therefore sent home with the minimum working crew and the sick or dying men. The two remaining ships were hit by a storm off the coast of Mozambique resulting in the total loss of the *Penelope* and her crew. The *Edward Bonaventure* eventually reached the East Indies, by which time her crew of 97 had been reduced to 34.

Unable to secure any trading contracts, they resorted instead to raiding Portuguese ships in an attempt to return home with something. The *Bonaventure* reached the island of St Helena in 1593 where she reprovisioned before setting sail for the final leg home. When further storms drove her off course, Lancaster attempted to reach Trinidad and succeeded in landing at a small island near Puerto Rico. Here the ship was mysteriously cut adrift with only five men and a boy onboard, and she was presumed lost at sea. Lancaster and a remaining handful of men finally reached England on 24 May 1594 to join those that had survived from the *Merchant Royal* which had miraculously made the journey home. The loss of life, ships and investors' money dampened even the most enthusiastic of merchants' ambitions and it was not until 1599 that news of Dutch success inspired a group of 101 London merchants to raise a joint investment of £30,000 to fund a further voyage to the East Indies.

English and Dutch East India Companies

In 1600 Queen Elizabeth I granted the newly formed Honourable East India Company its Royal Charter. The early HEIC fleets made profitable voyages but soon met with fierce opposition from

Flag of the Honourable East India Company. Before the red, white and blue national ensigns made their appearance around 1630, all English ships are generally thought to have flown striped ensigns with a St George's cross in the upper left canton. This tradition appears to have been continued by the East India Company's ships. When a royal proclamation of 1674 authorised the red ensign for merchant ships, the East India Company was restricted to using their ensigns in eastern waters and beyond the island of St Helena in the Atlantic. Various paintings of the period depict the ensign as having either nine, eleven or thirteen stripes.

the Dutch whose numerous small companies were already under strain from competition amongst themselves. The States General ordered consolidation of the Dutch companies and in 1602 the United Dutch East India Company, known as the Vereenigde Oost-Indische Compagnie or VOC, was founded.

The input of capital from individual investors and the scale of stock on the Amsterdam exchange gave the company immense financial power. It was also granted the exclusive trading rights from the Cape of Good Hope to the Straits of Magellan. To further enforce their monopoly on trade, they were also granted the power to negotiate treaties or wage war with local rulers by whatever means were necessary to secure cargoes.

At the height of its power in the mid-1600s the VOC had a fleet of 150 armed merchant men, 40 warships and an army of 16,000 soldiers to ensure the suppression of potential competition and to drive the Portuguese out of their established trading settlements, such as their stronghold of Malacca, which fell to the Dutch in 1641, giving them control of the eastern trade routes.

The wealth that poured into Amsterdam led to the city's rapid expansion and in 1661 the VOC started constructing a massive new shipyard, where three ships could be under construction at one time. The thousand-strong workforce could build a ship in 18 months, and nearly 1500 ships were built for the VOC over its 200 years of trading. There were carpenters' workshops, kilns for bending timbers, forges for the iron fixings and anchors, sailmakers' lofts, ropewalks and warehouses to store the various provisions to equip the ships for the voyage to South Africa, their principal base on the route eastwards. By 1650 they had established a fort in Table Bay and the settlement that grew up around it served as an essential haven where ships could take on fresh supplies of food and water, repairs could be undertaken, and crews recover from sickness and ordeals of the journey. From here most ships continued to Batavia on West Java (now Jakarta, Indonesia), which became the VOC headquarters in the East.

The island of St Helena also served as a welcome stopping point where ships could take on supplies of fresh water. First discovered by the Spanish in 1502 it became known to the British in 1588 when the English navigator Captain Thomas Cavendish of the *Desire* landed there during his world voyage. It was used by many countries before the Dutch annexed the island in 1633, but it was occupied by forces of the English East India Company in 1672, who took total control after a final skirmish with the

Flag of the Dutch East India Company (Vereenigde Oostindische Compagnie, or VOC). The upper stripe of the Dutch flag was originally orange but between 1630 to 1660 this gradually changed to red with the East India Company inserting its VOC monogram in the central stripe. Contemporary paintings also show the flag with the initial of the individual chamber of commerce above the VOC, such as A for Amsterdam, D for Delft, etc.

Duyfken, a yacht that accompanied *Hollandia*, *Mauritius* and *Amsterdam* on the first Dutch expedition to the East Indies in 1595. *Duyfken* was used on further voyages of exploration and in 1606 was the first recorded European ship to chart part of the Australian coast line, with her crew landing on the Cape York Peninsula.

Dutch in 1673. The island was later to become famous as the place of exile for Napoleon following his defeat at Waterloo in 1815, where he remained until his death in 1821. The island, which still remains under British rule, is one of the remotest inhabited islands in the world; measuring just ten miles by six, it lies 1100 miles off the coast of Africa with a further 2200 miles of ocean before reaching Brazil. A large part of the island's current population of 5000 are still direct descendants of British and Indian soldiers of the East India Company, which continued to control the island until the British government took over in 1834.

The fledgling Honourable East India Company did not have the financial backing or government support to defend its fleet or trading stations against the Dutch, and consequently failed to gain a lasting foothold in the Spice Islands during those early years. This often led to frustrating situations where local tribes were willing to assign all trading rights to the English in return for their protection against the exactions of the Dutch and Portuguese. Control of the Banda Islands is an example where attempts to safeguard the local inhabitants, who had made agreements with the English, led to much bloodshed through England's failure to supply sufficient force to defend the islands from the Dutch. By 1618 England's only remaining spice island of Pulo Ron was under siege by the Dutch, who succeeded in taking possession of it together with the neighbouring island of Lantore in 1619. The final blow came when the company

factors at Amboyna were massacred by the Dutch in 1623.

The English turned their attention instead to India, where they had already been successful in engagements with the Portuguese, driving them out of the west coast. By 1615 an expedition led by Captain William Hawkins and the ambassador from the court of King James I, Sir Thomas Roe, had reached Surat, where they secured an audience with the Mogul Emperor Jehangir. Having already established a reputation of being more powerful than the Portuguese, the party found favour with the Emperor by offering to secure safe passage for pilgrims travelling to Jedda. The alcoholic Emperor was so impressed with the drinking abilities of Captain Hawkins that he made him commander of his cavalry, bringing the encounter to a successful conclusion. The resulting freedom to travel with greater safety permitted renewed contact with the ancient trade routes, allowing access to silk, which was now being produced in the Persian Empire. With permission having been granted for the East India Company to trade, silk goods now found their way to the British station at Surat, which together with Indian cloth was becoming as important a commodity as spices. In 1629 the company was granted permission to build their headquarters at Surat, creating a foothold that would within a century lead to their eventual dominance of the Mogul Empire and subsequent exploitation of its resources.

The growing wealth of the HEIC allowed greater provision for military force and by the end of the 1600s the Dutch had been driven from mainland India and Ceylon. For the Dutch, holding on to their monopoly of the Spice Islands became an ever-increasing burden and, combined with their inability to trade with the increasingly important Indian market, this forced them to trade with China. But here too the squeeze was on. England had established a Chinese trading post in 1699, the year China opened its borders to foreign trade, and by 1715 had established a factory at Canton. Now it was the Dutch who were the newcomers; they were viewed with suspicion by the Chinese, making trade difficult. Back in home waters, war with France had taken a heavy toll on Dutch resources and the economy was in decline. Disasters added to this: four Dutch ships were lost on the way to Canton in 1781 with a further four between 1784 and 1790. By 1799 what was once the largest company in the world had been forced into bankruptcy.

The British East Indiaman *Northumberland* off Jamestown, St Helena. The ship was built in 1780 and this oil painting by Thomas Luny follows a common convention in portraying the ship in two positions. (National Maritime Museum BHC3519)

The huge wealth brought to Holland by the VOC was its lasting legacy, creating a state where the arts and culture flourished. Other nations were naturally eager to take the initially vast financial risks to enter the arena, but the eventual rule of India and growth in trade with China ensured England's success. By the mid-nineteenth century one-fifth of the world's population was under the authority of the East India Company, stretching across India, Burma, Singapore and Hong Kong.

The immense power it wielded became an increasing embarrassment to the British government, reaching a climax with the Indian rebellion of 1857. The crown took control of the Company's army and its Marine became the Indian navy. Complete control reverted to the crown in 1874 when their charter expired.

Whereas the ships of the Dutch VOC were designed and constructed in their own yard, the English East India Company in its earliest years

An anonymous oil painting of the HEIC shipyard at Deptford around 1660, showing its main facilities, the dock and two slipways. The ships fly the striped ensign of the Company but their general resemblance to warships in design and decoration is evident. (National Maritime Museum BHC1873)

The *Java* of 1815, the last East Indiaman, seen in her final incarnation as a coal hulk. (Author's collection)

Flag of the Danish East India Company (DAC).

relied on the spare capacity of warship-building yards. As demand for East India ships grew, the capacity of these yards proved insufficient. Around 1608 William Burrell, who held the post of Surveyor General for the East India Company, acquired land adjacent to the Navy yard at Deptford to build Company ships. Further land was purchased at Blackwall in 1618 where ships were built until 1650 when the yard was sold, although spare capacity still allowed the building of Company ships. In 1806 the area was enlarged to become the East India docks.

By the 1700s ships were being built at a number of commercial yards such as Barnard's in Ipswich and Buckler's Hard on the Beaulieu River, both of which also built ships for the Royal Navy. With the establishment of the Company in India, shipyards were established at Bombay and Calcutta. The tropical hardwoods used in their construction, such as teak, ensured the longevity of these vessels, an example being the *Java*. Her building was financed by the father of a young girl who had been travelling on an East India Company ship to China. During a stop at Java a party of passengers were put ashore for a picnic, but the convivial gathering soon met with disaster, when they were attacked by a group of natives who carried the girl away. An officer of the Indiaman led an armed party who successfully rescued the girl. Her father in gratitude built and equipped the ship as a gift to the officer. The *Java* was launched from the yard at Calcutta in 1813 and is recorded as having entered the service of the East India Company in 1824. For a number of years from 1841 the British Government chartered the ship as a troop carrier. Around 1856 she was purchased by Mr W H Smith of the firm Smith, Imossi & Co of Gibraltar, where she remained for over 80 years as a coal hulk. The picture shows her in 1939 shortly before being towed to the breaker's yard. Hundreds of people turned out to watch the departure of what was the last sail-powered East Indiaman afloat (note the wind powered pump rising from the main deck).

Footnote: While this book includes lists of Danish, French and Swedish East Indiamen, those of the Dutch and English companies are too numerous to be included in a book of this scope. The website www.historici.nl/Onderzoek/Projecten/DAS/voyages lists 8194 Dutch voyages between 1595 and 1795. Ships of the HEIC are listed in Rowan Hackman's *Ships of the East India Company*, published by the World Ship Society (Gravesend 2001).

Danish East India Company

The year 1616 saw the formation of the Danish East India Company and the establishment of their colony at Frederiksnagar (modern day Serampore), upstream from Calcutta on the Hugli river. Initially this became famous for its Protestant mission rather than a centre of commerce and it was not until 1620 that a successful trading post was established, by leasing land from the Nayak of Tanjore at Tranquebar on the Coromandel coast of India. The expedition was headed by Roland Crappé, a Dutchman who had been in the service of the VOC. He became governor at Tranquebar, establishing a fortress and factory facilities in preparation for trade. The venture was, however, beset with difficulties. Attacks from the Dutch and Portuguese were made no easier by numerous shipwrecks, continual internal disagreements and an inability to raise sufficient funds, which left little scope for success. Within its 34-year existence only seven ships returned to Copenhagen, and with cargoes that brought little profit.

By 1625 the Danes had effectively ceased trading for themselves, acting instead as carriers of Portuguese goods, which proved to be more profitable. The Danes established a factory at Masulipatnam, but problems within the company continued with the misappropriation of funds. Crappé negotiated with the Dutch to provide soldiers to defend the fort at Tranquebar, and in 1637 returned to Denmark, leaving the Dutchman Behrendt Pessart to govern the fortress. His subsequent mismanagement of affairs led to rising debts with his trading partners who eventually took him hostage until the debts were paid.

The year 1625 also marked Denmark's entry into the Thirty Years War, in which it suffered major defeats. In 1637 King Christian IV (ruled 1588-1648), in an effort to raise funds, sent Hans Trægaard on an expedition to negotiate trade with China, Japan and Siam (modern Thailand). He succeeded in establishing some trade with Canton but such success had little bearing on the troubles back home, where Jutland had been occupied by the Catholic League and large areas of Danish-held territory were relinquished to Sweden. Due to the company directors' continual struggle to raise funds during this period, the next voyage did not set out from Denmark until 1639, reaching Tranquebar after prolonged delays in 1640. On board was the colony's new governor Willum

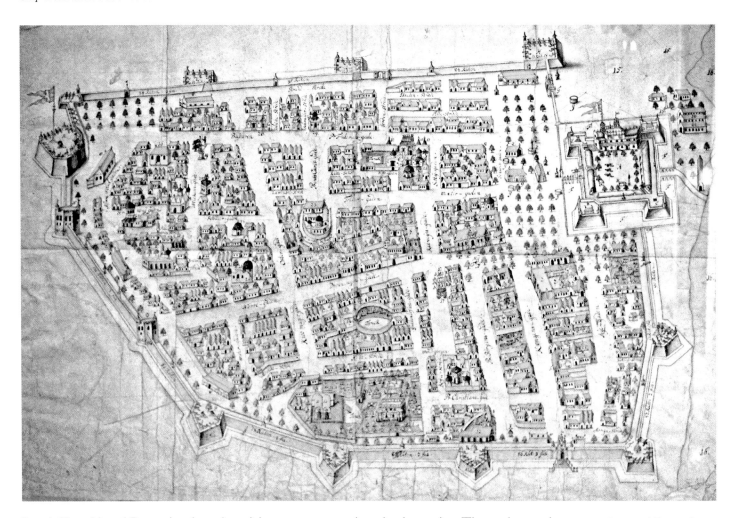

Leyel. He achieved Pessart's release by seizing one of his captor's ships as bargaining power for his exchange.

Leyel found that trading conditions were not particularly propitious due to his predecessor's misdemeanours, and further disputes with the Mogul traders prompted a return to their policy of raiding the Bengal fleets. When a peace treaty was signed in 1648, effectively putting a halt to the privateering from Tranquebar, the men mutinied, imprisoning Leyel. Povl Hansen Korsør, who led the uprising, took command and the colony resumed the life of their privateering exploits. Leyel was put on a passing ship and eventually found his way back to Denmark.

When Korsør died in 1655 the remaining Danes chose Eskild Andersen Kongsbakke as their leader. He soon proved himself as having greater loyalty to his country than his predecessors (who after all were of Dutch origin) for he made great efforts in fortifying the defences of the colony as it came under the threat of attack by the Nayak of Tanjore, who was attempting to extract increased rent by force. Kongsbakke's efforts ensured its retention under the Danish flag, albeit dependent

on continued privateering. The settlement became a refuge for people of all nationalities fleeing the constant troubles in the region. A map from the period shows that Muslim, Buddhist and Catholic places of worship coexisted within the fortified settlement, whose inhabitants continued to strengthen its defences. The turmoil of war back home ensured that Tranquebar became a forgotten backwater where Kongsbakke, as the number of mutineers slowly dwindled, became the last remaining Dane.

The defeats endured by Denmark against Sweden had led to a lack of confidence in the government, particularly amongst the growing merchant class, who suffered through the economic downturn and loss of foreign trade. At this time the decisions of the Danish monarchy were largely controlled by the powerful nobility. King Frederick III (ruled 1648-1670) took advantage of their unpopularity by overruling their authority and assuming control. In 1648 he formed an alliance with the Netherlands, and this combined force succeeded in regaining some territory from Sweden, providing tax levies that gave the country a sense of restored confidence

A map of Tranquebar dating from 1690. (Author's collection reproduced by courtesy of the Danish Maritime Museum)

under his leadership; this position allowed him to make the monarchy hereditary and in 1661 his power became absolute. He appointed his administrators in much the same way as the French Sun King, but perhaps through a remembrance of the uprising which placed him in power, he endeavoured to hold the respect of his subjects.

With mounting debts the Danish East India Company had already been dissolved in 1650, the largest creditor after the king being Poul Klingenberg. When reports of Kongsbakke's survival finally reached the king in 1668, Klingenberg was offered the *Agathe* (renamed the *Færø*) to mount an expedition in an effort to recoup their losses. The *Agathe*, a 54-gun ship built in 1653, was one of many Dutch ships loaned to Denmark during their alliance, and was brought into the Danish fleet under Admiral Cort Adelere along with eight other ships during his visit to the Netherlands in the same year. The ship set out on 20 October 1668 under the command of the admiral's son, Captain Silvert Adelere, and arrived at Tranquebar on 31 May 1669, with sufficient soldiers to ensure its defence and instructions to secure new trading agreements. Kongsbakke's misdemeanours were overlooked, but his marriage to a native woman precluded his return to Denmark. He died in 1674 amidst the native people who had enabled him to hold the colony without Danish help for fourteen years.

In 1670 an Octori (charter) was granted to form a new East India Company, which focused its attention on trade with China and enlarging the commercial role of Serampore by establishing a fort and factory named Dannemarnagore on the banks of the Hugli river in 1698. The company traded very successfully until the Great Northern War (1700-21) caused a drain on capital and resources. Dannemarnagore was abandoned in 1714 and by 1729 the shareholders were forced to dissolve the second company. Its ships and other assets were auctioned, raising sufficient funds to clear debts and retain a balance that would eventually be used to form another new company.

The Danes attempted to form a separate company based at Altona in April of 1728, with the intention to supply the German market. The port of Altona (now a suburb of Hamburg), together with Glückstad, formed part of the Danish-held territory of Slesvig-Holstein and already served as useful distribution points for the wares of the Danish whaling fleet into Germany, but the establishment of an East India company met with Austrian opposition. Their own East India business, the Oostende Company based in the Austrian Netherlands, had been forced to close a year earlier under pressure from the Dutch and British, and the proposed involvement of individuals from the Austrian company in the new Danish venture would have breached their agreements (see later section on the Oostende Company).

The convoluted undertakings of the Danes did not end there: in 1731 Danish ships were once again seen trading in Canton, and on 12 April 1732 the company was re-founded as the Danske Asiatische

The former Danish port of Glückstad on the banks of the Elbe. (Author's collection)

Dock and warehousing of the Danske Asiatisk Company forming their headquarters at Christianshavn, Copenhagen. (Author's collection)

Compagnie. They were granted a 40-year charter to trade with all countries east of the Cape of Good Hope and reinstated their warehouses at Canton. New headquarters were built at Christianshavn in Copenhagen, providing warehousing and shipbuilding facilities. Their first ship, named *Kongen af Danmark*, was launched from the yard in 1737. She proved to be very successful, remaining in service until 1803, by which time she had completed seven voyages to China.

By 1748 the success of the company was such that a substantial new warehouse was built at Christianshavn. This area of the city saw massive redevelopments at this time, its buildings displaying changing fashions in ornamentation, that will be looked at in a later chapter as they form an interesting correlation with ship ornamentation of the period.

Between 1732 and 1753 the DAC sent 60 ships to Asia, 32 to China and the remaining 28 to other destinations in the East Indies. Of these 19 made the return trip from the Indies and 24 from China, the remainder being lost at sea or stranded. Their factory at Canton comprised seven buildings, becoming the third largest after the British and Dutch, despite the lack of what could be considered as any ordered system of administration. Trading also commenced from Frederiksnagar (Serampore) in 1755 and continued from there and Canton until 1772, when the company lost its monopoly. Despite the competition from private investors, the DAC continued to send 40 ships to China and 41 to the East Indies between 1772 and 1791.

In 1801 the Danish fleet at Copenhagen suffered near-total destruction by the British, who feared that the Northern states were forming an alliance to control the Baltic trade. This would have had a detrimental effect on the supply of crucial naval stores for the British, and a significant advantage to the French. Denmark's allegiance to France during the Napoleonic wars led to a further attack on the city in 1807, when its remaining warships were removed to English ports and control was taken of its colonies. In 1800 the DAC had purchased six ships from the navy, which were decommissioned to trade as merchantmen, thus avoiding their confiscation. However, many DAC ships were also seized, along with their cargo, on their return journey to Denmark. The effect on trade was dramatic. In 1803 only eight ships set sail, five to the East Indies and three (*Norge, Arveprinsessen* and *Louisa Augusta*) to China. Of these, the *Arveprinsessen* was impounded on her return by the British, who rearmed her as a defence vessel at Copenhagen, together with *Kronprinsessen*. The *Norge* was formerly the Dutch vessel *Cromhout*, which had been taken by the British and sold to the DAC in 1798. Following her return to Copenhagen she voyaged again to China, but was seized by the British off the Cape in 1808. *Louisa Augusta* (ex-naval *Slesvig*) appears not to have made any further voyages for the DAC. Only two ships set sail in 1807 and four in 1808. In the same year *Arveprinsessen* and *Kronprinsessen* were disarmed and returned to the DAC.

DAC monogram from a coin minted at Tranquebar, 1730-1746.

With the defeat of Napoleon in 1815, control of the colonies was returned to Denmark and the ship *Antoinette* was sent to Canton on what was a private initiative to get Danish shipping back at sea. Having re-established trade links, she was followed in 1817 by *Norden*, which returned with a small cargo. In 1819 the DAC ship *Christianshavn* set sail for the company's factory at Canton. The voyage was a success and led to continued trade for the DAC. By this time Tranquebar had once more become something of a forgotten backwater, its community consisting of Danish officials who, having lived a life of colonial privilege, had no desire to return to a changing Europe. With most of India under their rule, in 1845 the British purchased Tranquebar and Serampore. A year earlier Denmark had allowed free trade to the East, ending the Asiatische Compagnie's monopoly.

Ships of the Danske Asiatische Compagnie

(As identified by the author which does not represent the complete fleet. Dates indicate commencement of voyage to the East Indies or China where known, or date when ship entered service)

First Charter, 1616-1650

Christian	1618	
Christianshavn	1639	Carried Willem Leyel as new Governor of Tranquebar
Færø (ex-Agatha)	1668	
Kjøbenhavn	1618	
Øresund	1617	Jacht sailed to Tranquebar
Perlen	1623	At Tranquebar 1624
Saayer	1644	
Solen	1639	
St Jacob	1636	
St Anne	1636	

Second Charter, 1670-1729

Christianus Quintus	1690	Caught fire at DAC Yard Christianhavn, 27 May
Dansborg	1678	Stranded in Kattegat
Den unge Jomfru	1725	
Fortuna	1673	
Færø	1670	
Gyldenløve	1710	
Haabet	1673	
Mageløs	1673	
Oldenborg	1672	Repaired at Bantam 1673, set out on another voyage 1677
Pheønix	1681	
Prins Wilhelm	1702, 1704	
Sophie Hedwig	1698	

Third Charter, 1732-1772

Anna Sophia	1750	
Croon Princen	1737	Caught in storm 1737
Christiansborg Slot	1742, 1745, 1750	
Cron Printz Christian	1730	
Disco	1742	
Dronning Juliane Maria	1753, 1761, 1771	
Dronning Sophia Magdalen	1753	
Dronning Sophia Magdalen	1762, 1764, 1766, 1768, 1770, 1772 Built 1761-2 for DAC	
Dronningen af Danmark	1737, 1742, 1751	
Fredensborg Slot	1764	
Fyen	1745	Navy ship launched 1736, purchased by DAC 1745

Grev Laurvig	1732	
Grev Moltke	1759	Built Sandefjord 1756
Kongen	1751	
Kongen af Danmark	1737, 1742, 1748	
Kronprinsessen	1744, 1751	
Kronprinsen af Danmark	1742	
Kronprinsessen af Danmark	1758	Ex-*Prince Conti* purchased London 1758
Kronprins Christian	1730	Ex-*Warberg* captured from Swedes. First DAC ship to sail direct to China
Prins Frederich	1760	Purchased Stockholm 1760, stranded Göteborg 1769
Princessen Louise	1751	
Rirernes Ønske	1762	Decoration by Møllerup
Sleswig	1733	Navy ship launched 1725, purchased DAC 1733
Warberg	1730	Built Karlskrona C Sheldon 1699, captured Marstrand 1719, handed to DAC 1730 (see *Kronprins Christian* above)

Fourth Charter, 1777-1785

Antionette	1815	Private venture
Arveprinsen	1803, 1803	Seized by British 1808 and rearmed at Copenhagen, returned 1810
Buttelever	1790	Provision ship
Casque	1806	Dutch, on loan as guard ship
Charlotte Amalia	1784	
Christianshavn	1800, 1807, 1819, 1826, 1833	Transferred to DAC 1800, returned to navy 1834
Danmark	1782	
Disco	1780, 1782, 1784	At Tranquebar, built 1777 Henrik Gerner
Dronning Juliane Maria	1777, 1780, 1783, 1789	Caught fire at sea and lost August 1789
Dronning Sophia Magdalen	1782	
Fredensborg Slot	1777	
Frederick VI	1800	Purchased from navy and disarmed 1800
Henriette	1800	Purchased from navy and disarmed 1800
Holsten	1800	Purchased from navy and disarmed 1800
Kronborg	1800	Purchased from navy and disarmed 1800
Kongen af Danmark	1777, 1780, 1782, 1789, 1801-3	
København	1808	
Kronprinsen	1802, 1808	At Batavia under escort by Casque
Kronprinsessen	1780, 1782, 1784, 1802, 1822	Seized by British 1808 at Copenhagen, returned 1810
Kronprinsen af Danmark	1780	
Kronprinsessen Maria	1795	Purchased from navy and disarmed 1795
Louisa Augusta	1798, 1803, 1806	Ex-naval *Slesvig* purchased 1798
Naiden	1817	Private venture
Norge	1806	Ex-Dutch *Cromhout* taken by British sold to DAC in 1798, confiscated again by British off the Cape 1808
Norden	1817	
Pommern	1795	
Prins Frederik	1774, 1788, 1780	
Prinsen af Augustenborg	1808	
Prinsessen Sophia Frederica	1780	Wrecked in an explosion off China 1780
Store Belt	1800	Purchased from navy and disarmed 1800
Vædier	1789	

French East India Company

The French had effectively been kept out of the East India trade by years of war that exhausted the county's capital. By the time the Treaty of the Pyrenees was signed in 1659, ending the war with Spain, its navy was down to 21 ships. A number of small companies had made some early attempts to establish trading posts, such La Compagnie Madagascar, which in 1643 took possession of an uninhabited island off Madagascar, known to the Portuguese as Mascarene, renaming it Île Bourbon after the ruling dynasty of France. The fragmented approach taken by the establishment of many small companies hampered development throughout the period of French trade in the East. In 1656 La Compagnie Madagascar, together with La Compagnie d'Orient, joined forces with La Compagnie da la Meilleraye, but this venture was also short-lived due in part to lack of investment. In 1664 the reformed Compagnie des Indes Orientales de Madagascar was given the concession to Île Bourbon. They initiated a colonisation scheme, which although slow, helped to maintained a presence on the island, whilst the settlement on Madagascar itself fell into decline.

The crowning of Louis XIV in 1661 marked the beginning of a new era for France, in which she would develop and flourish. In 1669 the king

Fortifications to the town of Port-Louis opposite Lorient where ships were loaded with stores and arms before embarking on their journeys to the East. The fort is now home to the museum of La Compagnie des Indes. (Author's collection)

entrusted the rebuilding of the navy to his finance minister Jean-Baptiste Colbert. The Dutch had become international suppliers of ships, and the French navy up to this period was a mixture of homespun and Dutch-supplied vessels. Colbert's reorganisation programme heralded a new age for the French navy. He established academies that soon designed and built their own ships. It was largely a period of experiment with its fair share of failures, but he had succeeded in laying down an ordered structure that by 1710 saw the adoption of design techniques that led to the founding of the school of naval architecture in 1741.

Colbert was also keen that France should not lose the opportunity to share in the lucrative East India trade. France was a big consumer of spices, relying on the Dutch and English for their supply. Louis XIV needed little persuasion from Colbert to realise the potential of such an enterprise and in 1664 granted the formation of the Compagnie Française des Indes Orientales. Colbert was left with the task of finding financial backers and the procurement of ships and men with experience of Eastern trade. François Caron, who had spent thirty years working for the Dutch VOC, joined the payroll of the new venture, which fashioned itself on the Dutch model. Despite its royal patronage, the company struggled to find backers, and by 1668 the king was still the biggest investor in the company, which remained under his control.

Colbert established the company's headquarters in the fortified Breton town of Port-Louis, with shipbuilding facilities at La Faouédic on the opposite bank of the Scorff estuary. La Faouédic rapidly grew into the shipbuilding and commercial hub of trade with the East and soon became known as the port of Lorient. In 1675 the company established a trading post in India with the settlement of Pondicherry, and an official Governor was posted to Île Bourbon in 1689.

The French, as those before them, found little welcome from their rivals, and Pondicherry fell to the Dutch in 1693. Little inroad had been made into the Dutch-dominated spice trade and although Pondicherry was regained in 1698, the company failed to expand further. By 1719 it was close to financial ruin.

French missionaries had been established in Siam as early as 1663, laying the foundation for links with China. In 1685 a group of Jesuit priests from the newly formed Mission Française de Chine set out from the port of Brest in a ship belonging to the mission, initially for Siam, then after travelling overland reached Peking on 7 February 1688, successfully establishing diplomatic links. On their return to France, they sought to encourage the formation of a French commercial venture, a challenge eventually taken up by a businessman from Marseilles called Jean Jourdan de Groucé. He formed the Société Jourdan and in 1698 his ship *L'Amphitrite* arrived in China. He managed not only to secure a cargo, but also established the first factory at Canton. The ship returned to France in 1700, and an auction of goods at Nantes followed on 4 October. Chinese goods had reached France before this date, with porcelain and lacquered work finding their way into the collections of the king, which undoubtedly added to the great success of the auction. Such earlier goods had been transported by the Compagnie Française des Indes Orientales via India, but Jourdan's venture clearly demonstrated the potential of direct trade with China, which lead to the formation of Compagnie Royal de la Chine on 7 November 1701.

The extravagances of the Sun King and the military expenses of the wars with Britain and the Netherlands created a tremendous drain on the country's economy, taking its toll on foreign trade. The Compagnie Royal de le Chine had begun to experience problems, with disputes amongst its directors causing the break up of the company. In 1712 it was reformed under the same name, but by 1715 was again experiencing financial difficulties. A number of smaller companies trading with the East were either struggling to survive or had become defunct. The Scottish economist John Law (1671-1729) perceived the problem as being a fragmented approach to trade, and sought to gather all the ventures together to form a united company. Under his initiative, Compagnie du Sénégal, Compagnie Royal de la Chine and Compagnie Française des Indes Orientales united to become the Compagnie des Indes on 23 May 1719. (It was also known as Compagnie Perpétuelle des Indes.) John Law also urged the establishment of a national bank for France. The ravages of war had left France with very little precious metals with which to mint coins. He believed that the issue of paper money backed by the king, would increase the availability of credit and in 1716 set up a general bank in which 75 per cent of the capital consisted of government bills. It became the Royal Bank in 1718. A year earlier he floated a joint-stock trading company called the Compagnie d'Occident which was granted a monopoly of trade with the West Indies and North America. Law exaggerated the wealth of American

colonies, leading to wild speculation, followed by a sudden loss of confidence which by 1720 had rendered the company's shares worthless. The collapse, known as the Mississippi Bubble, plunged France further into debt. Law was dismissed and forced to flee the country. He gambled his way around Europe, eventually dying of pneumonia some nine years later in Venice.

Law's East India company survived the crash, but following his departure, the decision was taken in 1723 that trade should be concentrated on India and commerce with China was to be organised as a separate venture. They resumed their former independence as Compagnie de la Chine and Compagnie des Indes, which maintained its presence in the Indian settlements of Pondicherry and Chandernagore on the Hugli river, together with Île Bourbon and the neighbouring island of Mauritius (Île de France), which came under French control in 1715. The Governorship of Île de France was in the hands of a sea captain from St Malo named Bertrand-François Mahé de La Bourdonnais. Under his leadership the island was transformed from a wretched settlement to a prospering community, and the capital (named Port-Louis) had become a major port and revictualling station, with facilities for shipbuilding and repairs.

A period of growth had finally come to the Indies companies. Shipbuilding at Lorient continued to expand, sending an average of nineteen ships a year to India and two to China. The company's success presented a serious threat to British supremacy, not only in trade but in the struggle for military control, as France sought to expand its interests in India. In 1742 Joseph François Dupleix was appointed Governor-General of all French territories in India. He pursued an aggressive policy against both the declining Mogul Empire and British-held territories. His victories were aided by La Bourdonnais, who in 1746 led a fleet nine ships from Île de France to India, where they defeated a British squadron, paving the way to the capture of Madras.

The French were finally defeated in the recapture of Bengal by Robert Clive in 1757. He first arrived in India as a civilian employee of the Honourable East India Company in 1743, but transferred to military service during the French troubles of 1756. In a series of victories he successfully wiped out the French military presence in India, seriously reducing its ability to trade there. French commerce with China then depended on ships sent from Pondicherry and Île de France. In

1761 Pondicherry was occupied by the British, leading to the total suspension of trade to Canton. In 1767 control of Île de France was handed over to the French Government.

The company was unable to support itself and when the French Government introduced free trade in 1769 they effectively lost their monopoly and the company was finally abolished. Attempts to trade direct to Canton continued with some success, but with the advent of the American War of Independence, commerce was again reduced as France directed its activities to the war. When peace was declared in 1783 Pierre-Jacques Mesié formed an association of private investors from the coastal trading towns, which led to the formation of the third Compagnie des Indes, but with the nation in a state of political and financial disorder it was unable to withstand the economic turmoil as the country spiralled headlong into revolution. The company went into liquidation and was dissolved on 15 April 1794.

With the fall of the House of Bourbon in 1793, Île Bourbon was renamed Réunion, only to be seized by the British during the Napoleonic Wars in 1810, along with Île de France. Pondicherry had already fallen to the British in 1793. Réunion and Pondicherry were returned following the Congress of Vienna in 1815, but Île de France remained under British control, who reverted the island's name to Mauritius.

Ships of the French East India Companies

(As identified by the author, which does not represent the complete fleet. Dates indicate commencement of voyage to East Indies or China where known, or date when ship entered service. The number of guns carried by the ship are listed where known)

Achille	1744	70	Condemned 1757
Actionnaire	1767	64	Built Lorient 1767, purchased by navy 1770, captured by British 1782
Auguste	1710		
Ajax	1762		Sold 1774
Astra	175	112	Captured by British 1755
Baleine	1741	40	Condemned 1753
Beaumont	1762		Purchased by navy 1770
Berryer	1759		Purchased by navy 1770
Bertin	1760	64	Captured by British 1761
Bertin	1761	56	Purchased by navy 1770
Bien-Aimé	1756	68	Wrecked 1758
Bien-Aimé	1769		Built Lorient 1769
Boulogne	1758	26	Captured by British 1762
Brillant	1757	60	Purchased by navy 1758
Bristol	1747	14	Captured by British 1761
Calypso	1756	10	Purchased by navy 1770
Centaure	1749		Wrecked 1749
Centaure	1751	70	Wrecked 1761
Chimère	1747	36	Captured by British 1747
Comte d'Argenson	1757	50	Purchased by navy 1770
Comte de Provence	1756	68	Built Lorient 1756, broken up 1766
Comte d'Argenson	1761		
Condé	1748		
Condé	1753	50	Purchased by navy 1770
Content	1747	60	Hulked 1749
Courier de Bourbon	1724		
Danae	1758	32	Built Lorient 1758, captured by British 1779
Dartmouth	1747	18	Captured by British 1747
Dauphin	1743	24	Captured by British 1745
Dauphin	1766		Purchased by navy 1770
Diligente	1756	26	Sold 1761
Dryade	1747		Purchased by navy 1770

Duc d'Aquitaine	1757		Built Lorient 1757, captured by British 1757
Duc de Berry	1755	44	Wrecked 1760
Duc de Béthune	1751		
Duc de Bourgogne	1752	54	Disarmed 1761
Duc de Chartres	1749	56	Captured by British 1757
Duc de Choiseul	1761		Purchased by navy 1770
Duc de Duras	1765	56	Purchased by navy 1769, renamed *Bonhomme Richard* 1779
Duc de Praslin	1764	24	Purchased by navy 1770
Duc d'Orléans	1753	54	Deleted from list 1761
Duc de Penthievre	1754	60	Captured by British 1756
Elephant	1758	20	Purchased by navy 1770
Favori	1743	40	Captured by British 1744
Fortuné	1757	60	Wrecked 1763
Fortune	1763		Wrecked 1763
François D'Argouges	1710		Jan 1710 sailed to East Indies, returned Feb 1712
Geraldus	1747	8	Captured by British 1747
Hercule	1746	48	
Hercule	1749	48	Captured by British
Indien	1768	64	Built Lorient 1768, purchased by navy 1770
Jason	1739	48	
Jason	1748	48	Built Lorient 1748, captured by British 1748
L'Utile	1761		Wrecked 1761
La Diane	1754		
Lys	1756		
Lys Brillac	1710		Jan 1710 sailed to East Indies, returned Feb 1712
Maré d'Estrees	1759	24	Sold 1759
Maré de Broglie	1774	64	Purchased by navy 1779
Marquis de Castres	1765	24	Sold 1770
Mars	1769		Built Lorient 1769, purchased by navy 1770
Massaic	1756		Built Lorient 1756, purchased by navy 1770
Maurepas	1692	46	Built Lorient, given to company in 1698, returned 1703, given back 1705, Jan 1710 sailed to East Indies, returned Feb 1712
Maurepas	1756		
Modeste	1747	18	Captured by British 1747
Orient	1756	80	Built Lorient 1756, purchased by the navy 1759, wrecked 1782
Pacifique	1757	16	Captured by British 1757
Paix	1762		Purchased by navy 1770
Penthièvre	1743		Purchased by navy 1770
Philibert	1741	40	Given away 1770
Pomone	1756	10	Purchased by navy 1770
Pondicherry	1754	56	Captured by British 1757
Prince du Conty	1745		Wrecked 1746
Saint Joseph	1755		Purchased by navy 1770
Saint Louis	1752	54	Purchased by navy 1770
Saint-Géran	1744		Wrecked 1744
Sechelles	1755	60	Wrecked 1760
Sylphide	1756	30	Sunk as blockship 1761
Thetis	1747	22	Captured by British 1747
Vengeur	1756	65	Built Lorient 1756
Venus	1728		
Vigilant	1747	20	Captured by British 1747
Villevault	1761	22	Captured by British 1762
Villevault	1762		Purchased by navy 1770

Oostende Company (Austrian East India Company)

Arms of the Oostende Company. (Author's collection)

The Austrian royal family of Habsburg had by 1500 created an empire consisting of Austria, Hungary and Bohemia and in 1516, through marriage into the Spanish royal family, a Habsburg became King of Spain. Members of the family had for centuries been elected head of the Holy Roman Empire and it was the uprising of Bohemian Protestants against their Catholic rulers that led to the Thirty Years War (1618-1648).

Fought mainly in Germany, the war eventually involved most European nations in a struggle for religious freedom and political power. The Thirty Years' War ended with the Peace of Westphalia, in which German rulers retained the right to determine the religious doctrine of their subjects. Sweden also increased its power as a Protestant country. France, fearing Habsburg dominance, had declared war on Spain, and this conflict continued until the Peace of the Pyrenees in 1659. When the last Habsburg king of Spain died in 1700, both the French and Austrian royal families claimed the throne, which led to the War of the Spanish Succession (1701-1714). In the event a French prince became King of Spain, but Spain's Italian territories and the area of the southern Netherlands (roughly modern Belgium) was transferred to the Austrian branch of the Habsburgs, thus providing them with a seaboard beyond their Austrian boundary. One year after the War of the Spanish Succession ended, in 1715 Scotland saw the first of two Jacobite risings that aimed to restore the Stuart family to the throne of Britain. After its failure, Jacobite and Irish supporters realised the considerable political advantage that could be gained in undermining the profits of the Protestant Dutch and British companies by trading from the Austrian Netherlands.

Ships from Oostende (Ostend in English) started sailing shortly after 1715. In the space of a few years the private investors had amassed a fleet of twenty-three ships (fifteen of which came from England and eight from the Netherlands), and thirty-four voyages had been made to China, the Coromandel coast, Surat and Bengal. The need to consolidate individual enterprises became apparent, prompting the Jacobite merchants to persuade the Holy Roman Emperor Charles VI of the advantages that were to be had in forming the Oostende Company, which received its official charter in 1722. Financed largely by silver from Jacobite exiles living in Spain, it smuggled tea and spices into England and Holland, thus breaking the trade barrier whereby such goods could only legally enter those countries in their own East India company ships. It was operated mainly by Scottish captains, among whom was Alexander Hume. As a former employee of the Honourable East India Company, Hume had firsthand knowledge of trading with the East. In the intervening years he had also built up contacts with merchants in Flanders and consequently was at the forefront of those early investors trading from Ostend. Hume had successfully obtained permission to trade with the Nawab of Bengal, where the deserted Danish fort of Dannemarnagore, on the banks of the Hugli river, served as a trading post.

Another Scotsman, Colin Campbell, also joined the company. Born in Edinburgh in 1686, he started his career as an officer in the Royal Navy during the War of Spanish Succession. He then served in the English East India Company, spending some time in India before becoming a victim of the South Sea Bubble (1720-23), losing most of his vast fortune and amassing considerable debts. He fled to the Austrian Netherlands to escape his debtors, where he joined the Oostende Company in 1723, serving with them until 1730, after which he became instrumental in the formation of the Swedish East India Company.

The first official ship of the company, named *Charles VI*, set out for the Indies in 1723. On board was a lawyer from Antwerp named André Cobbé, who had been appointed by the Austrian court to negotiate further trade with the Nawab of Bengal. Cobbé established a trading post at Bankuibazar on the opposite bank of the Hugli river to Dannemarnagore. Having secured a cargo, Hume returned to Ostend, leaving Cobbé as the appointed governor of the settlement. His attempts to negotiate further trading privileges were hampered by pressure placed on the Nawab by the Dutch and British companies. Losing patience, he attempted to exert his own pressure by holding local ships, and in the ensuing conflict he consolidated his forces in the old Danish fort. After a three-month siege he was eventually killed by wounds from cannon shot. His army surrendered on 24 June 1724 and accepted refuge from the neighbouring French trading post of Chandernagore.

When the news reached Ostend, Hume was appointed governor and returned to Bankuibazar in 1726, charged with restoring the reputation of the company with the Nawab. Naturally there was great opposition from the Dutch and British companies, whose governments continued to support their activities with aggressive diplomacy, culminating in a threat not to recognise Maria Theresa, the daughter of Charles VI, as his legitimate heir if he did not dissolve the company (having no male heir, Charles VI had declared his intention to overrule the Salic law which prohibited a woman from inheriting a kingdom). He finally met their demands and the company was dissolved in 1727. Ironically, that same year Hume finally succeeded in obtaining permission to trade from the Nawab of Bengal.

In the same year, representatives of the former company sailed to Copenhagen on board their ship *Josias van Aspen,* with a proposal to operate a department of the Danish East India Company from Altona. As pointed out in the earlier section on the Danish company, this scheme met with official approval, and the Danes went so far as to purchase a building on which a plaque was placed with the following inscription: *This is the new Ostindiske house to convey trade to Tranquebar, China and other territories.* The initiative was kept under the watchful eye of the Dutch and English who judged the *Josias van Asperen* an interloper. Pressure from them, combined with a lack of funding, ensured the rapid demise of the project.

Despite the closure of the company in 1727, there were reports of Oostende ships seen after this date sailing under Polish and Prussian flags. The *Apollo* was one such ship. Campbell notes in the logbook of his first voyage with the Swedish East India Company (1732-3) that an Englishman by the name of Peter Spendelow served as chief supercargo on three expeditions with the Oostende Company between 1724 and 1730, the last time on the *Apollo* when she sailed under the Prussian flag. She was later purchased in Hamburg by the Swedish East India Company, entering their service in 1735 as the *Tre Cronor.* The formation of the Swedish East India Company, which coincided with the closure of the Oostende Company,

aroused considerable suspicion both in Britain and the Netherlands, particularly with the engagement of Campbell by the Swedes.

Despite these concerns, in 1732 an agreement was signed between Austria and Britain granting permission for two ships to sail to China. This was endorsed by the Dutch in 1732 when the *Hertogh van Lorreyman* and the *Concordia* set sail for Canton, marking the final (official) voyage of the Austrian company's trading. The captain of the *Concordia* was charged with the task of removing all possessions of the abolished Oostende Company from the settlement. Before leaving, he also handed the attendant representative of the company, François de Schonamille, a letter from the Emperor appointing him as governor of the trading post.

Schonamille is reported to have hoisted the Austrian flag, which he kept flying at Bankuibazar for another eleven years, entering into trade that he financed through his own resources, allegedly with help from Danish and Swedish merchants. The log of the Swedish East India ship *Suecia,* which set sail from Göteborg on 25 January 1739, notes that it reached Bankuibazar on 13 November 'where some business was done' with the governor Schonamille.

During their trading period, the Oostende ships had to contend not only with attacks from their Dutch and English rivals, but also the constant threat of capture from the Algerines and other North African corsairs, generically known as Barbary Pirates. These posed a major threat to all merchantmen, capturing ships and holding their crews to ransom, which was rarely paid except by private means from the families of wealthy captains; this meant the majority were sold into slavery. Countries with weak navies were particularly vulnerable and between 1609 and 1616, at a time when the Royal Navy was in a poor state, no fewer than 460 English ships were taken by the Algerines and their crews sold into slavery. Their attacks were not restricted to shipping, with many reports of raids on coastal towns. The usual targets were Mediterranean islands and coasts, but at this time their depredations stretched to the English Channel. Local communities made attempts to raise ransom money: Barnstaple, for example, raised £240 in 1622 for the release of six local seamen. In 1625 attacks on fishing villages in Devon and Cornwall alone saw a thousand inhabitants taken into slavery. Women and children disappeared into harems, men were put to work rowing galleys or hard labour such as the building of Meknes (known as the Versailles of Morocco). It is estimated that over one million Europeans were taken into slavery during the peak of their operations during the seventeenth and early eighteenth centuries.

An account of one Oostende Company ship, the *Keyserinne Elisabeth* under the command of Captain Joseph de Gheselle, draws attention to a threat endured by all the merchant companies by describing how on 29 May 1724 they sighted two ships flying the Dutch flag. When they reached a quarter mile distance, they lowered the Dutch flag and raised the Algerian. After an hour's fight during which the Oostende ship sustained heavy losses, Captain Gheselle surrendered his ship, which was taken into Tangier, from where he wrote setting out the ransom demand for his return, his crew having already been sold into slavery. Five years later, a letter to the Oostende Company from the Brotherhood of the Holy Trinity states that they had secured the release of eighteen men, being the crew of an Ostend ship. This may well refer to the *Keyserinne Elisabeth*, as an earlier letter addressed to Gheselle in Ostend suggests they had secured his earlier release. Naval raids by the British, Dutch and French on Algiers saw short-term reductions in their activities. The largest of these was the Anglo-Dutch assault on the city in 1816 when, after nine hours of bombardment and the burning of the Algerian pirate fleet, they finally succeeded in freeing 1083 Christian slaves. However, it was not until 1830 when Algiers was captured and Algeria annexed to France that their activities finally ceased.

Swedish East India Company (SOIC)

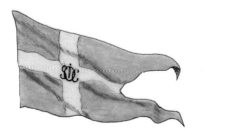

Swallow-tailed flag of the Svenska Ostindiska Companiet.

The 1600s saw a massive expansion in Swedish territories. Finland had been a part of it for centuries, but successive battles with the Danes had by 1658 brought in most of the area that makes up modern-day Sweden. In addition to this, during the Thirty Years' War (1618-48) the country had gained the Baltic seaboard areas of Pomerania and Wismar in northern Germany, together with present-day Latvia and Estonia. The Baltic Sea became known as 'The pond in the middle of Sweden'.

Despite this expansion, it was still a poor, mainly agriculture-based country with some mining and timber exports, lacking the economic resources to support the political and military power needed to maintain its inflated empire. The Great Northern War, which broke out in 1700, saw initial successes in Poland and Denmark that encouraged the Swedish king Charles XII to push further into Russia and try to take Moscow (a fatal decision, as Napoleon and Hitler would later discover). This led to a retreat that would eventually push the Swedes back across the Baltic. In 1718 Charles was shot during his campaign in Norway, leading to the peace treaty of Nystad in 1721.

Years of war left the country in a disastrous financial situation, but the death of Charles XII brought the opportunity for change. As the restless populace embarked on their 'bloodless revolution', political power shifted from the Crown to the Riksdag (Swedish parliament). This new era, known as the age of freedom, saw the founding of modern Swedish government and the country entered a new period of confidence in which trade was encouraged to grow.

Niclas Sahlgren (1701-1776) was the son of a merchant family in Göteborg who had many years' experience in trading Swedish products such as timber, iron and tar with Spain. Cadiz was home port for the Spanish silver fleets returning from South America, making the price of silver here lower than anywhere else in Europe. It also happened to be the only currency that China would accept in exchange for its valuable goods, having little use for the products that Europe had to offer. At the age of 16 Sahlgren was sent to Holland to work with a businessman associated with the VOC, giving him further insight into the world of commerce.

Sweden could see the wealth brought to other nations through their foreign trade and understood the potential of starting its own trading company. Another businessman, Hindrich König, had already approached the government but was opposed by those who felt Sweden's insufficient silver reserves would lead to foreign investment upon which the country would become dependent. In 1728 Niclas Sahlgren travelled to Ostend and met Colin Campbell, with the result that when the latter's contract with the Oostende Company ran out in 1731, he travelled straight to Sweden where he met Hindrich König. The formation of a company was proposed, but there was still further opposition, claiming that the road to economic recovery was through the manufacture of Swedish goods to supply its needs and through the export of the surplus. The possible flood of imports, many of which were regarded as useless luxuries that simply pandered to vanities and were of no benefit to the nation, would lead to a trade deficit. There was also the very real worry of the repercussions from Britain and the Netherlands, who would view Campbell's involvement simply as the Oostende Company starting up under a new name.

Despite such opposition, in 1731 König, in company with Campbell and Sahlgren, received his Royal Charter, giving them the sole power to trade east of the Cape of Good Hope. The charter made provision to alleviate the concerns of its objectors, by insisting upon the reselling of goods for export on their arrival in Sweden. In the final analysis East India ships contributed to the demand for Swedish goods, exporting them on the outward-bound voyages. Iron and steel goods rose to account for three-quarters of the country's total exports, along with tar and timber, demand for which also increased in the home market.

The company to be known as the Svenska Ost Indiska Companiet (SOIC) was to be based in Göteborg (Gothenburg to the English), and all ships were required to sail from and return to that port where the cargo was to be sold at public auction for export. To encourage the exportation of goods, all sales were free from domestic or export tax. During the first charter, which ran from 1731 to 1746, 90 per cent of goods were re-exported leaving only the profit in Sweden. Later, as fears subsided, a greater percentage remained in Sweden to meet the growing demand for oriental goods. As a further aid to re-exportation, all accounts were destroyed after each auction, helping to hinder tracing the origin of goods that found their way into England, Holland and France.

The SOIC ships were to be armed merchantmen, with the captains having the same authority as in the navy, and the crews subject to the same regulations, being exempt from military

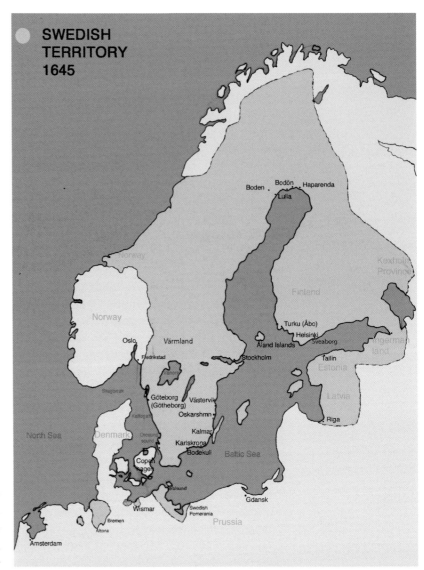

Swedish Territory in 1645.

service whilst serving in the company. They also adopted a swallow-tailed flag, more closely resembling the three-tongued naval ensign than the rectangular merchant flag, thus presenting an image of greater deterrence to attackers.

The company's intentions were represented to the maritime nations trading in the East, requesting that Swedish ships might enter their ports in times of crisis. With no bases of their own for revictualling or repairs, the Swedes had to rely on the goodwill of others, but their request was met with little sympathy from fellow traders operating in a market so fiercely competitive, and consequently the early voyages were undertaken knowing there would be few safe havens on the way. The first port of call was Cadiz, being one month's sailing time from Göteborg; it also served as the first and often only revictualling port before the six-month voyage to the East Indies.

Attempts to enter the established spice trade also presented difficulties; they sought instead to operate in the comparatively new China trade and soon established a good reputation with the Chinese who considered them as kinder and more honest than the British. A factory was established at Canton and cargoes, predominantly of tea with some silks, arrack and spices, were secured. Porcelain later became an important commodity – wealthy families would have their insignia and other motifs sent out to China to be reproduced in the glazed ware, many examples of which can be seen in the museum at Göteborg.

To cope with the demand for ships, Stockholm's two existing shipyards were joined by a further three. One of these, named the Terra Nova, built the first ship to be ordered by the SOIC. Originally built in 1725 as the *Terra Nova*, she was renamed *Friedericus Rex Sueciae*. The master shipwright at the yard was an Englishman named William Mackett, and before his retirement in 1749 six East Indiamen were built at the yard, including the original *Götheborg* of which a replica was to be built nearly three centuries later.

Friedericus Rex Sueciae, the company's first ship, set sail from Göteborg on 7 March 1732. On board was Colin Campbell, whose previous experience in navigation and trading with the East made him invaluable in ensuring the success of the venture. He carried with him letters from King Frederick I giving him the authority of Swedish ambassador to China, and in his capacity as supercargo he was responsible for the financial affairs of the voyage. After a passage of 33 days, they reached Cadiz, where Campbell negotiated the sale of their cargo of timber, tar, iron, potash and resin, with payment in silver. The ship was revictualled and ballasted with stone that would later be used in the construction of their trading post in Canton. They left Cadiz on 24 April.

After 60 days they rounded the Cape bound for Sunda, which they reached 48 days later on 10 August, and finally arrived at Canton 40 days after that on 19 September 1732. In his diary of the voyage Campbell describes their arrival and the suspicions of the Dutch and British towards the Swedish company, particularly as the Oostende ship *Hertogh van Lorreyman* had also recently anchored in the port and whose supercargoes were known to Campbell. The Ostenders were keen to

East India House Göteborg, alongside the Great Harbour Canal. Small lighters would transfer cargo from ships anchored in the deeper river for storage in the warehouses prior to sale by auction. The building now serves as the city museum, which has reconstructed the room where auctions took place. (Author's collection)

engage Campbell's help in obtaining introductions to enable them to trade, a service he refused to have any part in, fearful of raising suspicions of collusion between the two companies. He reacquainted himself with Chinese merchants with whom he had dealt on previous trips and after 120 days finally succeeded in gaining the necessary permissions to trade and reached agreement on prices for a cargo of tea, silks, porcelain and spices.

The season for embarking on the return journey was by now very late. The swift departure required to catch the last of the favourable winds soon met with disaster: when approaching the coast of Sumatra, the ship was intercepted by seven Dutch ships who demanded that the Swedes strike their colours. The ship was then siezed under suspicion of being in the service of the Oostende Company. Despite being shown their official passes, endorsed by the King of Sweden, the Dutch insisted on escorting the ship to Batavia under the orders of the Dutch Commissioner, to further question their authority to trade in the region. After a week of pointless cross-examination it was clear that the Dutch had no grounds to hold the ship and were doing so purely to delay the homeward passage of their competitor. The ship was finally released, and with all haste, rounded the Cape and headed for home. With the minimum of stops to make up time, lack of fresh food and water took its toll on the crew. Rather than enter the Channel, the ship took a course round Ireland and across the top of Scotland, by which time death and sickness amongst the crew forced the ship to put in at a Norwegian port and take on more crew for the final leg to Göteborg, which they reached on 17 September 1733. Despite the delays, the first voyage proved to be a financial and political success. Campbell continued to pursue his grievance with the Dutch at their illegal detention of his ship and succeeded in being granted compensation through the Dutch courts for loss of profits on their delayed cargo.

The *Friedericus Rex Sueciae* went on to make a total of five voyages to China. She was joined in 1733 by *Drottning Ulrica Eleonora*. Originally built in 1720, this ship was purchased from the Deptford yard of Bronsdon and Wells where she was undergoing repairs, having completed her fourth voyage for the British East India Company as the *Heathcote*. She made one passage for the SOIC. By then fifteen years old and having completed five voyages, she would have lasted beyond the expectations of her builders. In 1735

she was sold to the French and in May that year set sail for Ostend with soldiers recruited in Sweden to serve in the French army. The company's third ship was the *Apollo*; purchased from the Oostende Company, she was renamed the *Tre Cronor* and in 1736 made one voyage to Canton. By 1737 the company had completed the building of their own second ship, the *Suecia*. With the exception of two vessels purchased from the French, the next thirty-four ships to be used by the company were all constructed in Sweden, making a significant contribution to their shipbuilding industry.

The company was granted a total of five charters:

The First Charter, 1731 to 1746
The company made a total of twenty-two voyages to Canton and three to India using twelve ships. Four of these were wrecked, including the *Götheborg*.

The Second Charter, 1746 to 1766
Following the success of the first, further investors came forward allowing a total of thirty-five voyages to be made, all to Canton. Ten new ships were commissioned with a further three still in service from the previous charter; only one ship was lost.

The Third Charter, 1766 to 1786
The success of this was partly due to the American War of Independence and the collapse of the French East India Company, presenting Sweden with the opportunity to gain a greater share of the European market. By 1782 the company had reached the peak of its financial success. Thirty-nine voyages were made to Canton, seven new ships were commissioned with a further three still in service from the previous charter. The period was further blessed by not a single ship being lost.

The Fourth Charter, 1786 to 1806
The French Revolution and the subsequent rise of Napoleon led to a period of unsettled trading prospects. Sweden managed to send thirty-two ships to the East; eight new ships were commissioned, with a further four still in use from the previous charter; three were lost within the period and two sold on the outward journey. In stark contrast to the previous charter, the profits realised from a similar number of voyages was very small. American ships had entered the trade following their war of independence and, despite the pressures of war, Britain had still managed to

complete in excess of four hundred voyages during the period.

The Fifth Charter, 1806 to 1821
With the defeat of Napoleon's navy at Trafalgar, optimism in Sweden persuaded the company to invest in a fifth charter but poor results led to its dissolution in 1813 having made only two voyages. In the same year the English East India Company had relinquished its monopoly on trade with the East.

During the company's 82-year existence it mounted 132 expeditions with thirty-eight ships. As a concept, it would seem inconceivable that one company could produce sufficient wealth to turn a poor war-torn country into a thriving economy in which the arts and sciences would develop to an extent where they equalled those of other European nations; yet, starting from a country of limited resources it had within fifty years established itself in a highly competitive arena to become the third largest East India company in the world.

Ships of the Swedish East India Company (SOIC)
(The ships are in chronological order of their entry into the service of the SOIC. The number of voyages are the total during their period of service; where ships served for more than one charter the total is set in brackets, with the ship's entry in subsequent charters set in italics)

First Charter, 1731-1746	Built	Yard	
1 Fredericus Rex Suecciae	1724	Terra Nova, W Mackett	Entered service 1731; 5 trips 1745
2 Drottning Ulrica Eleonora	1720	Deptford, Bronsdon	Ex-HEIC *Heathcote* sold to SOIC 1733, 1 trip 1735, sold to French 1735
3 Tre Kronor		Ostende	Ship sold to SOIC 1735, 1 trip 1736
4 Sueccia	1735	Terra Nova, W Mackett	Built as *Stockholm*, SOIC 1737, 2 trips, wrecked 1740
5 Stockholm	1737	Clasons	3 trips, wrecked 1745
6 Götheborg	1738	Terra Nova, W Mackett	3 trips, wrecked 1745
7 Riddarhuset	1740	Clasons	2 trips 1748
8 Calmar	1741	Kalmar	3 trips 1748
9 Drottningen af Sverige	1742	Stockholm	Wrecked outward on 2nd trip, 1745
10 Cronprinsessan Lovisa Ulrica	1746	Djurgård	*(2 trips)*, 1st trip 1747
11 Freeden	1746	Terra Nova, W Mackett	*(2 trips)*, 1st trip 1747
12 Cronprinsen Adolph Frederic	1746	Stora Stad	*(3 trips)*, 1st trip 1748

Second Charter, 1746-1766	Built	Yard	
13 Prins Gustav	1746	Terra Nova, W Mackett	1 trip 1748
14 Götha Lijon	1746	Terra ?	3 trips 1754
11 Freeden	*1746*	*Terra Nova, W Mackett*	2nd trip 1748
15 Hoppet	1747	Terra Nova, W Mackett	2 trips 1754
10 Cronprinsessan Lovisa Ulrica	*1746*	*Djurgård*	(2 trips), 2nd trip 1748
16 Enigheten	1747	Djurgård	4 trips 1757
12 Cronprinsen Adolph Frederic	*1746*	*Stora Stad*	(3 trips), 3rd trip 1752
17 Prins Carl	1750	Clasons	6 trips 1766
18 Friederic Adolph (Prins)	1753	Terra Nova	4 trips wrecked 1761
19 Prinsessen Sophia Albertina	1753	Stora Stad	3 trips 1761
20 Stockholms Slott	1759	Stora Stad	*(7 trips)*, 3rd trip 1765
21 Riksens Ständer	1760	Terra Nova	*(4 trips)*, 3rd trip 1765
22 Finland	1762	Stora Stad	*(7 trips)*, 2nd trip 1764

Third Charter, 1766-1786

23 Adolph Frederic	1744	Stora Stad, J Holm as 60-gun ship 1760	
		Djurgård converted to SOIC, 7 trips 1786	
24 Lovisa Ulrica	1766	Djurgård	4 trips 1783
25 Cron Prins Gustaf	1767	Djurgård, F Chapman	*(7 trips)*, 6th trip 1785
21 Riksens Ständer	*1760*	*Terra Nova*	(4 trips), 4th trip 1768
20 Stockholms Slott	*1759*	*Stora Stad*	(7 trips), 7th trip 1778
22 Finland	*1762*	*Stora Stad*	(7 trips), 7th trip 1780
26 Drottning Sophia Magdalena	1771	Stora Stad	*(7 trips)*, 4th trip1783
27 Terra Nova II	1771	Terra Nova 4 trips 1786	
28 Gustaf III	1779	Djurgård	*(9 trips)*, 4th trip 1785
29 Gustaf Adolph	1783	Stora Stad	*(4 trips)*, 1st trip 1784

Fourth Charter, 1786-1806

29 Gustaf Adolph	*1783*	*Stora Stad*	(4 trips), 4th trip 1788
26 Drottning Sophis Magdalena	*1771*	*Stora Stad*	(7 trips), 7th trip 1795
30 Götheborg II	1788	Viken Göteborg	3 trips, wrecked 1796
25 Cron Prins Gustaf	*1767*	*Djurgård*	(7 trips), 7th trip 1788
31 Drottningen	1797	Viken	3 trips, wrecked 1803
32 Maria Carolina	1797		Bought from French, 3 trips 1806
33 Sophia Magdalena II	1798	Viken	2 trips, wrecked 1800
34 Östergöthland	1799	Norrköping	2 trips 1804
28 Gustaf III	*1779*	*Djurgård*	(9 trips), 9th trip 1804
35 Westergöthland	1799	Gamla Varvet Göteborg	Sold Amsterdam due to damage and captain's death, later seized by British, 1 trip 1799
36 Fredrica	1799		Bought from French, 2 trips 1806
37 Prinsessan	1802	Karlskrona	2 trips 1805
38 Wasa	1803	Karlskrona	1 trip 1805

PART II
~ Ship Decoration ~

The 70-gun ship
Ipswich, launched from
Portsmouth Dockyard
in 1730. (National
Maritime Museum
F9319-004)

1

~France~

The dominant position that Italy held in the arts since the Renaissance made it the essential place for the artists of Europe to study. By 1620 the strict concepts of Classicism were being adapted into a new variant where decoration ceased to be applied to an architectural design but became an intrinsic part of its make-up, giving a very three-dimensional feel of flowing lines and a visual effect that covered the underlying structure rather than being bound by it. Classical themes from Roman mythology were interpreted in a theatrical manner, creating a rich and flamboyant effect of abundance and grandeur. Technical ability had flourished with an assurance that held no limits. Sculptures of allegorical figures were created to apparently float on air, leaving the viewer in awe and wonderment. Pietro da Cortona (1599-1667) and Gian Lorenzo Bernini (1598-1680) were the established masters of this style that came to be known as the High Baroque.

Among the artists who went to study in Italy was Charles Le Brun (1619-1690). He was greatly influenced by the work of Cortona and by the 1660s had developed the French variant that became the foundation of the Louis XIV court style. His innovations in both art and architecture created a harmony to which the symbolic imagery of a divine hierarchy could appear as a glorious vision, and his promotion to Director of the Paris Academie de Beaux Arts in 1648 gave him the position to encourage its development.

Typical decorative motif associated with the Sun King Louis XIV. (Author's collection, from Cape Horners Museum, St Malo)

When Louis XIV took the throne in 1661 he set about creating a palace that would express his ideal of a king with absolute power. Le Brun together with Le Vau and Le Nôtre had already shown their pre-eminence in architectural thinking and were employed as early as 1668 to convert Louis XIII's hunting lodge at Versailles into a new palace.

When the treaty of Nijmegen was signed in 1678 by the Netherlands and her allies, it set the seal on French supremacy in Europe. Louis relocated his residence to Versailles where he continued to employ the greatest artistic talent that France had to offer, creating a vision of excellence from which he could administer his supreme command. Work continued throughout his reign and by the time of his death in 1715 the French Baroque style had been established as equal to that of contemporary Rome. The Palace of Versailles had become the model to emulate in its innovative layout and scale of grandeur. It had an amazing influence throughout Europe – even William of Orange, Louis's implacable enemy, chose the French style to rebuild the courts of Holland, and after assuming the throne of England in 1688 he set about improving the palaces there in the same manner.

Baroque sculpture, Cliveden House, Buckinghamshire. (Author's collection)

Stern of a Dutch-built ship for the French navy, one of ten authorised in 1665. This pen and ink sketch by Willem van de Velde the elder displays a decorative composition typical of Dutch ships from the mid-1600s. (National Maritime Museum PY3881)

Louis XIV regarded art and architecture as having an important political role, serving to impress the population with its splendour and ideological imagery, whilst also underlining its imposing authority to keep them firmly in their place. This was a theme not only evident in buildings, but in the decoration of his ships, conveying to the world the message of the Sun King's absolute power. In Jean-Baptiste Colbert (1619-1683) he found the perfect statesman: the son of a draper, Colbert had risen to the position of financial adviser to Cardinal Mazarin, who on his deathbed recommended Colbert's services to the king. Colbert was appointed minister of finance in 1665 and soon instigated a sweeping set of changes with the intention of making France economically self-sufficient. He set up chambers of commerce, paying particular interest to international trade, which effectively left the internal economy locked into a medieval system of guilds. Despite the Sun King's incredible extravagances, Colbert managed to maintain some degree of financial solvency and as part of his duties in the financial affairs of the king, took control of all building work. He had already engaged Le Brun during the rebuilding of the Louvre and now put him in control at Versailles. Le Brun's input was immense – not only in his own work, but in overseeing virtually every aspect of

other contributors, which undoubtedly resulted in the unified completion of this vision.

There seemed no limit to the organising powers of Colbert. In 1669 Louis XIV appointed him Minister of Marine and under his masterly direction every aspect of the navy was totally reorganised, from the conditions and training of its men, to the design and construction of its ships. This resulted in the end of French reliance on Holland, which acted as supplier of ships to many navies in the 1600s.

He reconstructed the naval base at Toulon, making it the largest in France, and set up naval schools at Rochefort, St Malo and Dieppe. Dunkirk had been purchased from Charles II of England in 1666 and rapidly took over from Le Havre as the principal port on the Channel. The fulfillment of Colbert's vision of his new navy is aptly expressed in a statement he made to the commander of the French fleet at Toulon: 'Nothing can be more impressive, nor wholly suited to glorify the king's majesty, than a ship of the fleet bearing the most splendid ornamentation to behold upon the sea.' To this end he established sculpture academies at Toulon, Rochefort and Brest to provide professional training in the art of ship-carving. They soon became centres of excellence, creating ship ornamentation of

Stern carvings from the galley *La Favorite* (launched 1688, lost 1704). The piece was carved at the Toulon sculpture academy showing an interplay of bandwork and foliage, where the former creates a framework for the foliage and figures to emerge. This interplay was a device commonly used by Le Brun where he retains a Classical sense of proportion that has not been swamped by an overlay of imagery but still exudes the voluptuousness of prosperity

The portrait at the base of the panel is believed to be Madame de Maintenon, with whom the king had been having a liaison since 1683. (Author's collection by courtesy of the Brest Maritime Museum)

outstanding quality. The integrity of design and competence of craftsmanship can still be admired in some of the finest examples of maritime sculpture that survive to this day.

Le Brun was made responsible for overseeing the design and ornamentation of all warships, and his influence is very clearly seen in surviving work, thus demonstrating how a figure so influential in the decorative arts of buildings was also responsible for the style and subject matter in maritime applications. At each of the royal dockyards Colbert appointed a master carver who, in theory at least, was responsible for the design of such work. However, a regulation issued in 1674 instructs master carvers and painters to make accurate and detailed drawings of their work, which would then come under the scrutiny of Le Brun. This effectively ended the previous regime where each dockyard tended to develop its own style. By establishing the position of overseer, a unified vision of ship ornamentation was created.

The Baroque sculptor Pierre Puget (1620-1694) had for much of his life also been closely involved with ship decoration. He spent his early years in the carving workshops of Marseilles, which was the home port of the French galley fleet. These lateen rigged vessels were usually rowed by convicts and later slaves (even Indians transported

One of a set of silver candleholders designed by Le Brun that stood in the king's audience chamber at Versailles in the 1680s. Detailed drawings such as this were then presented to the leading goldsmiths of the day such as Ballin and de Launay for manufacture. The entwined dolphins and cherubs could easily be adapted to ship ornamentation, displaying the Baroque's theatrical nature in becoming part of the structure rather than applied to it.

This simple example demonstrates the essential principles of Baroque art, where an interplay of movement directs the emotions of the viewer without losing sight of the underlying structure and order behind it. Here the base is held firm. The griffin creatures look out, unmoved by the activity they support, evoking a sense of guardianship and authority. They also offer a point of stillness which settles an otherwise wandering mind to focus fully on the expressiveness of the piece. The watery nature of the fish rise up to the weightless flight of the cherubs, drawing one up both physically and emotionally to the light that would have burned in the holder above. In this way the underlying principles and structure create the maximum emotional effect in the experience of the viewer.

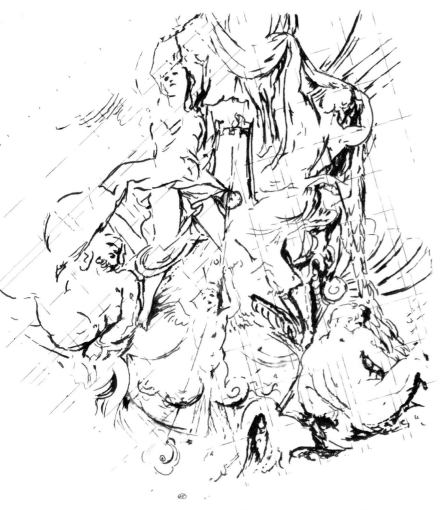

An initial sketch for ship's decoration after Charles Le Brun (1619-1690), displaying his mastery of composition and ability to comprehend three-dimensional concepts. The mass of movement is centred around an underlying structure that gives direction to the viewer. The powerful seated figures offer support to those rising above. From potential chaos one's sight and emotions are lifted up ultimately to the heavens, shedding the shackles of an earth-bound existence.

from the French colonies in America were tried); the galleys were fast and relatively cheap to build, but still displayed a wealth of carved work. When the British took the Danish battle fleet to prevent it falling under Napoleon's control, Denmark quickly rearmed itself with smaller versions of these craft. Rowing vessels also formed the basis of Sweden's inshore fleet, reformed by Fredrik af Chapman (1721-1808) on his return from France in 1757.

The galley fleet was organised as a separate corps under the command of the land army. The 'galleys ordinary' had up to 26 banks of oars and formed the main body of the squadron while the General and Lieutenant General commanded 'galleys extraordinary' having more than 26 banks of oars and considerably richer ornamentation. The General's flagship galley took the name *Réale*, the most resplendent of which was Louis XIV's *Grande Réale*. Built at Marseilles in 1676, the vessel's carvings are attributed mainly to Jean Mathias, master carver at that port from 1676 to 1706 and have survived to this day, beautifully preserved as testament to the superb craftsmanship that was exhibited on such craft. At 171 feet in length, the ship experienced problems with its longitudinal rigidity and was replaced in 1688. Many of the carvings were reused on this replacement and in turn on its successor, the *Réale* of 1694, by which time the fleet's value as a fighting force was in decline. The *Réale*s had become little more than a symbol of prestige,

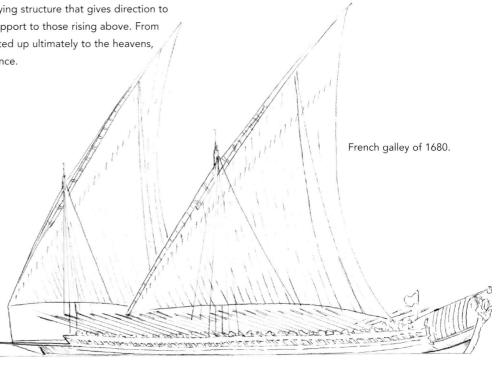

French galley of 1680.

The stern of a model representing the chebec *Le Requin* (built Toulon 1750) provides a typical example of decoration to such vessels. The depiction of a figure riding on a scallop shell is usually identified with Venus (the Roman Aphrodite) as she is delivered to the shore. However, the other attendants in the composition suggest an allusion to the nereid Galatea, as she rides in her cockleshell car drawn by dolphins. Above her head she holds an arch of drapery, the attribute of the Roman god of air, Aura. She is attended by nereids (water nymphs) and a winged figure symbolising an attendant to Aura, whose swiftness enabled Galatea to escape a falling rock thrown at her by Polyphemus, a legend that may allude to the qualities of the ship.

amidst a fleet whose effectiveness depended on smaller vessels capable of fast attack in shallow waters, working to support the battle fleet of larger heavier armed sailing vessels.

The galley fleet was dissolved in 1748, with all those still serviceable moved to Toulon. The Marseilles carver Antoine Gibert was transferred two years later and became master carver at Toulon in 1760. Gibert returned to Marseilles in 1753 to retrieve a stock of carvings that had been removed from scrapped galleys for their reuse at Toulon, where smaller galley-like vessels known as chebecs were still being construction.

There are carvings currently on display at the maritime museum in Brest which are thought to have originated from the sculpture academy at Toulon. It was probably a graduation piece for an apprentice studying at Toulon, possibly using Gibert's retrieved carvings as a model since the density and proportions of the composition are remarkably similar to what is known about galley decoration. The fluid nature of the composition

Carving from the sculpture academy for ship-carvers, now at Brest but believed to originate from Toulon in about 1730-1750. The figure is carried by a dolphin, which suggests that she is the nereid Amphitrite, who was delivered to Neptune as his bride in this manner, perhaps speeded by the wind, depicted here by the arch of drapery. (Author's collection)

A sketch by Pierre Puget for the ornamentation of the *Argos*. (Author's collection)

stands as a superb example of Baroque sculpture, exhibiting the workmanship of someone who has truly mastered his craft.

In 1638 Puget travelled to Italy where he also studied under Cortona and was greatly inspired by the works of Michelangelo and Bernini. He returned to France in 1643 to carry out ship decoration at the workshops in Marseilles. He spent the years 1661-1665 working in Genoa where he established his reputation as a sculptor of great originality. On his return to France he worked on both civic sculpture in Marseilles and ship decoration at Toulon. By 1670 he had become overseer at Toulon, giving him responsibility for the design work.

In December of the same year Le Brun refused the designs of Puget as 'very handsome but not at all convenient to ships.' The minister was more precise in further indicating that Puget 'was to set his mind to getting rid of huge figures that hindered their sailing ability.' Apparent inaction led to Le Brun issuing an order in September 1673 indicating that sterns would not be allowed to carry figures that would affect the stability of the ship, but were to have lighter forms of decoration. Ships already displaying large figurative work had the extreme examples removed. Curiously, figureheads escaped this order, with ships such as *Laurier* of 1678 having a group figurehead. The order of 1673 would have made Puget directly accountable to Le Brun, a situation he would have found intolerable – he was after all an artist of exceptional talent not only as a sculptor but also as a very accomplished painter, and it was his intention that the decorative composition of ships

should consist of both art forms. He resigned in 1679, returning to architectural sculpture. His style remained faithful to the Italian school, bringing him little favour at Versailles. His influence on the design of carved work in the ships of Toulon can be seen from drawings that survive showing figurative work of truly monumental proportions. He returned to his home town of Marseilles, designing architectural projects for the community, providing another example of the common thread that runs through the application of the decorative arts, where the decoration of a nation's ships was shown to be as important as royal palaces, civic buildings and aristocratic houses by employing the same great designers and craftsmen of the day. Unfortunately in Puget's case, it would appear to be followed without a practical regard for the ship's intended purpose.

From 1672 to 1678 France was at war with the Netherlands, giving an opportunity to see how

Pierre Puget design for *La Madame* 1669. The designs attributed to Puget are often drawn as a means of expressing ideas rather than working drawings. Constructional details were clearly seen as the concern of those who dealt with such matters. The flowing exuberance of his designs encapsulates the grand theatre of Baroque's self-assuredness in a wonderful display of imagery whose appearance in land context must have been breathtaking. He endeavoured to pour the same degree of lavish decoration onto the stern of his ships with little regard to their seaworthiness; the hindrance they posed to the practicalities of sailing the ship were clearly of secondary importance.

their ships performed. Colbert set about establishing a comparison in the abilities of each nation's ships leading to his son Colbert de Seignelay (1651-1690) compiling a report which indicated that French ships were overburdened with large decorations compared to Dutch and English ships. This confirmation of Le Brun's views probably led to the order of 1674 and the subsequent period of research into naval architecture. In practice, the effect was not to change ornamentation dramatically, with each yard maintaining some individuality of style, set within the unified vision of Le Brun.

The appointment of master carvers for each yard took place around the time of the naval order, with particular attention given to the three principal yards where the sculpture academies had been established. The first master carver to be appointed at Brest, in 1674, was René d'Augère (1642-1703). In 1678 he provided designs for *Le Souverain*. Although the composition still retains large figurative work, there is a marked reduction in the sheer volume of carving compared to that of Puget. His design for the figurehead of *Le Neptune* of 1679 is a superb example of his masterful draughtsmanship and sense of composition; it also indicates the transformation of ship design from Dutch to purely French, not only in the direction

of its decorative style, but also innovations in the technical advancement of their ship design.

The post at Rochefort was given to Claude Buirette (1639-1694), whose propensity for large armorial compositions set the style of ornamentation at the yard. Buirette's son Claude-Ambroise (1663-1743) was appointed master carver at Port-Louis in 1698, rising to the position of master carver at Rochefort in 1712. Buirette's second son Thomas (born 1664) also worked as a sculptor at Rochefort. Following the death of Claude-Ambroise, the post of master carver at Rochefort remained empty for some years. In 1743 a carver from the French colony in Quebec named Pierre-Noël Levasseur (1690-1770) came to Rochefort to further his training. After a brief return to Quebec, he came back to Rochefort in 1746 to be appointed to the post. His talents were also called upon by the chamber of commerce in La Rochelle, where he carved a number of maritime-themed sculptures to the facade of their building in 1763 and shortly before his death in 1769. Some well-ornamented ships' sterns carved in stone can still be seen.

Another carver whose family continued the tradition was Philippe Caffieri (1634-1716). Originally from Rome, he became acquainted with

Above: The 80-gun *Paris* was launched at Toulon in 1668 with ornamentation by Pierre Puget. As a skilled painter and sculptor, Puget often combined both mediums, with the *tableau de poupe* providing a convenient surface for large painted scenes. The spiral columns and grandiose balcony forming the quarter gallery point to Puget's reliance upon examples used ashore, rather than more imaginative adaptations for maritime use. (From Carr Laughton, *Old Ship Figureheads & Sterns*)

Left: Many of Puget's creations were heavily criticised by seamen as dangerously impractical – Admiral Duquesne refused to go to sea in Puget's *Royal Louis* – and *Paris* was rebuilt as *Royal Thérèse* a few years after her launch. However, as depicted in this van de Velde drawing, the decorative scheme still provides a theatrical performance that refuses to be bound by the limitations of practicality. (National Maritime Museum PZ7270)

Le Brun during his appointment as a sculptor at Versailles, where he completed a number of sculptures in wood. When it was decided that the Grand Canal at the palace was to have gondolas amongst its pleasures, Caffieri was the obvious choice to decorate such craft. A close friendship clearly formed between the two: in 1663 Philippe married Le Brun's cousin Françoise Renault de Beauvallon, and Le Brun's wife Suzanne Butay (herself from a family of sculptors) became godmother to a number of the Caffieri children. In 1687 Philippe was appointed master carver at Le Havre. He was also given the responsibility for all carved work at the Dunkirk yard.

Drawings detailing Philippe's designs for the Versailles gondolas carry the hallmarks of his Italian origin, together with some fifteen drawings that survive from his time at Le Havre. A drawing which details carved work for the frigate *L'Amphytrite*, built at Dunkirk in 1700, is signed by the designer René Levasseur, which suggests that Philippe carved from his design. Of his five sons three followed in their father's footsteps, the eldest, François (1667-1729), succeeded Philippe in 1714, followed by his grandson Charles Philippe (1695-1766) and great grandson Charles-Marie (1736-1777). Many drawings of François and Charles Philippe Caffieri's work survive, giving a useful reference to the decorative style and motifs of their periods and the degree of drawing skill that each possessed.

The Swedish artist Carl August Ehrensvärd also travelled to France in 1766 where he made a series of sketches depicting ship decoration. The example reproduced here is a detail of decoration

A sketch taken from a drawing by Le Brun for a quarter gallery, demonstrating the quintessential French style that here creates a delicate balance between asymmetric waywardness with its naturalistic forms, whilst still maintaining an elegant sense of Classical symmetry. Such constructional elements together with the use of palm leaves would date the design to the latter end of Le Brun's career.

from an unidentified ship, in which he has captured the exuberance of Baroque design, showing the French penchant for group figures, and the distinctive arrangement of head rails terminating behind the cathead, giving further opportunity for added decoration. Forward of this is a putto-like figure in the form of a herm that supports the cathead, or *bossoir* in French. This projecting timber enables the anchor to be lifted clear of the ship's side, although the mass of decoration at the termination of the head rails must have still been very susceptible to damage. The head timbers in French are called *jambettes* ('small legs'), which are often fashioned as balusters, as in this example.

Colbert's death in 1683 also signalled the decline of Le Brun's influence and the beginning of a move away from the Classical unity which underpinned the added exuberance of Baroque style. In 1690 Jean Bérain (1639-1711) succeeded Le Brun as overseer of ship ornamentation. He had become a leading creative force within the royal court and was to be responsible for furthering the development of Le Brun's work into a new light form. The distinctive features of this were the

Carl August Ehrensvärd, pen and ink drawing of unidentified French ship. (Göteborg Maritime Museum SMG/M/73)

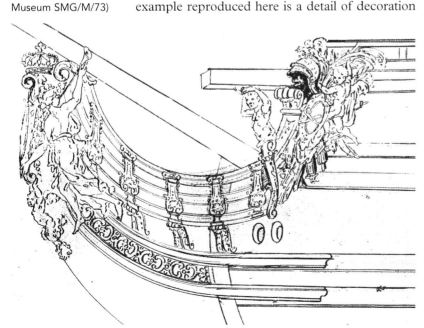

An example of Le Brun's style of Grotesque ornamentation.

Bérain's reworking of a similar composition indicating his lighter approach in form and density. Bandwork has started to appear within the design

Soleil Royal of 1689, which although attributed to Bérain, were executed whilst Le Brun still held the post of Overseer. The carving work was entrusted to the court sculptor Antoine Corsevoix, indicating once more the importance that the French placed on ensuring that the best artisans possible were engaged from conception to completion of their decorative work The density of decorative composition is considerably lighter, with the introduction of banded panels that put greater emphasis on the vertical and horizontal structure of the ship rather than relying on the theatrical ingenuity of High Baroque to encapsulate the underlying form within its grand purpose.

Colbert's son, de Seignelay, set Bérain the task of standardising ship decoration. Similar orders were being issued at much the same time by the English Admiralty in an effort to reduce the cost and sheer bulk of carved work that was seen to be having an adverse effect on the ship's efficiency. Although he had no previous experience of working with the practicalities of naval architecture, the format of his style was perfectly suited to ship decoration, where the use of panelling and fretwork emphasised the horizontals and verticals of the architecture. Bandwork panels framed

In 1696 Bérain was commissioned to design a coach for the Swedish King Charles XI. This drawing shows the decorative arrangement for the rear framing of the coach. The espagnolette head in the centre of the bottom crosspiece is a motif that will also appear on his maritime designs. The lion figures are also interesting in that they adopt the rather subdued demeanour that is also prevalent in the rare cases when such creatures are used in French figureheads. The composition of the upper crossbeam could easily be transposed directly to the tafferel of a ship. Other motifs, such as the patera in the upright sections (small formalised flowers which create breaks in the panelling) will also come to be a feature in ship ornamentation.

reworking of Le Brun's grotesques. This type of ornamentation was first seen in Roman art of the 1400s where lightly scrolling foliage would evolve into fantastical figures and mythical creatures such as the sphinx and griffin. To this formula Le Brun added bandwork, a device used to contain or frame a design into set panels. Bérain's reworking of the bandwork and foliate forms harks back to an earlier combination of the forms known as Arabesque, and his work has been misleadingly described as such. In his development of the style, the bandwork will abruptly change direction, evolving into grotesque masks or foliate forms.

The transition between the two masters begins to show itself in detailed drawings that exist for *Le*

gallery rails, and interweaving foliage linked quarter piece figures to the tafferel, developing an ornamental language that compensated for the lack of large figurative work. He created the perfect balance between the artistic value of ornamentation and the functionality of a ship. Between 1681 and his death in 1711, he produced over one hundred designs, accounting for the vast majority of ships built within that period. The influence of his work at Versailles and elsewhere continued as his style developed, adding new elements such as 'chinoiserie' and the more abstract forms of 'rocaille'. Panels framed in light bandwork would be intertwined with shells and naturalistic foliage, on which were woven Classical figures holding festoons or lightly worked drapery. Engravings of his designs were first published in the 1680s, leading to the spread of his style throughout Europe.

It is clear from the surviving drawings that Le Brun and Bérain were men of vision – not just as an initial concept, but complete in every detail. A craftsman following their drawings could confidently execute the work, as every intention has been clearly expressed, in a way that shows that the image held in the designer's mind was complete. There are no 'fuzzy' areas that betray an inability to visualise quite how a certain part will work. A lack of such clarity invariably manifests itself in drawings as little more than a limp expression of a vague idea, leaving the craftsman to sort out the detail necessary to create a cohesive composition.

An incident that occurred in 1741 demonstrates how distinctive the decoration of French ships had become. On 24 March the British 44-gun ship *Anglesea* was cruising in the approaches to the Channel. She was to be joined by the *Augusta*, which had put into Kinsale to land some sick crew members. The *Anglesea*, seeing an approaching sail, assumed it to be the *Augusta* and piped to dinner, giving the vessel no further heed. The approaching ship turned out to be the 56-gun *Apollon* belonging to the French navy but fitted out as a privateer; she carried no colours. It was not until the vessel was fast approaching, that she yawed slightly revealing decorations on her quarter gallery which immediately identified her as French. In the confusion that followed, the British captain ordered the foresail to be set, which had the unfortunate effect of burying the gun ports of the leeward lower deck into the sea, causing the ship to take on a considerable amount of water.

The *Apollon* poured fire onto the *Anglesea*, leaving 60 men dead or wounded. Among the fatalities were Captain Elton and the ship's master. In retrospect, the *Anglesea* should have passed under the enemy's stern to gain an advantage, but with the ship now half full of water, and the *Apollon* having engaged on her leeward side, the *Anglesea* struck her colours and was taken as a prize. The subsequent court martial of the second lieutenant reads as follows:

> It was unanimously of the opinion that Captain Elton deceased, did not give timely directions for getting his ship clear or in proper posture of defence, nor did he afterwards behave like an officer or seaman, which was the cause of the ship being left to Lieutenant Phillips in such distress and confusion. And that Phillips late second lieutenant of the said ship, by not endeavouring to the utmost of his power after Captain Elton's death to put the ship in order of fighting, not encouraging the inferior officers and common men to fight courageously, and by yielding to the enemy, falls under part of the tenth article. They do sentence him to death, to be shot by a platoon of musketeers on the forecastle … But having regard to the distress and confusion the ship was in when he came to the command, and being a young man and unexperienced, they beg leave to recommend him for mercy.

The recommendation was ignored, and he was duly shot. This somewhat harsh decision was possibly swayed by rumours that Phillips had shown Jacobite tendencies – the Navy contained known sympathisers – at a time when the threat of invasion was very great.

The *Apollon* was built at Rochefort in 1740 and later served in North America, being present during the French defence of Louisbourg, which came under siege from the British. On 28 January 1758 the French sank the *Apollon* along with three other ships in the mouth of the harbour to blockade the entrance.

A sketch showing the stern of *L'Apollon* was drawn by the Swedish artist Karl August Ehrensvärd during his studies in France. The centrepiece of the tafferel is remarkably similar to that of *Le Soleil Royal* (1689) in depicting Apollo driving his chariot across the firmament. Such

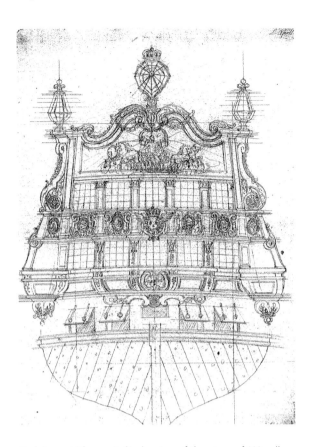

Carl August Ehrensvärd's drawing of the stern of *L'Apollon*.
(Göteborg Maritime Museum SMG B 3)

imagery, not surprisingly, was frequently used to uphold Louis XIV's aspirations as the Sun King. Above him festoons of foliage are lightly draped around two deeply scrolling volutes not dissimilar to the previous example of the Swedish royal coach (1696). The quarter pieces consist of two consoles whose scrolling ends enfold a sunflower, creating a further reference to Louis XIV. Bandwork panels form the solid balustrading to the quarter gallery with royal insignia occupying the central position, while the corresponding panel below it is in the form of a cartouche displaying the vessel's name, a feature that would become synonymous with French sterns; similarly the *cul de lamp* (or pendants) that form the lower termination of the quarter pieces are a quintessentially French appendage.

Although Ehrensvärd does not indicate the age or designer of the work, it bears all the hallmarks of Bérain's work from the 1690s. In his collection of sketches Ehrensvärd would appear to be recording the development of French decorative styles, rather than simply sketching the ships of his own time, possibly in an effort to understand the progressive construction and make up of composition. A long-standing tradition in the

Bérain's design for the stern of the 64-gun ship *Le Brillant* of 1690. The main rail to the tafferel is formed of a flat section which then sweeps down to form supports for the stern lights. The curved sections are decorated with patera rosettes whilst the centre section has a pelmet of lambrequin, a repeating pattern of short swags imitating woven fabric. Bérain combined this popular element from the earlier Grotesque period with espagnolette to become a trademark of his interior designs and here adapted it to a maritime composition. Caryatid figures form the quarter pieces where they serve to support the stern lights, unveil a portrait of the king and return the lower structure of the quarter gallery back to the fashion piece. Solid balustrading to the upper open gallery is decorated in set panels of bandwork and foliate forms, which again is a key feature of Bérain's decorative compositions. The central panel on the quarterdeck has become established as an escutcheon housing an emblem of the crown with the corresponding panel on the upper deck reserved for the vessel's name. The oval panels known as médaillons du vaisseau lead to the quarter galleries.

teaching of art students is the practice of copying the drawings or paintings of the great masters, in order to gain an understanding of the various techniques and forms of expression that their style encapsulates. It is therefore a very useful exercise in understanding period styles and an invaluable preliminary aid in attempting to carve works that represent them.

In this collage of decorative motifs Ehrensvärd

Bérain's design for the quarter galleries of the 64-gun ship *Le Brillant* of 1690. The caryatid figure on the left is taken from Bérain's designs for King Charles XI of Sweden's coach of 1696. In classical architecture these figures formed supporting columns, and Bérain has used the device here to provide an aesthetic support to the stern lanterns. The upper finishing to the quarter gallery is surmounted by the regal crown beneath which a scrolling pediment acts to frame a motif depicting the Sun King. A false light to the quarterdeck is set within inward curving panels decorated with acanthus leaves to form the upper section of *les bouteilles*, which in conjunction with the *cul de lamp* create what was to become the distinctive shape of French quarter galleries. The central panel above the lower finishing houses the monarch's cypher, with simple mouldings that help to accentuate the inward curve of the gallery. Note also the use of patera in the mouldings on the side of the ship.

Drawing by Carl August Ehrensvärd of the French *L'Assuré*. (Göteborg Maritime Museum SMG 31070)

appears to be studying the compositional elements of Bérain. He also appears to be making an attempt at replicating the drawing style of Bérain, where the relaxed looseness of line depicts a sense of movement that is very similar to preliminary sketches by Bérain. Gradually a confidence in the formation of designs is attained through this practice, and a fluidity of movement in the drapery above the figure is beginning to emerge.

Bt the time the 5-year-old Louis XV succeeded the Sun King in 1715 Bérain's lighter style of decoration was well established, providing the basis from which new styles would develop in a climate that heralded an end to the formal restraints of the previous regime. The change in monarch coincided with the appointment of a new overseer to the master carvers, following Bérain's death in 1711. Antoine-François Vassé accepted the post, as the succession of master carvers at Dunkirk passed from Philippe Caffieri to his son François following his father's death in 1714. Three years later, François relinquished this post to his son Charles, in order to take up the post of master carver at Brest.

The period from 1715 to the mid-1720s became known as Regency style after the Duc d'Orléans who ruled as Regent until 1723. It is characterised by a continual move away from the ordered hierarchical court style, free of nationalistic symbolism and constraints of Classical motifs. Subject matter became more naturalistic with the

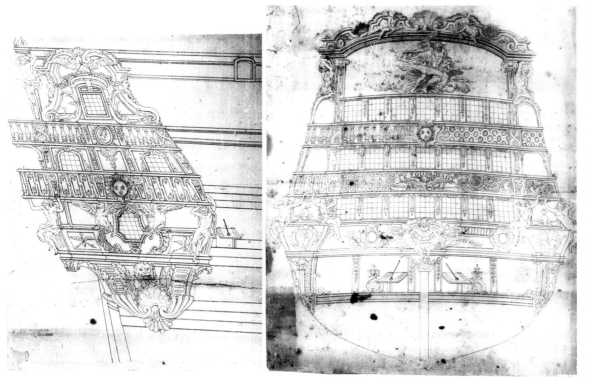

The 110-gun ship *Foudroyant* of 1723 was launched from the yard at Brest with ornamentation by Antoine-François Vassé. His composition shows the continuing influence of Bérain in the gallery formation, but Vassé has elaborated the decorative composition with the reintroduction of figurative work. It is known that Vassé was a great admirer of Puget, and elements of this design, such as the two putti astride the tafferel, are taken almost directly from Puget's design for the *Royal Thérèse* (see earlier illustration) while figures to the quarter pieces have progressed to the elegance and fluidity of design that are the hallmarks of the Vassé style. (Danish Archives, Copenhagen)

use of scallop shells, foliage and bandwork designs. Acanthus patterns were lighter, springing from bandwork in a less continuous pattern that could change direction or diminish into a natural ending.

Antoine-François Vassé (1681-1736) was a student at the carving academy in Toulon. His talent was soon realised and it is a testament to the success of the academy system set up by Colbert that it produced so many skilled craftsmen. That in his short life Vassé rose to the position of overseer is also a mark of his exceptional talent as an artist and designer. He had been employed at Versailles assisting with designs for the chapel before accepting the position of overseer in 1711. The Regent transferred the hub of French society from Versailles to Paris where, in 1718, Vassé designed and executed the panelling for the Hôtel de Toulouse. This and other private residences such as the Hôtel d'Assy became the settings where the sophisticated urban society of Paris could experience the most advanced decorative fashions, of which Vassé and Gilles-Marie Oppenard (1672-1742) were the leading exponents.

Their designs introduced a fluidity of movement, interpreting forms in an increasingly naturalistic manner that moved away from a formalised structure. Exotic motifs influenced by the many artefacts imported by the East India company inspired the compositions of 'chinoiserie'

and 'arabesques' and shell-like structures that formed the medium of 'rocaille', a term first coined in the publication of *Premier livre de forme rocquaille et cartel* in 1736 by Jean Mondon (died 1760). Asymmetric compositions were also a major feature of their work, paving the way for the advent of the Rococo style.

Ship decoration called for less frivolous motifs, and the approach of Vassé for the decoration of *Foudroyant* of 1723 was to reintroduce figurative work on a grand and vibrant scale, but unlike those of Puget, they are tucked well into the body of the composition to retain a practical ability to work the ship. These are balanced by bandwork panels in the tradition of Bérain but the overall effect is one of fluidity and an easing of contours.

François Caffieri's design for *La Néréide* was approved in 1723 and displays a confident use of the curves and reverse curves that characterise the Regency style. An *espagnolette* head set into a semi-circular pediment forms the upper finishing and piercing to the curved section creates a naturalistic shell-like appearance. Margent drops and festoons of husks cascade down the outer edges of the gallery where a stylised dolphin creates a continuity of composition as it turns onto the stern walkway. This has solid balustrading consisting of a raised framework inset with scallop shells and lightly scrolling foliage. The pattern is repeated in the waist

La Néréide, François Caffieri 1723. The succession from Philippe Caffieri to his son François saw the appointment of a new master carver willing to embrace the innovations of Vassé. He was highly accomplished in adapting the Regency style to ship decoration, as his design for the 42 gun ship *La Néréide* demonstrates. The ship was built at Rochefort in 1722-1724, where François stood in as master carver, his main seat of office being Brest.

of the quarter gallery where a *médaillon aveugle* balances a wreath port on the side of the ship.

Scallop shells are also incorporated into the scrollwork around the wreath light where further festoons of husks complement those above, creating a balance between shells and foliage, in a delicate application that maintains an air of elegance. The lower finishing terminates in the traditional *cul de lamp* above which the body of the quarter gallery is held in a bowl-shaped pattern known as 'gadrooning'. Acanthus leaves emerge from here, tightly hugging the swelling form of the gallery.

In Caffieri's design for *Le Gloire* the naturalistic influence of Vassé can be seen in the use of palms

for the foliate forms. The slender waving leaves adapt well to asymmetric compositions often combined with shells. The theme is continued by Caffieri with the use of palm trees to form the quarter pieces or *figures de poupe*. Their use is generally associated with triumphal processions and as such work very well in this location, acting as supporters to the main rail, which creates the effect of a canopy over the figure of winged victory resting on the clouds. Her left hand is placed on the globe which is her dominion, whilst the other raises a laurel branch denoting glory and honour. At the base of the palms a panoply of armour rests in a manner that suggest a sense of basking in the

François Caffieri's design for the 46-gun ship *Le Gloire* built at Le Havre in 1726.

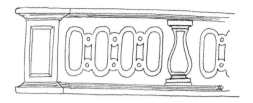

Le Soleil Royal 1689.

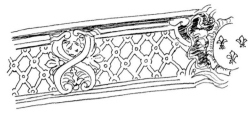

Le Foudroyant 1723.

glory of victory. Such gladiatorial helmets when set with a shield signify Mars, the Roman god of war. The two small lights in the *tableau de poupe* are framed in bandwork that still manages to introduce an element of doubling back in a neat design of which Bérain would have been proud, with arched mouldings to the lights creating a wave-like effect that forms the perfect base for the figure floating on clouds. The two central lights lead out to an open walkway, which extends beyond the stern in typical French fashion.

The solid balustrading to the walkway has a mixture of decorative features such as the cable moulding, below which is a band of basket-weave. Basket-weave appears in the borders of porcelain and silverware at this time, where advances in rolling mill technology helped to replicate repeating patterns. For the wood carver this repetitive task was still cut by hand, but such work is not without its uses. By learning how to create given shapes in the least number of cuts, it provides a good discipline in working efficiently, and as such is an excellent task for apprentices. The rhythm that is created by such work helps develop an ease of movement in the co-ordination of hands and tools, encouraging a sense of confidence in their use.

This small addition of basket-weave is also an indication of the emerging fashion of *Fêtes Champêtres* and the style known as Pastoral, which evoked a highly romanticised ideal of simple country life, often depicted in rustic scenes of contented and well turned out animals and peasants. Fashionable figures in society (such as the mistress to Louis XV, Madame de Pompadour, and Marie Antoinette, who married the future Louis XVI in 1770) amused themselves with such role playing, while the real peasants of France starved. The paintings of François Boucher (1703-1770) depicted such pastoral scenes and provided the basis of designs for printed textiles and porcelain, but would not find their way into the inappropriate setting of ship ornamentation.

Decoration to the balustrading continues with a repeating framework of oval forms, which are inset with alternating palmettes and fleur-de-lys. This type of framework is known as a diaper pattern and most commonly consists of repeating circles, ovals or lozenge shapes; it was to became a characteristic motif of the Regency style, although its origins are much older, having gained popularity in Tudor times.

Bérain used the device as early as 1689 in his design for *Le Soleil Royal* and in this form diaper-pattern frameworks became a characteristic motif of French ships until the late 1750s. Vassé adapted the device on *Le Foudroyant* in 1723 where the pattern repeats horizontally and vertically to create a lattice effect. In this form the device becomes a motif used in Rococo compositions where the resulting contours help to emphasise the structure of curved forms. The centrepiece of the balustrade consists of a large rocaille-inspired cartouche that houses the vessel's name, this being flanked by two wreath ports whose borders create the impression of a cartouche. In theory, the inclusion of these apertures could provide two additional stern-chaser guns.

Juste-Aurèle Meissonnier (1695-1750) succeeded Bérain and his son (also Jean) as architectural designer to Louis XV in 1726, having worked previously in the decorative arts specialising as a goldsmith. Meissonnier and Vassé were early contemporaries in what later became known as the rocaille style, developing the aquatic motifs of shells and rocks of almost coral-like forms into compositions where the scrollwork and foliage continued to ease the structure away from the constraints of horizontals and verticals.

Meissonnier continued to develop the asymmetrical direction through the reversal of C- and S-shaped scrolls to emerge as wave-like forms that rise and fall with the liquidity of constant movement. His incredibly inventive designs for gold and silverware, together with furniture and interior decoration, were first published in 1723, to

This example illustrates a number of Rococo's key features such as the asymmetry achieved by the reversal of C-scrolls, the use of palms as foliate forms, pierced shells creating the base of the structure and the naturalistic representation of the interspersed flowers.

create the basis of the Rococo style. To this were added the naturalistic shell forms now known as rocaille; the slender palms and foliate forms of Vassé were already established motifs. Chinese goods imported through the East India companies and subsequently popularised as chinoiserie, in part through the adoption of motifs by Bérain, already presented a sense of asymmetry and exotic

subjects that were readily absorbed into the genre of Rococo. The light frivolity of its forms matched the atmosphere of the age, where society cast away the formalities of the old order to simply indulge in its riches.

Ship decoration throughout the Regency period and the years leading up to Rococo's heyday in France, came under the scrutiny of Vassé, who seems to have stopped short of approving designs that went beyond his own development of the asymmetrical style, enabling the decoration of what were after all ships of war to retain a sense of disciplined order. The light gay nature of what had become Rococo's frivolous subject matter was generally confined to interior decoration, with only the stronger elements of asymmetry finding its way into French architectural design.

With the death of François Caffieri in 1729, the posts of master carver at Brest and Dunkirk were passed to his son Charles Philippe. His early designs would have come under the scrutiny of Vassé to ensure the decorative structure remained faithful to his artistic direction. When Vassé died in 1736, the post of master overseer was not continued; instead, the responsibility for design returned to the earlier system where the master carver for each arsenal took control.

Right: Pen and ink sketch by Carl August Ehrensvärd depicting the stern of *La Couronne*. (Göteborg Maritime Museum SMG/M/73 12676)

Work in the style of Meissonnier illustrating the fluidity and balance that he managed to maintain in his confident construction of asymmetric forms. The examples are details taken from Mondon's designs published in 1736, displaying his development of the rocaille.

The 30-gun frigate *La Renommée* of 1744 stands as a typical example of the decorative style developed by C P Caffieri, where decorative motifs are kept firmly in their place and displayed as intricate details that do not detract from the underlying sense of order.

While the artistic taste of Louis XV's court continued in the Rococo fashion, leading figures such as the architect François Blondel (1705-1774) and the designer Nicholas Cochin (1715-1790) began to ridicule the disparate excesses of the style, calling for a return to dignity. It was also the period of the 'Grand Tour' when the archaeological discoveries at Herculaneum and Pompeii had awakened a renewed interest in Classicism, a style encouraged by Blondel and Cochin as they endeavoured to restore a sense of the principles that underpinned what they saw as the golden age of French art. By the 1750s the wayward aimlessness of Rococo had reached the opposite extreme of the Sun King's vision. The glory of his empire was also crumbling fast, following the War of the Austrian Succession and the Seven Years War that had left the country in political and economic turmoil.

Although Rococo continued to have an influence in Europe up to the 1770s, it had run its course in France, where the political climate had become more serious. It was time for art to sober up and Neoclassicism became the order of the day, providing a path of disciplined structure for society to tread. The early designs of C P Caffieri were essentially re-workings of Vassé, but he began to develop his own style with a shift towards Neoclassicism as early as 1740, by which time his designs are devoid of any asymmetry beyond a wistful return to the curving nature of the Regency style. This he kept firmly in check by a supporting framework of formal mouldings and applied decorative motifs.

The 30-gun frigate *La Renommée* of 1744 stands as a typical example of the decorative style developed by C P Caffieri. The rigid structure of this creates a stark contrast to the flowing naturalism of his father's work. Classical composure remained a hallmark of his designs from the 1740s until his death in 1766.

The 74-gun *Monarque* was built at Brest to a design by Jacques-Luc Coulomb in 1745-47; the master carver at Brest at the time was Charles Caffieri. The ship was taken by Hawke off Finisterre in 1747 and this drawing shows her decorative work as captured. The draughtsman has managed to capture the general sense and feel of the composition; interestingly, this displays a greater range of decorative motifs than frigates of the period, which adhere more vigorously to the concepts of Neoclassicism. (National Maritime Museum J3201)

Obedience to the Neoclassical regime gives *La Renommée* an air of military precision that will not tolerate any deviation from its set path. Neoclassicists were keen on the extensive use of intricate mouldings, such as the cornice which forms the top section of the tafferel, and delicate motifs carved in very light relief, such as anthemion (stylised acanthus flower) vases, urns, palmettes, candelabra forms and mythical creatures such as the sphinx. The two remnants in this design from the earlier naturalistic style are the two swelling pilasters that form the quarter pieces and the shell-inspired cartouche. The winged figure holding two trumpets typically denotes Fame, more commonly blowing both, or blowing one to sound out victories whilst the other hand holds a branch of palms denoting the peace that will follow victory.

Renommée proved to be one of the fastest frigates in the French navy and was used to deliver dispatches to the French fort at Louisbourg in April 1745, but was forced to retire when she encountered a British blockading squadron. She returned to France with news of the blockade, whereupon the 64-gun *Vigilante* was despatched with stores for the besieged fortress; this ship was, however, captured by the British on 19 May.

During a passage to San Domingo in 1747, *Renommée* was taken by the *Dover*, having been severely crippled the day before in an encounter with the *Victory*. She served in the British navy as the *Renown* and proved to be faster than anything in the fleet at that time. During a rebuild in 1757 she was strengthened to take a heavier armament, as a result of which her sailing ability suffered, but she continued to be of use, serving in the Leeward Islands in 1759. In 1762 she was back in home waters and captured the 26-gun *Guirlande* whilst cruising in the Channel. *Renommée* was finally broken up in 1771.

The drawings of C P Caffieri were often turned into their three-dimensional form by the sculptor Jacques-Étienne Collet (1721-1808), who worked as a carver at Brest from 1752 to 1800. He was regarded as the greatest figurative carver at the arsenal, and a number of wax maquettes survive as testament to the superb quality of his work. The sense of movement and expression of his figures helped to restore a balance in the otherwise sombre demeanour of Caffieri's designs. Collet received little formal recognition of his talent, preferring perhaps to remain in the background whilst those around him rose to positions of importance.

Collet's son Yves-Étienne (1761-1843) joined the sculpture academy at Brest when only 9 years of age. His artistic talents flourished under the guidance of his father, who encouraged the aspiring student to continue his studies in Paris at the Academie de Beaux Arts, 'to absorb and become proficient in the new styles'. He returned to Brest in 1784 and was appointed to the post of master carver in 1797. He was to be the last master carver at Brest, the position being dissolved on his retirement at the age of 79 in 1840.

Despite the reputation of Rococo having suffered under the criticism of Cochin and Blondel, it still found favour in the French court. Madame de Pompadour remained a patron of the style, commissioning many works up to her death in 1764. Her taste would inevitably influence the style of design, which became more subdued as

Mars as depicted in the superb carving of Yves-Étienne Collet. (Author's collection by courtesy of the Brest Maritime Museum)

Quarter gallery ornamentation to Augustin Pic's 1753 model of a 74-gun ship.

Drawings of Augustin Pic's model of 1753 showing the stern and quarter gallery decoration for a 74-gun ship. Many elements of the ornamentation bear a striking resemblance to a model constructed at Rochefort two years earlier known as the *Dauphin Royal*. The model was the result of an order issued by the Secretary of State for the Marine to the master shipwright and sculptor at Rochefort, to produce a model that would express what they considered to be their ideal: 'A ship fit to bear the name of a future sovereign'.

she pursued the pastoral idyll. With such patronage, a number of carvers took advantage of the lack of overseer to present designs that demonstrated a desire to retain a sense of luxuriant elegance, whilst avoiding the excesses that led to the art form's eventual decline.

One such artist was the sculptor Jean Lange (1671-1761), who held the post of master carver at Toulon from 1736 to 1760 and most notably produced the decoration for *Le Sérieux*, *La Pléiade* and *Le Foudroyant*. His work was influenced by the style of Vassé, which ensured the continuation of Rococo-inspired compositions on the ships of Toulon through to the 1760s. The more subdued forms of Rococo that developed through the increasing influence of Classicism manifested in compositions reminiscent of the Regency style. Carvers continued to produce this style of composition up to the 1770s, no doubt helped by Madame de Pompadour's continuing patronage maintaining its presence in high society.

A good example survives in the exquisite model of a 74-gun ship on display at the museum in Brest, which is a masterpiece of practical ornamentation. Built in 1753 by the Rochefort assistant shipwright Augustin Pic, the decoration is a good example of the continuation of naturalistic style prior to the total acceptance of Neoclassicism. Here the influence of Rococo has subsided to leave a swelling voluptuousness and elegance reminiscent of the Regency period. During Augustin Pic's time at Rochefort, the master carver

at the yard was Victor Bourguignon, who would almost certainly have been responsible for the ornamentation of both Pic's 74-gun model and an earlier but similar model of *Dauphin Royal*.

The town of Rochefort was created to serve the arsenal that was established by Colbert in 1665. Many of its buildings still exist, including the *corderie*

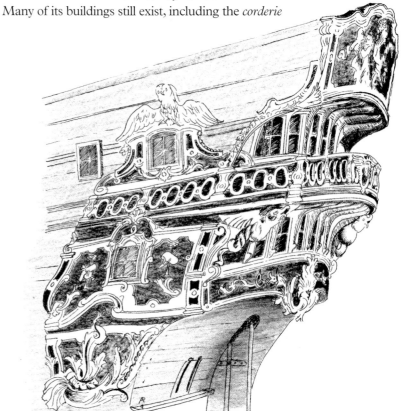

The Rochefort *corderie* (ropewalk) completed in 1669. When approached from the river, it appears as a magnificent palace, while the back, which faces the former dockyard, remains utilitarian. The Admiral's fountain settles in the soft ground to the left of the *corderie*. (Author's collection)

(ropewalk), which when completed in 1669 was the longest building in Europe. A walk through the town provides valuable insight into the progression of ornamentation within a naval town, where sculptors from the arsenal's academy would invariably be employed in the creation of its civic art.

One such example still stands, relating directly to the two models. The town suffered severe water shortages in 1750, due in part to the ageing vitrified pipes constantly breaking in the soft unstable ground of this marshy area. They were replaced with lead pipes and a series of new fountains to supply the town. Bourguignon was commissioned to provide a sculpture which stands at the fountain in the town's square. Bourguignon chose as his theme Neptune and a water nymph, and to represent the meeting of the Ocean and the Charente the two engage in a show of strength wonderfully illustrated as they arm-wrestle, looking intently into each other eyes. The water remains sweet so long as she matches his strength to prevent the mingling of their waters. The style of ornamental motifs and the expressive nature of the figurative work both closely resemble that of the two models.

During Carl August Ehrensvärd's visit to Brest in 1766 he made some pen and ink drawings of *La Couronne*. The presentation of the drawing is similar to that of C P Caffieri, who also employed the heavy use of washes to create shading. They present a curious mixture of styles, which may be representative of the time, or simply a continuation of his studies in the development of French decoration. The general composition and style of motifs originate from Bérain. It even uses a device employed by Bérain where two alternative layouts for the gallery balustrading are displayed either side of the centreline on the same drawing. The tafferel, however, paints a very different picture. The main rail springs from two cornucopia of flowers held by winged figures, creating a romantic feel indicative of the Pastoral form of decoration of the mid-1700s. The fluid line of the scrollwork surmounting the rail is also reminiscent of this period.

An 80-gun ship named *Couronne* was built to a design by Antoine Groignard at Brest in 1766, being the tenth vessel to take the name. The earlier ships were as follows:

1636	the first modern man of war built in France
1664-1675	galley
1669-1712	80-gun ship
1674-1677	6-gun fireship
1677-1686	galley
1686-1696	galley
1697-1716	galley
1697-1716	32-gun ship
1749-1766	74-gun ship built at Rochefort to a design by Blaise Geslain
1766-1796	80-gun ship

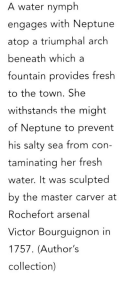

A water nymph engages with Neptune atop a triumphal arch beneath which a fountain provides fresh to the town. She withstands the might of Neptune to prevent his salty sea from contaminating her fresh water. It was sculpted by the master carver at Rochefort arsenal Victor Bourguignon in 1757. (Author's collection)

The 74-gun ship may possibly have been in the process of being broken up when Ehrensvärd was at Brest; if so, the replacement vessel under construction may have re-used some carvings or other sound remnants of the earlier ship. The style of decoration in Ehrensvärd's drawing certainly dates from this period, being remarkably similar to that of the 74-gun ship *Intrepide* built to a Blaise Ollivier design at Brest in the same year.

The 80-gun ship is worthy of mention as it highlights the chequered history that befell so many ships. Launched at Brest in 1766, she was present at the Battle of Ushant in July of 1778 and served as the flagship for de Guichen against Rodney during their engagements off Martinique in 1780. Damage caused by fire in April of 1781 resulted in her being rebuilt at Brest between June and September of that year. In 1792 she was renamed *Ça Ira* by the revolutionary regime (probably with republican alterations to her decoration at the same time) and in August of

Above: Detail of figurative work to the stern of *Le Dauphin Royal*. This large scale and beautifully decorated model was based on a 110-gun ship designed by the master shipwright at Rochefort, Antoine Groignard, in 1751. The model, which is displayed at the maritime museum in Rochefort, is believed to have been for instruction purposes only as there is no record of this vessel having been built. (Author's collection)

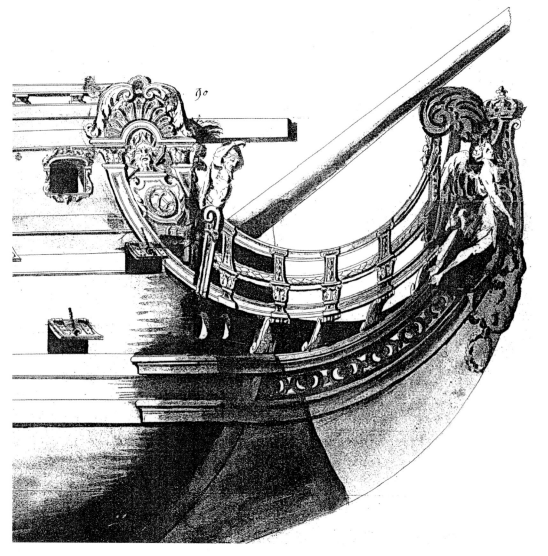

Left: Pen and ink sketch by Carl August Ehrensvärd depicting the bow of *La Couronne*. The design of the figurehead with winged figures acting as supporters to the crown and crest is similar to C P Caffieri's design for *Le Diadéme* of 1756 for which Jacques-Étienne Collet produced a wax maquette before executing the carved work. The fretwork design between the upper and lower cheeks also follows the same repeating pattern as used on *Le Diadéme*. (Göteborg Maritime Museum SMG/M/73 12675)

1793 she was captured by the British, only to be retaken by the French in December of the same year. On 14 April 1795 she was involved in an engagement with the frigate *Inconstant* under the command of Thomas Fremantle and the 64-gun *Agamemnon* commanded by Horatio Nelson. She was boarded by men from the *Agamemnon* and taken into the British navy, but being considered to too badly damaged for active service, was used as a floating hospital at San Fiorenzo (modern Saint-Florent), where on 11 April 1796 the ship was destroyed by an accidental fire.

With the abolition of the post of Overseer in 1736, the development of carving styles slowly became subject to the vagaries of local knowledge, although the navy offered to fund aspiring sculptors from the regions to develop their talent and absorb new academic styles in Paris. Pierre Philippe Lubet (1721-1797) came as a student to the arsenal at Brest in 1736, and after eleven years' service he was admitted to study in Paris; on his return to Brest in 1751 he was named second sculptor under C P Caffieri. Caffieri's son Charles-Marie (1736-1777) was similarly funded and went to Paris in 1756. He returned in 1766, presumably to see his ailing father who died the same year. The post of master carver was awarded to Lubet with Charles-Marie becoming second carver.

Both Lubet and Caffieri's time in Paris was spent during the heyday of Neoclassicism and their designs reflect the sombre nature of the idiom. The minimal amount of carving that adorned ships of the period is a reflection not only of the restrained nature of Neoclassicism, but also changing attitudes within the navy office towards the relevance of decoration. Efficiency in ship design was now paramount, with a utilitarian view of aesthetics as a consequence. Charles-Marie Caffieri submitted his first design in 1766, for the 64-gun ship *Vengeur*. The stern and quarter galleries were devoid of any figurative work, decoration being composed of drapery and mouldings. The art of the ship-carver had all but gone, while the joiner's work also came under threat by his innovation of casting balustrades to the stern walk in metal.

Metal grilles had been proposed for *Le Sérieux*, built at Toulon in 1740, but with the cost of casting being three times that of wooden fabrication, its use at that time was overruled. Charles-Marie's enthusiasm for the new material may have been fuelled by the friendship with his cousin Philippe Caffieri (1714-1774), a celebrated bronze-caster

who was working in Paris during the time Charles-Marie studied there. Philippe cast bronze inlay work for the artist Louis-Joseph Le Lorrain, who was a fellow student of Charles-Marie at the art academy. Lorrain belonged to the circle of artists and intellectuals who met at the fashionable salons. Commissions from such influential circles ensured acceptance of his at times brutally minimalistic portrayal of Classical symmetry, a style that clearly influenced the work of Charles-Marie and Lubet.

In 1777 the secretary of marine, Gabriel de Sartine, wrote to the commodore of the port of Brest, the Count d'Orvilliers, stating that 'The ornamentation no longer holds a political message, and is no longer an artistic necessity. It is an accessory that adds little to the fulfilment of the ship's purpose and a reduction in the spending of this kind will bring about the most scrupulous economy.' The argument was taken up by the commander and officers at Rochefort, where the *intendant*, François-Ambroise d'Aubenton, added that the allegorical figures that were common on the head of ships were slow and costly to produce and only served to make French ships easily recognisable from a distance, as most other nations had only a lion. If only a lion was used, it meant in effect that they could be moved from one ship to be reused on another, where the universal figure was not specific to the ship's name.

The Commissioner of the navy Daniel Lescallier (1743-1822) commented that 'Female figures astride the stem in an attitude that often appeared forced were uncomely. A more practical and morally correct image would be a bounding lion, with or without attributes.' For a man clearly concerned with the moral aspect of design, this last remark hints at a compromise between his personal wishes and that of mainstream French society in its desire to portray themselves as the most virile and sensual nation on earth. To this end French lions often presented their sexual organs not only in full view, but fully erect in a display befitting the self-image held by its males. A model of the 108-gun *Sans Pareil* ('without equal'), launched at Toulon in 1760, provides a typical example of such figures. He also criticised the current quality of carving, expressing the desire to return to the previous regime whereby the master carver would submit a model of the proposed decorations to an overseer, who would uphold the standard of work. He proposed as an example of good work and the type of lion to be employed as that displayed on *L'Actif* of 1752. Here the lion presents a countenance of military might, with his genitalia not obviously rising to the occasion.

Such discussions led to a ministerial instruction in January 1777 stating categorically that: 'Figureheads are to be replaced with lions, holding a shield which should bear the arms of France. Where ships are named after a province, the shield may bear the arms of that province.' A further ministerial instruction was issued in 1786, ordering a standard design for the decoration of each class of ship. The master carver at Brest, Pierre Philippe Lubet, was appointed to fulfill the task, having submitted designs the previous year for *Le Superbe*, which had been suggested as an example of decoration for all the arsenals. The horseshoe-shaped stern of this two-decked ship provided little scope for inventive compositions, which were inevitably reduced to applied mouldings devoid of any figurative work. A balustraded walkway and modest cartouche bearing the ship's name fixed to the upper counter completed the design. Greater scope for artistic expression was allowed at the ship's head, where the figurehead was replaced with what was still an impressively large composition of foliate forms around a crowned shield bearing the arms of France. The termination of the main rail also retained some decoration. Despite the issue of the two orders, it is clear from drawings that exist from subsequent ships that they were not strictly adhered to, as was the case in Britain where similar orders proved unpopular among the captains and crew.

During this period, the yard at Rochefort built a number of very successful frigates to the design of their master shipwright Chevillard. His 32-gun frigate *Hermione* was launched in April of 1779 and on 29 March 1780 set sail as part of a force sent to aid America in its War of Independence. On board was the Marquis de La Fayette, who commanded a force of 5500 men and five frigates. *Hermione* fought a spirited engagement with a British convoy off Louisbourg, and was one element of the French sea power that played a crucial role in the eventual surrender of the British army at Yorktown in 1781, ensuring American independence. The ship returned to France in 1782. After a brief spell of service in India she sailed for home, but was wrecked off Croisic in 1793.

In 1997 the keel was laid for a replica of the *Hermione*, in the same dock where the original ship had been built two hundred years earlier. This

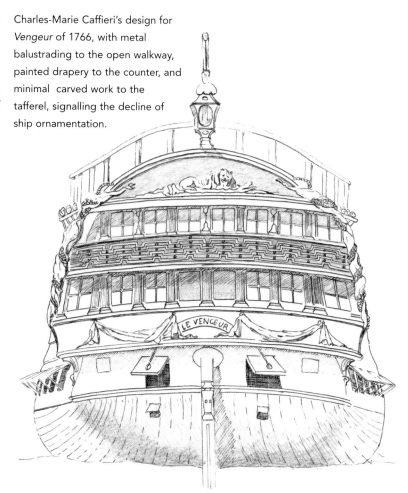

Charles-Marie Caffieri's design for *Vengeur* of 1766, with metal balustrading to the open walkway, painted drapery to the counter, and minimal carved work to the tafferel, signalling the decline of ship ornamentation.

historic moment was the start of what turned out to be a fifteen-year project to launch a frigate from the Rochefort yard. In 2010, along with a number of French sculptors, I was approached to submit designs based on our historical research for the figurehead. The ship had so far been based on plans held at Greenwich, which were taken off *Hermione*'s sister ship *Concorde* which had been captured by the British in 1783.

The primary reason for taking off a ship's lines, particularly at this period, was for the purpose of comparing hull-forms with British ships. The plans held at Greenwich therefore concentrate on the lines of the ship, with a cursory sketch depicting a lion figurehead. As a result I centred my research on French models and documentation that still exist from the period, all of which conform to the ministerial decree of 1777 in being uncrowned, but holding the arms of France before them. The lion's mane tends to be less tightly curled than English or Dutch counterparts, and the expression is not of the 'attacking Bulldog' but more aloof, giving an air of superiority (see colour plates 1 and 2).

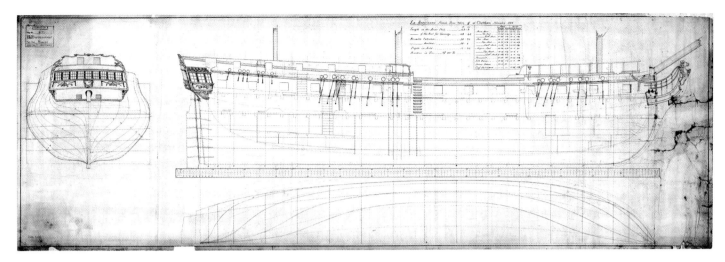

The 32-gun frigate *Magicienne* was launched from the Toulon yard in 1777. She was captured in 1781 and her lines taken off at Chatham in 1783. Her stern displays the minimal carving typical of the period, but the figurehead is of interest in depicting a lion that conforms to the ministerial decree of 1777. In compiling my research for the figurehead of the replica frigate *Hermione*, *Magicienne* served as one of seventeen examples that were compared to arrive at the final design. As part of this process, the profile of each figure was superimposed onto the stem of the *Hermione* to evaluate the artistic merit with regard to stance and bulk in relation to the shape of *Hermione's* lines. *Magicienne* proved to be a good match. (National Maritime Museum J6647)

Following the submission of my research and a maquette of the proposed design, which was presented before a court in Rochefort, I was awarded the contract and in May of 2011 took up residence in Rochefort where over the next seven months the figure was carved and fitted to the ship.

In arriving at the final design for the lion, the process was much as it would have been in 1780. Firstly, due regard was taken of the ministerial decree of the time, which established that the male lion would be uncrowned and hold the arms of France before him. By looking at known examples of the period, details such as the flowing rather than tightly curled mane were established, to suit the fashion of the time – 70 per cent of examples found from frigates built at Rochefort had this

feature, along with the mane extending onto the *cagouille*. This brings the design to the second consideration, which is that it must fit the constructional shape of the stem head and be clear of fixing points for the standing rigging. A drawing detailing the profile from each of the known lions, such as *San Pareil*, *Nymphe*, *Babet*, *Lutine* and *Cleopâtre*, were superimposed onto the stem of the *Hermione* to see which would best meet these practicalities.

The austere form of Neoclassicism took a further turn in 1792 when all royal regalia were removed by order of the new regime of the French Revolution, who viewed attributes of royalty as marks of slavery which the republican eye could not look upon. Ships' names and their figureheads were replaced with subjects that reflected republican values. The sculptor Nicolas Delizy (1758-1814) conceived the image of an eagle, the adoption of which as a national symbol soon took the regime on the same course as so many who have chosen the device, as the history of Napoleon reveals. The three arsenals of Brest, Toulon and Rochefort continued to operate their sculpture academies through to the 1890s when the role of master carver ceased with their closure.

Many of the buildings at the former Rochefort yard still stand, including the last ship-carvers' studio. Built in 1806, it occupies the same site as the original building, to the rear of the former slipways. The volume of carving had by this date diminished considerably, but it was still felt necessary to train carvers. The atelier doubled as a gallery to house carvings from former ships, saved for posterity and to offer both instruction and inspiration for apprentices. The atelier continued to operate until 1891.

The sculptors' atelier of 1806 still stands in the former Rochefort arsenal. (Author's collection)

Initial roughing out of the lion, which is formed from three sections: the centre part which sits on top of the stem head, with two outer pieces fixed to each side of the stem. (Author's collection)

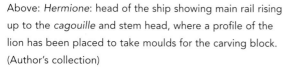

Above: *Hermione*: head of the ship showing main rail rising up to the *cagouille* and stem head, where a profile of the lion has been placed to take moulds for the carving block. (Author's collection)

The centre section and port side fixed together, nearing completion; the starboard side stands on its own. (Author's collection)

Left: The three sections making up the lion are here fixed together, showing the cut-out splayed to fit the tapering section of the stem and splayed section caused by the *cagouille*. The completed lion now primed and undercoated is ready for final fixing to the ship. At this stage it weighed approximately 750 kilos. (Author's collection)

CARVERS OF THE FRENCH NAVY

OVERSEERS

Le Brun, Charles	(1619-1690)	Held post 1669-1690
Bérain, Jean	(1639-1711)	Held post 1690-1711
Antoine-François Vassé	(1681-1736)	Held post 1711-1736

CARVERS

Brest

René D'Augère	(1643-1703)	Master carver 1674-1683
Jean Legeret	(1628-1688)	Master carver 1683-1688
Nicolas Renard	(1654-1720)	Master carver 1688-1717
François Caffieri	(1667-1729)	Master carver 1717-1729
Charles Philippe Caffieri	(1695-1766)	Master carver 1729-1766
Pierre Philippe Lubet	(1721-1797)	Master carver 1766-1797
Charles-Marie Caffieri	(1736-1777)	Second carver under Lubet 1766-1775
Jacques-Étienne Collet	(1721-1808)	Sculptor working at Brest 1752-1800
Yves-Étienne Collet	(1761-1843)	Master carver 1797-1840, last master carver

Dunkirk

Philippe Caffieri	(1634-1714)	Master carver 1687-1716
François Caffieri	(1667-1729)	Master carver 1714-1717
Charles P Caffieri	(1695-1766)	Master carver 1717-1729

Le Havre

Philippe Caffieri	1687-1691	Carried out carved work to *Le Brillant* 1690
François Caffieri	1726	Due to absence of a master carver

Lorient

Louis Hubac	(17??-18??)	Carver 1817-1820

Marseilles

Jean Mathias	(16??-1706)	Master carver 1676-1706
François Caravaque	(16??-1698)	Carving 1698
Jean-Baptiste Olérys		Carving 1688
Jean Caravaque	(1673-1754)	Master carver 1706-1748
Antoine Gibert	(1716-1789)	Carver 1743-1750

Port-Louis

Claude-Ambroise Buirette	(1663-1743)	Master carver 1698-1712

Rochefort

Claude Buirette	(1639-1694)	Carver 1669-1694
Pierre Turreau	(1638-1676)	Carver
Claude-Ambroise Buirette	(1663-1743)	Master carver 1712-1743
François Caffieri	(1667-1729)	Stood in as master carver 1720-1724
Pierre-Noel Levassuer	(1690-1770)	Apprentice 1743-46, carver 1746-63
Victor Bourguignon		Master carver 1750s
Nicolas Delizy	(1758-1814)	Master carver 1789-1814
Jean-Joseph Parenteau	(1774-18??)	Carver 1817-1839
Louis-Adolphe Vambourg	(1801-1844)	Master carver 1839-1840

Toulon

Pierre Puget	(1620-1694)	Master carver 1670-1679
Christopher Veyrier	(1637-1689)	Carver
François Girardon	(1628-1715)	Carver
Romaut Longueneux	(1638-1718)	Carver
Antoine-François Vassé	(1681-1736)	Master carver 1711-1736
Bernard Toro	(1661-1731)	Carver 1718-1731
Jean Ange Maucard		Carver 1731-1760
Jean Lange	(1671-1761)	Master carver 1736-1760
Antoine Gibert	(1716-1789)	Master carver 1760-1789
Nicolas Delizy	(1758-1814)	Carver
Félix Brun	(1763-1831)	Master carver 1789-1831
Charles Dupin	(1784-1873)	Master carver 1831-1873

COLOUR PLATES

Plate 1: The *Hermione* replica at Rochefort, with figurehead researched and carved by the author: the completed lion fixed to the stem head. His feet rest on the lower cheek (*jottereaux*) while the upper cheek rises to form the hair bracket on the *cagouille*. The main head rail terminates behind the cat head (*bossoir*) in the traditional French manner, while a bracket known as the *arc boutant soutenant le bossoir* provides support to the cat head, which on a British ship would be taken by the termination of the main or middle rail (*herpes*). The head timbers (*jambettes*) are here painted white together with the hawse holes for the anchor cables. Rounded mouldings to the cheeks have been cut away where gammoning (lacings) to the bowsprit terminate in the slots below on the cutwater (*see page 60*).

Plate 2: Launch of the replica French frigate *Hermione*, 6 July 2012. (Both: Author's collection)

Plate 3: Stern board from the fluyt *Abraham's Offerhande* of 1639 depicting the scene from the Old Testament when Abraham was ordered by God as a test of his faith to sacrifice his son Isaac. He is about to obey the command, when an angel appears to stop the sacrifice. The coat of arms at the top depict the vessel's home port of Hindelopen. Such scenes were popularised by the engravings of artists such as Pieter Hendrickszoon Schut (*see page 70*).

The figures and decoration are individually carved pieces, attached to six oak boards. Overall the board measures 1750mm high by 930mm wide, representing the decoration of a medium-sized coastal trader that foundered off the Danish coast around 1700. The board now hangs in the church of Söndre Harritslev in northwest Jutland. (Author's collection)

Plate 4: A close-up of the stern of the *Zeven Provinciën* from the famous painting of the Four Days Battle by Abraham Storck. Launched from the Delftshaven yard in 1665, the ship was to become the favourite flagship of Admiral Michiel Adrienszoon de Ruyter. The painting shows a typical Dutch colour scheme and accurately depicts the main decorative feature of this ship's stern – the heraldic lion of the Dutch republic surrounded by seven small shields bearing the arms of the individual provinces, after which the ship was named. (National Maritime Museum BHC0286)

Plate 5: Stern of the *Gouden Leeuw*, launched from the Amsterdam yard in 1666. The painting by Abraham Storck shows the vessel whilst serving as Admiral Tromp's flagship during the battle of Texel in 1673. The Dutch predilection for large heraldic or pictorial compositions on the tafferel illustrative of the ship's name – in this case a golden lion – facilitates the identification of individual ships. (National Maritime Museum BHC0307)

Plate 6: In its adoption of French ornamentation, the *Rotterdam* of about 1724 ceases to employ the *slijngerlist*, but retains closed galleries. Although the use of brackets on the counter has survived, the traditional grotesques have been replaced with acanthus leaves, while their replacement between the lights take the form of more elegantly composed figures. Figures to the quarter pieces extend down to the lower counter in typical French manner, with a shield bearing the insignia of the Rotterdam chamber of the VOC forming the centrepiece. The quarter galleries have also adopted the recognisable *bouteilles* shape with an oval window of the French fashion to the upper finishing (*see page 80*). (Image reproduced by courtesy of Rotterdam Maritime Museum)

Plate 7: Model of the Dutch yacht *Prince van Orange* of 1764, still retaining predominantly Baroque ornamentation, with only a hint of neoclassical influence (*see also page 91*). (National Maritime Museum BHC0307)

Plate 8: Phineas Pett's *Sovereign of the Seas* launched in 1637 with carved work by John and Mathias Christmas. This is half of a joint painting with the ship's builder Peter Pett. Although the portrait of Pett is attributed to Peter Lely, the ship is thought to have been painted later and its authorship has been disputed (*see page 96*). (National Maritime Museum BHC2949)

Plate 9: The First Rate three-decker *St Michael* launched from Portsmouth Dockyard in 1669 with carved work typical of the Restoration period (*see page 108*). (National Maritime Museum F9219-005)

Plate 10: The 90-gun ship *St George* was launched from the Portsmouth yard in 1701. William III's cypher RWR forms the centrepiece of the upper deck gallery, amidst tightly curling acanthus 'cut through' to emphasising the three-dimensional effect of the design. Such lavish displays of Baroque ornamentation would soon come under the scrutiny of Admiralty orders intended to restrict expenditure on decorative work. (Henry Huddleston Rogers Collection, Annapolis; by courtesy of Grant Walker)

PLATE I

PLATE 2

PLATE 3

PLATE 4

PLATE 5

PLATE 6

PLATE 7

SLR0206

PLATE 8

PLATE 9

PLATE 10

2

～The Netherlands～

In the sixteenth century Brussels was the capital of the Spanish-ruled Netherlands, with Antwerp as the seat of commerce. This deep-water port provided access via the North Sea to the Baltic and Mediterranean, creating a hub of commercial enterprise, where the merchant classes prospered. The wealthy and discriminating society that arose provided a ready market for luxury goods and their patronage of the arts led to a flourishing of creative talent, which had a ready source of inspiration from the influx of exotic imports around them. The craftsmen of Antwerp became famous throughout Europe for all manner of

goods, including lace work, silverware, stained glass, musical instruments, tapestries, glassware and printed books, which included many pattern books of motifs that greatly influenced the decorative arts of northern Europe.

Dutch ships had always been highly decorated, with the design of even their most modest inland trading vessels incorporating a wonderful balance of practicality and artistic ornamentation. When those early merchants set sail for the East in the 1590s, the Mannerist style was predominant in northern Europe. This development of Classical concepts originated in Italy during the Renaissance, where architects wishing to break the bonds of Classical constraint presented new orders of capitals, cornices and ornamentation, opening the door to greater inventiveness. This playful rearrangement of Classical concepts seemed to suit the Dutch temperament, where it was developed into an independent style of Flemish Mannerism. The unconstrained nature of this showed a total irreverence to any Classical precepts, and the more bizarre elements were further developed into a style known as Netherlands Grotesque.

Strapwork that in Mannerist compositions took the form of yielding leather to create a supporting structure, now appeared as cold forged iron, encaging soft fleshy figures, that appear in stark contrast to the harsh solidity of their entrapping framework. Bizarre sproutings of delicate foliage, fruit, exotic birds and grotesque masks helped to further soften the solid ground, in a mixture of Classical functionality and wayward playful forms.

Cornelis Bos (1510-1560), a founder of the movement, had travelled to Rome in 1548, where he studied the designs used in the Vatican Loggias. These were derived from Classical Roman compositions, buried for centuries in underground ruins. When unearthed from what appeared to be a cave or 'grotto', these unfamilar forms were termed 'grotesques'.

While not necessarily relevant to ship ornamentation, mention of such divergent forms provides a backdrop to the development of the

applied arts at a time when the northern Netherlands, led by the province of Holland, were fighting to free themselves from Habsburg Spain. Motifs expressing the emotions of the times chart the changing values and nature of a nation that eventually gained its independence as the United Provinces in 1648. Their trading centre of Antwerp, which remained under Spanish rule, then shifted to Amsterdam, where the Dutch government (the States General) organised the maritime affairs of the new republic into five regions: the Admiralty of Amsterdam, the Admiralty of the Maas (seated in Rotterdam), the Admiralty of Zeeland (based in Vlissingen, and later in Middelburg), the Admiralty of Friesland (first in Dokkum and then in Harlingen), and the Admiralty of the Noorderkwartier (seated in Hoorn, and later in Enkhuizen). Each college was responsible for the maintenance and building of its ships, with that of the Maas also being charged with the management and construction of the highly decorated Stadholder's and state *jachts* (one of these was presented to King Charles II, from which the English term 'yacht' derives). The regions were not bound by central regulation and therefore each admiralty controlled the decoration of its ships, commissioning its own sculptors, working to designs that were approved by the governing bodies of each region.

Whereas France developed academies to train its ship-carvers, the United Provinces relied instead on the guilds. This was a system dating back to the Middle Ages whereby skilled tradesman and artisans grouped themselves together to form a governing body, which then controlled all aspects of economic life in that trade. Acceptance into the guild was dependent on quality of work, providing the customer with some assurance of quality control, whilst protecting the tradesman from outside competition. In return for such support, a guild member was expected to take on apprentices, to further the skill of his particular trade.

Painters, sculptors, woodcarvers, frame makers and art dealers had been part of the saddlers' guild, along with trades such as weavers and house painters, but in 1611 they formed the Guild of St Luke to focus their direction on the liberal arts. An apprenticeship usually lasted six years, during which time a talented student would be expected to travel to the great centres or art, such as Rome, to learn from the established masters.

The wealth of this new nation grew dramatically through its sea trade. The arts continued to flourish with the patronage of an increasingly wealthy merchant class, allowing it to develop in quite a different direction from the Catholic south. By 1610 a new style was already evolving, which was very much a result of these anti-establishment times, and became known as the Auricular style. A fundamental element of the style was the use of naturalistic forms such as the ear and smooth flowing sinewy lines that melt and merge into grotesque masks, fish, sea creatures, shells and

The development of Mannerism into the Auricular: carving to a doorway in Stockholm, where many Dutch craftsmen were employed during the first half of the 1600s. (Author's collection)

The sinewy lines of this mask melt and merge into organic shapes that are formulated into the Auricular style. The pole passing through a pivot seated in the figure's mouth extends down to the ship's tiller. By swinging the pole from left to right, the tiller is moved in the opposite direction, thereby steering the ship in the same direction as the staff is put over. This system of steerage, known as the tiller and whipstaff, was the forerunner of the wheel. This example is taken from the *Vasa* of 1628. (Author's collection)

other forms familiar to a water-borne nation, all of which could be poured onto the rounded flowing lines of their ships as naturally as flowers blossoming on a tree.

Alongside the Auricular fashion the Classical traditions evolved, particularly within court circles and the architecture of national institutions. The leader of this movement was Jacob van Campen (1595-1657), who designed the Mauritshuis in 1633, setting the style for Classical symmetry in Holland. Ship design at this period did not lend itself to the clean-cut lines necessary for the adoption of such architectural restraint and so continued to display the Mannerist and Auricular forms, which gradually adapted and receded into the emerging Baroque. Such elements begin to appear in ship decoration by the mid-1650s with heavy festoons and scrolling acanthus that gained

Ornamental detail to Amsterdam City Hall by Artus Quellin. Cherubim in their Christian context belong to the first hierarchy of angels and as such these winged infants represent Divine Wisdom. By the Baroque period they had been taken beyond their ecclesiastical settings, where, as cherubs, these ethereal winged infants embrace the secular world. (Author's collection)

a certain plumpness so recognisable in the Dutch propensity for a voluptuous fullness in their forms.

An important figure in early Dutch Baroque art was Artus Quellin I (1609-1668). As a young man he trained as a sculptor and in 1630 travelled to Rome to study with the master of High Baroque, François Duquesnoy, who in turn had studied with Bernini. He returned to Holland in 1639 and by 1648 had established a studio in Amsterdam, where Jacob van Campen had begun work on what is considered to be his masterpiece, the Amsterdam City Hall. By 1650 Quellin had been engaged to carry out decorative work for the project. The richness of his compositions imparts a feeling of generous abundance – cherubs hold cornucopia of exotic fruits, festoons of flowers encircle fish and game to invoke scenes that must have mirrored the wealthy air of a merchant city, alive with vibrant energy and enthusiastic inventiveness.

A stroll down practically any canalside street in Amsterdam will reveal examples of ornamentation that celebrates the wealth of a nation built on trade and its affinity with the sea. The theatrical nature of Flemish Mannerism allowed its artists to readily embrace the emergence of Baroque. The adaptation of applied decoration from architectural purposes to ship ornamentation became second nature, particularly given the profusion of maritime themes. As the Dutch navy relied on the employment of sculptors who gained their instruction through the established guilds, their sphere of employment went beyond the naval yards to encompass ecclesiastical and municipal projects, underlining the commonality of civic and ship ornamentation. However, such divergence in the work of sculptors does make tracing their involvement in ship decoration a difficult task, as biographers and historians tend to cite their achievements based on surviving examples, which are funerary and architectural monuments. For many artists their work on ships has been forgotten.

A leading example is that of the sculptor Rombout Verhulst (1624-1696). In 1646 he moved from his birthplace of Mechelen to Amsterdam, to become Artus Quellin's leading assistant during the construction of the City Hall. From 1657 to 1663 he was based in Leiden, where alongside his ecclesiastical and municipal commissions he also carried out carved work to state jachts, by which time the quality of his work defined him as one of the most talented Dutch sculptors of the day. He was particularly renowned for his portraits, the expressive nature of which ensured the demand for his work throughout the country, including the tombs of Lieutenant-Admiral Willem Joseph van Ghent in 1676 and Admiral Michiel de Ruyter in 1681.

This ornamentation over a doorway to Helligand's Church in Copenhagen was completed by Dutch craftsmen in 1622. The motifs displayed are in the Flemish Mannerist style, arranged in a composition that perfectly illustrates the commonality that exists between civic and ship ornamentation. The supporting figures mirror the arrangement of strongmen to the quarter pieces and the curved pediment could easily perform the function of a tafferel. (Author's collection)

Hollandia of 1665 displays the typical layout of a Dutch stern from 1640 through to the 1660s. A characteristic of Dutch sterns is the curved line of the gallery whose outer edges then rise up to meet the quarter galleries, creating a distinctive shape known as a *slijngerlist*. Although the style of motif has moved on from the Mannerist, the format of the composition remains the same, bearing a striking resemblance to the doorway pictured opposite, which could be transposed directly onto the ship. Large figures known on Dutch ships as 'strongmen' form the quarter pieces, below which cherubs ride on the backs of dolphins, as the stern gallery spreads out to reach that of the quarters.

Windows to the quarterdeck appear on the stern only as very small lights, leading to the characteristic deep tafferel – the term derives from *tafel*, meaning 'table', and *tafe'reel* in Dutch denotes a scene. However, the decorated area whose centrepiece is reserved for an emblem depicting the province of the ship or figurative representation of the vessel's name is best described as the 'the great board'. This term is the Swedish definition for the area below the tafferel proper, *bord* being Swedish for 'table' (or 'board', as it also is in Dutch). Here the arms of Amsterdam are depicted. The shield is supported on the starboard side by a figure representing justice, blindfolded to signify her impartiality and carrying a sword, the emblem of her power. On the port side sits Ceres holding a corn sheaf and horn of plenty, symbols of fertility and abundance. Above the great board a seated figure forms the centrepiece of the tafferel, flanked by two lions. (Author's collection)

A typical warship of this period is the *Hollandia*, famous as the flagship of de Ruyter (1607-1676). A born leader and skilled naval tactician, he commanded in many successful engagements, not only against the English, but supporting the Portuguese in their war against Spain and the Danes in their quarrels with Sweden. Denmark and Sweden regularly disputed jurisdiction of the narrow Öresund sound which gave access to the Baltic because the dominant power could control the lucrative tolls on all shipping passing through. The supply of timber, tar and other naval supplies from the Baltic was essential to meet the needs of Holland's navy and its vast fishing and commercial fleets, while trade and naval competition with England inevitably drew both maritime powers into involvement with the Baltic states.

By the beginning of the seventeenth century the Dutch had developed a type of vessel known as a *fluyt*. The term first appears in 1595 when the Hoorn historian T Velius recorded 'the building of the first Fluyten being four times as long as wide'. Their bluff bows and rounded stern created a hull shape that maximised cargo space. Rigged for ease of handling by small crews, they also provided low running costs, making them popular bulk carriers. Variants were developed to cater for carrying grain, with no upper deck to facilitate loading, or with deeper draught for timber carriers and with strengthened bows for the whaling fleets. Fluyts were soon operating in the North Sea trade, transporting goods such as coal from the Tyne and working the fisheries. Those operating in the Baltic took on a pronounced tumblehome – the curving in of the topsides above the waterline – to take advantage of the toll rules, whereby vessels were charged by the width of their weather deck. This led to a virtual monopoly of Dutch shipping in the Baltic trade. In an effort to curb their dominance, England passed the Navigation Act in 1651 restricting the carriage of cargoes to its ports in non-English ships, effectively banning Dutch ships from English trade. They also sought to control ships passing through the English Channel and by allowing their warships to stop and search foreign ships. Not surprisingly, the first Anglo-Dutch war broke out the following year.

The approach in providing decorative work to the rounded stern of the fluyt, with its lack of galleries and narrow tafferel, was in general to create a condensed version of the standard format, where the stern board displayed the coat of arms of her home port, or symbolic representation of the vessel's name. Large figurative work formed the quarter pieces, with the introduction of a *slijngerlist* (the characteristic curved line of the gallery whose outer edges then rise up to meet the quarter galleries of Dutch sterns) to form the entrance port for the tiller. The rudder head, which stands beyond the stern presented an arrangement common to smaller barges of the Netherlands and adopted their traditional form of decoration known as a *roerkoppen* where a human or animal head is placed on top of the rudder stock, or occasionally a complete animal such as a beaver or crocodile is depicted climbing up onto the tiller.

Biblical scenes were also very popular, with their ability to relate a story in pictures. Such scenes became widely available through the engravings of artists such as Pieter Hendrickszn Schut (1619-1660) and Claes Jansen Visscher (1587-1652). The composition of many stern boards that survive are direct three-dimensional interpretations of their engravings.

The intricacy and quality of carvings naturally depended on the size of ship and wealth of the owner. In the case of the VOC the large cargo carrying capacity of the fluyt presented an attractive proposition. Despite their light construction and inability to be heavily armed, the company employed over 400 fluyts between 1620

and 1790, with decorative work to equal the quality, if not quantity, of their armed merchantmen.

Since the birth of the nation, Dutch merchants had played a dominant role in its political life and, with little landowning nobility, they also became the principal patrons of the arts, creating circumstances very different from the rest of Europe. They turned for inspiration to the achievements of their own people, creating art that was accessible, less academic, and depicting simple scenes from everyday life. Portraiture in particular developed to an advanced state of realism. Artists such as Thomas de Keyser (1597-1667) injected a vibrancy that would be further developed by Rembrandt (1606-1669). Merchants also filled the gap left in the reformation of its religious system, in becoming patrons of ecclesiastical commissions. The engravings of Schut and Visscher typically depict stories in a manner that was accessible to all, as shown in the style of carving applied to fluyts (see colour plate 3).

The fluyt *Graaf Floris* of about 1640. The narrow stern of the fluyt shows a condensed version of the standard composition of stern ornament, with tafferel ornament around the lantern, with figure to the great board flanked by two mermaids as strongmen. The rudder head has a carving known as a *roerkoppen* and above the entry port for the tiller is a richly decorated garland of shells which terminate at the *slijngerlist*. See also colour plate 3.

The stern of a 60-gun ship of 1665 illustrating the transition from Mannerist to Baroque ornamentation. The distinctive *slijngerlist* rail persisted up until the mid-1720s, together with the fashion for heavily carved brackets below the gallery, which had been dropped in France, England and the Baltic states by 1700 in favour of simple mouldings.

By 1650 the rich, dense style of Artus Quellin's Baroque ornamentation is also evident in the composition of carved work to the ships of the Netherlands and in the Baltic States where ships were supplied or built by the Dutch. The woodcarver Grinling Gibbons (1648-1721), born

to English parents living in Holland, studied with Quellin before the family returned to England in 1667. Quellin's influence is clearly visible in Gibbons's work, who in turn contributed much to the decoration of royal palaces, churches and public monuments in England. Quellin's cousin (Artus II) was also an established sculptor and assisted Artus I on the City Hall in Amsterdam. His sons Arnold and Thomas came to England to work on various projects with Gibbons, contributing to the considerable influence Dutch artists were to have on the country at this period. Whilst in England, Thomas married Anna Maria Cocques and in 1689 the couple moved to Copenhagen to oversee numerous commissions that his father had received in Scandinavia.

The freedom from convention allowed artists of the new republic to embrace subjects previously considered below the attention of the established world of fine art. Through the painting of seascapes a vast body of knowledge on the appearance of ships during this period has been preserved in the drawings of artists such as

When built in 1646 the 58-gun *Brederode* was the most powerful ship in the Dutch navy. She served as Admiral Maerten Tromp's flagship in the Battle of the Kentish Knock in 1652 and at the Battle of Scheveningen the following year in which Tromp was killed during an engagement off Terheide. Tromp was well respected on both sides, being a popular leader amongst his men and admired for his tactical skill. The drawing by Willem van de Velde the elder provides an impression of the stern carvings which were produced during the period when Willem van Douwe was master carver at the Rotterdam yard. (National Maritime Museum PY1720)

the elder Willem van de Velde (1611-93). The son of a naval captain, Willem spent part of his youth at sea, which undoubtedly gave him the practical knowledge to accurately depict the nature of a ship when he later devoted his time to artistic endeavours. He became the official artist to the Dutch fleet, recording battle scenes to provide on-the-spot accounts of their engagements. As such they provide a useful confirmation of general trends in the carved work that are better illustrated in the intricate drawings he made of particular ships, which often include sketched notes of individual carvings, taken while the ships were at rest.

In 1672 he travelled to England with his son Willem van de Velde II (1633-1707), who had trained under his father and the marine artist Simon de Vlieger (1600-1653) to become a well respected painter of maritime scenes. In 1674 Charles II engaged Willem the elder at a yearly fee of £100 'For the taking and making draughts of sea fights' and similarly for Willem the younger 'To put the said draughts into colours'.

The Dutch republic had become the most powerful Protestant nation in Europe through the wealth that continued to pour in from its trading companies. Amsterdam expanded as a centre for commerce and banking. In 1661 the VOC constructed its own shipyard on the man-made island of Oostenburg. This district formed one of three areas created from reclaimed land to cope with the needs of the growing city.

The dominance of France, however, presented an ever-growing threat, as the armies of Louis XIV forced their way into neighbouring lands. The United Provinces were invaded in 1672 and after a series of disasters, leadership of the resistance passed to William of Orange who was eventually able to check the advance of France in 1678. A year earlier, William had married Mary, daughter of James, who was brother to King Charles II of England, potentially uniting the two Protestant countries. The Catholic James succeeded Charles in 1685, but his autocratic, pro-French policies earned him widespread hatred. Encouraged by James's political opponents, in 1688 William landed at Brixham with an Anglo-Dutch army to launch the 'Glorious Revolution'. James II fled to France, leaving the throne of England vacant. In 1688 at the request of Parliament, William and Mary assumed the English crown. Now head of the combined countries, William embarked on a rebuilding programme of his royal palaces in

Top: Detail of a Delftware tile designed by Daniel Marot around 1694.

Bottom: Detail from Bérain's design for the Swedish coach of 1696.

Holland and England, to reflect the heightened status of his court. Despite the bitter war that had continued with France, he paradoxically favoured the French court style and endeavoured to introduce the style in his building programme.

An influential figure of the time was Daniel Marot (1663-1752). His father Jean was an accomplished French architect and Daniel followed to become a great exponent of the French court style. As a Huguenot Daniel was forced into exile along with many other artists and craftsmen during the French persecution of Protestants. They travelled north to the states of the Netherlands, Germany and Scandinavia, or crossed into Switzerland. Marot went to Holland when exiled in 1685 and was soon employed by William to work on the Het Loo palace in the Netherlands and Hampton Court in England, where he continued to develop his 'Marotesque' style of Baroque ornamentation, often employing fellow Huguenot craftsmen under his close direction.

His work shows a significant influence from Bérain, particularly in the use of bandwork. He also adopted the principles established by Le Brun in overseeing every aspect of a project from architectural conception through to the consideration of the smallest detail. The homogeneous result of this unity of vision provided a pre-eminence that would in time enable fellow artists to absorb elements of French Baroque into a style that still retained distinctly Dutch characteristics. In 1698 he returned to Holland and in 1702 his works were published as *Oeuvres de Sieur Marot*, illustrating designs for furniture, upholstery, curtains, porcelain, fireplaces, overmantels, cornices and all manner of applied decorative work. The book was expanded in 1712, helping to spread his style throughout the Protestant north as far as Sweden.

The influence of Marot's designs were to take a while to filter through to ship ornamentation, the style of which continued to be dominated by Italian Baroque, in compositions designed by sculptors such as the van Douwe family. Willem van Douwe (1620-1689) established a sculpture atelier with his brother Michiel in his hometown of Rotterdam. In 1655 Willem married Emmerentia Waerdeniers. With the imminent birth of their first child, they moved to the 'ship makers harbour' in 1659 where he was employed as a woodcarver, and shortly after moved into the admiralty yard, where in August of that year, their son François was born. Surviving payment records show that Willem completed sculptures for a transport jacht in 1661 and a year later for a bezaan jacht. The town of Rotterdam commissioned him to carry out the ornamentation of their new 'Stad jacht' in 1682, in which year his wife died following the birth of their ninth child. The following year he married Akida van Hoogstraaten with whom he had a further two children. Apparently François was by this time receiving sufficient commissions in his own name to feel that he could support a wife and family, for in the same year he married Christina van der Poll.

Of Willem's eleven children, six died in infancy, but his eldest son François continued the family business, possibly with a brother called Franciscus Carolus, although with so little documentation of his existence, one might speculate whether it is simply a Latinised version of François. Drawings signed 'FC' are, however, of a different style, bearing a greater similarity to the work of François's son Willem junior

On his father's death, François took over what had become the most prominent studio in Rotterdam. From 1694 to 1720 he played an important part in St Luke's guild, and was the first among the stone- and woodcarvers to head the guild. He was commissioned by the winemakers' and coopers' guilds both as an artist to paint portraits of their members, and as a sculptor to produce work in stone and wood for their chambers. His accomplishment as an artist included many fine paintings of landscapes and still-life studies. The competence of his drawing and painting is clearly displayed in the many sketches that survive showing his compositions for ship ornamentation, all of which from 1683 to 1695 display rich voluptuous compositions inspired by the Italian Baroque, typified in the work of Artus Quellin. His talents as a painter would later coincide with the increased use of the medium in ship ornamentation and the introduction by the turn of the century of French-inspired Baroque.

In 1688 William of Orange combined the fleets of England and the Republic in the fight against Louis XIV. With his land forces focusing on the defence of the Netherlands, the war at sea came under the control of England, which must have caused much consternation among the Dutch flag officers, who after decades of war against them, now had to submit to the command of English admirals.

William's combined rule of England and the the Dutch Republic is alluded to in naval ornamentation by the lion figureheads of Dutch ships wearing the English crown, a detail that is apparent in the figurehead of *William Rex*. The model known by this name represents a typical 74-gun ship of the period rather than a specific vessel and was constructed for the Admiralty of Zeeland at their Vlissingen yard in 1698 to a design by its head shipwright Adriaen de Vriend. Zeeland was the first province to proclaim William III as its Stadholder, effectively opening the gate for his rise to power, and ensuring his popularity in the region. Although it later became hereditary, the Stadholder was an elected leader, and William was only king in Britain – hence the symbolism of the English crown worn by the republican Dutch lion.

Originally displayed in the admiralty's assembly chamber at Vlissingen, the model serves as a valuable record of the design, rig and decoration of a ship from the period. The superb carvings were executed by the sculptor Cornelis Moerman (1683-1758), for which he received the sum of 24 Flemish pounds.

The history of his family also provides a fascinating insight to the hardships faced by people at that time. Cornelis was the second of eight children born to Willem Moerman (1660-1727) and Marijte Vermeer (1657-1697). His father arrived in Holland as a refugee, having fled from the Spanish Netherlands. He was granted ownership of a piece of land on the island of Rosenburg, which formed part of the shifting sandbanks of the Maas estuary. The constantly slipping sand that formed the edge of the island rose to an area of marshland that would partially flood. Through the ingenuity and dogged perseverance of the residents this was systematically dyked and drained to eventually form land that the families could cultivate in order to subsist.

His elder brother, Jan Willemsz, joined the service of the VOC and rose to the position of captain. He died on board the VOC ship *The Dam* whilst returning from India in 1729. His widow appears to have been left destitute, but she remarried the following year, presumably in an attempt to provide support for her three children. Her two sons joined the VOC; the younger died while serving as a sailor in India at the age of 14 in 1740; the elder was stationed at Batavia where he died in 1747. They also had a daughter who tragically was found 'dead and burned' presumably as a result of a house fire at the age of 26 in 1745. Cornelis married in 1714, his wife Gretel giving birth to thirteen children, the first of whom died within a year. They named their second child after the first, Maartje, who thankfully lived to the age of 72. Their third child, a boy, died at the age of 8, and a further four died before reaching the age of 5, while their eleventh, a boy named Jan,

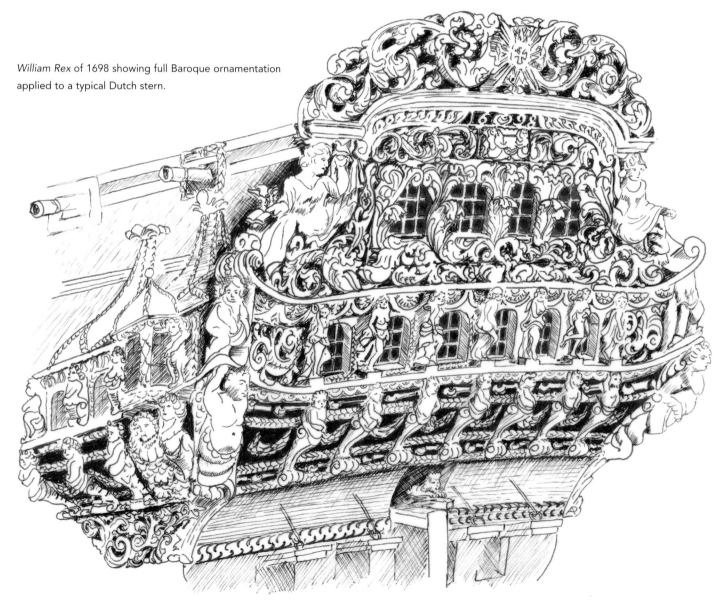

William Rex of 1698 showing full Baroque ornamentation applied to a typical Dutch stern.

survived just fifteen days. When Gretel died in 1775 at the age of 81, of her thirteen children only Maartje is known to have still been alive.

With Baroque ornamentation now fully embraced, the earlier motifs taken from biblical and secular scenes diminish in favour of more unified compositions. The large figurative pieces no longer sit in isolation, but nestle amidst the scrolling acanthus and foliate forms that provide a cohesive quality to the assembled parts. The fine quality of the carved work is worthy of a detailed description particularly as the model was produced at such a large scale (the model measures 15 feet in length).

On Dutch ships of the period, the term *tafferel* is generally used to describe the 'great board', and so what the English consider the tafferel becomes the upper tafferel. When this is 'cut through' to create a fretwork effect such as on the *William Rex*, it is then called the 'upper *hakkebord*'. The encircled St George's cross in the centre of the tafferel (of the Order of the Garter) alludes to the House of Orange and has in its four quarters the monogram RWR standing for *Regnat William Rex* (King William reigns). Richly scrolling acanthus intertwines in a very dense composition reminiscent of early Le Brun but more comparable to Italian Baroque, which continued to display this style of very three-dimensional foliage well into the 1690s. The Austrian painter Paul Schor studied in Rome under Bernini and Cortona in 1640, where he would have been exposed to the same forms of artistic expression as Artus Quellin, who returned home from Italy a year earlier. The strong sculptural feel of Schor's work influenced the German decorative artists of Augsburg and Nürnberg, where a very similar style of vigorous, tightly packed acanthus also persisted into the late 1690s, whereas the French fashion had developed into a much lighter density of ornamentation by this period.

A curved quarter-round moulding creates a break between the *hakkebord* and the gallery to the quarterdeck, beneath which two seated figures recline to form the quarter pieces, in a very naturalistic pose typical of Baroque figurative work. A ribbon moulding incorporates the year in which the model was built, below which are the arms of Zealand. The mullions between the windows of the quarterdeck are pilasters of a foliate form whose luxuriant growth threatens to engulf the lights completely, while their upper leaves curl over to create the sense of capitals that follow the curved

top of the windows behind, any remaining space to the gallery being packed with scrolling acanthus.

Mermen with intricately twisting tails and two cherub-type figures support the *slijngerlist* of the gallery to the upper deck. They are depicted in the lively flamboyant manner that typifies Baroque figurative work and are joined by a series of sensuously posed nymphets whose loose drapery reveals the femininity of their curvaceous forms. Above the windows to the gallery runs a moulding of repeating lunettes. This type of semi-circular ornament infilled with foliate forms became a popular decorative motif with woodcarvers of the mid-1600s. Corbelled brackets to the upper counter take the form of herms in various expressive poses, between which are festoons, leaf mouldings and a smaller repeating line of lunettes.

The ornamental theme continues onto the quarter galleries, which at this period are confined to the upper deck. Their roof neatly diverges into two onion-shaped spires drawing the galleries back to the ship's side. This was a fairly common arrangement on Dutch-designed ships from 1630 until the turn of the century and commonly expressed in English as 'fayed' to the ship's side.

With no expense spared in the construction of this model, it is interesting to note that with the exception of royal insignia, the date and the arms of Zealand, all the carvings are painted yellow rather than gilded. In general terms, the purpose of producing such models was to create an accurate record of a particular ship or class of ship, to present a new design for approval, or for the purposes of presentation to dignitaries. In all these cases they represent a showpiece that served to glorify the skills of the shipwright and the superb craftsmanship of the modelmaker and as such were completed to the highest standards of decorative finish. Such models have always been highly prized as exquisite pieces of art and although they provide an accurate record of ship design and rig, it is doubtful if the initial expense of gilding, coupled with the continuous cost of maintenance, would have been either practical or economically viable for a full size ship on anything other than a private yacht or flagship of the fleet. In all probability the painted carvings of the *William Rex* model present an accurate record of the finish as applied to actual Dutch ships of the period.

Pigment studies carried out on the model reveal that it has only been painted twice. The top layer is a zinc-based paint, which was not introduced until

Briel, launched
Rotterdam 1695 with
carved work by
François van Douwe
senior. (From Carr
Laughton, *Old Ship
Figureheads & Sterns*)

the 1850s, so this probably stems from a restoration carried out to the model around 1890. The original paint colour was a gold ochre. Ochre is an earth pigment consisting of decomposed rock which on heating becomes darker and redder in colour; when produced from lead-tin the colour ranges from lemon yellow to reddish yellow. The micaceous mineral orpiment creates a luminescent quality and was therefore often used as a substitute for gilding. Conservation undertaken in Stockholm on the *Vasa* (1628) revealed that her carvings were realistically coloured – particularly the figurative work, with flesh tones to the skin and appropriate colours to their dress. Gilding was reserved for coats of arms and detailing to ornamental patterns, edging to cloaks, belts, etc.

A greater complexity of painted work would appear to have been commonplace at the beginning of the century. Puget extended the use of the medium by combining a mixture of painted scenes and carved work in the ornamentation of French ships. The Dutch *Eendracht* of 1664 and the *Gouda* of 1670 also had a combination of painted and carved ornamentation. It is known

that the Dutch artists Reinier Nooms (1623-1668) and Pieter Cornelis Verschuier were commissioned to carry out painted work on ships. Both Pieter and his son Lieve Verschuier (1630-1686) were also commissioned to provide paintings and etchings of ships in naval operations and state occasions. Although recognised primarily for such paintings, Lieve was also appointed sculptor to the Admiralty of the Maas in 1674. As such he would have been a contemporary of Willem van Douwe senior and also active during the early years of the career of his son François senior. Lieve had studied in Italy around 1655 to gain first-hand knowledge of the Italian Baroque, which presumably influenced his carving work.

François van Douwe senior clearly followed the changing fashions of artistic expression with a keen interest, be they from Italy or France. As an accomplished sculptor and painter, this extended to the development of both mediums, which he enthusiastically embraced, combining both in his compositions. One such example was his design for *Briel* of 1695. The ship is named after an area on the Maas estuary close to Rosenburg, the provincial arms of which appear on the stern (possibly in painted form).

The reclining figures forming the quarter pieces no longer represent heroic mythological or biblical characters, but portray simple country peasants, having the composure of the pastoral idyll. The French landscape painter Claude Gellée (known as Claude Lorrain 1600-1682) studied in Italy, where he became absorbed in the beauty of the landscape surrounding the Bay of Naples and its rich association with Classical grandeur and the Arcadian idyll. The style became fashionable in the

omitting carved brackets to the counters, the previously vertically accentuated format is broken, making way for some sweeping changes that are apparent on the ornamentation for the 74-gun ship *Rotterdam* of 1703, which displays a distinct shift towards French-inspired Baroque. The beloved carved brackets to the counter have been omitted in favour of a repeating oval pattern as developed by Bérain, while the use of palms as foliate forms are reminiscent of François Caffieri's designs, creating a far lighter and naturalistic feel to the composition, which again expresses the somewhat

The gradual introduction of French Baroque can be seen in the designs of François van Douwe senior for *Gelderland* of 1699 (left) and *Rotterdam* of 1703. Some elements of the Dutch tradition remain, such as the arms of each ship's province displayed on the tafferel (great board) and the arms of the United Provinces displayed on the counter – a device that occurs on many ships between the official recognition of the union in 1648 and the invasion of French revolutionary forces in 1795. The figurative work on both ships has returned to representations of characters from Classical mythology.

1699

1703

Netherlands through the work of Nicolaes Berchem (1620-1682), who also studied in Italy during the 1640s. On his return to the Netherlands he worked principally in Haarlem, painting idealised rural scenes of pastoral tranquility. Berchem became very successful in his own lifetime, influencing many landscape artists, with van Douwe clearly among them. In the composition for *Briel*, van Douwe has skillfully brought the idealised figures to life by transposing them into three-dimensional forms. Stylised dolphins support the figures to complete the quarter pieces. The Order of the Garter representing the House of Orange forms the centre piece of the tafferel, with accompanying decorative work that complements the composure of the figures in naturalistic, flowing forms.

In his design for the *Gelderland* of 1699, the figurative work has returned to characters from Classical mythology, which, combined with the lighter density of carved work, suggests a move towards French-inspired compositions. By

less exuberant approach favoured by Bérain. The *slijngerlist*, such a distinctive feature of Dutch sterns, has also been modified, giving a gently curving line to the counter.

The death of William III in 1702 did not end opposition to French ambitions. In the same year an alliance of European powers refused to accept a member of Louis XIV's Bourbon family on the throne in Madrid, precipitating the War of Spanish Succession. The *Gelderland* served as part of the Anglo-Dutch fleet at the Battle of Malaga in 1704 under the command of Lieutenant Philip Schrijver (1649-1711). The war dragged on until 1713, leaving both the United Provinces and France exhausted. By then the Netherlands had ceased to be a major political or military power, and the lack of compensation given to the Dutch at the peace steepened the decline of their navy. With few resources to build new ships, the navy relied on the longevity of its existing fleet, which Schrijver's son Cornelis (1687-1768) noted had proved to be inferior to that of the British. (Cornelis would later be instrumental in the introduction of British building methods to the ships of Amsterdam.) During the intervening period (1713-1728), the Dutch admiralties built around nineteen ships of 50-74 guns and about twelve ships of 22-44 guns, intended primarily to replace ageing vessels. Nevertheless, despite these new additions, the fleet of 89 ships of the line at the start of the war was reduced to 44 by 1730. The majority of ships built during this period were to designs by Jan van Rheen, the master shipwright at the Amsterdam yard, and by Paulus van Zwijndregt (1681-1749) at the Rotterdam yard. Unfortunately, little documentation exists showing how their vessels were ornamented during this period.

With France no longer a threat and naval operations with the British fleet no longer a necessity, emphasis was placed once more on rebuilding the nation's wealth through trade. The VOC yards of Amsterdam, Middelburg, Rotterdam, Delfshaven, Hoorn and Enkhuizen all worked to the same guidelines as laid down by the directors of the company, known as the Heeren XVII (The Seventeen Lords). As a commercial enterprise with a view to maximising profit, the VOC had realised the advantages of standardising ship design as early as 1697, with the consequence

that ships could be produced in a remarkably short space of time by the most economical means. (A hull could be built and launched in three months, compared to nine in an average yard.) Models that survive of Dutch East Indiamen show that by the 1720s they had adopted the horseshoe stern, the introduction of which effectively eliminated the use of large figurative work to the quarter pieces, and provided a more practical arrangement of carvings.

The transition to this arrangement can be seen on English ships from the 1680s, where it was common to extend the tafferel to the fullest extent of the quarters, thus giving the appearance of widening the stern, with the quarter figures appearing to come inboard, when in fact they simply mask the narrowing of the quarter galleries which still do not rise to the height of the quarterdeck. Several examples are illustrated later in the book, such as the Science Museum's Navy Board model of a British 60-gun ship whose dimensions correspond to the *Dunkirk* of 1704. It displays a tafferel that curves down onto the quarter pieces creating the effect of an elliptical stern, but still retaining strongmen, which due to the loss of height have been reduced to two crouching figures.

De Jonge Jacob, a Dutch East Indiaman of 1724.

A model known as the VOC ship *De Jonge Jacob* of 1724 provides a good example of what was to become a standard format of an elliptical stern for Dutch Indiamen from 1720 to 1740. Decoration to the tafferel makes great use of bandwork intertwined with naturalistic foliage, the general composition of which takes its inspiration from the work of Marot. The lighter density of carved work shows a shift to embracing the influence of French Baroque, whilst other elements, such as the retention of the *slijngerlist* and Mannerist-inspired figures to decorate the brackets, remain distinctly Dutch.

signify the arms of Jacob de Witt, first statesman of the United Provinces, who was born in Dordrecht and whose family shield bears a hare and two hounds. A further shield forms the centrepiece of the tafferel, which traditionally depicts the vessel's provenance, while the banner below would display the vessel's name.

A drawing signed Franciscus Carolus van Douwe depicts what would appear to be an attempt to show how a jacht could be ornamented to fit with the changing fashion adopted on VOC ships. It shows the stern and quarter view of a 'Staten jacht' (royal yacht) from the period where

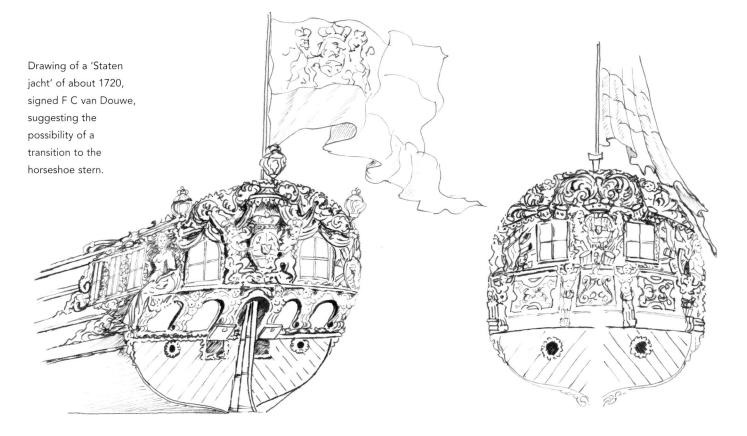

Drawing of a 'Staten jacht' of about 1720, signed F C van Douwe, suggesting the possibility of a transition to the horseshoe stern.

The composition of the cartouche around the two oval lights is interesting in that it still maintains elements of the Auricular style that will soon re-emerge as Rococo. Foliage between the windows has undergone a transformation of conformity compared to the wayward abandon of the *William Rex* days, while brackets to the counter continue to be ornately carved. Between the brackets, a coat of arms sits above the rudder head. Identification of this is unresolved: the red and white vertically striped flag of Dordrecht has as its supporters two griffins, but here the shield contains three indistinct images. Although the name *Jonge Jacob* often refers to the biblical character, the shield may

the shape of the stern is heading towards the elliptical shape, but interestingly gives two options. One retains the *hoekman*, or quarter figures, sitting beyond a continuous curve, whilst the second crudely flattens the figure to fit within it. Although attributed to Franciscus Carolus, the quality of drawing and suggested use of drapery is consistent with that of Willem van Douwe junior (born 1690) rather than the far more accomplished style of his father François. (A number of known works by Willem junior also employ the same technique of offering the option of fitting the figurative work within an elliptical stern.)

Similar uncertainty surrounds the authorship

and date of a design for the VOC ship *Rotterdam* of about 1724 (see colour plate 6). VOC records list two ships named *Rotterdam* during this period: the first, launched in 1716, was wrecked in 1722; the second, launched in 1741, was condemned in 1761. It was common to perpetuate the name of lost ships, but one would expect the namesake to be launched, say, two rather than twenty years after the loss of the first. The drawing may therefore represent a ship proposed during the intervening period. At this time, both François and his son Willem junior were employed by the Rotterdam admiralty. Designs submitted by Willem junior appear from 1720 in a far less accomplished hand than that of his father, suggesting that the *Rotterdam* may be the work of his father. The design fully embraces the French Baroque, but set in the now popular elliptical stern, the solid outline of which has been achieved by seating the large figurative work within a composition of scrolling foliage, taking the horseshoe shape as its outer border, thus neatly solving the problem faced in the previous example of how to include figurative work. In order to achieve the effect of a *tableau de poupe*, the central window of the quarterdeck has been omitted, creating sufficient space to depict a scene relevant to the ship's name. Interestingly, this takes the form of a large painting of the Rotterdam roadstead rather than carved work.

François was by now an accomplished and well-respected artist, so if the general design was the work of his son, François may still have been responsible for the painted work and perhaps the decision to include the medium in the decorative composition, a practice that became an increasing feature of Dutch ornamentation, particularly on the royal jachts. The flamboyant style of decoration depicted on the *Rotterdam* would appear more akin to the lavishness laid upon the state jachts than generally seen on merchantmen of the period, which tend to show a marked reduction in figurative work. Such a reduction would be in line with naval fashions, through the emerging designs of Paulus van Zwijndregt, whose lighter style bears the influence of Daniel Marot.

By 1725 Zwijndregt was submitting ship plans with his already distinctive style of decoration, which typically consisted of simple mouldings and set panels of lightly scrolling acanthus, devoid of any figurative work. They were clearly composed from a naval architect's perspective, where efficiency of the ship becomes the foremost consideration. His designs maintained the general outline of a stern that narrows at the level of the quarterdeck, but the ornamentation and layout of galleries that are added to this traditional arrangement create a very different emphasis, which in some respects mirror the Classical ideals of Palladianism. In his design for the *Maas* of 1728 he introduced arcading pilasters, topped by com-

De Maas launched Rotterdam 1728 to a design by Paulus van Zwijndregt.

positions of lightly scrolling foliage, which cleverly reintroduces the solidity of Dutch Baroque in a startling new form, but without alienating the composition from the comforting familiarity of its Dutch origins. The head rails are set on a *cagouille*, in the French style, but terminate under the cathead in the Dutch fashion, upon which a lion with tightly curling mane forms the figurehead.

In contrast to the lightly balanced compositions of Paulus van Zwijndregt, those of Willem van Douwe continued in the traditional mode, with compositions consisting of rich, densely packed acanthus and figurative work. His designs for the VOC ship *De Boot* of 1733 has lost all trace of the French influence displayed on earlier ships. His drawings show little regard for accuracy, providing

A sketch taken from Willem van Douwe's design for the stern of the VOC ship *De Boot* of 1733.

On his father's death in 1735, Willem junior effectively inherited the position of carver to the admiralty, which seems to have been the common practice. The Admiralty of the Maas appear to have been unimpressed by van Douwe's continued attempts to persuade them of the benefits of the elliptical stern, apparently favouring designs submitted by Paulus van Zwijndregt, who had been employed at the yard since the beginning of the 1700s. Willem van Douwe's time in post was short-lived, with many of his designs submitted to the VOC rather than the naval yard. In 1741 he moved to Gouda, at the same time the admiralty deciding that in future carved work should be put out to tender, rather than automatically appointing Willem junior's son François junior (1720-1799) as his father's successor.

a hastily drawn general impression of a proposed design. Anything beyond the decoration is clearly of little concern, with details such as the placing of gun ports added as a reluctant gesture to acknowledge that they will have to fit somewhere. In his defence, the speed with which these ships were built would not allow for detailed study, nor would it be necessary for a competent carver, who could simply be left to get on with his section of the work.

De Boot made two trips to Batavia, but on the return leg of her third voyage to Ceylon she was wrecked off Start Point on the South Devon coast. Many of the crew were rescued and taken to Dartmouth, but the ship became a total loss. In 1736 Willem submitted designs for another VOC ship, the *Rynhuyse*, which displays a move towards the changing fashions. The upper tafferel is still 'cut through' to form a *hakkebord* in similar fashion to *De Boot*, but the large figures have been replaced by two eagles placed on the turn of the quarter pieces; the elliptical shape of the stern is then continued in a diminishing line down to the lower counter, where carved brackets have been replaced by simple moulded panels.

A contemporary of François van Douwe senior

Marot. Their collaboration appears to have been a success, as in 1701 he was engaged on Marot's next project, the Het Loo Palace in Apeldoorn. Bogemaker's career as a ship-carver appears to have begun around 1716, with commissions for state jachts that continued through to 1734. Unfortunately, evidence of his work has not survived to see how much it may have been influenced by Marot.

was the sculptor Anthony Bogemaker (1659-1735), who was also employed by the Admiralty of the Maas. Having trained in the Hague with the sculptor Jan Blommendal (1650-1707), he qualified as a master sculptor in 1680 but, dissatisfied with the support offered to sculptors by the Guild of St Luke, in 1697 he joined the Confrerie Pictura, an organisation founded in 1656 to provide an alternative to the guild (a decision no doubt influenced by his teacher, who had been a member since 1675). Blommendal had in turn trained under Rombout Verhulst, thus continuing the link between the most eminent of sculptors' involvement with the ornamentation of ships.

Like Verhulst, Blommendal also made a great number of funerary monuments. The character of his work is less intense than Verhulst, a good example being that of Admiral Johan van Brakel for St Laurens Church, Rotterdam in 1691. Similarly, Bogemaker's early work consisted of civic commissions of increasing importance. By 1694 he was employed on the parliament building in The Hague known as the Trèves Hall, which was undergoing a total renovation to designs by Daniel

In 1732 Marot came in contact with the admiralty directly, when he was commissioned to design the decorative work for a new jacht for the Stadholder of The Hague. The work was to be carved by Michiel van Calraet (1679-1748), a sculptor who was already working under the direction of Marot on the City Hall in The Hague. Calraet's father, Pieter Janszoon van Calraet (1620-1722), studied as a woodcarver in Utrecht before establishing his studio in Dordrecht, where his six sons all became recognised painters and sculptors.

His eldest brother Abraham Calraet (1642-1722) studied under the Dordrecht sculptors Aemilius and Samuel Huppe and subsequently worked as a woodcarver, but he is best remembered for his work as a still-life painter, having later studied with the artist Aelbert Cuyp. Michiel moved to The Hague in 1720, where as an already well respected sculptor he played an important role in the Guild of St Luke, receiving many commissions from the municipality and the admiralty, during a period when it sought to address problems facing the design of its ships.

Detail taken from the frontage of a house on the Herensgracht, Amsterdam. Many notable families like the Schrijvers took up residence in this fashionable canal side street, in houses with frontages designed by the leading architects of the day. This example, designed by Daniel Marot in 1730, displays an elegance and fluidity of movement that by 1720 began to be accepted in the decoration of Dutch ships. (Author's collection)

Memorial to Vice Admiral Isaac Sweers (1622-1673) carved by Rombout Verhulst in 1674 (Oude Kerke Amsterdam). Verhulst had previously worked with Artus Quellin on the Amsterdam City Hall, where his reputation was such that he was able to sign his own work. (Author's collection)

To cross the shallow waters of the Zuider Zee (present day Ijsselmeer) the larger vessels of the Dutch navy and VOC had to be supported by floats known as camels and towed to deeper water. This encouraged broad, flat-bottomed hull forms and had always imposed a significant constraint on ship design, but during the reign of William III, when the existing fleet was allied to England in the war against France, it became clear that Dutch naval architecture had failed to keep up with other navies. Amsterdam's master shipwright Gerbrand Slegt made some attempts at improvement but, with his ability and honesty repeatedly questioned, he was forced to resign in 1726.

Following the death of his father in 1711, Cornelis Schrijver (1686-1768) was promoted to Lieutenant-Admiral and in 1724 given command of *Wageningen*. This 36-gun frigate was launched from the Amsterdam yard in 1723, to a design by Gerbrand Slegt in an attempt to produce a ship to match the speed of her English equivalents. As a captain in the recent war, Cornelis was aware of the shortcomings in Dutch ship design and therefore eager to test the performance of the new ship, which was put into service providing protection for the VOC fleet.

Although she was successful in capturing an Algerian pirate ship and setting fire to another, it was clear that better designs were needed. Schrijver placed the views of his captains before the admiralty, which now conceded the need to bring in British expertise. He obtained permission to travel in secret to England, where he found three shipwrights at the royal dockyard in Portsmouth willing to come to the Netherlands. The dockyard authorities, however, learned of the plan and prevented the termination of their employment.

In 1728 one of the shipwrights, Charles Bentham, deserted from Portsmouth and travelled to Amsterdam, where he was appointed assistant shipwright under Thomas Davis, another Englishman, who had previously been employed in Naples, before working his way along the Danube to finally arrive in Holland. They were later joined by John May (1694-1779), a shipwright originally from Chatham, who had been working in Toulon. This odd band of expatriates would in a short time assert a great influence in the shipbuilding of Amsterdam. Eight apprentices were assigned to learn British shipbuilding methods, where the time-honoured role of shipwrights building by eye and instinct had been renounced in favour of proto-naval architects, with the ability to set designs on paper based on calculations providing a methodical system for improvement.

Davis proposed the building of larger vessels. By increasing the proportion between length and breadth and using a lighter structure, he reduced the weight, which would in turn reduce the vessel's draught and increase its speed. Davis's first ship, the 64-gun *Provincie van Utrecht* was launched in 1728, and was observed with keen interest by both the British and other Dutch admiralties. An opportunity to test her performance came the following year, when the *Provincie van Utrecht* under the command of Cornelis Schrijver formed part of an Anglo-Dutch squadron in which a ship renowned for her speed, the 70-gun *Monmouth*, was also present. During a four-day period when the squadron was awaiting orders, the two vessels were pitched against each other, and under varying weather conditions they proved to be equally matched, neither proving superior to the other.

The design of each new vessel produced by Davis was committed to paper to allow for future consultation. A drawing that survives of the *Provincie van Utrecht*'s stern shows a mixture of English naval architecture to which a profusion of Dutch-inspired ornamentation has been applied. A cherub forms the centrepiece of the tafferel, with ferocious lions at the turn of the quarters. Above the cherub and down the quarter pieces are a panoply of military trophies, the haphazard nature of which are neatly ordered in Davis's later designs. A stern gallery has been introduced, but extends only as far as the centre section of the upper deck, perhaps as a compromise between

Bentham's desire for a full gallery and the Dutch reluctance to embrace such a feature.

A painting of Davis's fourth ship, the 50-gun *Prins Friso* of 1730, shows an almost identical stern, again having an open gallery to the centre section only of the upper deck, with a wealth of carved work to the tafferel and quarter pieces. The *Prins Friso* was built at the Harlingen yard to act as flagship to the Admiralty of Friesland's fleet. She participated as part of the Anglo-Dutch fleet off the French coast in 1744, along with three other ships designed by Davis and five by Bentham, including the 64-gun *Damaiten* of 1742 under the command of the now Vice-Admiral Cornelis Schrijver.

Following the success of Davis's earlier ships, the *Boekenrode* of 1732 displays a far greater acceptance of British conventions in the layout of the stern and quarter galleries. The Classical nature imposed by such details as balustrading to the open gallery of the quarterdeck, and the panoply of military trophies to that of the upper deck, has restrained the joyful waywardness normally associated with Dutch ships. Only the tafferel and quarter pieces continue to exhibit a playful profusion of curvaceous aquatic creatures, in the rich density of peculiarly Dutch

Sketch showing the general layout of stern and quarter galleries for Thomas Davis's 52-gun ship *Boekenrode*. The keel was laid at the Amsterdam yard in 1729, with the ship finally launched in 1732; she was stricken from the navy lists in 1758. Mermaids form the quarter pieces, their twin tails entwining in half-human, half-aquatic form, and a series of four cherubs or water nymphs adorn the tafferel, creating a playful scene in contrast to the military trophies and Classicism imposed by the columns and balustrading. The United Provinces are represented in the central motif on the counter, with the nation's arms consisting of a lion holding seven arrows surrounded by the flags of each province.

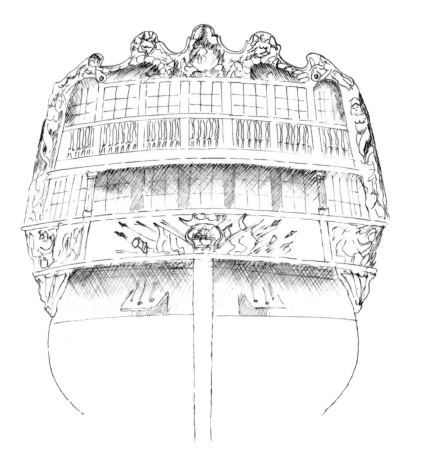

A drawing of Bentham's stern for the standardisation of VOC ships, showing the stern of the largest class of 150 feet. The composition is in essence an British stern, which unfortunately gives little indication as to the style of decoration beyond an outline of the tafferel; the shape of this suggests compositions of Dutch form, the outline being very similar to that of Davis's ship the *Boekenrode*. The open gallery to the quarterdeck shows blank panels below the top rail. As open balustrading would be considered an architectural element and detailed in a similar manner to the windows and columns, it may be assumed that this, in common with the other blank areas, would have received carved ornamentation. A completed model representing the same class of ship differs in showing oval mouldings to the quarterdeck, with carving only to the upper counter consisting of a cartouche to house the vessel's name. It also shows the gallery to the quarterdeck as closed. Such alterations were presumably a result of consultation with the Heeren XVII.

proportions. A lion drawn in the British manner forms the figurehead for the ship, which was the tenth of sixteen designed and launched by Davis in the seven years that he was employed at the yard in Amsterdam.

In 1735 Davis was succeeded by his former assistant Charles Bentham. The success of Bentham's frigates and lighter ships of the line established such a good reputation that by 1742 he was called upon by the VOC. They had in the previous year bought two of his ships from the navy, and now wished to standardise their ship construction in the British fashion. He prepared plans for each class of ship to fulfill this function; the accompanying sketch is taken from such a plan, representing the largest class of East Indiaman at 150 feet with a capacity of 1100 tons. As the drawing relates to a class of ship rather than a specific vessel, it does not detail carved work, but leaves blank areas where carving would be applied. Bentham also introduced the practice of producing models, as a visual aid to both apprentices and the admiralty board who ultimately approved the design.

A model dated 1742 accompanies the previous plan, to depict the largest class of East Indiaman, and shows a lion figurehead, with quarter galleries and stern layout typical of those employed in British ships of the period, but with some variations to the original plan, by adopting the Dutch preference for a closed gallery to the quarterdeck. Strongmen representing Mercury and Neptune stand full height on the quarter pieces, with the arms of Amsterdam and the VOC chamber of Amsterdam forming the centrepiece to the tafferel. The lower finishing to the quarter gallery terminates in a fish's tail, whilst the upper comprises a central cartouche, flanked by luxuriant foliage, the no-nonsense boldness of which is indicative of Dutch craftsmanship.

In 1969 the wreck was discovered of Bentham's East Indiaman *Amsterdam*. Launched in 1748, she was the twentieth ship built to his designs, but was unfortunately lost on her maiden voyage. Driven off course by strong winds, she lost her rudder on a sand bank off the Sussex coast, but her captain managed to sail her off and anchored in the shelter of Hastings Bay, waiting for the storm to abate. Fever had broken out on the ship soon after she set sail from Texel and by now fifty men had died, with a further forty unable to rise from their hammocks. Sickness and diarrhoea combined with the lack of ventilation to make conditions on board unbearable and the captain, fearing the whole crew would succumb to the unidentified illness, decided to beach the ship. The surviving men were taken ashore, together with the cargo of silver carried to pay for goods bought in Asia. The ship became stuck firmly in the deep soft mud, making attempts to refloat her impossible; the VOC reluctantly declared her a total loss.

Despite such tragedies, the three classes of ship designed for the VOC by Bentham proved to be very successful in their performance and seaworthiness. Comfort aboard was improved, particularly in the tropics where Bentham designed a ventilation system to provide an air flow to the lower decks.

During the 1980s sufficient information was gathered to build a replica ship, which is now berthed as a permanent exhibit at the maritime museum in Amsterdam. The carved work follows the basic composition of Bentham's model of 1742, which, having insignia relating to Amsterdam, was appropriate for the replica. Van der Meer, the master shipwright for the project, served as a model for the head of Neptune, continuing a tradition where contemporary characters would have been imortalised by their workmates.

The master shipwrights of navy yards beyond Amsterdam continued with their own methods, considering the British-designed ships of too deep a draught for their shallow waters. The opposition they displayed prevented the introduction of one uniform ship design for the five admiralties. Rotterdam continued to employ Paulus van Zwijndregt as their master shipwright. He considered the presence of the British shipwrights an insult, and in 1738 submitted designs to champion his own innovations, which he proposed as the 'New Dutch Method'.

Bentham had established the procedure of submitting a model to accompany his designs for approval by the admiralty board. In order to give a comparable presentation, Zwijndregt also had a model constructed, ironically in Britain where the quality of workmanship benefited from a longer tradition of modelmaking than in the United Provinces. The carving is best viewed as a British interpretation of the design, as it lacks confidence in displaying the Dutch fullness of form, but it serves very well as an example of Zwijndregt's proposed layout for the stern, to which the carved work was to be applied. It clearly portrays Zwijndregt's different style of composition, which in common with the previous example, returns to the concepts of Classicism. The figurehead appears to be of standard British design, which may be the result of the modelmaker's interpretation rather than Zwijndregt's intention. The head rails adopt the French convention of terminating in a *cagouille*, so that the hair bracket and junction of the rails are visible beyond the lion when viewed head on.

Anchor from the *Amsterdam*, now at St Katherine's Dock, London. (Author's collection)

A drawing taken from Paulus van Zwijndregt's model of 1738 to demonstrate his 'New Dutch Method'. (Author's collection)

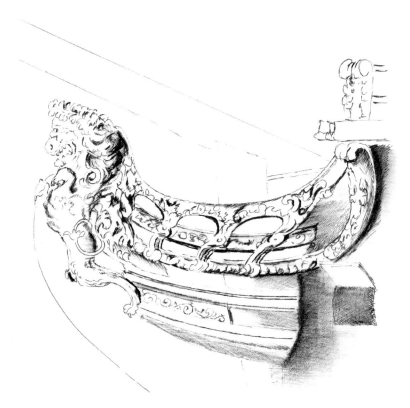

missioned François van Douwe to design a new choir screen, for which he carved the moulds in wood, to be cast in brass. The church continued to employ both ship-carvers, commissioning van der Beke to carve a new pulpit while further sculptural work was given to van Douwe. Much of the original church interior was lost during bombing raids in 1940, but the screen has since been restored, together with Jan Blommendal's funerary work.

In 1737 the office of Stadholder was made hereditary in the House of Orange, for both the male and female line. In the same year Princess Carolina was born, only to be relegated to second in line by the birth of her brother a year later; the next two ships to be launched were to be named in their honour. Van der Beke was successful in submitting the lowest tender for the carved work to

The lion figurehead to Paulus van Zwijndregt's 54-gun ship *Rotterdam* of 1745. The style of ornament to the head rails is typical to many of Zwijndregt's ships, with ornate carving to the rails flowing onto the head timbers, terminating on a *cagouille* in the French fashion. The lion is also a common choice of figure, in a style as set out in the model depicting his 'New Dutch Method', having a strong upper body that further expands into a mass of flowing mane which almost obscures the crown on his head.

A year after the submission of Zwijndregt's proposed 'New Dutch Method' his 54-gun ship *Dordrecht* was launched from the Rotterdam yard, with ornamentation that closely follows the composition as proposed in his model. She had a long career, serving as part of an Anglo-Dutch fleet in 1744 before being sold in 1783. Zwijndregt's next two ships, the 66-gun *Rotterdam* of 1741 and the 56-gun ship *Schiedam* of 1745, continued with the same style of decoration to the stern and quarter galleries. The sculptor Solomon de Visser (1678-1745) was commissioned to carry out the carved work to both ships, which both carried lion figureheads of a similar style to the *Rotterdam*.

The Zwijndregt family clearly found favour with the Rotterdam Admiralty, and they appointed Leendert (active 1745-1763) and Pieter (1711-1790) who designed both men of war and many state jachts, creating a dynasty of shipbuilders that spanned over eighty years. The van Douwe family also maintained a presence at the Rotterdam yard, through François junior (son of Willem junior) alongside other carvers competing for the naval contracts, such as Jan Baptist van der Beke (1712-1773), who trained under the Antwerp sculptor Jean-Joseph van der Gught. He received his first major commission in 1748 for carved work to a new organ for the St Laurens Church in Rotterdam. The same church had in 1711 com-

Detail taken from the brass choir screen of St Laurens Church, Rotterdam. The original moulds were carved by François van Douwe senior (1659-1735), revealing scroll work and foliage inspired by the work of Bérain and Marot. Other sections of the screen were decorated with compositions of palms, gadrooning and *guilloche* moulds, all very much in the French style. Van der Beke's work was sadly destroyed through bombing raids on the town, but the 'Marotesque' influence of Van Douwe's work shows in decorative design he provided for the ship *Princess Carolina*. (Author's collection)

both ships, the first of which, the 56-gun *Princess Carolina* was built at Rotterdam to a design by Paulus van Zwijndregt and launched in 1748. She was captured by HMS *Bellona* in 1780, at which time her lines were taken off, providing some record of her decorative work. She served in the British navy as the *Princess Caroline* until 1783 when she was hulked at Sheerness as a receiving ship before being broken up in 1799.

Paulus van Zwijndregt's vision of artistic perfection clearly rested on the precepts of Classicism, where architecture was meant to reflect the harmony of the universe in abiding by the natural laws that upheld it. He had as a supreme example Jacob van Campen's City Hall, where divine proportion underpinned a structure that manifested this harmony, to which was added the earthly delights of creation in a celebration of the abundance offered by the creator.

The degree to which Zwijndregt as naval architect and van der Beke as carver collaborated in the ornamental designs is unknown, but the composition of Zwijndregt's sterns and van der

Beke's carvings take elements that can be found on the City Hall, such as the festoons of shells that appear on *Princess Carolina*, which being some hundred years later than the City Hall, also includes later developments in the arts, namely ornamentation inspired by the French Baroque, which appears on the majority of Zwijndregt's designs. The delicacy of line and lightness of density would have naturally appealed to his sense of harmonic proportion.

Leendert van Zwijndregt was employed at the Rotterdam yard from 1745. His period in office spanned the changing fashions as Baroque ornament began to embrace rocaille and Rococo-inspired motifs. The admiralty adoption of this does not appear before the mid-1750s and then generally restricted to the smaller frigates, with Paulus van Zwijndregt's more Classically inspired Baroque still dominating the ornamentation of larger vessels.

The van Douwe family presence at the yard was maintained by Johannes Hubertus, who submitted designs in 1764 for the jacht *Willem V*

Princess Carolina, designed by Paulus van Zwijndregt in 1748 with carved work by Jan Baptist van der Beke. Bandwork decoration to the cove is in the 'Marotesque' style, with the arms of the admiralty of the United Provinces forming the centrepiece, above which the continuous line of lights forms a standard feature of Zwijndregt's designs. Festoons between the foot and breast rails of the quarter gallery are unusual in being composed of sea shells between vertical drops of drapery, while large volutes replace figurative work to the quarters. Zwijndregt's designs are typically devoid of any figurative work.

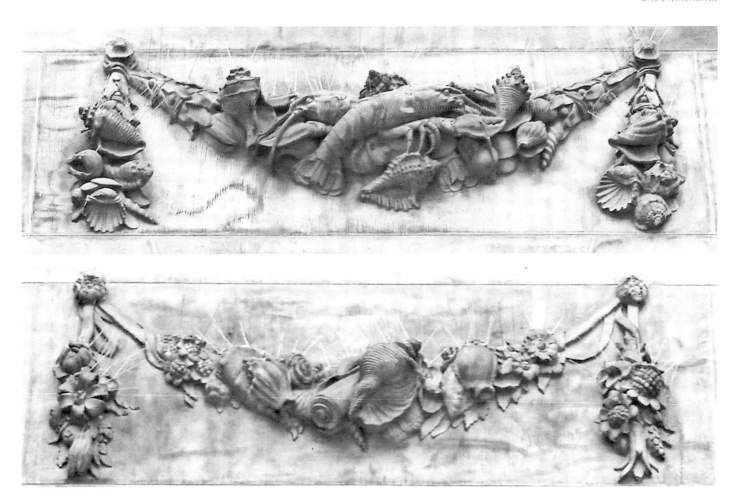

Festoons to the stern of Paulus van Zwijndregt's ship *Princess Carolina* clearly take their inspiration from the many examples that adorn the exterior of the City Hall in Amsterdam. The stone carvings designed by Artus Quellin are now over 360 years old, but thanks to the quality of the stone are still in remarkably good condition, having retained their intricate detail (helped by the later addition of spikes to deter perching birds). (Author's collection)

Rococo ornamentation in the style of Balthasar Maystre's early work, applied to a frigate of the Amsterdam Admiralty around 1755-1765. (From Carr Laughton, *Old Ship Figureheads & Sterns*)

that hint at the influence of Rococo, while still maintaining a more dignified regal presence, while the Rococo theme was further developed by the sculptor Balthasar Maystre (1729-1803). He was active at the Amsterdam yard, where John May succeeded to the post of master shipwright following Bentham's death in 1758. May had eight sons, one of whom became an admiral in the Dutch navy, while William (1725-1807) continued the family shipbuilding business, creating a continued British presence in Dutch ship design for over eighty years. The frigate illustrated here may be the result of their collaboration, as the style of drawing resembles similar examples from the Rotterdam yard, where Maystre commenced work around 1755, submitting Rococo-inspired designs through to 1770 and the advent of Neoclassicism. John May's 36-gun frigate *Mars* of 1769 also displays Rococo ornamentation by Maystre, clearly expressing his mastery of the new style.

The drawings of Leendert van Zwijndregt initially continue the style set by Paulus, but his design for a 46-gun ship of 1745 includes an innovation of his own, whereby a large sculptural work rising to the height of two decks is placed in the centre of the stern. This feature is repeated on his design for the 60-gun ship *Mars*, launched from

the Rotterdam yard in 1763, by which time the arrangement of galleries had adopted the British pattern, with a balustraded walkway to the quarterdeck, connecting to a quarter gallery that now extends up to this level. A preliminary sketch of the stern, dated 1760, is held in the archives of the Rotterdam Maritime Museum, and shows the stern with the same sea creature on the starboard quarter, but with the figure of Mars located on the corresponding port side, leaving the galleries with a clear run of lights. The figure appears insignificant compared to the scale of the ship, and the move to the central position certainly gives the Roman god of war a mightier stature. Balthasar Maystre was commissioned to carry out the carved work, testing his talents on such a monumental scale.

Ornamentation to the ships of the VOC continued in the rich, voluptuous Baroque tradition, many fine examples of which can be seen in the designs of P Vlaming, who was employed by the VOC from 1750 to 1780. During the fashionable period of Rococo they included its asymmetrical waywardness, together with the naturalistic forms of rocaille, creating what in modern terms would be defined as their 'mission statement' expressed as 'the generation of wealth and abundance'. The state jachts, naturally wishing to

The port side of the drawing shows the general layout to the stern of Leendert van Zwijndregt's 60-gun ship *Mars* as an initial sketch dated 1760. The starboard side and central figure shows the stern layout as captured by the British in 1781, when the sea creature to the starboard quarter replaced that of Mars on the portside. Large figurative work placed centrally on the stern was a feature of Leendert's designs, and the decision to include it here was presumably taken before the ship's launch in 1763. The ship served in the Royal Navy as *Prince Edward* before being sold in 1784.

A Dutch jacht from the 1750s displaying an exquisite composition of lively Baroque ornament, as it embraced the motifs of Rococo's asymmetrical forms and the naturalistic shell-like ornament of rocaille (see also colour plate 7).

project the same image, also continued with the Baroque style. A drawing of the jacht *Johanna Francisca* of 1770 by J B Eekhout displays a delicate rocaille-inspired design, while those of Willem van Gendt continue to show Rococo ornamentation to admiralty jachts as late as 1775. Such vessels provided an outlet for carvers to express the playful imaginings of a creative mind, standing in stark contrast to the admiralty warships, which by 1776 had been universally confined to the balanced equanimity of Neoclassical motifs, fittingly projecting their statement of clear-headed discipline, capable of defending the values of its people.

The head of the 50/56-gun ship *Berschermer* was built at Enkhuizen in 1784 for the Admiralty of the Noorderkwartier. The drawing is attributed to Jan Rood, an artist from Enkhuizen who recorded many ships, generally in pen and ink wash. Although the drawing takes the form of a sculptor's draught, it is not known if Jan only recorded completed ships. (National Maritime Museum PAG9651)

For Pieter van Zwijndregt, who carried on from Leendert, it was an easy task to seamlessly mutate the classical Baroque structure of Paulus to the more sober Neoclassical style. Maystre also appears to have coped with the change, providing Neoclassical designs from 1771, to which he still managed to include some lively figurative work, such as to the 54-gun *Hercules* of 1781.

The 68-gun *Pieter Paulus* was launched from the Rotterdam yard of the Maas Admiralty in 1798, representing the last ship for which Evert Maystre provided the carved work. She was renamed *Utrecht* in 1807 and was finally broken up in 1815. Balthasar Maystre was joined by his son Evert (1756-1799) in 1781, both producing clearly defined compositions in the Neoclassical style. Evert managed to inject a sense of buoyant liveliness into the otherwise stolid sensibility of the idiom, composed mainly of military trophies and insignia held together by delicate mouldings, margent drops of diminishing husk ornament and swags of thin-lipped foliage or drapery. A little more leeway was given to the figureheads, which commonly depicted the heroic figures after which the ships of the period were often named.

The Maystres were joined by the very talented artist Johannes Keerbergen, who began submitting designs to the Admiralty of the Maas around 1780. As a fine draughtsman, his designs invariably show the ship as an artistic portrait with the vessel afloat on the waves, with pen and ink washes to emphasise shadows. As an accomplished sculptor, his designs take advantage of any opportunity to include large figurative work, such as the *Staaten Generaal*, a 76-gun ship launched from the Rotterdam yard in 1788. The quality of his drawing clearly demonstrates his ability to visualise the compositions three-dimensionally, while other designers such as P Glavimans and Jan Guidici continued to produce ornamentation that fell strictly in line with the minimal precepts of Neoclassicism similar to those of Balthasar Maystre's later designs.

Keerbergen's time in office spanned the 'French period' when the United Provinces were invaded by France in 1795. The country was reorganised to become the Batavian Republic, then in 1806 Napoleon installed his brother Louis as King of the Netherlands, occupying the Amsterdam City Hall as his royal palace. In 1813 the Prince of Orange, who had been in exile in London, returned following the retreat of the French to become King Willem I.

The marking of such events maintained Keerbergen's career as a ship-carver through to 1825, by which time the tight constraints of Neoclassicism had eased to allow the return of more expressive creativity. Keerbergen's design for *d'Comercie* of 1806 features large figurative work to the quarter pieces and centrepiece to the tafferel, amidst mouldings and decorative motifs that maintain a sense of elegance and grandeur. This expressive quality in his work continued through to the end of his career, by which time ornamentation applied to ships of other nations had become weary in comparison.

The warship *Pieter Paulus* 1799 with carved work by Evert Maystre (1756-1799). Panelled balustrading to the quarterdeck extends beyond the stern to create an open walkway, decorated with a repeating pattern of festoons and wreaths carved in shallow relief. Brackets that support the projecting walkway take the form of herms whose pedestals run the length of the mullions. By the 1760s the quarter galleries had extended up to the quarterdeck which here connect to the stern gallery. A panoply motif forms the centrepiece of the tafferel, carved in deep relief surmounted by acanthus volutes mirrored to create an arch onto the quarter pieces, providing some sense of movement in an otherwise typically sombre Neoclassical design.

The 74-gun *Washington* was launched from the Amsterdam yard in 1795 to a design by Cornelis Mast. The flags of the seven provinces forming the centrepiece of the tafferel have been joined by two lions and a centurion, with further figurative work to the quarter pieces creating a decorative composition unusually ornate for such a late period, possibly as a result of the 1795 French invasion of the United Provinces, which then became the Batavian Republic. The ship surrendered to the British in 1799 and was renamed the *Prince of Orange* after the Dutch ruler who had sought exile in London. (National Maritime Museum F5800-004)

DUTCH SHIP-CARVERS

Rotterdam (the Maas)		Active for admiralty
	Pieter Verschuier	1647
1634-1686	Lieve Verschuier	1674-1686
1620-1689	Willem van Douwe senior	1683-1689?
1659-1738	François Douwe senior	1683-1703
1663-1748	Anthoney Bogemaker	1716-1734
1678-1745	Salomon de Visser	1742-1745
1671-1760	Dingeman van der Vis	1730-1758 ?
1679-1748	Michiel van Calraet (Kalraat)	1732
1690-17??	Willem van Douwe junior	1725-1745
1712-1773	Jan Baptist van de Beke	1749-1752
1720-1799	François Douwe junior	1730-1731
1729-1803	Balthasar Maystre	1741-1803
17?? -17??	Johannes Hubertus van Douwe	1764
1756-1799	Evert Maystre	1781-1799
17??-18??	Johannes Keerbergen	1783-1825
	Pieter Franciscus Luijpen	1800

Amsterdam
1729-1803	Balthasar Maystre	
	J H van Blitterswijk	

Zeeland
Vlissingen (Flushing)
1657-1758	Cornelis Moerman	1698

Leiden
	Hermanus van Groen	1699-1720
1624-1696	Rombout Verhulst	1658-1669
	Gerrit Goosman	

DUTCH SHIPWRIGHTS

Amsterdam
1662-1723	Hendrik Cardinaal
1692-1722	Jan van Rheen
1723-1726	Gerbrand Slegt
1726	Jacob Papegaaij
1729-1740	Thomas Davis
1735-1755	Charles Bentham
1754-1778	John May
1779-1782	Willem Lodewijk van Ghent
1782	Booy
1783-1785	Cornelis Mast & William May

Friesland
1782	Sjoerd Jouwerts stapert
1781, 1782, 1794	J Swerus

Harlingen

1761-1769	W Lodewijk van Genth
1779	J Swerus
1783	Pieter Tetrode
1796-1797	P Schuijt

Maas, Dordrecht, Goringchem

1702	Van Leeuwen
1703-1763	Paulus van Zwijndrecht
1752-1763	Leendert van Zwijndrecht
1767-1782	Pieter van Zwijndrecht (1711-1790)
1770	P Glavimans (1753-1820)
1781	Jacob Spaan

Noorderkwartier

1708	Cornelis Willemsz Blauwvlag (Medemblik)
1725	Gerbrand Slegt
1725	Jan Pool (1725 Medemblik, 1725 Enkhuizen)
1753	Baes (Enkhuizen)
1779-1786	J Hand (1779/1784 Medemblik, 1780 Enkhuizen, 1786 Hoorn)
1797	Mooij

Zeeland

1699	Adriaen Davidsen Flushing (Vlissingen)
1723-1733	Hendrik Raas
1796	Crul
1798	P Scuit Flushing

3

⟨Great Britain⟩

Detail of a gallery in Hatfield House, Hertfordshire; built in 1607-1611, it provides a showpiece for the developing Jacobean style. Caryatid figures support an entablature with mock capitals, below which are a series of linked arches known as arcading. Strapwork which formerly acted as a border now stretches to an entire panel, while the panel adjacent to it is decorated in an earlier style with a grotesque mask and linear strapwork.

Queen's House Greenwich, 1620. (Wikimedia Commons)

Prior to 1620 each craftsman in England was effectively his own designer, plucking elements of post-Gothic and Mannerist styles, then mixing them with the Renaissance influences that had spread to the country through the 1500s. This carefree approach was not tethered by the correct usage of Classical application; he simply chose elements that appealed to his artistic eye, creating individual and sometimes eccentric results, which in their way captured the lively enthusiasm of the age.

Ship decoration reflected the predominant trends, with those of the Tudor period (1485-1603) displaying Mannerist influences. Following the death of Elizabeth in 1603 the succession passed to the Scottish house of Stuart, heralding the Jacobean period (1603-1649) that covered the reigns of James I and Charles I, which with regard to decoration, in general terms, saw the transition from Mannerist to Renaissance-inspired designs – arcading symmetry and the repeating interlaced bands known as *guilloche*, mixed with caryatids and allegorical figures combined in a haphazard fashion.

All this was to be changed through the influence of Inigo Jones (1573-1652). By 1613 he had made two trips to Italy where he studied the works of Andrea Palladio (1508-1580), an Italian architect who set out the precepts of Classical architecture in a form which bears his name. On his return to England Jones worked for the crown, and in 1620 designed the Queen's House at Greenwich. This stands as the first true Classical building in England, and marked the beginning of architectural practice where drawings would be produced instructing the craftsmen in every detail of the work, to achieve a pure form.

Supporters of the Jacobean style ensured that it continued to flourish into the mid-1600s and little evidence survives suggesting that the Classical influence found its way into ship decoration in any formal sense. When Charles I ascended the throne in 1625, the nation inherited a king in constant opposition with its parliament, as he sought to continue his father's policy of increasing the power of the sovereign. In 1629 he dissolved parliament to begin eleven years of direct rule.

The showpiece of Charles I's navy was the *Sovereign of the Seas*. Considerably larger than any previous ship, she was also the culmination of many advances in the design of her hull and rig, among them being her method of steering, which departed from the established tiller and whipstaff arrangement to a system of relieving tackles. She was the first ship in the world to carry 100 truck-mounted guns on three complete battery decks and, with a length at keel of 127 feet the largest yet built.

Designed by Phineas Pett, she was laid down at Woolwich in 1636 under the supervision of his son Peter Pett and launched in 1637. The final cost of £65,486.16s.9d was more than three times her original estimate. Her carved works were of an unequalled scale and are worthy of special attention. Despite Charles I's many political shortcomings, he deserves credit as England's first great royal patron of the arts. In 1632 he appointed the Flemish artist Anthony van Dyck (1599-1641) as court painter. The works of van Dyck, who had studied under Rubens, defined the style of English portrait painting. He became a revered and influential figure at court and was ennobled for his service.

If England lagged behind in the introduction of the latest styles in architectural ornament, this was certainly not the case with the appointment of van Dyck. His fast dashing strokes were viewed as a modernistic approach that created a sense of Baroque grandeur, whilst maintaining a balance of refined elegance. England was also very much in the forefront of the dramatic arts, where the sense of theatricality in van Dyck's work was readily accepted.

In 1622 the playwright Ben Jonson (1572-1637) staged the *Masque of Augres* with sets, stage machinery and costumes designed by Inigo Jones. Masques were extravagant and ephemeral, one- or two-time productions after which the sets and machines were discarded. Van Dyck was well acquainted with Ben Jonson, Inigo Jones and the dramatist Thomas Heywood, for whom he may well have provided theatrical sets. Heywood was also called upon by the crown to record important state events in prose to match the splendour of the occasion. This talent combined with his scholarly knowledge of the Classics made him the perfect choice to devise the iconography – the subject matter for the decoration – of the *Sovereign of the*

The showpiece of Charles I's navy, the *Sovereign of the Seas* as depicted in an engraving by John Payne following her launch in 1637 (see also colour plate 8). (National Maritime Museum A6719)

Seas, which was then to be interpreted into their decorative forms by the court painter Sir Anthony van Dyck. Thomas Heywood recorded the scenarios depicted in the carved work with detailed explanations for onlookers to fully appreciate the significance of the imagery; this was then published for maximum public impact.

The figurehead depicted King Edgar the Peaceful conquering the seven provincial kings, the significance of which is enshrined in a motto cast into the barrel of each cannon: *Carolus Edgari sceptrum stabilivit aquarum* (Charles has firmly grasped Edgar's sceptre of the seas). The stem of the ship was further embellished with numerous figures to provide a continuous sequence of decorative motifs, which Heywood goes on to describe:

Upon the stemme-head there is a cupid or a child resembling him, bestriding, and bridling a Lyon, which importeth that sufferance may curbe Insolence and Innocence restraine violence; which alludeth to the great mercy of the King, whose Type is a proper Embleme of that great Majesty, whose Mercy is above all his Workes.

On the bulkhead right forward stand six severall statues in sundry postures; their figures representing Consilium, that is Counsel: Cura, that is Care: Conamen, that is Industry, and unanimous indeavour in one compartment: Counsell holding in her hand a closed or folded Scrole; Care a Sea-compasse; Conamen, or Industry a Lint stock fired. Upon the other, to correspond with the former, is Vis, which implyth strength; holding a sword Virtus, or Virtue, a sphearicall globe; and Victoria or Victory, a wreath of lawrell.

The moral is, that in all high enterprizes there ought to be first Councell to undertake; the Care, to manage; and Industry, to performe; and in the next place, where there is Ability and Strength to oppose, and Virtue to direct, Victory consequently is alwayes at hand ready to crowne the undertaking.

Upon the hances of the waste are four Figures with their severall propertie: Jupiter riding upon his Eagle, with his Trisulk (from which hee darteth Thunder) in his hand:

Mars with his Sword and target, a Foxe being his Embleme: Neptune with his Sea-horse, Dolphin and Trident: and lastly Aeolus upon a Camelion (a beast that liveth onely by Ayre) with the foure Winds, his Ministers or Agents, the East call'd Eurus, Subsolanus, and Apeliotes: the North-winde, Septemtrio, Aquilo, or Boreas the West, Zephyrus, Favonius, Lybsm and Africus: the South, Auster, or Notus.

I come now to the sterne, where you shall perceive upon the upright of the upper Counter, standeth Victory in the middle of a Frontispiece, with this generall Motto *Validis incumbite remis*: It is so plaine, that I shall not need to give it any English interpretation: Her wings are equally disply'd; on one Arme she weareth a Crowne, on the other a Laurell, which imply Riches and Honour: in her two hands she holdeth two Mottoes.

Heywood goes on to describe 'Hercules, on the sinister side, with his club in hand' and 'Jason industrious with his Oare upon the water'. On the lower counter of the stern is an inscription which translates as 'He, who Seas, Windes and Navies doth protect, Great Charles, thy great ship in her course direct.'

In addition to the most notable sculptures described above, the stern had numerous caryatid figures forming mullions and brackets to arcading galleries inset with allegorical figures and mythical beasts. Also, of course, the quarter galleries were richly ornamented and a continuous band of carved work ran the entire length of the upper gun deck, all richly carved and gilded in the prevailing Jacobean style.

Thomas continues in his report to praise the various master craftsmen, most notably the ship-carvers:

The master carvers are John and Mathias Christmas and sons of that most excellent workman Master Garret Christmas, some two years since deceased, who, as they succeed him in place, so they have strived to exceed him in his art: the work better commending them than my pen is in any way able.

Let me not here forget a prime Officer, Master Francis Sheldon, Clerke of the

Check, whose industry and care, in looking to the workmen imployed in the architecture, hath been a great furtherance to expedite the business.

The Christmas family are recorded as having worked as ship-carvers from 1590 to 1668, at Harwich, Woolwich, Sheerness and Chatham, where Gerrard (or Garret) was master carver from 1631 to 1622, when he was succeeded by his sons John and Mathias. Both of these also worked in stone, contributing to work at palaces in Greenwich and Whitehall. More will be heard of Francis Sheldon in the coming chapters.

Charles took a great interest in the Navy but without parliament he had little recourse to funding. He overcame this by the unpopular measure of demanding 'Ship Money' from seaports and later inland towns. The struggle between king and parliament eventually led to civil war and the emergence of Oliver Cromwell (1599-1658), whose rise to power from a humble member of parliament, ironically, led to his virtual dictatorship as Lord Protector. Charles was executed in 1649 and under Cromwell all royal imagery was removed from the ships of what was

now the Commonwealth Navy. Although his puritan regime's belief in the profanity of adornment demanded restraint, the decoration of existing ships escaped with little alteration beyond royal insignia being removed and replaced with equally rich and lavishly carved imagery, which now depicted Cromwell's might. It was proposed to rename the Navy's largest ship *Commonwealth*, but finally she became known simply as *Sovereign*.

In 1652 she under went a major refit, at which time reports suggest she was cut down to a two-decker to improve what was generally considered to be her poor sailing ability, but a commissioner's report of 1651 recommended that:

> The gratings and upper deck amidships be taken down, the upper state room be taken away, the forecastle to be lowered to six feet high and the works abaft to be taken down proportionately to the waist. The half deck to be shortened, also the head to be made shorter and the galleries to be altered as may be comely and most convenient for service.

If the alterations were completed as this report, she would have achieved greater stability without the loss of her third gun deck.

With the restoration of the monarchy in 1660 the *Sovereign* was rebuilt, by which time the carver Thomas Fletcher (on the recommendation of Peter Pett) had been appointed master carver at Chatham. He was paid the sum of £109, presumably for restoring the carvings to their royal stature. The names of Thomas, Matthew and John Fletcher appear in Admiralty accounts as carvers to the Thames and Medway yards of Deptford, Woolwich, Sheerness and Chatham, where they were responsible for the production of carved works to many ships following the Restoration. Any family relationship is unknown, but the dates suggest that Matthew and John were the sons of Thomas.

The bulk of Matthew and John's employment was as a result of Samuel Pepys's report to James II (who was his own Lord High Admiral) in 1685 which found that 85 per cent of the fleet was unfit for service, prompting a programme of overhauling and rebuilding of the major warships. John started work at Chatham shortly after the report, completing repairs to twenty-one vessels in 1687. A detailed account exists for the repairs to *Montague* of 1654 and *Hampton Court* of 1678 which provides a valuable insight, not only as to costs, but also into the size and location of decoration:

Flags and cyphers of the Commonwealth. From 1649 men of war were instructed to wear a St George's cross on a white field as the national ensign; at the same time every warship was to carry on her stern an escutcheon containing in one compartment a red cross and in the other a harp.

The example shown here seems to have been suggested as a flag of command instead of the Union: a flag bearing the arms of England and Ireland (gold harp on a blue field) in two escutcheons on a red field within a compartment. In the case of a vice- or rear-admiral the compartment seems to have been without ornamentation; in that of an admiral it was encircled by a green laurel wreath. Ships of the Commonwealth period can often be identified by insignia such as this ensign being incorporated into the carved work.

Upper deck ports	19 @ 17/- each	£16.0.3
Quarter ditto	5 @ 12/- each	£3.0.0
Taffrells 10ft long 2ft deep 6^1/$_2$in Thick	2 @ 55/- each	£5.10.0
Brackets 3^1/$_2$ft long 7in Thick	11 @ 9/- each	£4.19.0
Peeces of buttons for Topps of ye gallerys 5ft long, 4in thick	9 @ 3/- each	£1.7.0
Wing for ye support 3ft long 4in Thick		£ 9.0
A Lyon for ye Head 15^1/$_2$ft long 2ft Thick		£4.10.0
Brackets 5ft long 10in Broad	8 @ 14/-each	£5.12.0
A mask for ye cats		£ 7.0
Bulkhead brackets for ye forecastle 6ft long 5in broad	4 @ 11/- each	£2.4.0
Brackets for ye steerage 8^1/$_2$ft long 5in thick	3 @ 12/- each	£ 1.16.0
Brackets for ye bulkhead 6^1/$_2$ft long 4in thick	3 @ 10/- each	£1.10.0
Belfrey capp 4^1/$_2$ft broad 2in thick		£2.5.0
Hansings 4^1/$_2$ft long 9in thick	2 @ 7/- each	£ 14.0
Knightheads	2 @ 5/- each	£ 10.0
Head brackets 5ft long 6^1/$_2$in broad (Head timbers)		£ 12.0
Head brackets 5^1/$_2$ft long 8in thick		£ 12.0
One whole port of four quarters 5^1/$_2$ft thick 71in broad and 3ft diameter to ye outside of ye port		£1.10.0
Hawse piece in ye waist 3ft long 6in broad		£ 8.0
Ports 5 ft diameter, cut leaves and flowers	6 @ 18/- each	£5.8.0
Gallery brackets 4^1/$_2$ft long 8in broad	6 @ 9/- each	£2.14.0
A support for ye cathead 13ft long 15in broad		£2.10.0
Bulkhead bracket 2ft long ^{1}/$_2$in thick	3 @ 5/- each	£1.1.0
A dogg for ye hansings 3^1/$_2$ft long		£1.2.0
Knightheads	3 @ 5/- each	£ 15.0
		————
		£77.8.0

Figurehead of the 80-gun ship *Naseby* of 1655: a likeness of Oliver Cromwell riding over the representatives of six nations. (National Maritime Museum F9221-006)

The cost of gilding such monumental works was immense, and in an effort to cut expenditure – and presumably to conform with Cromwellian puritanical beliefs – gilding to warships during the early years of the Commonwealth was not permitted. To what extent the order was adhered to is hard to say: contemporary ship models usually show all carved work gilded, but it should be borne in mind that these were display items and made as decorative as possible. Also, those surviving from the Commonwealth period were usually altered after the Restoration and therefore do not show the ship as first completed.

Carved work to newly built ships tended to be restricted to the stern, quarter galleries and head, with only the hance pieces and perhaps wreath ports decorating the ships' sides; this still amounted to a considerable degree of ornament. The efforts made by Charles I to improve the Navy shrink into insignificance compared to the astounding building programme of the Cromwellian era. During the Commonwealth period more than half of Britain's total expenditure went on naval affairs. The fact that this exceeded the country's total income appears to have been ignored in the desire to fulfill the Cromwellian dream.

The largest ship of the Commonwealth fleet was the *Naseby*. This 80-gun ship was launched at Woolwich in 1655 to a design by Francis Sheldon (1612-1692). She was some four feet longer than the *Sovereign*, having a length at the keel of 131 feet. The experience gained by Sheldon through his involvement with the *Sovereign* undoubtedly stood him in good stead, as the *Naseby* proved to be a very successful ship. There are a number of similarities in the themes applied to the carved works, particularly the figurehead, where Cromwell exhibited his supremacy by having it carved in his own likeness. He is depicted mounted on horseback trampling the six nations of Scotland, Ireland, England, Holland, Spain and France underfoot.

Description of the Carved Work to *Naseby*

The stern carvings show little development in style of decoration or richness of application from earlier ships of the Jacobean period, with a mixture of Classical motifs carved in the Mannerist style. Motifs such as the cupid astride a lion are themes taken from the *Sovereign*. Both ships were built at Woolwich, where Mathias Christmas was master carver up to his death in 1654, when his son-in-law Thomas Fletcher was appointed to the post. Carving for the ship would have commenced long before the ship's launch, so it is possible that both carvers worked on the ship. (Thomas Fletcher was later responsible for replacing carvings on both ships after the Restoration.)

The crowning of the tafferel is supported by two animals that resemble hippocamps; with the head of a horse and tail of a fish, these beasts draw Poseidon's chariot through the sea. In Greek mythology Poseidon was originally god of earthquakes and later of the sea, being attended with chthonic (Underworld) creatures, not seahorses. He is also said to have fathered the winged horse Pegasus, so the winged hippocamp may therefore symbolise an earlier Classical connection.

The cross of St George takes the place of royal insignia forming the centrepiece of the tafferel, above which sits a figure blowing two trumpets. This Renaissance motif represents Fame, who is supported on each side by a sphinx. The ancient Egyptians depicted this mythical beast as a lion with a human head, symbolising power and vigilance. The Greeks endowed the figure with the torso of a woman displaying her naked breasts and it is in this form that the figure became a Classical motif of the Renaissance that symbolised the seat of arcane knowledge. The strapwork volutes upon which they sit extend to form a cartouche around

the cross of St George, thus forming a bond between the two. A belt around the cross bears the commonwealth motto *Pax quæritur bello* (peace is sought by war).

Four lights now appear within the tafferel, two of which take the form of a sunflower. A Greek myth describes how the love between Clytia, a daughter of Oceanus and Tethys, and the sun god Apollo was thwarted when he turned his attentions to her sister Leucothea. Clytia's jealousy resulted in her sister's death, but Apollo continued to reject her love. In grief she pined away to be transformed into the flower that always faces the sun as in a pledge to her undying love. Van Dyck used this symbolism in his 'Self portrait with a sunflower' to acknowledge the devotion to his patron Charles I. It is tempting to suggest that this may have been included by carvers with royalist sympathies. The motif is replicated on the upper and middle decks. In theory, all these openings could be used for stern-chase guns, providing a bitter twist to the tale. Those to the middle deck are held by mermen with a particularly mischievous grin whilst the figure of Justice sits in the central panel. Between them sit two further mermen, one holding the cross of St George, the other that of St Andrew, signifying the union with Scotland in 1652.

Caryatid figures form mullions between the windows. Standing one upon the other, they resemble circus performers with expressively caricatured faces. Such touches help one to remember that all this work was carved by men who lived and breathed the same air as us, sharing a common sense of humour, creating ships that sailed on the same seas.

The standing figure on the port quarter piece is a representation of Mars, god of war, depicted in his Roman armour. On the starboard quarter stands Minerva, goddess of wisdom and good government. When appearing with Mars, she acts as an antidote to the destructive powers of war. Continuing down the quarter pieces are two seated figures. With their contemplative demeanour, they may represent such attributes as Counsel and Care.

The main visual reference for this model, made in 1943 by Robert Spence, is a drawing by Willem van de Velde showing the ship when renamed *Royal Charles*. With the exception of a few details it complies perfectly with the model, the differences being such details as in the drawing Mars turns his head towards Minerva and the two seated figures are clearly female, their attributes of an alluring physical nature.

Below them are two cherub-like figures riding on the backs of lions, the symbolism of this simple motif being 'he who rides the lion can never dismount'. The same motif was used on the *Sovereign of the Seas*, where Heywood notes that the figure is a cupid or a child resembling him, explaining the significance of this combination thus: 'That sufferance may curb insolence and innocence restrain violence'. The figure astride the lion on the *Naseby*'s port side appears to be winged, whilst the starboard figure carries what appears to be a quiver and arrows, which are the attributes of Cupid, the son of Venus and god of love. The addition of trumpets being blown introduces the element of Fame; such figures

appear as attributes of Britannia, heralding her fame, having tamed the king of beasts (or perhaps Cromwell's dominion over the royalist lion). As an attribute of Britannia, the motif first appears on the *Antelope* of 1619 but did not become popular until the Restoration period, when it even found its way onto figureheads. Examples of this are the *Coronation* of 1685 and the *Lion* of 1670, where the lion figurehead has seated behind him a cupid-like figure holding onto his tail.

The solid panelling between the upper and middle decks has as its centrepiece two cherubs (from the model it is hard to tell if they are winged but the van de Velde drawing shows them as female and winged) riding the backs of dolphins whilst unfurling a banner which does not appear to have any recognisable insignia, possibly due to its miniscule size on the model, as the van de Velde drawing shows three lines of text, but unfortunately too small to read. The outer panels are decorated with winged figures riding hippocamps; the figure on the port side looks back whilst the starboard one looks down. The significance of this is uncertain (van de Velde shows both looking straight ahead). The hippocamp is an attribute of Poseidon (in Greek mythology, Neptune in Roman), employed to draw his chariot through the waves. This mythical beast of land and sea on occasion appears alone with a figure on his back, dispensing the fruits of both land and sea from a horn of plenty. As such, the motif signifies prosperity, being the happy consequence of victory.

The van de Velde drawing shows the vessel without stern lanterns, which allows all the carved work to be seen and reveals the central cartouche crowning the tafferel as a thistle with two crossed leaves from the same plant. It also shows the Commonwealth arms and motto blanked out, confirming the work of the crew after the Restoration, as described by Pepys.

A contract drawn up in 1655 with the painting contractor Richard Isaacson for the ships *London* and *Henry* gives an insight to the finishing of the *Naseby*:

The figurehead, quarter piece figures and coat of arms were to be gilded, other carvings to be painted gold colour in oil, on a black ground. Their heads, sterns galleries, rails, brackets and ports, their sides, timberheads and planksheers all to be primed and blacked as well as ever hath

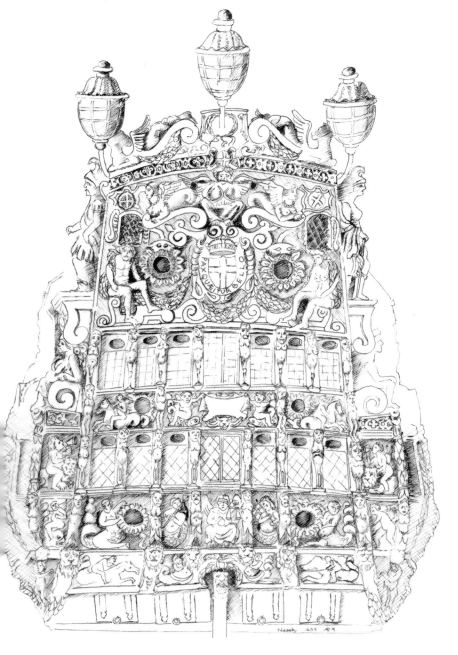

Stern of the 80-gun ship Naseby of 1655. With a length of keel at 131 feet her builder's measurement tonnage was 1228; by comparison, the 100-gun Sovereign of the Seas, with a keel length of 127 feet but greater breadth, measured 1683 tons.

been used in the Navy. Their great cabins and state rooms to be walnut tree colour in oil, grained and revailed, and what is proper to be gilded similar to the *Naseby*. Their round houses and other cabins to be stone colour and green.

The *Naseby* was instrumental in defeating Dutch forces during confrontations over access to Baltic trade, an event that would lead to Sheldon becoming influential in future Swedish naval architecture. Trade with the Baltic was essential to both the Dutch and English fleets, which depended on the northern states for the supply of timber, particularly for masts and spars, and other naval stores. Pepys records in his diary that in 1663 he secured a contract for the supply of 40,000 deals of Scandinavian timber and £3000 worth of masts for the Navy. Pepys in his role of Clerk of the Acts to the Admiralty conducted a thorough investigation into the various measurements of masts supplied by merchants in Göteborg compared to those of New England, the ratio of their diameter to length, the proper method of preserving them, whether wet or dry; as a result, in July of 1664 he signed a contract with Sir William Warren to supply a thousand 'Gottenburg masts'. Wood tar (known as Stockholm tar) and turpentine were also essential commodities, both of which were the prime materials used for the preservation of timber and rope.

It was therefore in the interest of both the Dutch and English to maintain stable trading conditions in the region – particularly for Cromwell, who regarded trade with the Baltic as essential in view of his country's already volatile economic state. When Dutch forces allied to Denmark took control of the Öresund Sound in 1658, an English squadron commanded by Montague (Lord Sandwich), with the *Naseby* as his flagship, was sent to intervene.

Cromwell died in 1658 to be succeeded by his son Richard who did not posses the strength to rule a divided nation. Both Montague and his cousin Pepys had been followers of Cromwell, but they too were turning their allegiance as 'Reformation had proved but ruin, freedom of conscience but fiercer oppression, commonwealth in the hands of money grabbers and positions achieved through bribes.' Montague returned to England in the *Naseby* intending to effect a *coup d'état* for the king, but the royalist uprising he had expected had been quelled by the Commonwealth's 'New Model Army'.

He lay low until the riots of the trade apprentices and the arrival of the Duke of Albemarle's army in London demanded the reinstatement of the long parliament.

Montague regained his position as commander of the fleet that set sail in March of 1660 with both Pepys and Montague aboard the *Naseby*. On 1 May the exiled Charles was invited by parliament to return. Setting a course for Holland, Pepys recalls in his diary that 'Sunday was spent making ready for the new era, with the fleet's painters and tailors hard at work removing the commonwealth harps from their ships and cutting yellow cloth into crowns and C.R.s.'

Pepys also describes in detail his time ashore in The Hague where many English were in exile and finally the moment when the king came aboard the *Naseby*. Having dined in the coach, he marked the inauguration of a new regime by re-christening the *Naseby* with his own name as the *Royal Charles*. In gratitude for their service, Charles gave £500 to the crew and officers; Pepys received £100 (equal to twice his annual income).

As part of the new regime, Pepys was made Clerk of the Acts to what was now the Royal Navy. As such, his most immediate priority was to tackle the Navy's considerable debts. With Cromwell's largely naval wars against both Holland and Spain having ceased, this was achieved partly by the decommissioning of ships in a period of retrenchment. He also became committed to exposing the corruption of the Navy's administrators, who had established monopolies for the supply of materials such as masts, hemp, sail cloth and other bulk stores for their own profit.

In this pursuit he found an ally in the young Anthony Deane (1633-1721) who, as assistant shipwright at Woolwich, promised to discover 'the abuses that the king suffered in the short measurement of timber' and also to make him a model of a ship so he could become acquainted with its various parts. They rode to Epping Forest to see how timber was hewn and to the Forest of Dean to allow Pepys acquaint himself with the value of its areas when drafting contracts for the extraction of timber. For imported goods Deane made him aware of the various wares such as Dram, Swinsound, Christiania and the manner in which the Swedes cut and sawed them. As an ambitious young shipwright, Deane was also keen to end the monopoly held by the Pett family in constructing the king's ships and to further the advancement of design through the application of mathematical principles.

With the restoration of the monarchy in 1660, ship-carvers were once again kept busy removing all Commonwealth insignia, reinstating the royal coats of arms and related imagery. The figurehead of the ex-*Naseby* survived until 1663, when Pepys recorded that it was pulled down and burnt, in a formal ceremony attended by three Commissioners of the Navy and the Rochester band. Thomas Fletcher, the master carver at Chatham, was paid the sum of £51.16s.0d for work associated with changing the name of the *Naseby* to *Royal Charles*. The standard cost of carving a lion figurehead during this period stood at £40, with £12 to carve the king's arms. As the figurehead was replaced with a relatively simple representation of Neptune, it is feasible that the sum paid could have covered the replacement of these two major motifs.

On 23 February 1665 Charles II declared war on Holland following grievances that had festered on both sides since the end of the First Anglo-Dutch War in 1652. The *Royal Charles* set sail for the Dutch coast on 21 April 1665, hoping to entice the enemy out to battle. Pepys prayed that 'God may go with them': unfortunately, what did not go with them was enough beer (the daily ration was a gallon per man per day). With insufficient victuals, on 8 May the thirsty sailors headed for home.

As Clerk of the Acts Pepys had the onerous task of ensuring that the fleet was supplied with all it required to keep the sea, from clothing to beef, peas and beer. With the country in financial ruin and suppliers in many cases not having been paid for two to three years, he struggled to obtain sufficient credit to maintain a fighting force, but by 30 May 1665 109 warships and 28 fireships had been re-victualled and were waiting to engage the Dutch at the Battle of Lowestoft.

The king's brother, the Duke of York, having

Michiel Adriaenszoon de Ruyter (1607-1676), mastermind of the Medway raid. (Author's collection)

been appointed Lord High Admiral, commanded the fleet from the *Royal Charles*. During the battle that took place on 3 June, the *Royal Charles* came close to being boarded by the crew of the Dutch flagship *Eendracht*. In the engagement that followed three noblemen were killed at the Duke's side by a single chain shot, with a splinter of skull embedding itself in the hand of the Duke. The *Royal Charles* was in danger of being sunk under the intensive bombardment from the *Eendracht* until, through circumstances that still remain a mystery, the *Eendracht* blew up with the loss of some four hundred lives.

John Leadman (the master carver at Woolwich from 1659 to 1682) was paid £200 for carrying out carved work to the *Royal Charles* in 1667. This represents almost half the allotted sum for the decorative work of a First Rate ship and was presumably for extensive repairs following action in the Four Days' Battle in June 1666 and the St James' Day Fight on 25 July 1666, as the ship is not recorded in fleet action again after that.

In 1667 de Ruyter made his audacious attack on the Medway. After successfully capturing Sheerness fort, de Witt and van Ghent proceeded upriver towards Chatham where the severe scarcity of manpower offered little defence. By the end of Cromwell's rule the unaffordable cost of the forces that upheld his military might had become painfully obvious. By 1659 the Navy Board owed £500,000 in wages alone. Unpaid crews were issued with tickets, effectively promissory notes that would be honoured with interest when funds permitted. Faced with imminent starvation, many sailors sold the notes at heavy discounts in their desperation for ready cash.

By 1667 the Navy's total debt was approaching £2,300,000. Hoping for peace, the government consequently laid out their intentions on 6 March to lay up the battle fleet, as there were insufficient men or stores to commission the ships. Instead, it resolved to strengthen shore defences and encourage privateering to plunder Holland's merchant fleet (an opportunity soon realised by Pepys, who bought shares in such a vessel – unfortunately his hired captain was not too particular as to which ships he plundered, and the venture was condemned by the prize courts when it was presented with the proceeds taken from two Swedish merchantmen).

When the Dutch fleet sailed up the Medway most of the British ships were partially dismantled or actually laid up and unmanned. Despite the unfavourable odds, the few that were present fought doggedly. Captain Dowglass, a land officer ordered to command the *Royal Oak*, held his position to the last, perishing with the vessel when it was burnt by a Dutch fireship. The *Loyal London*, *Mathias* and *Old James* were also destroyed by fire, while the *Royal Charles* and the *Unity* were taken as prizes.

Travellers fleeing to London spoke of English seamen standing on the decks of the Dutch ships, shouting to their countrymen that they had hitherto fought for tickets, but now they would fight for dollars. The *Royal Charles* was towed back to Holland where, to further humiliate the English, she was put on public display. Once more the king's insignia was removed, this time to be saved as a trophy of war, where it still survives in Amsterdam as a valuable record of carving from this period. Its construction reveals that the timber used had been salvaged from masts and spars of other ships (items that require good quality

Note issued to Captain Parks of the *Norfolk* for heaving onboard 92 tons of ballast, 29 December 1803; similar notes exist for the *Hermes*, *Neptune*, *Valiant*, and many more. (Author's collection)

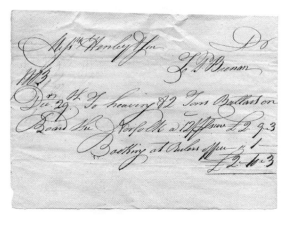

straight-grained timber).

Incidentally, many country houses in England also benefited from the recycling of ships' timbers. My workshop was for some years in the grounds of an Oxfordshire estate whose owners during the 1800s had dealings in the shipbreaking business, together with the supply of stone ballast that was transported by barge down the Thames to London, then returning with salvaged timber. Renovation work on the house revealed the use of many ships' timbers, including sections of masts as columns in the outbuildings. I have experimented with using such timber for carving, but without much success. The constant pressure masts endure through their working life leads to the timber delaminating at their annular growth rings. When cut into planks for carved panels, many sections came apart like layers of an onion. I can only assume timbers reused for carving had endured a relatively short life as masts and spars.

Considering that the reign of Charles II commenced with the country in dire financial straights, circumstances further compounded by the costly wars with Holland (Second Dutch War 1665-67, Third Dutch War 1672-74) during which time the country also had to contend with the plague (1665) and the Great Fire of London (1666), it is hardly surprising that the optimistic enthusiasm that marked his return as king would later turn to despondency. But let us for now return to 1660 when the restoration of the monarchy heralded a magnanimous era of royal patronage to the arts.

Charles had returned from exile in France and the Netherlands full of enthusiasm for the artistic endeavours he had encountered, particularly the Baroque, which would be manifest in England as the Restoration style. His accession announced the return of a joyous atmosphere to a country previously forced to endure a strict puritan regime. The Restoration style mirrored this fervour with the voluptuousness of the Dutch-inspired naturalistic and lively forms, woven into compositions full of the grace and symmetry displayed by such artists as Puget and Le Brun.

The States General of Holland presented Charles with a 'jacht' named *Mary*. Derived from the Dutch word for hunting, a jacht was designed for speed and manoeuvrability; in war they were used for scouting – 'to hunt out the enemy' – but their main peacetime role was as fast and comfortable passenger transports, usually for the wealthy and important. The *Mary* was originally built in Amsterdam for the VOC and was finished to a high degree of decoration. During his exile in Holland Charles had discovered the pastime of yachting and became a competent helmsman in these beautifully decorated pleasure boats. Willem van de Velde was presented with a similar vessel in which to follow the Dutch fleet and record naval battles.

Carvings to the *Mary* were presumably adapted to suit its new owner, as a drawing by van de Velde the younger shows the inclusion of the Stuart royal insignia on the stern, with the figurehead depicted as a unicorn. This mythical beast was used as supporter to the royal arms in Scotland while England had adopted the lion and

dragon. With the accession of James VI of Scotland to the throne as James I of England in 1603, the supporters were changed to the lion and unicorn, heralding the Stuart period.

A list of her fittings from a contemporary report would appear to confirm this as it includes: 'One copper horn for her figurehead, 12 lime blocks for carving and 1013 books of gold for the gilding'. With a book of gold containing twenty-five three-inch squares, this represents an area of 1580 square feet of gold. By the time gold is applied to intricate shapes, the area actually covered is reduced to approximately a quarter, which compares reasonably with the area of carving that such a yacht would carry. At current prices this represents approximately £12,000 in value, putting into perspective the degree of lavishness that was bestowed on such craft.

The first most notable English architect to embrace the burgeoning Baroque style was Sir Christopher Wren (1632-1723). This largely self-taught architect originally trained as a scientist, but had gained some notoriety as an architect with his design for the Sheldonian Theatre in Oxford. In 1664 he embarked on a tour of Holland, Flanders and France to further his interest in architecture. On his return in 1665 he found favour with Charles for his knowledge of the new Baroque style that was sweeping through Europe. The Great Fire of London in 1666 provided the opportunity for a rebuilding programme that would elevate Wren's reputation to one of the greatest architects in British history. He developed many new solutions to architectural problems, with most of his decorative sources derived from a mixture of Dutch, French and Italian Classicism. The pure Classical style set by Inigo Jones and his own understanding of the Italian Baroque ensured that his work maintained a restrained sense of academic Classicism (an element that would in time prevail in ship decoration). The economic constraints following the fire also contributed to curbing the introduction of lavish Baroque designs, which do not appear in his work until the end of his life.

Another important figure was Grinling Gibbons, who arrived from Holland in 1667. His father had been a tailor and it is possible that through his connections Grinling was accepted into the Drapers' Guild on 19 January 1672. A year earlier he had moved to Deptford where he is recorded as working as a ship-carver. With the Thames being a main highway through the city, most stately homes and

A model of the *Mary* showing the unicorn figurehead and the royal arms on the tafferel. (National Maritime Museum F9231-003)

royal palaces were built close to the river. The possession of a barge or shallop became a social necessity, complete with luxuriant fittings and decoration. The wealthy Livery Companies, descendants of the medieval guilds, also possessed such craft and Grinling's entry to the Drapers' Company undoubtedly provided him with the opportunity to decorate their barges and halls. The Oxford carver Jonathon Mayne, who later worked on many prestigious projects with Gibbons and Wren, also worked on the decoration of barges, completing carved work for a new Lord Mayor's barge in 1687 and for the Fishmongers' Company in 1691.

A note issued by one William Lowndes in 1689 gives authority to pay £725.1s.3d to:

John Loftus	(Barge builder)
Alexander Fort	(Joiner)
Grinling Gibbons	(Carver)
William Ireland	(Glazier)

'upon their warrants for building of barges for his Majesty'. (This may refer to the shallop built for Queen Mary in the same year which is now on display at Greenwich.)

The remarkable quality of his work soon came to the attention of the king and he began working for the crown. The combined talents of Wren and Gibbons were used on many projects in a partnership that lasted over forty years. In 1682 Gibbons was commissioned by King Charles to carve a panel as acknowledgement of the friendship and confirm the alliance between Charles and Cosimo III de' Medici, Grand Duke of Tuscany (1642-1723). The completed panel was shipped to Italy onboard the Fourth Rate *Woolwich*, but on arrival the ship was held in quarantine for one month for fear that it might carry the plague. The panel survives in Italy as testament not only to his compositional skill, but is personally signed by Gibbons indicating that the superb craftsmanship was wholly by his hand. The demand for his work was such that in 1686 Gibbons signed a contract jointly with Arnold Quellin to carry out an altarpiece for Wren to be installed at the Palace at Whitehall. The work was to be completed within two months and to meet the deadline Gibbons and Quellin employed the services of an additional fifty carvers.

In 1693 he suceeded Henry Phillips (with whom he had worked at Windsor castle) as Master Carver and Sculptor in wood to the crown, whose duties included the carved work for state barges.

He held the position until 1721, when he was succeeded by James Richards (died 1759). His equally superb work is displayed on Prince Frederick's barge of 1731. This barge, designed by William Kent, is one of the few surviving examples of ship-carving of the period, and clearly shows the splendour of the Baroque art equal in design and craftsmanship to those of France, with tapestries to the ceiling of the barge and internal furniture designed by Daniel Marot.

Decorative work to the earlier and smaller Queen Mary shallop is extremely modest by comparison, since its purpose was to convey the Queen to the royal yacht rather than for parades on the river. The royal coat of arms sits within a cartouche at the stern, with relief carved work running the length of the gunwale in a composition that conveys an elegant sense of balance. William III's insignia alone are represented on the transom, set amidst a composition of palms, ribbons and oak leaves. In its depth of relief, the work is reminiscent of Gibbons's earlier work, lacking the intricate detail which he developed later, and would on any account be inappropriate for such practical applications. It does demonstrate a unity of style that would have been appreciated by Mary, with her knowledge of French fashions.

But all this takes us beyond the reign of Charles, where decoration to ships of the early Restoration period generally continued much as before, along with closed galleries to the stern. If lights appeared at the quarterdeck level, they were small, as depicted on the *Naseby*, leaving the deep tafferel clear for royal insignia or allegorical figures relating to the ship's name. Quarter galleries also remained below the quarterdeck, thus maintaining the narrowing of the stern at this level, the *Resolution* being a typical example.

This 70-gun Third Rate ship was built at Harwich in 1667 to an early design by Anthony Deane. King Charles and the Duke of York both agreed that it was the best warship yet built. Such approval secured Deane's position as an up and coming naval architect and effectively ended the monopoly held by the Pett family. With Pepys's help, Deane was given the position of master shipwright at Harwich.

The carved work was carried out by the Woolwich carver Gerrard Christmas, who worked at Harwich from 1666 until his death in 1668. Two years later the ship was in Plymouth, where the carver Robert Reynolds carried out repairs to both the *Resolution* and the *Mary*. On her return from a

An example of the very three-dimensional quality and intricacy of detail that came to epitomise Gibbons's work ashore. His earlier work displays greater simplicity, providing designs that would have been more suited to the working environment of a ship. (Image reproduced courtesy of Bristol Public Library)

Stern of the *Resolution* redrawn from a painting by William van de Velde the younger. From a decorative perspective, the composition conforms to the standard format shared by Dutch and English ships of the period.

successful campaign to deal with Algerian pirates, she was damaged during an engagement with the Dutch off the Isle of Wight in 1672. She put in to Portsmouth where Allen Lewis was paid the sum of £20.18.0d for repairs to her carved work. After an eventful career, sadly, she foundered on the Goodwin Sands during the Great Storm of 1703.

Sir Anthony Deane was to become one of the foremost ship designers of the day. In 1670, at the request of Samuel Pepys, he produced his celebrated work *A Doctrine of Naval Architecture*. He became adviser not only to the English navy, but also those of Denmark, Sweden and Russia. Deane introduced to his drawings horizontal lines or waterlines, which added to the previous system of vertical sections denoting the ship's frames, creating a method of determining the ship's hull shape with much greater accuracy: indeed, Deane is credited with being the first English shipwright capable of establishing a ship's draught of water prior to its launch and therefore able to calculate its stability. This led to the refinement of ships' lines and improvements in their design.

The appearance of a First Rate ship from the same period as the *Resolution* can be appreciated in the model of the *Prince*, a 100-gun ship built at Chatham by Phineas Pett in 1670. Currently displayed at the Science Museum in London, it is one of the finest models to have survived from that era. The carving to the stern agrees with a drawing by van de Velde, thus confirming its authenticity and providing a detailed insight into the decorative schemes of this period. The composition of the carving follows the standard format dictated by the dominant framing, adorned with caryatid figures and grotesques harking back to the Renaissance. This has the effect of compartmentalising the structure into squares for windows or decorative motifs, all of which have been described earlier.

The tafferel bears the Stuart arms with lion and unicorn supporters, attended by two cherubs that hover rather stiffly in an attempt to give the sense of flight. The arms, however, display a greater fluidity of movement and the composition of the quarter figures shows a move towards the

A model of the *Prince*. Designed by Phineas Pett, this three-decked 100-gun ship was launched at Chatham in 1670. The model depicts the layout before the addition of windows to the quarterdeck. Here the quarter galleries can be seen on the middle and upper decks, which also have closed galleries to the stern. Note the elaborate carving inboard of the tafferel. Such a wealth of decoration was similarly repeated on the quarterdeck bulkhead. Gun ports to the quarter- and upper decks are decorated with wreaths; restricting orders at the turn of the century will lead to their disappearance by 1710.

Figurehead of the *Prince* model. Equestrian figureheads were restricted to ships named after members of the royal family, further reference to which is made on the quarter galleries, which are crowned with ostrich feathers. The use of this motif was confined to the heir apparent to the English crown, whether he was the Prince of Wales or not. The stern carries the royal coat of arms of 1606-1688 with the monograms I R (for Jacobus Rex) and H P (Hendricus Princepus). (Photographs of the *Prince* model taken by the author from the Science Museum, London, ref 1898–56, and reproduced by their kind permission)

confidence expressed in Baroque ornamentation in the constructs of its composition and naturalistic sense of movement. Above the arms a richly ornamented panel of cherubs and foliage intertwine in the curvaceous manner beloved by the Restoration period. Between 1673 and 1674 Thomas Fletcher was paid the sum of £935 for work on the *Prince*, *St Michael* (1671), *St Andrew* (1670), *London* (1670), *Katherine* (1671; colour plate 9) and the king's yacht (1672). His skill in mastering the Mannerist style on the *Naseby* must clearly have progressed to embracing the Baroque; although he would appear to have been paid well, he had to wait two years to receive the money!

In 1672 Charles once again declared war on Holland, and the newly built *Prince* was present at the Battle of Sole Bay as flagship to the Lord High Admiral, the Duke of York. The battle ended with the defeat of the Dutch, but the *Prince* was so badly damaged that the Duke was obliged to shift his flag temporarily to the *St Michael*; there are, however, no reports of repairs to the carved work. In 1692 she was rebuilt at Chatham as the *Royal William* (effectively broken up with any sound timbers being reused). As the *Royal William* she is listed as having been broken up in 1714, to be replaced by a new ship of the same name in 1719.

Prior to 1670 windows in the stern at the quarterdeck tended to be squeezed into gaps between the decoration, but after this date they

The quarter pieces to the *Prince* are decorated with large figures that still reflect the influence of the 'strongmen' that dominated this position in the composition of Dutch sterns. The quality of carving does differ, however, in that it captures a greater sense of movement and emotional expressiveness, acknowledging that the carvers have grasped a sense of the Baroque's propensity to display emotion. It portrays a powerful figure, ready to protect the contrasting delicate and vulnerable female form. There is a feeling of balance and weight in the figures that hitherto appeared stiff and inanimate, and as such is fundamental to the power of Baroque ornamentation.

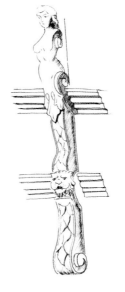

begin to appear as a feature that interrupts the large area traditionally reserved for the royal coat of arms or allegorical figures (this area was commonly termed 'the great board' on Dutch ships, or 'the frontispiece' on English). In an effort to secure sufficient space for a compressed version of such insignia, the windows initially appear as a narrow band, but their introduction soon led to an open gallery at this level, which in turn, saw the removal of galleries to the middle deck of three-decked ships. Quarter galleries for the time being rose as far as the upper deck, often displaying the distinctive 'bottle shape' with their elongated roof, leading decoration back to the fashion piece such as those of the *Prince*.

The reduction in the height of the tafferel called for designs employing seated figures or standing figures in compositions of a smaller proportion than previously adopted. In many respects this compression of space produced designs of far greater ingenuity. This fortunately coincided with the acceptance of the structured approach of emerging Baroque and Classical influences. The very three-dimensional effect of Baroque forms, coupled with its propensity to create the shape it decorates rather than be bound by the underlying structure, helped produce some beautifully proportioned designs, brimming with lively expressiveness.

An early example of this transition can be seen in the *Grafton* of 1679. This Third Rate 70-gun ship illustrates the development of the stern from the initial introduction of small windows to the quarterdeck, to fully embracing a stern gallery at

The lower finishing to the quarter gallery is unusual from a constructional view point in having a gun port set within it. The composition of its decoration takes the form of two angelic figures, their wings spreading to carry the gallery. It is a small Baroque addition amidst other decorative motifs that conform to the conventions of the time, but again indicates an understanding and readiness to embrace new concepts in the portrayal of ornamental motifs.

Ornamentation forming the mullions also begins to display elements of the Baroque, where the herm figures exhibit a greater sense of realism in their emotional expression. The accompanying drawing shows how the figure would develop, shifting away from decoration simply overlaid on constructional members, towards adopting a more natural pose, leaving the viewer unaware of the underlying structure to concentrate simply on the artistic form.

this level, which has become an open walkway. The earliest known example of this French-inspired feature is on the *St Michael* of 1669.

Although the gallery to the quarterdeck on the *Grafton* had become an open walkway, it still retains its vertical framing, setting the decoration into compartmentalised panels.

The tafferel now extends to the full width of the quarter galleries, supported by two large figures creating the quarter pieces. This widening of the tafferel forms the basis of the next transition of the stern, where the quarter galleries will extend up to the quarterdeck and finally link with the stern gallery. The presence of the large quarter piece figures on the *Grafton* indicates that her quarter galleries are still restricted to the upper deck, the roof of which will terminate behind the figures.

The *Grafton* was built at Woolwich in 1679 by Thomas Shish, with the carved works executed by John Leadman. He was one of the leading carvers for the Navy in the seventeenth century, working at Woolwich and Deptford, and has been mentioned previously for his work in 1667 to alter carvings on the *Naseby* when she was renamed *Royal Charles*. The original Admiralty model of the ship survives in the Henry Huddleston Rogers Collection at the US Naval Academy in Annapolis. The ornamentation to the stern and starboard quarter gallery was heavily restored during the 1920s, but it does provide a good example of the transition to an open gallery on the quarterdeck and subsequent widening of the tafferel.

A shield bearing quartered arms forms the centrepiece of the tafferel, above which a crown is held by two cherubs. The shield bears the arms of Henry Fitzroy, Duke of Grafton, who was the second son of King Charles II by Barbara Villiers, the Countess of Castlemaine. The crown above the shield, or more correctly a coronet with five visible pearls, denotes the rank of earl, a title he was granted in 1672 as Earl of Euston (and subsequently Duke of Grafton in 1675). He was made a naval captain at an early age and promoted to vice-admiral when he was nineteen.

Frames to the counter are decorated with the model's original caryatid figures, still very much in the Renaissance style. These have been replicated between the galleries, but attempts have been made to interrupt the monotonous lines of figures by the introduction of margent drops composed of husks. The inclusion of them in this position is an assumption made by the model's restorer, based on an original section of framing that formed the corner piece of the counter and quarter gallery. Between the framing are inset panels of densely scrolling acanthus. Here the restorer has replicated the design of an existing panel to the quarter gallery, substituting the royal coat of arms in the central panel with the corresponding panel on the upper deck displaying the Admiralty badge, which is an educated guess based on what was the accepted practice of the period. The lower finishing to the quarter galleries together with the framing are similarly decorated; the upper finishing which forms a bottle-shaped roof, has a central panel framed by two cherubs holding a crown above a seated figure, presumably of King Charles. A finial to the roof takes the form of the Prince of Wales feathers.

Although it cannot be seen, the quarterdeck bulkhead has a further shield, carved and gilded to depict the Dartmouth coat of arms, quartered with those of the Washington coat of arms and

Stern of the 70-gun ship *Grafton* built at Woolwich in 1679 with carved work by John Leadman. Grinling Gibbons was a close friend of the Grafton family who, interestingly, visited Gibbons during the building of the ship. With such close connections, it is tempting to suggest he may have been asked to contribute to the decorative composition. This badly damaged model was heavily restored in the 1920s, so the only carving that can be accepted as original are the lower caryatid figures and the panels between the two rows of lights. It does, however, serve to demonstrate the basic layout of the stern, with a well-educated guess at the ornamentation.

surcharged with the blazon of Villiers. George Legge became Baron Dartmouth in 1682. These arms incorporate those of the Washington family because Legge's mother Elizabeth was a Washington (the coronet of a baron has four visible pearls only). This was presumably added later, as the *Grafton* was the flagship of Admiral Lord Dartmouth during an expedition of seventeen vessels in 1683-4 to effect the dismantling and evacuation of Tangier. This port in present-day Morocco was part of Catherine of Braganza's dowry when she married Charles II, but its continued occupation by British troops was expensive and made almost untenable by local opposition.

The *Grafton* was one of the huge 'Thirty Ships' building programme of 1677 that Pepys was instrumental in pushing through parliament. As such it would have held a special significance to him when, on 9 August 1683, he joined the ship at Spithead bound for Tangiers. Pepys had been closely involved with trying to turn the colony into a viable naval base, but this was to be his only visit to a place which for many years had proved to be a great source of income to him. With neither Portugal nor Spain interested in taking over the colony, his task now was to see the destruction of its defences so that it could not become an impregnable base for the Barbary pirates, and to evacuate the garrison.

After completing the mission, the *Grafton* was in need of repair, and on 27 April 1686 Pepys visited Chatham to discover what he later described as the 'wretched state of his ships'. He inspected the *Grafton*, which was then in dock, and noted 'Not with standing that she had been built in the King's yard all of English timber and plank, not hastily built, and having been at sea, now shows signs of decay.' He was shown the *Kent* afloat, 'The King going upon the stage of her side and seeing and feeling the rotten condition of her timbers and treenails with his own hand.' Returning to London that evening, their yacht was caught in a violent storm. Pepys recalls that:

> They passed not one ship in their passage with their ports shut, except their hailing caused them to be so. Or upon the *St Andrew* and *Grafton* in dock, neither shipwright or assistant nor any other officer minding it till, sending for Dummer we required him to see it done. Such negligence with their ports either open in wet weather

or closed in dry, occasioning that a succession of heat and moisture that has ruined them.

Despite Pepys's criticism of her condition in 1686, the *Grafton* went on to see a good deal of action, being present at the Battle of Beachy Head in 1690 under the command of Henry, Duke of Grafton, and in the same year she took part in the landing of troops at Queens Harbour, Cork. Henry chose to fight for William of Orange against his uncle James II, but during the storming of Cork he suffered a bullet wound, from which he died in October of the same year. Two years later *Grafton*, under the command of William Bokenham, was present at the defeat of the French fleet off Barfleur. In 1699 the ship is listed as having been rebuilt at Rotherhithe Initially, the term 'rebuild' was generally considered to imply that the ship was dry-docked to replace her rotten timbers, such as planking, framing and fastenings, although it also provided the opportunity to lengthen or modify the shape of the hull to incorporate new developments in design. By the early eighteenth century, however, the term was little more than an administrative fiction to allow for the construction of a new vessel. The old ship would be dismantled completely, with any serviceable timbers (and carvings) reused in the production of what was essentially a newly built ship. The rebuilt *Grafton* of 1700 served at the Battle of Vigo Bay in 1702 and at the capture of Gibraltar in 1704. In 1707 she was taken by Forbin's Dunkirk squadron off Beachy Head and remained in French service until 1744 when she was broken up.

The *Britannia* provides a further example of the effect on stern design created by the introduction of an open stern gallery to the quarterdeck, which consequently led to the closing of the middle deck's gallery. Unlike the *Grafton*, *Britannia*'s gallery framing on both the quarter- and upper deck levels has been removed, creating a clear space across each gallery. This structural change begins to accentuate horizontals, leading to a move away from the dominant compartmentalising of decoration bought about by the vertical framing. This 100-gun three-decked ship was built by Phineas Pett at Chatham three years after the *Grafton*, in 1682.

Her carved work was executed by Thomas Fletcher. Having previously provided carved works for the renaming of *Sovereign* (ex-*Sovereign of the Seas* of 1637), the *Royal Charles* (ex-*Naseby* of

1655) and the *Prince* (1670), his reputation was by now well established and seemingly able to adapt to the changing fashions in artistic expression. Thomas was by now a very wealthy man. For his work on the *Britannia* he received the sum of £895.19s.4d. His interests had clearly extended beyond carving, for at the time of his death in 1684 property mentioned in his will included the lease from St Bartholemew's Hospital for shops, outhouses, bankside gardens and a wharf. He owned a farm at Cliffe that extended to 12 acres of woodland, a further plot of 87 acres plus a property in Chatham.

The tafferel of the *Britannia* once again depicts a gruesome scene of an enemy being trampled beneath the feet of two horsemen, both of whom are armed with swords and pistols. In the background is a panoply of military trophies. The quarter figures depict Hercules, valiant with his club, administering blows to a wretched-looking figure below. The large quarter figures appear out of proportion to those of the tafferel – a trait that is common with other ships of the period, most of which were rebuilds from vessels originating from 1678 to 1682.

The general composition appears as an eagerly awaited attempt to embrace the concepts of Baroque, where the figurative work, although rather stiff in its execution, tumbles down in a continuous scene from the tafferel to the quarter pieces so that the artistic expression overrules the restraints of structural concerns. The wonderfully three-dimensional effect is achieved by the carvings being 'cut through' to remove (wherever practical) any solid background. A style much loved and expertly achieved by the late Restoration period, this can be appreciated in the example shown here of a chair back that has animated figures of similarly 'lanky' proportions to the stern

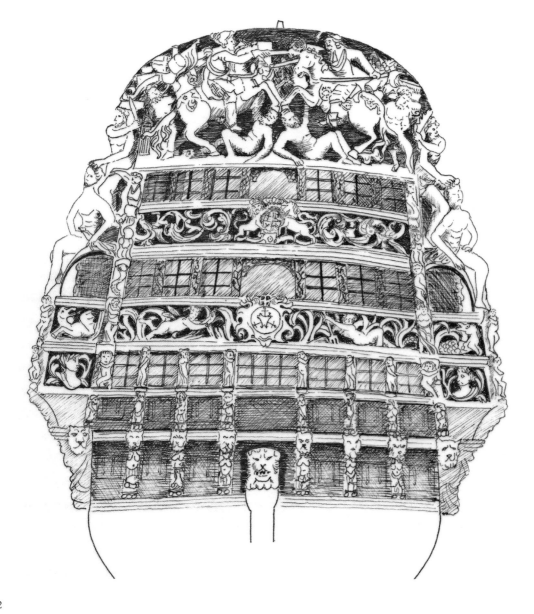

Stern of a model in the Henry Huddleston Rogers Collection, Annapolis depicting the *Britannia* of 1682 but after the ship's rebuild in 1701.

Jacobean-style chair from the last quarter of the seventeenth century, reproduced courtesy of The Red House, Bristol. (Author's collection)

of *Britannia*. This fretwork effect was often used on Dutch ships of the same period, as described in the previous section, where the tafferel is then called a *hakkebord*.

Vertical framing to the counters and lower decks are decorated with the usual caryatid figures still prevalent in the Restoration period, while those to the fashion pieces have a freshness that suggests the enthusiasm associated with new ideas. The subject matter has also changed to cherubs, putti and female figures in well-executed drapery rather than the busty caricature of earlier caryatids, suggesting they are a later addition.

Such alterations highlight the difficulty in dating the decorative composition of ship models and to some extent paintings and drawings from this period. A clue can be found in the records of payments made to carvers, by indicating the extent to which decorative work was renewed or repaired. It is reasonable to assume that small alterations or repairs would have been carried out sympathetically to the grand scheme, and therefore insignificant with regard to decorative style.

The problem is greater if the vessel undergoes a rebuild. The task is then to ascertain to what extent the carving has remained intact or been altered. The *Britannia* underwent a refit in 1688 following the accession of William and Mary and in 1691 the ship was 'girdled' (her beam increased), but no records have yet been found of payments made to carvers. There are, however, references to a 'Great Repair' in 1701. This coincides with payments made to Mathew Fletcher, who became master carver at Chatham on the death of Thomas in 1689. Mathew was

finally paid £328.14s.7d in 1703 for carved work to *Britannia*. He was assisted by Joseph Wymhurst, who had been carving at Chatham since 1700, and was paid £172.6s.8d for his contribution to the project. These figures represent a considerable amount of work, so what alterations could have been made?

The head of the Annapolis *Britannia* model showing the figurehead of the ship's rebuild in 1701. (By courtesy of Grant Walker)

The figurehead is certainly from a later period, depicting an intricate and exceptionally well carved figure of a man on horseback. His demeanour is of one who remains calm and steadfast in the execution of his duty, looking straight ahead as his rearing horse tramples upon five crowned heads. The expressive quality of such small-scale carving is outstanding, but the figures to the tafferel are equally as good, the artistic style of which would suggest they are of the same hand and period.

The stern presents a different picture. Alterations to the galleries are a reasonable

The quarter galleries of the Annapolis model of *Britannia*. (By courtesy of Grant Walker)

assumption given the fact that both have become open. A painting by Isaac Sailmaker (1633-1721) follows the common convention of two-view ship portraits showing both stern and quarter gallery. Such paintings were commonly commissioned to show how a proposed ship would look, or to record her completion. The gallery to her quarterdeck is closed, while that of her upper deck is possibly open, but with her vertical framing intact. The removal of vertical framing and the endless rows of caryatid figures agrees with the changing layout of ships at the turn of the century, and a greater understanding of the naturalistic precepts of the Baroque, when faced with the task of ornamenting the structural changes. A later painting attributed to Peter Monamy (1681-1749) clearly shows open galleries to both decks; the ship also flies the Union Flag, dating it to after the Union with Scotland in 1707 and therefore the rebuild.

Expenditure is always a consideration within the public purse, as the Admiralty orders pertaining to decorative work demonstrate by their encouragement to reuse or retain existing carvings. Caryatids to the unaltered lower decks remain, while their later counterparts decorate the fashion pieces. An uninterrupted composition of scrolling acanthus decorates the central panel of the quarterdeck, with the royal arms forming the centrepiece; these include the arms of Nassau (lion *rampant* in the centre of the shield), a device used by William and Mary and Queen Anne up to the Scottish Union in 1707 and are therefore clearly later additions. The acanthus panel is similarly replicated between the rails of the

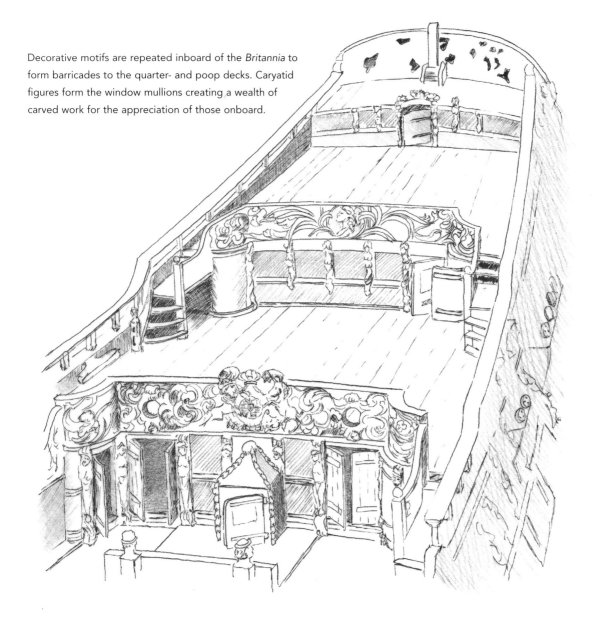

Decorative motifs are repeated inboard of the *Britannia* to form barricades to the quarter- and poop decks. Caryatid figures form the window mullions creating a wealth of carved work for the appreciation of those onboard.

Details of carved work on the Annapolis *Britannia* model: poop bulkhead; royal arms on the quarterdeck stern rail; beakhead bulkhead carvings. (By courtesy of Grant Walker)

quarterdeck bulkhead, here also with the royal arms forming the centrepiece. In both positions the acanthus has lost the frenetic temperament associated with the earlier Restoration period, suggesting that it is of a later date than the ship's launch.

Two male portraits are placed near the base of the quarter pieces. These would presumably have been changed from Charles II to William (Mary having died in 1694) and are decorated with palms rather than acanthus. The central panel to the stern gallery of the upper deck has a similar motif of leaves, here depicted as waving reeds, with a central cartouche displaying Admiralty insignia. Nymph-like figures swim amid the reeds, with mythical beasts that extend the composition onto the quarters, in a further attempt to stress the horizontal nature of the design. Such aquatic scenes are common on the ships of William and Mary, but the reeds are rarely depicted with such confident naturalism. A similar panel with a male portrait as its centrepiece is replicated between the rails of the poop deck bulkhead.

Palms are very much an innovation taken from French ships rather than of Dutch or English origin and point to Mary's admiration of the French Baroque. She was instrumental in the employment of Huguenot craftsmen in the alterations to Hampton Court, where similar motifs are found. They also appear on the stern of her shallop of 1689. Palms first appear as an alternative motif to acanthus on British ships around 1700. As is so often the case, fashions acceptable within high society take a while to filter down to general use, and even then in a more moderate form. The confident use of the motif on *Britannia* is accentuated by cutting them clear of the background, a feature they share with the acanthus panel and tafferel figures, helping to create a cohesive quality to the various decorative elements of the stern.

By the time Charles died in 1685 the Baroque-influenced style he introduced had become the predominant form of decoration to adorn English ships. Flowing curvaceous forms of the Restoration style began to adopt the lively sense of movement that is associated with the Baroque. Rich festoons of fruit and flowers entwined with shells, epitomised by the designs of Grinling Gibbons, were showered upon allegorical figures attended by sea nymphs and dolphins. Foliate forms were used more frequently, forming bands of richly scrolling acanthus, creating compositions that continued through the turbulent years of his brother James II's reign.

The Glorious Revolution of 1688 that brought William and Mary to the throne was followed by a constitutional settlement that limited royal prerogative, in effect ending the struggle between crown and parliament. The monarch was to govern under the statutes of parliament, thus relinquishing his divine right, so that the king as well as the people now came under the rule of law.

The alliance with Holland through William's accession to the crown inevitably led to England's declaration of war on France. The containment of Louis XIV's expansionist ambitions across Europe was William's prime passion, demanding that his time was spent with his armies. He did not share the enthusiasm of Charles II for theatre or music and his interest in art was limited. He did, however, embark on a rebuilding programme at his royal palaces, to create residences that befitted his new position. Mary was very taken with the French court style, particularly through the work of Marot and other Huguenot craftsmen, many of whom were already employed in England during the

reign of Charles II. Designs began to display an integrity achieved through the sense of order that is so dominant in the court style of Louis XIV.

It is encouraging to note that when reason is allowed to operate, the innate desire of man to search for artistic beauty and harmony seemingly has the power to cut across the political and religious landscape. We see the anti-French Protestant court of William and Mary appreciating the same artistic qualities as the pro-French

Decorative details about 1680: ribband festoon of exotic fruit and flowers; undulate band of scrolling acanthus taken from between the gallery rails of a Fourth Rate 56-gun ship of 1680; stylised dolphin of the same period.

Model of a 60-gun ship of around 1690-1705 – the dimensions are of a ship of the 1690s but the royal cypher suggests Queen Anne's reign. (Author's collection reproduced by courtesy of the Science Museum, London)

Catholic court of Charles and James. Coming via Holland this was perhaps unavoidably tinged with Dutch characteristics and the revolution certainly extended the period of Dutch influence in England.

Such national characteristics inevitably have a bearing on the arts, manifest either as a natural support for, or defiant suppression of, what is seen as a foreign influence. The reserved English nature halted the glorification of churches in High Baroque style and, perhaps encouraged by the war with France, increased interest in Italy. This ensured that architectural design continued to follow the Classical precepts favoured by Wren, who shunned the extremes of fashion and guarded against such novelties in which 'fancy blinds judgement'.

The decorative composition on the model of a 60-gun ship from the 1690s (but made around 1702-1704) stands as a good example of the late Restoration style, which incorporates many aspects of Baroque influence. Very rich in its density of composition, the dominant motif consists of an undulate band of scrolling acanthus, which takes its inspiration from the Italian rather than French Baroque. From an architectural perspective, the model is interesting in that it shows the quarter gallery with windows to the stern forming a continuous line of lights to the upper deck. The artist has accentuated this

widening of the gallery by continuing the scrolling acanthus in an unbroken line below the lights. The mullions at this level have dropped the caryatid figures in preference to margent drops of leaves and flowers. This development of the festoon appears in the work of Grinling Gibbons during the 1670s to decorate verticals.

The figures to the fashion pieces have extended to the width of the quarter galleries, employing a very well executed design combining a seated figure within a console, to give the profile of a continued curve of the tafferel. The decoration of this displays a superb composition, given the narrow constraints placed upon it. The confident use of perspective creates a wonderful three-dimensional effect with the lightness and movement of its figures producing a good example of Baroque ornamentation.

Mullions to the windows of the quarterdeck continue to adopt the use of caryatid figures of the previous age, with a further undulate band of scrolling acanthus typical of the Restoration style. A similar design is applied to the lower counter, creating an overall effect of a very dense composition, the contrasting red ground helping in some small measure to allow the intricate detail to be appreciated.

The composition lacks any of the bandwork or other devices to be seen on French ships of the period, maintaining a predominantly Italian-inspired design. The naval order of 1703 restricting the amount of carving included the demise of wreath ports, which are still in evidence on this model, suggesting that it pre-dates the order, or at least before the order became effective. It also bears the 'AR' monogram of Queen Anne, who came to the throne in 1702, further suggesting that the Restoration style continued, alongside more subdued compositions that were appearing after the Glorious Revolution.

Lower finishing to the quarter gallery takes the form of uncurling acanthus leaves. The figure sitting on the console holds a shield bearing the cross of St George. The upper finishing terminates with a crown below which is the monogram AR dating the model in the earliest years of Queen Anne's reign (1702) prior to the naval orders restricting the amount of carved work taking any effect.

A line from the running rigging sits precariously close to the gilded carving, providing a good example of how the practicalities of sailing the ship are of paramount importance to the crew, where the siting of such blocks is determined by the efficiency of the rig and not the preservation of carved work which, should it prove to snag the line would be swiftly removed before placing the ship in jeopardy. (Author's collection reproduced by courtesy of the Science Museum, London)

William and Mary's reign marked the high point not only of Baroque art in Britain, but also of the expenditure on its production. In 1691 the Clerk of the Cheque was instructed to monitor the quality of carved work and control its cost. Future Admiralty orders were to set out tables of payments that would be allowed for both carved and painted work, marking the start of a programme that would attempt to reduce the cost of their production. It also marked a point at which the efficiency of ships was becoming increasingly under review and the reduction in cost was also an attempt to reduce what some regarded as impractical forms of decoration.

In 1700 the cost of carved work might range from £900 for a First Rate ship to £50 for a Sixth Rate. An Admiralty order issued in 1700 gave the following reasons for reducing these figures to £500 for a First Rate down to £25 for a Sixth:

H.M. ships are found to have carved works in their cabin coaches and other improper places, which upon any prospect of action are torn to pieces by the sailors, and consequently a very unnecessary charge; and where as upon examination of the bills passed for carved works for new ships and ships rebuilt for some time backward, some are thought to be very extravagant and few of a rate observed to agree one with other, which renders it absolutely necessary to have some regulation made therein.

We have, upon mature consideration had thereof, thought it fit not only to prohibit for the future the putting up of any carved work in the cabin coaches and other improper places of H.M. ships, but also to put a limitation to the charges of said works by establishing such sums for the several rates and ranks of ships as are not to be exceeded when any of the said ships shall be built or rebuilt.

Likewise in the reparation of H.M. ships for the time to come you are carefully to survey their carved work and save what can be saved and will or may be made to serve again so as H.M. may have the benefit thereof in as full and ample manner as is hereby intended.

This was a sobering message that was not received kindly; indeed, ships built after the order show little sign of complying with it.

A good representation of the William and Mary period is a model of a small Fifth Rate ship of 30 guns preserved in the Henry Huddleston Rogers Collection. The tafferel has as its centrepiece a lion's head supported by two thinly coiling volutes, from which emerge contrastingly large acanthus leaves. This modification became a popular motif, a variation of which can be seen in the accompanying illustration of a bale tomb.

The acanthus leaves in the lower part of the tafferel move in an outward direction, providing a contrasting sense of movement to the volutes that draw inwards as supporters to the lion. Two herms form the fashion pieces, the pedestals of which are decorated with coin moulding, extending the figures down to the bottom of the lights, which have caryatid figures forming the mullions. Between the rails of the upper deck are portraits of William and Mary with their cypher forming the central panel, but with the M removed to display only the W of William. This provides a useful clue to dating the ship as Mary died in 1694 but William survived until 1702.

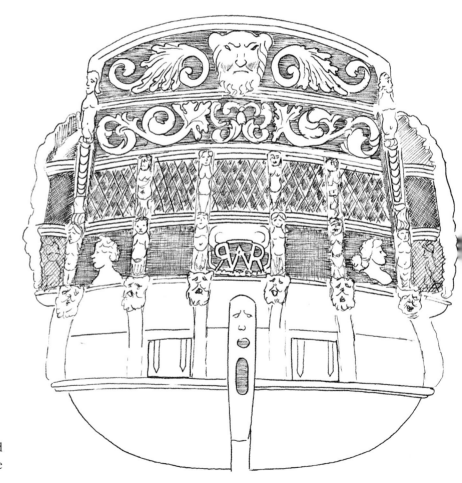

An example of a small Fifth Rate 30-gun ship of the William and Mary period. The drawing is from a contemporary model in the Rogers Collection which, somewhat unusually, is constructed from olive wood.

Bale tomb of William Thomas, who died in 1697 at the age of 103; from Quenington, Gloucestershire. Lyre end and bale originally represented corded bales of cloth.

The Restoration period experimented with many adaptations of the acanthus leaf, as can be seen in its inclusion in a scroll which forms what is known as the lyre-shaped end to William Thomas's tomb, but can more readily be described as a volute, in which is entwined a horn of plenty dispensing exotic fruits. The cartouche also became a feature of the Restoration style, here depicted in a less curvaceous manner than is typical of the period. A somewhat naive representation of a cherub completes both the outer border and inner content of the composition. The representational style of these motifs can all be found on ship models of the period.

By 1689 Wren was nearing sixty and had held the post of surveyor general for twenty years. His first task under the new regime was the remodelling of Hampton Court, but it was the building of Chelsea and Greenwich veterans' hospitals that offered the greatest scope for entirely new designs. The war with France was creating ever increasing casualties, and the only existing provision for aged and maimed seamen was the Chatham Chest, a pension arrangement whereby every serving sailor contributed 6d from his monthly wages; it had been established by Francis Drake after the defeat of the Spanish Armada, but was inadequate to meet the present situation. Mary pressed for the building of a hospital at Greenwich, and although she died before work could begin, William honoured her wishes.

It was also a period in which a new generation of architects, namely Nicholas Hawksmoor (1661-1736) and John Vanbrugh (1664-1726), came to the fore. Both were students of Wren, who in his

Pediment decoration to the King William Court of the Old Royal Naval College, Greenwich. Originally the Royal Hospital for Seamen, it was designed and begun by Wren, but completed by Hawksmoor and Vanbrugh in 1712. The nautical theme and shape of composition could be directly transposed to the tafferel of a ship, serving as a full-scale model of how such compositions would have been executed. The resplendent vitality of the piece captures the majesty of the age, with the lion and unicorn sitting in royal repose, unmoved by the mythical figures and sea creatures whipped into turmoil by the four winds. Reeds and water lilies are used as an alternative to formalised acanthus foliage, adding to the sense of naturalism. An early example of their use can be found in the decoration of the *Britannia* of 1682. (Author's collection)

design wished to develop a sense of spatial awareness. His students were keen exponents of the Baroque and can be credited with expanding Wren's vision into a monumental sense of theatricality through Baroque ornament. The buildings provide many examples of sculptural compositions ideally suited to their use on ships of the period, providing some excellent three-dimensional models of how such work might have appeared.

The first academy to offer artistic training was not founded in Britain until 1711, by which time the French academies had been established for some fifty years. Consequently, foreign artists seized the opportunity to seek patronage in England, where the country's growing wealth was creating a society eager to embrace the arts. The only options open to an aspiring English artist were to take an apprenticeship with a master craftsman through the guilds or with an established artist, or to seek instruction abroad.

The work of Wren and his successors had established the pre-eminence in civic architecture of largely Italian-inspired Baroque, initiated by the

warmer relations with the Papacy in Rome enjoyed by the court of Charles II and James II, while the established traditions mixed with imported goods continued to have an effect amidst the houses of wealthy merchants and the landed gentry who had risen to power and wealth in the preceding decades. Queen Mary in particular was keen to cultivate the arts, introducing many influences from Holland such as Delftware. This now-familiar blue and white glazed pottery perfected by the Dutch was during this period decorated with Chinese-inspired motifs to satisfy the growing demand for oriental goods that were being imported through the East India companies, all adding to an exotic abundance of imagery that so suited the Baroque age, but tempered by the recent history that allowed English versions to develop independently of continental Europe.

Carvers attached to navy yards were often from families who had established themselves in such positions for generations. Few would have had the resources to travel abroad, or inclination to learn from an artist beyond the sphere of the ship-

The earlier illustration of the figurehead of the *Prince* provides a good model with which to compare the alteration in carved work bought about by official restrictions. On this model of the *Captain* of 1708 the head decoration has been reduced to mouldings fixed to the head timbers (described in the order as brackets) and hair bracket. A relatively simple panel forms a trailboard between the upper and lower cheeks.

HEAD ARRANGEMENT AND LION FIGUREHEAD, *CAPTAIN* 1708

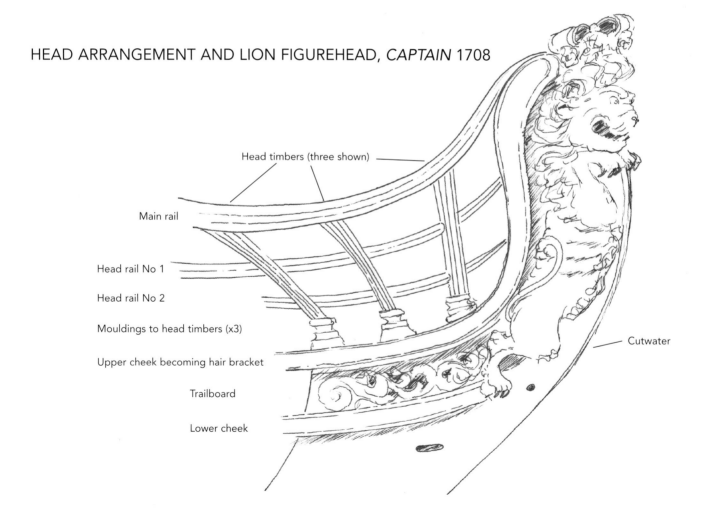

Head timbers (three shown)

Main rail

Head rail No 1

Head rail No 2

Mouldings to head timbers (x3)

Upper cheek becoming hair bracket

Trailboard

Lower cheek

Cutwater

carving fraternity. Their training, together with apprenticeship to the master ship-carver, would therefore have followed the traditional route. Left to their own devices, the introduction of new concepts from abroad would have been slow and largely secondhand. The problem was often compounded by the practice of reusing carvings from an existing vessel during the rebuilding process that created its successor. The resultant compositions often manifest themselves as a somewhat random collection of varied concepts that were only now beginning to develop into a unified vision, albeit with an air of idiosyncratic Englishness.

Great emphasis was placed on figurative work, particularly during the 1680s and 1690s. Although inaccurate in a Classical sense, they still bear the mark of skilled craftsmen, able to achieve emotive qualities through an honest simplicity of form such as those described on the *Britannia*. These often very animated characters bring a quality of lively realism to the compositions, creating their own sense of Baroque theatricality, whilst stopping short of excessive drama, thus creating art forms quite different from those found on French ships of the period, and at this point also developing independently of the Netherlands.

The crowning of Queen Anne in 1702 represents a turning point in the style and ornamentation of English ships. Whilst Baroque continued to develop for the first quarter of the century, there were murmurings of disapproval amongst critics who saw the proficiency of Baroque artists blossom into what they considered to be the excesses of an extravagant style. These were views that the Navy Board could exploit in their desire to reduce the ornamentation of ships. The apparent non-compliance with their earlier ruling led to a further order being issued in 1703: 'That carved works be reduced to only a lion and trail board for the head, with mouldings instead of brackets placed against the timbers.'

A model of the *Captain* demonstrates how the order was to be implemented. The first *Captain* was built to a design by Shish at Woolwich in 1678, with a rebuild commencing at Portsmouth in 1705. In the same year the yard at Portsmouth engaged the carver Robert Smith to work on various ships that came in for rebuilds during the War of the Spanish Succession. Smith was paid the sum of £53.1s.6d for carved work to the *Captain*, a Third Rate ship of 70 guns launched in 1708. The model was built by a young shipwright at

Portsmouth but not completed until after 1714, as it includes the GR cypher of George I. Details such as the carving could, therefore, have been taken from the completed ship. In 1718 the *Captain* was at Cape Passaro where Sir George Byng defeated the Spanish fleet. She was broken up in 1722.

The order of 1703 continues:

That the stern have only a tafferel and two quarter pieces, and in lieu of brackets between the lights of the stern, galleries and bulkheads, to have mouldings fixed against the timbers; that the Joiner's work inside the sides of the great cabin, coach, wardroom, and round house of each ship be fixed only with slit deals without any sort of moulding or cornice and the painting be only plain colour.

We have considered these propositions and very well approving thereof do hereby desire and direct you to cause the same to be put in execution as soon as it conveniently may be, and that no other carvers, joiners or painters works be allowed or put in any H.M. ships for the future, without particular and especial orders for the same.

Although the *Captain* had stern galleries to the upper and quarterdeck, those of the quarterdeck remain unconnected to the stern, an arrangement that would soon change as the layout of sterns continued to develop. This model's compliance with every letter of the law may well represent the Admiralty's ideal, but the order was very unpopular and frequently not adhered to. Dispensations were sought for more elaborate figureheads to three-decked ships, with changes to the stern being dictated more by further developments in ship design and changing fashions in ornamental style than obedience to the regulations.

First and Second Rate ships in particular resisted any reduction to their carved work, as demonstrated in the accompanying example. The model represents a Second Rate 90-gun ship built in accordance with the Establishment laid down in 1706, which attempted to standardise the dimensions, if not the design, of the larger rates. The model corresponds most closely to the *Neptune*, rebuilt at Blackwall in 1710, and the *Ossory*, rebuilt at Deptford in 1711. Such dates concur with the royal insignia depicted on the tafferel, as used by

Queen Anne between 1707 and 1714

This three-decked ship displays a number of features introduced during Anne's reign. Quarter galleries to her middle, upper and quarterdecks now link with those of the stern. Carved work to the lower finishing complies with the restrictive order, but she continues to display a considerable amount of carved work to the upper counter, in panels below the breast rail of the upper deck and along the ship's side. Balustrading appears for the first time, here set between panelled framing forming the upper finishing and to the walkway of the quarter gallery. This Classical baluster has been represented in the form that would have been most common to craftsmen of the day – the barley twist – made popular during the Restoration period. The introduction of balustrades points to the growing enthusiasm for Classicism.

In many respects decoration to the stern can claim to obey the restrictive order, in that the bulk of decorative work is confined to the tafferel and quarter pieces. The style of this can be described as Baroque, although seriously lacking in the vitality associated with the genre. The artist does not appear to have come to terms with the diminishing size of the tafferel by persisting with the over-large portrayal of the subject matter – although this may

be the result of re-using figures during the rebuild from the original ship (*Ossory* of 1682 with carved work by Allen Lewis or the *Neptune* of 1683 with carved work by John Leadman).

Figures previously on the fashion piece have been replaced with simple pilasters. This widening of the tafferel led to the introduction of a cove under its bottom edge, which in effect formed the demarcation line of the tafferel and to accord with the 1703 order, work above the cove could be carved, whilst ornamentation below 'should' be

Stern of a model of the *Captain* built at in Portsmouth 1708 (Author's collection reproduced courtesy of the Science Museum, London; inv no 1917-2)

This model of a 90-gun ship of 1710 continues to carry carved work to the ship's side and upper gun ports, flouting the restrictive order of 1703. The insides of the gun port lids are painted with masks with an oriental demeanour. (Author's collection reproduced courtesy of the Science Museum, London; inv no 1931-19)

Quarter gallery of the Science Museum's model of *Captain*. The modelmaker's use of plain veneers to indicate pilasters and panelling mirrors the changing taste associated with the Queen Anne style, where such simple forms of decoration were making an appearance alongside the ornately decorated Baroque. The art of marquetry was also becoming fashionable for use in furniture, flooring, etc. (Author's collection reproduced courtesy of the Science Museum, London; inv no 1917-2)

The stern of the 90-gun ship of 1710. A shield forming the centrepiece to the tafferel contains the royal standard of Queen Anne, the outer edge of which may have been inscribed with her motto SEMPER EADEM, 'Always the same'. (Author's collection reproduced courtesy of the Science Museum, London; inv no 1931-19)

The stern of the 90-gun ship of 1710. With all the quarter galleries coming aft to link with the stern, decorative emphasis has now firmly shifted to horizontal compositions. The replacement of carved work to window mullions with pilasters detracts the eye from such junctions, creating an almost seamless transition of decorative work from fashion piece to outer edge of the quarters. A row of oriental figures is painted across the counter. (Author's collection reproduced courtesy of the Science Museum, London; inv no 1931-19)

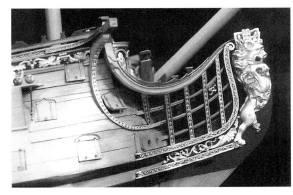

Further oriental figures can be seen on the roundhouse to the beakhead bulkhead; the insides of the gun port lids are similarly decorated with oriental faces. The unusually deep head is a peculiar feature of three-deckers in the reign of Queen Anne and George I, prompting to the introduction of a fourth rail. The brackets and cheeks go somewhat further than simple mouldings, while carving to the ship's side pays no attention to the restrictive order. The top edge of the main rail incorporates an exquisitely scalloped support for the 'bumpkin', giving three positions in which this spar can be supported as it holds the clew of a square sail set below the bowsprit. (Author's collection reproduced courtesy of the Science Museum, London; inv no 1931-19)

only painted. Although carved on this model, the convention generally came to be accepted.

The gallery to the quarterdeck is interesting in showing an open walkway that projects beyond the stern. This was common on French ships (and there are a few examples on Restoration-era English ships), but the model marks its earliest introduction as a regular feature on British sterns, together with the use of an open balustrade as previously described. The projecting walkway to the upper deck employs relief carved panels depicting military trophies, while the central panel carries the royal arms of Queen Anne following the Union with Scotland, at which time Scottish warships were absorbed into the Royal Navy. The same arms form the centrepiece of the tafferel.

During the later part of Queen Anne's reign Royal Navy ships began to display decorative motifs that reflected the country's trade with the East. Decoration to the counter of this model illustrates the crossover of motifs from East India company ships, with this warship embracing the emerging fashion for oriental-inspired designs. Motifs depicting oriental figures are set within arcading panels to the lower counter. These predominantly painted motifs would comply with the restrictive order, while the upper counter has carved work depicting an aquatic scene similar to earlier examples described on the ships of William and Mary. Decoration at this level has taken precedence over the gun ports, whose lids assume a continuation of the decorative composition. In contrast to the tafferel, the composition here is well executed, the definition of the relatively small-scale figures having been increased by the contrasting black background. This is particularly effective and seems to have become the accepted regime, as confirmed in an order of 1715:

> You are to use good husbandry in the painted works and not to refresh oftener to the weather than once in a year or two. And the inboard works that are from the weather only upon rebuilding and great repairs, or after a return from a long foreign voyage when the ship hath not been refreshed abroad and that the outsides of the ship be painted of the usual colour yellow and the ground black and that the inside and out be a plain colour only, except such part of the head stern and galleries as are usually friezed.

A further development in ship design was the introduction of the screen bulkhead. As stern galleries to the quarterdeck became open, those of the middle deck were closed. This strengthening of the lower decks was considered enough to allow the removal of framing to the stern of the quarter- and upper decks. The gallery had effectively moved inboard of the stern. A lightly constructed bulkhead was then sufficient to form a partition to the cabin. During action the screen could be stowed, thus reducing injury from flying glass and saving the cost of its replacement. Stern-chase guns could also be more readily deployed. Screen bulkheads first appear around 1705, their introduction coinciding with the adoption of pilasters, which provided the perfect form of decoration to screens that required lightness of construction.

Palladio

While Europe was poised to follow French Baroque's evolution into the excesses of Rococo, by 1715 Palladianism had become an influential force in English architecture. The Venetian architect Andrea Palladio (1508-1580) rediscovered what he argued were the true precepts of

Classical architecture, where the systematic use of the five orders is intended to restrain the desire for wayward expression, thus creating forms that bring the viewer to a point of rest. Balance and proportion are paramount, creating a natural order where each form is appropriate to its use, in unadorned harmony.

Its effects were soon visible in ship ornamentation. The areas where carving was prohibited by the 1703 order were ideally suited to the Palladian style. Carved panelling below the breast rails of galleries was replaced with balustrading. Open galleries could be supported with columns and pilasters fixed to screen bulkheads or form mullions between windows. By 1714 this had become the standard format, with elaborately painted frieze work below the cove and to the counters. Quarter galleries invariably mirrored the sterns, with mock balusters to closed galleries, painted work below the breast rails, and carved work restricted to the upper and lower finishings.

While the works of Palladio described in detail the principles of Classical correctness, they gave no indication of interior decoration. This gap was largely filled by the architect William Kent (1685-1748). He was a great admirer of Inigo Jones and had travelled to Italy to study at first hand the

Model of a 60-gun ship built in accordance with the dimensions laid down in the 1719 Establishment. Pilasters and balustrades now dominate the galleries. A simplified composition of seated figures forms the tafferel, with the quarter pieces becoming the last vestige of monumental work, here appearing as obstinate relics of a bygone age. Painted frieze work to the counters takes on a Classical demeanour. (Author's collection reproduced courtesy of the Science Museum, London; inv no 1899-32)

Detail from the stern of the Prince Frederick barge of 1731. The exquisite decorative work was designed by William Kent and carved by Grinling Gibbons's successor as master carver to the crown, James Richards. (Author's collection)

works of Palladio. On his return in 1720 he gained the patronage of Lord Burlington, who became the guiding light of the Palladian movement. Kent was a brilliant designer whose influence spread through all aspects of the decorative arts. The

Baroque style he developed maintained a sense of grandeur without being irreverent to the Classical structure of Palladianism. His furniture and applied decoration used delicately scrolling acanthus, surmounted with scallop shells and festoons of flowers, all of which are employed in ship decoration – margents of leaf and flower designs replace brackets, *guilloche*, wave scroll and husk mouldings surmount frames amidst columns and balusters. Prince Frederick's barge at Greenwich survives as a superb example of his work. Designed by Kent in 1731, the exquisite carving was beautifully executed by James Richards, who succeeded Grinling Gibbons as master carver to the crown in 1721, and the mass of gilded work was completed by Paul Petit. The barge was built by John Hall, builder of many ceremonial barges, including the City barge of 1722, the Drapers' Company barge of 1733 and the Haberdashers' barge of 1738.

Kent's drawings, many of which still exist, superbly illustrated every detail of the carved work,

One of the hallmarks of Palladian architecture is this three-panelled window, the central light arched and supported by columns, with the outer edges in this instance decorated with pilasters, the capitals to both of which are of the Ionic order and balusters to the balcony of the single vase type, with simple square base and abacus. This example is from Waterperry House, Oxfordshire, 1740. (Author's collection)

The Palladian window first appears on British ships around 1719 and is shown here on a model of a 50-gun ship built between 1736 and 1742 by which time the decorative compositions that accompanied the Classical foundation had reached the grace and fluidity witnessed here. (Author's collection reproduced courtesy of the Science Museum, London; inv no 1909-123)

providing the carver with a crystal-clear picture of what was expected. The drawings are devoid of any ambiguities to be sorted out on the way, allowing this wonderfully unified vision to be realised.

James Richards worked on many projects with William Kent, including that of his patron Lord Burlington (1649-1753) at Burlington House, London, and at Houghton Hall, Norfolk for Sir Robert Walpole, providing carving to interior furnishings such as wall panelling, tables, mirror frames and so on designed by Kent; these often included marine motifs such as stylised dolphins and scallop shells, detailing to which he developed into a distinctive style of 'ruched' or horizontal veining, creating a rippled effect.

⟶ The Use of Columns ⟵ and Balusters

Although not always adhered to either in general architecture or ship ornamentation, the use of columns with their associated base, pedestal, capital, abacus and entablature, were in strict Classical usage supposed to be employed in accordance with the function and hence importance of the building. Through the ages various architects set out the principle of their use, including Isaac Ware (died 1766), whose work spanned the Palladian and later Neoclassical period being therefore of greatest relevance to ship ornament. His advice on the use of the five orders of architecture was as follows.

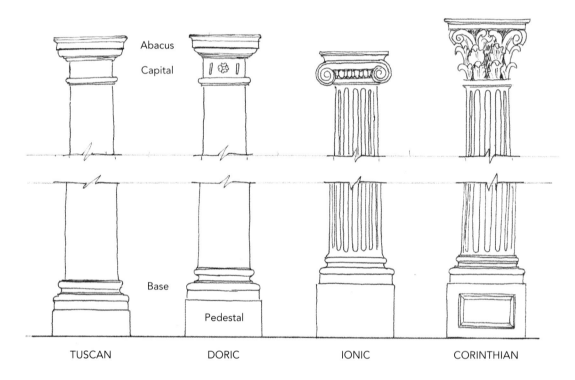

TUSCAN   DORIC   IONIC   CORINTHIAN

COLUMNS AND BALUSTERS

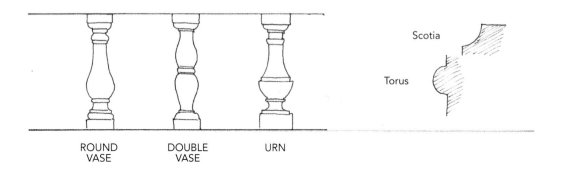

ROUND   DOUBLE   URN
VASE   VASE

The Tuscan was the simplest form, having a plain base, and a column which thickens slightly at its mid-point so as when viewed from a distance, its outer edges do not appear 'concave', with a capital that takes the form of simple mouldings, upon which the abacus creates a rounded or square support to the entablature. Its use was restricted to simple domestic buildings, and being considered a solid male form, also suitable for fortifications, prisons, etc.

The Doric takes a similar form, but includes a pedestal to the base, and some ornamentation between the banded mouldings. The column can also be fluted, depending upon the importance of its position. Its strong male form made it suitable for military structures and formal civic buildings.

The Ionic, again, has the addition of a pedestal, fluted column, generally of a tapering profile and capital formed of volutes, producing a slender 'female' form, emanating a sense of peace and calm, and therefore suitable for buildings connected to the arts, temples, noble houses, etc.

The Corinthian had a pedestal, tapering fluted column and capital consisting of acanthus leaves arranged in two rows with curling stalks that settle beneath the abacus, generally of a concave form. Ware described it as 'The order giving the utmost elegance to a building'; for use in buildings of grandeur.

The Composite order was, as the name suggests a mixture, and generally viewed as 'richly tricked, a borrower of beauty and the poorer for it'. Although it makes an ostentatious appearance in Baroque architecture and later Neoclassical ornament, its use on ships is negligible.

Balusters with a varying degree of decoration were developed for use with each order of capital, in their simplest form consisting of a single round 'vase' with plain square base and abacus. The 'double vase' set one vase upturned, upon the lower, joined with mouldings ranging from a simple bead moulding to 'Torus' and 'Scotia' moulds. When set flat against a wall, the column or pillar becomes a 'pilaster'; the use of balusters in this context could be a half-round section baluster, or more often the square-sectioned 'urn' baluster, which sits more convincingly when halved. When balusters are joined to form a balustrade, as on the stern of a ship, flat planks were often cut to the profile of a vase or urn baluster, for use in the narrow confines of a walkway.

The *Jersey* of 1736 displays the beauty of form that can be achieved when individual elements no longer stand alone but create a unified vision based on harmonic principles. The omission of detail to the carved work of the stern allows the underlying sense of proportion to be appreciated. This in turn provides the opportunity for the viewer to come to a point of rest, and connect with the natural harmony described by Palladio. One can assume the stern carvings would be similar to those of the previous example, to create a composition that does not rely on a mish-mash of unconnected and ill-proportioned motifs but, under the guidelines of Palladio's ideal, emerges as a unified style of decoration.

The only vestige of English eccentricity is the inclusion of four spindles in the old Restoration style, mischievously placed among the balusters like a sweet to tempt the disciplined Palladian from his authoritarian path. This partial inclusion of spiral twist balusters also appears in staircases of domestic architecture, an example being Queen's Square, Bath, also of the early Georgian period.

Jersey was launched from Plymouth as a Fourth Rate 60-gun ship in 1736. An Admiralty order of

Quarter gallery to the 60-gun *Jersey* of 1736, based on the Admiralty draught. Romanesque arcading decorates the lower finishing before terminating in a fishtail. A scaled roof covers the Palladio window, crowned with gadrooning which supports three balloon finials to form the upper finishing.

HMS JERSEY 1736

1727 had relaxed the restrictions on figureheads, permitting the use of heads other than lions on the smaller rates. This gave rise to the emergence of many individual figures, but *Jersey* stayed with the lion, for which the carver Cuthbert Mattingly received the sum of £17.10s.0d. Cuthbert worked at Plymouth from 1736 to 1760, when he moved to Portsmouth. He was joined by his son William in 1773, to whom he handed over the business in the late 1780s. The carver Maynard Nicholls was also working at Plymouth between 1735 and 1736, receiving £16.10s.0d for his contribution to work on the *Jersey*.

The rising cost of carving caused the Navy Board to issue a new schedule of prices in 1737. It is possible that Mattingly did not receive payment for his lion until this date as the price paid is exactly as this new schedule:

Guns	Lion			Trailboard			Tafferel			Quarter pieces			Total		
	£	s	d	£	s	d	£	s	d	£	s	d	£	s	d
100	44.	8.	0	7.	4.	0	55.	8.	0	57.	12.	0	166.	12.	0
90	39.	0.	0	5.	6.	0	45.	0.	0	47.	8.	0	136.	14.	0
80	31.	14.	0	4.	5.	0	38.	16.	0	40.	0.	0	114.	15.	0
70	23.	18.	0	2.	16.	2	30.	18.	0	30.	4.	0	87.	16.	2
60	17.	10.	0	2.	11.	2	22.	16.	0	22.	10.	0	65.	7.	2
50	13.	2.	0	2.	1.	5	16.	4.	0	16.	4.	0	47.	11.	5
40	10.	2.	0	1.	13.	4	12.	7.	0	13.	0.	0	37.	2.	4
20	7.	4.	0	1.	4.	8	9.	8.	0	10.	7.	0	28.	3.	8

The *Jersey* was built under the 1733 Establishment where, in response to concerns about the growth in size of foreign ships, the dimensions of ships were reviewed, leading to the replacement of many 50-gun ships with 60s. The earlier 50-gun *Jersey* of 1698 was hulked in 1731 to be replaced by the new *Jersey*. This highlights the general move away from rebuilding to a preference for new construction, while the old vessels continued to survive as hulks – dismasted and in harbour service as receiving ships (for crews awaiting assignment to their new ship), hospital ships or store ships. The *Jersey* of 1698 served as a hulk until 1763 when she was finally sunk as a breakwater; similarly the *Jersey* of 1736 was served as a hospital ship from 1771 and finally abandoned in 1783 after three years as a prison hulk.

The policy of retaining rather than breaking up old hulls and then reusing their carvings must have made it easier to create a cohesive quality to the decorative compositions on new ships. The order of 1703 stipulated the use of pine in lieu of oak, which being easier and therefore quicker to carve, allowed elaborate figures to still be produced within the ever-diminishing sums allowed by the Navy Board. However, the use of less durable timber reduced their serviceable life to little more than twenty years, effectively curtailing the benefit of their reuse. Lime, the favoured timber of Grinling Gibbons and largely introduced by him, was also used, but with a similar detrimental effect on the longevity of carvings. While the best wood possible for intricate carving, it is not a durable timber when exposed to the elements.

The active career of the *Jersey* began with the war against Spain (1739-1748) and in 1741 she formed part of Sir Edward Vernon's fleet during the attack on Cartagena. She went on to serve in the Mediterranean after the French entered the war in 1744 and in 1745 she was badly damaged in an engagement with the French 74-gun *St Esprit*. In 1759 she again saw action during the

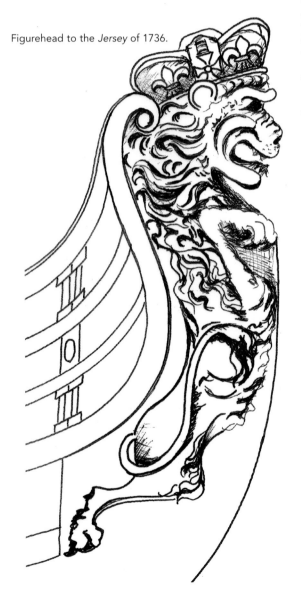

Figurehead to the *Jersey* of 1736.

Right: Stern of the *Jersey* built at Plymouth in 1736. She illustrates the adoption of a cove that terminates at the fashion pieces, with two secondary arches spanning the stern lights of the quarter pieces. The fashion pieces are here decorated with two fluted columns with Corinthian capitals; a year later, the Admiralty allowed the use of terms at this position. Pilasters with Ionic capitals form mullions to the lights. The balusters are unusual in showing the single vase shape, but upturned, having their thinner section at the base, while those in line with the pilasters are of the barley twist pattern, associated more with the Restoration period.

Detail from a console table from 1740 utilising many of the motifs favoured by Kent, such as the scallop shell, festoons, central bust and foliage presenting a sense of abundance without becoming over-indulgent.

supports at this position, as an alternative to columns. The term is more commonly described as a herm, being a tapered pillar which terminates into a male or female bust, and was a motif much used by William Kent in Palladian ornamentation. Their use in this position can be found on later ships such as the *Isis* of 1774 through to the *Leopard* of 1790.

The imaginative designs of William Kent continued to work their way into ship ornamentation, creating a semblance of composure, while still retaining the lively expressiveness of the Baroque. A balance was achieved that perfectly complemented the structure of Palladianism, softening the austerity of its architecture with measured delight. The influence of the Palladian movement in England was far-reaching, establishing a style that influenced developments abroad, thus reversing the trend of imported ideas shaping British fashions.

Figurative work tended to dominate ship ornamentation, in compositions to suit the ever-diminishing size of tafferels and quarter pieces. As a consequence, little space remained for the inclusion of foliate forms, beyond the occasional festoon, to be draped around a central motif, or shell design, or incorporated into painted work to the counters.

blockade of Toulon where she received severe damage aloft, but no record exists of repairs being required to her carved work.

The *Jersey* illustrates a development of the English stern that appeared around 1730 where the cove of the tafferel ended at the fashion piece, with a secondary arch over the stern light of each quarter gallery. This detail spread to Holland when Thomas Davis and Charles Bentham were employed at the Amsterdam yards, and can be seen in their designs of the period. An Admiralty order issued in 1737 allowed the use of 'terms' as

Among the many Navy Board models hidden away in the store of the National Maritime Museum, Greenwich, is that of 64-gun ship of the 1741 Establishment. The exquisitely carved and finely detailed model provides an accurate insight into the density and compositional make up of the period and is worthy of some analysis. A heraldic shield adorned with scrolling acanthus and palms forms the centrepiece of the tafferel. It bears the arms of Great Yarmouth, from which the identity of the ship in all probability can be taken as the *Yarmouth*. Ordered in 1740, she was built at Deptford as a 64-gun ship and launched in 1745.

Carved decoration to the stern consists almost entirely of figurative work in a superb composition that requires some ingenuity to fit within the confines of the narrow tafferel, the tight structure of which fulfils the practical aspects of the ship's sailing ability, whilst still maintaining a pleasing sense of proportion. The counters are decorated with a painted frieze depicting nymph-like figures in an aquatic scene. Bearing in mind the minute scale (1/48th) in which the artist has to work, the painting is very fine, with flesh tones to the figures who move amidst waving green reeds, set on a deep blue background, giving a

Drawing showing the stern of a Navy Board model of the *Yarmouth*, a 64-gun ship launched at Deptford in 1745. The model is in the National Maritime Museum, Greenwich, ref no SLR 0454 (see colour plate 12).

clear example of how the actual vessel would appear. With the ship lying at anchor, dappled light reflecting off the surface of the sea would dance across these figures, creating a magical illusion of them becoming alive in the water below.

The narrow quarter pieces of the elliptical stern are decorated with putti playing musical instruments; standing on heads and shoulders, they rise up to the tafferel with a playful sense of movement. At the turn of the quarter piece are two C-shaped scrolls. This Rococo-inspired motif is the only representation of the genre, but serves as a reminder of its existence in fashionable circles ashore. Two cherubs holding shields bearing the cross of St George ride on dolphins above the fashion pieces, which are unadorned, to maintain a clear demarcation of architectural and sculptural areas. Tritons act as supporters to the shield, blowing conch shells by which act they have the power to quell storms or raise a fair wind. In the other hand they hold a banner bearing the cypher of King George II, beneath which two enormous arms rise out of the ocean depths to form supports for the stern lights

The galleries present a purely Classical countenance, devoid of any decoration beyond architectural embellishments. This was to become the standard layout in accordance with the order of 1703. Breast and foot rails to the open walkway support square-sectioned balusters, below which pilasters representing the Doric order form the window mullions.

The *Yarmouth*'s first recorded action was during Anson's engagement with the French fleet under their Admiral Jonquière off Cape Finistère in 1747, when she was instrumental in the capture of the French East India Company ship *Vigilant*. (The previously captured 64-gun *Vigilant* also formed part of Anson's fleet.) *Yarmouth* served in Indian waters during 1758-9, where she was in action against the French off Cuddalore in April 1758 and Pondicherry in September 1759. In the next war from 1779 she formed part of Rodney's fleet in the West Indies where she was in action against the French off Grenada and Dominique in 1780 and 1782. The following year, having served for nearly forty years in tropical waters, she was hulked and served as a receiving ship until sold (to be broken up) in 1801.

At the time of *Yarmouth*'s construction, carvers working at Deptford included Thomas Burrough, who started work there in 1740 and became master carver at the yard in 1757, a position he held until 1788. A surviving description of work that he completed to the *Cambridge* of 1755 has similarities to the *Yarmouth* in so much as it consists almost entirely of figurative work, but of a more serious nature than the frolicking cherubs of *Yarmouth*. He describes Mars, Jupiter and Mercury with their proper attributes, the only lightening of subject matter being a cherub attendant described as 'boy with fish and seaweeds, together with scrolls and foliage', a theme that does occur on the *Yarmouth*, making him the most likely creator of her carved work.

The Chichley family, although based at Chatham and Sheerness, also carried out work at Deptford. Richard Chichley is recorded as having worked on the *Yarmouth* in 1764. This was during the period after she ended her service in India, and presumably was sent to Deptford for repairs before embarking on her career in the West Indies.

～East Indiamen～

Little has thus far been mentioned on the decoration of East India ships. With so many built at the same yards as warships, employing the same carvers, the difference in their decorative work is negligible. Thomas Burrough is known to have carried out carved work to East India ships built at the merchant yards in Deptford, including Bronsdon & Wells. Barnard built ships for the Navy and East India Company at their yards on the Orwell. In 1742 they took over the tenancy of the royal dockyard at Harwich to build ships for the Navy and in 1763 purchased their own yard in Deptford, where East India ships were built, among them the *Arniston* with carved work by Batton and Glover. Navy ships also came in for repair, and later new ships were built for the fleet. The majority of East India ships were owned by a syndicate of shareholders, who assigned a ship's husband to arrange both the building of the ship and its charter. In times of peace, yards that normally concentrated on wartime naval work were keen to attract such commissions, so it is easy to see that cross-fertilisation of ideas occurred.

In contrast to the Classical and Baroque-inspired decoration of the *Yarmouth*, the East Indiaman *Somerset* of 1738 draws on a mixture of Rococo and Classical motifs. The model (again hidden away in the depths of the National Marime Museum stores) shows how closely this merchantman follows Admiralty notions relating to carved work. Mouldings are used in conjunction with balusters and pilasters; carving is restricted to the quarter pieces and tafferel, with painted work to the counter, etc. The quality of carving on the model is, unfortunately, very poor, but the accompanying drawing which has been taken from the model serves to provide a guide to the general style of decoration. Figurative work to the tafferel has been supplemented with C-scrolls and reverse curves to emulate the asymmetric quality of Rococo ornamentation. The reserved application of this shows a hesitancy on the part of the designer to stray from the time-honoured sense of symmetry.

Whilst the 1730s saw the emerging Rococo spread across Europe, it was never taken seriously in England, where it was viewed as a product of the frivolous French. Its immodest forms were generally kept indoors. Even here, to remain within the bounds of good taste, it was employed sparingly to soften the rigidity of Classicism. *Somerset* is a good example of its use in this context, where the designer has tentatively acknowledged the new style without straying beyond the bounds of his own limited understanding, or public acceptance. The master carver Mathias Lock (1724-1769) was the first English designer to gain a confident understanding of the genre's complex nature. His pattern book of designs, published in 1740, provided an invaluable guide for British craftsmen to follow the new and distinctly foreign genre, transcribed to what he considered an acceptable level of decadence.

The Admiralty issued a further order in 1742, relating mainly to the strengthening of the ship's stern and head, but it also required that the quarter pieces and tafferels be made as small and light as possible. As this fashion already held sway, the order was specifically directed to ships in dockyard hands for repair or rebuilding, to establish a procedure for the renewal or removal of older carvings. The

Quarter gallery of the East Indiaman *Somerset* of 1738. For the stern, see drawing in the Glossary.

importance of decorative work was clearly waning for an Admiralty whose financial constraints demanded durability and efficiency over aesthetic quality, setting the tone of a utilitarian attitude that has come to dominate our modern world. The order's unpopularity ensured that the maximum amount of carving permissible continued to be applied, with subject matter and motifs following the developing trends of fashionable society.

Decorative motifs to the quarter gallery follow the same pattern as the stern, with armorial panoplies forming painted decoration to the lower finishing, with similar designs replicated along the ship's side. Herms form the quarter pieces, presenting a mixture of figurative work and mouldings when viewed from the side. The coin and crescent moulding that decorates the herm's pedestal continues as a coin moulding on the capping of the tafferel. Balusters are of painted effect, in a style to replicate flat timber, rather than turned, to accommodate the varying lengths required to produce the radiating nature of their formation, a task that would be beyond the technical ability of turning.

Design from Chippendale's pattern book *The Gentleman and Cabinet-Maker's Director*, first published in 1754.

The *Somerset* completed a total of four voyages to India whilst in the service of the East India Company from 1738 to 1747, by which time the stresses on her hull, combined with the effects of damage by worm, would have put her in a condition that her owners would consider expendable. She was sold for breaking up in 1750.

The token use of Rococo ornament on the *Somerset* serves to illustrate the minimal extent to which the genre found its way onto ships, while the imported goods of the East India companies continued to provide artists with inspiration for household items. By the mid-century their exotic motifs had developed into the fashion for chinoiserie. Mandarin figures, dragons, pagodas and distinctive foliage with its spiralling tendril forms began to decorate porcelain, tapestry, furniture and plaster mouldings. The shock of the new is often made palatable by slowly introducing it to an already accepted taste. Thomas Chippendale (1718-1779), for whom Mathias Lock was employed as a carver, merged chinoiserie motifs with the asymmetry of Rococo, publishing his designs in 1754. The whimsical absurdity of their gaudy nature confined their use

famous example in England was built at Kew gardens in 1761 by Sir William Chambers (1723-1808) – where traditional Chinese ornamentation to suit the scale of application was reproduced in a purer form.

The advent of Chinese decoration on ships begins, as previously described, around 1710 with the introduction of painted figures to counters and inside gun port lids. During the 1730s and 1740s the manes and tails of lion figureheads take on the tight double curls, with wrinkled snouts and bulging eyes so reminiscent of their Chinese counterparts. The forms of chinoiserie made acceptable for outdoor use through structures such as the pagoda began to make an appearance on ships around 1745.

A Navy Board model representing a 70-gun ship of the 1745 Establishment provides a good example, where balustrading to the galleries of the quarterdeck take the form of latticework. Furniture designed by William Linnell (1703-1763) and his son John (1729-1796) incorporated similar designs for chair backs and screens. This father and son team were responsible for the earliest examples of chinoiserie interiors in Britain, their

Quarter gallery and head of a Navy Board model of a 70-gun ship built to the 1745 Establishment. Elements of chinoiserie appear in the design of balustrading and the dragon-like creature chasing the lion figurehead. (Author's collection reproduced courtesy of the Science Museum, London; inv no 1934-549)

to such objects that could be kept indoors, where they could be enjoyed in close company.

The aura of mystery that comes with such foreign goods continued to hold an attraction, creating a desire for ornament that could be displayed beyond the drawing room. The Chinese garden and pagoda became fashionable – the most

most celebrated being a bedroom commissioned by the 4th Duke and Duchess of Beaufort for Badminton House, Gloucestershire, in 1754. Chinoiserie-inspired motifs continue on the trailboards, where a dragon chases the lion figurehead, which by this period has begun to lose the doubling-back curls.

Seven ships of this rate were built under the 1745 Establishment, the first being launched in 1748 and the last in 1751. With such a modern form of decoration, identification of the ship most likely points to the *Swiftsure*, launched 1750, or the *Buckingham* 1751. Both ships were built at Deptford, where the master carver was Thomas Burrough.

In 1761 the *Buckingham* was engaged together with the *Swiftsure* in an operation to capture Belle Isle off the Brittany coast. On their second attempt, troops were able to land, and after three days of engagement French troops were driven from the town. After intense bombardment from the ships, the walls of the citadel were breached and the governor offered his surrender. Possession of the island lasted till the end of the war. Later that year the fleet focused their attention on the Isle d'Aix, which protected the mouth of the Charente and the naval base of Rochefort. The shallow waters of the area were further defended by flat-bottomed vessels known as prames, carrying between 10 and 20 guns. Although they attempted to interfere with the operations, fortifications on the island were effectively destroyed. The *Buckingham* was sent to Chatham in 1764, where Richard Chichley received payment, presumably for repairs to her carved work. She went on to serve in the West Indies, but she foundered at sea on 11 November 1779.

Another ship present during the blockades of French ports during the Seven Years War was the *Royal George*. This 100-gun ship was launched from Woolwich in 1756, with carved work also by Thomas Burrough. Although the official budget for a First Rate ship was set at £166.12s.0d, Burrough received the astonishing sum of £424.7s.0d for the ornamentation of the ship, which included a group figurehead (see dustjacket of this book and colour plate 13). As Admiral Hawke's flagship, the ship led the chase that routed the French fleet at Quiberon Bay in 1759, and in the following war the ship saw action in the 'Midnight Battle' off Cape St Vincent in January 1780. In stark contrast, she was to meet an inglorious end two years later, when she formed part of a fleet that was gathering at Spithead prior to setting sail with supplies and troops for the relief of Gibraltar, then besieged by the Spaniards. Whilst at anchor, sails were set to force the ship to heel over in order to carry out repairs to the hull. Bad seamanship and an increase in wind strength caused the ship to overset, and she sank in sight of the fleet and the base at Portsmouth; 900 souls were lost, including women and children onboard,

and Rear Admiral Kempenfelt.

In 1769 the carver Luke Lightfoot completed the most extravagant example of a chinoiserie interior in England. His design for the Chinese Room at Claydon House, Buckinghamshire creates a striking contrast to the exterior, the simple Classical proportions of which are typical of the early Georgian period. (George I succeeded Queen Anne on her death in 1714 and George II reigned from 1727 to 1760.) The contrasting styles mirror the divergent taste among fashionable society of the time. Palladianism had not only awakened an interest in the Classical world but also provided a model to uphold what many regarded as good taste amidst the wanton waywardness of Rococo and the diverse expressions resulting in chinoiserie.

Amidst such conflicting tastes, architects like Isaac Ware created compositions that attempted to offer an appreciation of the perfect sense of balance and tension that could be achieved in well-executed asymmetry. He built in the Palladian style but was not averse to the inclusion of Rococo-inspired ornamentation on the grounds that it was 'an allowable use of imagination'. He designed Wrotham Park in 1754 for Admiral Byng, who presumably found no objection to the occasional hint of asymmetry also appearing in ship ornamentation.

⁓Neoclassicism⁓

An association of gentlemen known as the 'Society of Dilettanti' promoted what they considered to be 'the correction of taste' towards an appreciation of Classical art by sponsoring travel and books relating to Classical antiquities. Their endeavours coincided with archaeological discoveries at Herculaneum, Paestum and Pompeii (1738-1756), heralding the age of the 'Grand Tour' and a greater enthusiasm for all things Classical.

One such person who embarked upon the 'Grand Tour' was the architect James Stuart (1713-1778). He spent the years 1751-1755 in Athens studying the architecture and ornamentation of Classical Greece. He produced the first study of the subject and by 1757 was designing work in the radically new Neoclassical style. The movement was soon joined by Robert Adam (1728-1792); having studied in Italy, he returned to publish designs from Classical antiquity and the Renaissance. He criticised the Palladians for their improper use of interior decorative schemes. Archaeological discoveries made at the ancient

Neoclassical motifs that came to define the 'Adam style'. Slender scrolling foliage known as the candelabra form are draped which equally delicate swags of drapery, the ends tied with ribbons, a motif frequently used as a device to draw a composition to a close, or encircle objects such as mirrors. Mythical creatures such as griffins or, in this case sphinxes, provide figurative work. The stand to the left is crowned with an anthemion, one of the principal motifs of Neoclassical ornament, loosely based upon the flower of the honeysuckle; a further example appears above the urn.

Drawing showing the stern of a model in the Rogers Collection at Annapolis depicting the 38-gun frigate *Minerva* of 1780; it displays Neoclassical designs typical of the Adam style.

sites had enabled him to undertake a meticulous study of the artefacts from which he was able to create a unified style. The motifs that were to become his trademarks were, typically, intricate mouldings of palmettes and anthemions, oval patera, often draped with slender festoons and swags, candelabra, vases and urns. This he considered to be a true representation of Classical ornament, and therefore the only authentic accompaniment to Classical architecture.

The style had its critics, who perceived its motifs as having little substance or sense of scale. The minute detail of the decorative forms appeared ill-proportioned to the imposing dimensions of the rooms they were to adorn. The success of the Adam style rested on his artistic ability to select specific motifs from his studies at the ancient sites, and modify them to create compositions of his own making. What appears as a set formula to his designs allowed them to be widely copied, but in less skilful hands the resultant compositions can appear as a collection of parts assembled purely to fill space rather than create an *ambiance* inspired by artistic flair and imaginative use of a medium.

But by 1760 Neoclassicism had taken over, where no doubt the simplicity of its repeating patterns met with the approval of an Admiralty keen to reduce the cost of decorative work still further. The adoption of Neoclassicism in ship ornamentation was initially restricted to the lesser rates, where the delicate nature of the motifs corresponded reasonably well with the small scale of the ship's stern. At this level of application, the genre maintained an acceptable degree of elegance, with the diminishing amount of carved work supplemented by an increase in painted decoration, in an effort to preserve a sense of measured splendour.

A fine example is a model at Annapolis of the 38-gun Fifth Rate *Minerva* of 1780, which is not only beautifully decorated but also shows the hull of the frigate sheathed in copper, a protective measure introduced in the 1770s. All decoration on and below the counter consists of painted work, with carved work confined to the tafferel and quarter pieces. Here figurative work is executed with the same delicate sense of detail and scale as the accompanying mouldings and relief carved work. The narrow dimension of the tafferel has forced the lion and unicorn to adopt a crouching position, making them appear somewhat subdued. Two nymphs hold a portrait of King George III whose monogram appears on the counter. The cove carries carved work of a foliate form with relief carved ribbons and urns on the quarters, where two further nymphs hold shields depicting the Admiralty badge. Warriors in Greek attire form the quarter pieces, with painted drapery to the counter

The manner in which the larger rates differed is exemplified by a description of carved work on a three-decker Second Rate submitted by the carvers Elizabeth Chichley and William Savage. In a letter sent to the Navy Board on 22 September 1772 they requested payment as follows:

Elizabeth Chichley and William Savage to the Board.

We beg leave humbly to acquaint you that we have performed the following carved works for His Majesty's ship PRINCE GEORGE at Chatham

A new head piece
Cut with Prince George in a rich roman dress, holding in his right hand a batton, in his left hand a coronet setting on the globe in a large scallop shell supposed to be glideing over the sea, drawn by a dolphin on the starboard side with a sea nymph rideing on it holding the rains with a bunch of seaweed in one hand and supporting the shell with the other - on the larboard side is a sea horse supposed to be drawing the shell, a sea nymph rideing on him holding the rains with a bunch of seaweeds in one hand and supporting the shell with the other. On each side in front is a large zephyrus blowing, supposed to be supporting the shell, all richly ornamented with seaweeds.

20 feet in long, 5 feet 6 inches in broad and 5 feet 6 inches in thick   **£90.0s.0d**

A large cove
In the middle of the cove is a large cypher representing Prince George, with a coronet on the top. On each side is a large bow knot of ribbon holding festoons of flowers, trophies etc. richly ornamented supported at each, and by a genious, supposed to be flying blowing a trumpet sounding Prince George's praise.
20 feet long, 3 feet in broad,
9 inches in thick   **£10.10s.0d**

Capitals
Four large Corinthian capitals fitted in elm carved with three fronts each, 16 inches each front at 2s.8d per inch according to the customary price, each cap at £6.8s.0d
  £25.12s.0d per cap

Two brackets to support the columns cut with bracket scrowle shell flute and beeds each measuring 4 feet 6 inches in long, 1 foot 3 inches in broad and 1 foot 7 inches in thick.

Two brackets for above each cut with bracket scrowls, a large eagle devouring a serpent and other ornaments each measureing 4 feet 4 inches in long, 3 feet in broad and 1 foot 6 inches in thick.

Two canterlevers cut with bracket scrowls, leafs and festoons of flowers etc. measureing 5 feet 6 inches in long, 1 foot 6 inches in broad and 4 inches in thick.

Two peases to the lower part of the lower finishing ornamented with leaf etc.
The four items above
  £14.10s.0d

There fore pray you be pleased to grant an order fore our being paid for the same and humbly remain Honorable Sirs Yours most obedient servants.

The term 'cove' somewhat misleadingly refers to the tafferel, the description of which naturally includes a larger number of figures than that of the *Minerva* frigate, but the theme of the composition is not dissimilar. The inclusion of bracket scrolls and seaweed as a foliate form exhibit the desire for greater expressiveness than that favoured by Neoclassicism, and when motifs of the genre are mentioned, such as festoons of flowers, the emphasis is still placed on the requirement to be 'richly ornamented'. No mention is made of the quarter or fashion pieces, suggesting that this section of the work was contracted out to other carvers, while work to the counters would have consisted of a painted frieze

With one or two exceptions, the ship's name does not appear on the stern of British ships before 1770, unlike the Dutch where it is invariably

displayed, and on French ships where the name was presented within an elaborately carved cartouche. An Admiralty order of 1771 stated that 'Henceforth ships should have their names painted on their counter in letters 1 foot high and enclosed in a compartment'. The order was strongly objected to on the grounds that it was 'Frenchifying our navy'. The following year the order was amended: 'Name to be painted without a compartment in letters as large as the counter will allow'. As a consequence the upper counter became devoid of any carved or painted ornamentation.

Although the relationship between Elizabeth and Richard Chichley is unknown, she was in all probability his daughter, with Abigail as his wife. Richard was master carver at the Chatham and Sheerness dockyards from 1713 to 1770. Abigail worked alongside him from around 1737-43. Abigail's early work seems to have been mainly on repairs to existing ships, but from 1741 she was paid for work to new vessels at both Chatham and Sheerness, such as the 70-gun *Sterling Castle* of 1742. Richard produced a phenomenal amount of carving during his long period of office. From 1764 his accounts show him as being in partnership with Elizabeth; this was during the period when the *Victory* was under construction at Chatham, for which Richard was commissioned to carry out the carved work.

Work began on the *Victory* in 1758, followed by a number of years spent weathering in frame before her eventual launch on 7 May 1765. This period in which her timbers were allowed to fully season undoubtedly added to her longevity and eventual use as Nelson's flagship 40 years later. She was to carry a group figurehead to personify the strength and greatness of the nation. The team were clearly daunted by the mass of work involved and sought assistance. William Savage, who had been employed as a carver at both Chatham and Sheerness, was well known to Richard, having worked alongside Abigail at those yards. Richard petitioned the Navy Board to allow him to take William into the partnership in order to complete the carved work to the ship, doubtless assisted by a team of lesser carvers and apprentices. From 1768 to 1769 Richard and Elizabeth assisted Thomas Burrough at the Deptford yard, by which time Richard must have been around 80 (Richard had also worked there in 1760 on the *Yarmouth*). William Savage succeeded to the post of master carver at Chatham on Richard's death in 1771. His

A model depicting the original figurehead for the *Victory* of 1765. Although this is attributed to William Savage, the contract for the ship's carved work was given to the partnership of Richard and Elizabeth Chichley, who took William into the partnership to assist with the carved work. The figurehead was replaced in 1802 to a design by the carver George Williams, which by the 1980s had come to the end of its life. The decision was then taken to replace it with a replica of Williams's figure in order to preserve the ship's appearance as at the Battle of Trafalgar. (National Maritime Museum L2400-003)

The stern of the 50-gun ship *Trusty*, built at Hilhouse yard, Bristol in 1782. Her ornamentation presents a superbly succinct composition, providing the perfect balance of ornamental motifs, complementing the graceful lines of the ship with uncluttered clarity. She was converted to a troop ship in 1799 with her armament reduced to 26 guns, but resumed service as a 50-gun ship in 1802. In 1807 she was hulked at Chatham where she served as a prison ship before being broken up in 1815.

widow Abigail and William Savage requested that outstanding payments were made out to them as partners; the records of Elizabeth's work at the yard seems to have ceased around 1777.

The Admiralty called on the services of merchant yards for contract shipbuilding during the constant years of war with France. As an example, *Trusty* was built at Hilhouse's yard at Bristol in 1781. The composition of her carving is typical of the larger rates from 1745 to 1790, which retain predominantly figurative work, well proportioned, and exhibiting superb artistry in their expressiveness and practical application. They are clearly visible from afar, while presenting a clean uncluttered line to the stern. Geometric designs were frequently used as an alternative to balustrades, with designs of oriental origins that soften the rigidity of Classical columns and mouldings. The ship follows the principles set out in the Admiralty order of 1737, which permitted the use of terms to decorate the fashion piece, while warriors in Classical attire form the quarter pieces. Foliate forms are less dominant; their inclusion recedes into the background, creating a balance with the figurative work. Such considerations make for a remarkably unified composition that fulfils its ultimate purpose, in presenting a picture of assured confidence in the abilities and intentions of the nation it represents.

By 1790 Neoclassical ornamentation was softening into what would become the Regency style, which reflected influences drawn from images that came into the public consciousness through Napoleon's Egyptian campaign and Nelson's victory at the Battle of the Nile (1798). The furniture-maker Thomas Sheraton (1751-1806) adapted the motifs popularised by Adam into a form that encompassed emerging fashions from France. Scrolling leaves and volutes were reintroduced to inject a feeling of

The stern of a model in the Rogers Collection of an East India Company ship of the late 1780s displaying late Neoclassical ornamentation that shows the influence of Sheraton in its use of scrolls and volutes.

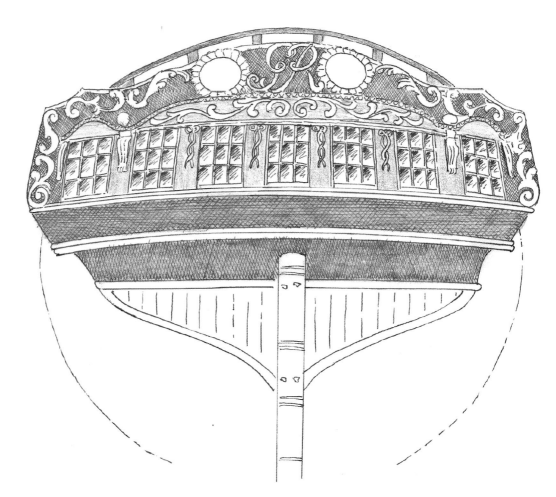

The stern of the 32-gun frigate *Triton*, built in 1796 by Barnard, Deptford. This highly experimental ship was built of fir, and surviving information suggests that it was not a success. The ship was hulked at Woolwich in 1800 before being moved to Plymouth in 1803, where she served as a receiving ship before being sold in 1814. Unfortunately, little is known of the carvers that worked for Barnard, but *Triton* displays decorative motifs consisting of scrolling foliage introduced to Neoclassicism creating an element of the Regency style.

naturalism to the otherwise formalised motifs derived from Egyptian influences.

The ornamentation of the East Indiaman from the 1780-1790 period shown here reveals a greater acceptance of Neoclassicism than her naval counterpart and, compared to the smaller frigate previously described, emphasis has been placed on the weight of the ornamentation to help balance its relationship with the scale of the vessel. The layout of the stern remains identical to a warship of the period, with a cove line below the tafferel, here decorated with a repeating pattern of patera mouldings. An egg and dart moulding follows the edge of the cove and although not drawn, is repeated around the windows. The ship also adopts the principle of terms to decorate the fashion piece, while large volutes are placed on the quarters, reflecting the refinements introduced by Sheraton.

The Regency period proper spans the years 1811 to 1820 when the Prince Regent ruled in place of his father (George III), but the Regency style is generally considered to have evolved in the 1790s and continued through to the end of King George IV's reign in 1830, marking an end not only to the Georgian era, but also to all ship-carving beyond figureheads and token gestures at stern ornament. The Regency style continued the Classical theme, but ironically drew on the Empire style of Napoleon while carefully omitting his personal devices, creating a sense of military uniformity that relied on the solidity of geometric forms. Furniture adopted the sabre style of leg, with lion's paw feet, with little to soften the harshness beyond scrolls and volutes. The complex curves of a ship's hull did little to attract the style beyond the application of random motifs to form compositions made up of of ill-fitting parts. The *Triton* of 1796 illustrates this, with ornamentation that lacks any sense of artistic cohesion. Enthusiasm within the Navy for advancement in the sciences had raced ahead of artistic concerns. It is unfortunate that the applied arts stuck firmly to fashions ashore, rather than embrace the emergence of new hull forms, upon which artistry could have been applied to a much greater effect. But development of the ship-carver's art was deemed to be of little importance. This led to the continued use ill-matched adoptions of existing motifs amidst the Navy's continued cuts in expenditure for such work.

In 1796 an order was issued directing the dockyards to 'explode' carved work aboard His Majesty's ships, both on those being built and those under repair. Although the order appears to have been disobeyed at every opportunity, busts rather than full figures were generally fitted to the smaller rates. A further order was issued the following year to ensure closer control on the yards' activities, directing the yards to submit designs for all carved work to heads and sterns. Continuing failure to comply with the spirit of the regulation forced the Board to issue a further order in 1799 for estimates to accompany the designs. Dockyards needed to be reminded of this again in 1806 due to their non-compliance, and by 1809 the Board had lost all patience, stating categorically that unauthorised carved work would not be paid for.

Carving was increasingly undertaken by contracted carvers as the Royal Navy ceased to employ their own craftsmen, leading to the total demise of naval carvers by around 1815. By this time the amount allowed for carving a figurehead for a 100-gun ship had been reduced from the £100 rate set in 1773 to £50 and for a 64-gun ship from £25 to £6 for an equivalent-sized 50-gun ship. With such meagre renumeration, the golden age of the ship-carver was at an end.

Carvers at Naval Dockyards 1615-1800

The majority of information is taken from P N Thomas's book British Figurehead and Ship Carvers, *to which additions have been made and dates altered following my own research.*
The dates in many cases indicate the period in which a carver worked at a certain yard,
and not an indication of continuous service at that location.

Master carvers to the crown
1661-1693	Henry Phillips
1693-1721	Grinling Gibbons
1721-1759	James Richards

Portsmouth
1660-1667	Samuel Ive (died 1667)
1668-1669	Robert Reynolds
1670-1705	Lewis Allen, master carver (died 1705)
1679	Lewis Sawyer
1696-1698	Thomas Coward
1705-1724	Robert Smith
1724-1753	William Smith
1760-1807	Cuthbert Mattingly (father of William)
1773-1807	William Mattingly (from the 1780s he was in partnership with Jones
1778-1790	[Christian name unknown] Jones (replaced by Hellyer in 1790)
1790	Edward Hellyer

Plymouth
1691	John Pippin
1691-1701	Anthony Allen (died 1701)
1701-1728	Phillip Read
1735-1736	Maynard Nicholls
1737-1760	Cuthbert Mattingly
1753-1770	Thomas Pierce (died 1770)
1770-1790	Samuel Dickerson
1790-1828	James Dickerson (master carver from 1794)
1797-1815	William Dickerson
1797-1815	Kingston Pavey
1832-1860	Frederick Dickerson

Deptford

1659-1679	John Leadman
1667-1721	Grinling Gibbons, master carver to the crown 1693-1721
1679-1705	Joseph Helby
1687-1692	John Fletcher
1693-1704	Mathew Fletcher
1696-	Richard Walker
1698	Abigail Chichley
1700-1715	Thomas Davidson, master carver 1710-1715 in partnership
1700-1715	John Carter, master carver 1710-1712 (died 1712)
1716-1739	Joseph Wade, master carver 1716-1739 (died 1743)
1740	[Christian name unknown] Goddard
1740-1788	Thomas Burrough, master carver at Deptford 1757-1788
1751-1760	Richard Chichley (*Buckingham* and *Yarmouth*)
1768-1769	Richard and Elizabeth Chichley
1797-1822	Nathaniel Keast
1797-1822	George Whitfield
1790-1810	William Montague Burrough

Woolwich

1608	Sebastian Vicars
1615-1666	Gerrard (Garret) Christmas
1659-1679	John Leadman
1679-1705	Joseph Helby
1687-1704	Mathew Fletcher
1710-1721	Robert Jones
1716-1739	Joseph Wade, master carver 1716-1739 (died 1743)
1740-1788	Thomas Burrough
1767-1777	Richard (until 1770) and Elizabeth Chichley (until 1777)
1790-1810	William Montague Burrough

Chatham

1593-1613	Sebastian Vicars
1613-1622	Gerrard (Garret) Christmas
1622-1654	John and Mathias Christmas
1654-1689	Thomas Fletcher
1687-1693	John Fletcher
1688-1713	Mathew (Matthias) Fletcher
1700-1706	Joseph Wymhurst/Mathew Fletcher partnership
1700-1710	Thomas Davidson (taken into partnership by Joseph Wymhurst)
1700-1710	John Carter (taken into partnership by Joseph Wymhurst)
1713-1737	Richard Chichley, carver at Chatham and Sheerness
1737-1743	Richard & Abigail Chichley
1744-1764	Richard Chichley, carver at Chatham and Sheerness
1764-1770	Richard & Elizabeth Chichley/William Savage (1765-6)
1765-1766	Edward Savage
1770-1777	William Savage, in partnership with Elizabeth Chichley
1777-1783	William Savage
1784-1820	George Williams
1797	Jeremiah Carraway, journeyman carver
1797	John Morley, journeyman carver

Sheerness

1693-1704	Mathew Fletcher
1713-1737	Richard Chichley, carver at Chatham and Sheerness
1740-1743	Abigail and Richard Chichley
1764-1770	Richard and Elizabeth Chichley
1770-1777	William Savage in partnership with Elizabeth Chichley
1777-1783	William Savage
1802-1820	George Williams

Carvers employed at merchant yards 1615-1800
where ships were built for the Navy under contract from the Admiralty

Blackwall

1666-1668	William Christmas

Deptford, Barnard & Co yard

1790	Batton & Glover

Harwich

1666-1668	Gerrard Christmas 1668
1668	James Christmas
1771	William Savage/Elizabeth Chichley

Bucklers Hard

1698	Richard Herring, master shipwright
1745	James Wyatt, master shipwright
1749-1789	Henry Adam, master shipwright and ship-carver
1790-1813	Balthasar Adam, master shipwright and ship-carver
1790-1813	Edward Adam, master shipwright and ship-carver

Kinsale

1696-1700	Henry Christmas, master carver
1696-1703	Abraham Hunt

Bristol

1666-1667	Richard Cord
1815	Robert Price Williams
1830	John Bailey
1868-1914	John Robert Anderson
1869	Williams and Anderson

Lydney

1666-1667	Richard Cord

Milford Haven   (Pembroke)

1800 ?	James Dickerson (worked mainly at Plymouth)

4

~Denmark~

Denmark's close association with the Netherlands through their trading links invariably led to many Dutch influences in architecture and the applied arts. The expansion of Copenhagen as the seat of power also led to the employment of Dutch craftsmen on the construction of its ships and buildings. An early example is Copenhagen's stock exchange, designed in 1613 by Hans van Steenwinkel the younger (1587-1639), where Mannerist motifs combine with figurative work of Renaissance demeanour, giving an ease of line compared to the intensity of pure Mannerism.

The decorative composition illustrates the move away from the earlier Mannerist style which originated in Italy as a development of Renaissance art, primarily to import an emotional response to the reasoned coolness of Classical harmony. In Northern Europe it developed ultimately into the bizarre extremes of Netherlandish Grotesque – perhaps as an outlet for expressing the emotional torture of troubled times, sweetened with the pleasures of the flesh or religious ecstasy. Its vibrant form ultimately became the forerunner of Baroque, but not before the over-indulgent imagery was restrained by a return to Classical principles, allowing elements of Renaissance composure to reappear.

A shift in artistic style invariably mirrors the changing mood of a nation. In 1625 Denmark joined the turmoil of the Thirty Years War (1618-48), withdrawing in 1629 after defeats by the Catholic League. In three ensuing wars between 1643 and 1658 the Danes suffered huge losses of territory to Sweden, leading to a lack of confidence in the government of the aristocracy, who attempted to limit the power of the king in order to protect their own interests.

King Frederick III took advantage of their unpopularity by forming an alliance with Holland, which led to a Danish victory in the next Swedish conflict of 1658. This success was attributed to the strength of the monarchy, which was made hereditary in 1661. The rule of the monarch became absolute, with many aspects of the autocratic French regime implemented in an effort to create a sense of order and stability. In practice, absolutist rule led to the loss of autonomy for outlying regions, as all decisions came from Copenhagen, leading to economic stagnation.

Although the decorative influence in Denmark can said to be Dutch, ship design was not entirely so. Shipwrights from England had been employed in Denmark since at least the 1570s, but after Christian IV came to the throne in 1596 he turned

Copenhagen Stock Exchange, 1613-31. The caryatid figures could transpose directly onto the brackets and mullions of a ship from the same period. (Author's collection)

Facade of a building in Assens, northern Jutland, from about 1624. Craftsmen and their patrons were not always ready to accept changing fashions, with the result that examples of Netherlandish-inspired Mannerism persisted into the 1630s in the form of grotesques intertwined with strap work. Elements of this are reminiscent of the Auricular style that remained popular in Holland through to the 1640s. (Author's collection)

to Scotland for expertise. In 1597 he appointed the Scots David Balfour and Daniel Sinclair as master shipwrights, and they dominated Danish naval construction until the 1630s. A set of ship's plans from the period illustrates Balfour's skill, but unfortunately give no indication of the decoration of the ship. In 1645, after consultation with Charles I of England, Christian appointed an Englishman, James Robbins, who built the 100-gun ship *Sophia Amalia* in Norway as part of the Danish-Norwegian fleet. A model of the ship survives in the Norwegian naval museum at Horten displaying decorative compositions in the Renaissance style, where panels of scrolling acanthus adorn a stern which takes the English form. The figurehead is on a grand scale, depicting a charioteer in a bright red coat, his gilded chariot drawn by two powerful horses, similarly gilded.

He went on to build the *Tre Løver* (Three Lions) at the Bremerholm yard, Copenhagen in 1657. In the same year the shipwright Thomas Lindsey is also recorded as working in Copenhagen. The following year he filled Robbins's now vacant post at Christiania (modern Oslo) in Norway. Well-executed and finely detailed carvings of lions reputedly from the ship, survive in the Royal Danish Naval Museum (Orlogsmuseet) in Copenhagen. Baltasar Ellertsen is recorded as the master carver at Bremerholm in 1652, so they are possibly by his hand or that of the assistant carver who is recorded as Lauritz Hansen Worm. The ship was present at the Battle of Køge Bay (1677) after which she served as accommodation for workers at the Christiansø yard until she sank in 1686.

In 1663 the Norwegian Cort Adeler was appointed General Admiral to the fleet and given the task of rebuilding the navy. Having previously served as a naval officer in the Netherlands, he had ten years earlier arranged for the loan of Dutch ships to the Danish fleet. Having first-hand experience of Dutch administration and familiarity with their ships, his reorganisation programme was consequently influenced by their methods. The fleet was fitted out with the help of the Dutch navy and the employment of their shipwrights. Greater emphasis was placed on this task when Christian V ascended the throne in 1670, which hastened much needed preparation for the Scanian War of 1675-1679 in which Sweden, allied to France, opposed Holland, Spain and Denmark. During the conflict the Danes attempted, unsuccessfully, to regain territory lost to Sweden prior to 1658, but their navy proved its worth in the Battle of Køge Bay when it won its first major victory without calling on Dutch assistance. During the battle the Swedish ship *Den Flyvende Ulv* was captured and later served in the Danish Asiatic Company, voyaging to Tranquebar in 1681.

With renewed confidence in the navy's effectiveness, the yards were enlarged to support a rebuilding programme. The port of Copenhagen was extended northwards to replace Bremerholm with the building of Nyholm in 1680 and the enlargement of Holmen to form the royal dockyard of Copenhagen. The Norwegian yard of Frederikshald was moved to Christiansand in 1687 and a navy yard established at the trading town of Glückstadt in the Danish-held territory of

Pencil and pen wash sketch by Willem van de Velde the younger depicting the 63-gun Danish ship *Hannibal* of 1646, designed by James Robbins. She was renamed *Svanen* in 1658. (National Maritime Museum PZ7256)

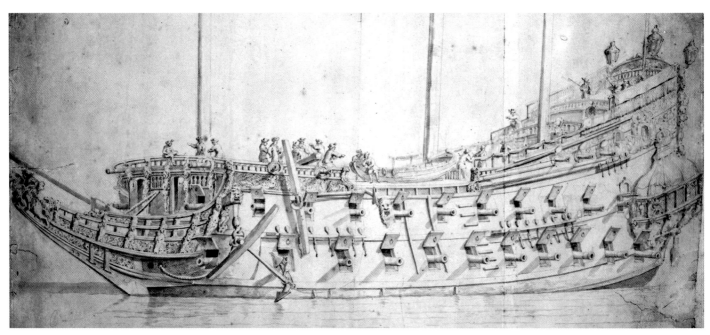

The Toll house at Glückstadt. (Author's collection)

Holstein, where customs duties were levied on ships bound for Hamburg.

During the rebuilding programme the anchor forge at Bremerholm was converted into Holmen's church, where Ellertsen's colleague Lauritz Hansen Worm was buried in 1674. His son Tyge Lauritzen Worm had been apprenticed to the yard, and in 1669 received his first assignment to execute the carved work for a frigate and a First Rate ship under construction at the Norwegian yard of Hovedøya near Christiania. Four assistants travelled with him to complete the task. Tyge Worm later returned to Copenhagen: a natural assumption would be around the time of his father's death. He was serving as master carver there by 1687 and records from 1694 describe him as a royal carver, indicating that he may also have undertaken commissions for the royal household. A draught of the frigate *Hummeren* of 1664 illustrates the style of ship favoured by Admiral Adeler, with typical Dutch lines and the style of decoration that would have been executed by Danish carvers of the period, still heavily influenced by the Dutch style.

It is not known if Ellertsen or Worm carried out commissions for the church, but with so few examples of ship decoration surviving from the period, their contemporaries in the ecclesiastical world can provide a reasonably accurate record of the style of carving that would also have been found on ships of the period, when journeyman carvers would often seek employment in both domains. For example, Peder Jensen Kolding worked as a journeyman carver between 1635 and 1675, and surviving pieces of his work provide a useful record of the artistic style as it developed from Mannerist to Baroque.

The year 1686 saw the arrival in Denmark of Francis Sheldon. Having made his reputation in England with the successful *Naseby*, Sheldon went

The stern of *Hummeren*, built at Glückstad and launched in 1664, displays the typically Dutch *slijngerlist* and generously curvaceous proportions to the scrolling forms, which have progressed from the Renaissance-inspired compositions towards the Baroque. The blank area of the tafferel would presumably have contained a painted composition.

Support brackets to the pulpit of Horsens Church, Denmark, carved by Peder Jensen Kolding in 1667-1670. The Renaissance style of his carving draws inspiration from Dutch examples of the genre. The dominant motifs of Mannerism have here subsided beneath the composure of Renaissance structure. The figures have in turn begun to take on the naturalistic expressiveness of Baroque. Kolding, who was an active carver from 1635, gradually developed his Renaissance style to embrace the Baroque.

The curving structure of the pulpit perfectly matches that of a ship's stern, with the caryatid figures forming ornamental brackets, the style and form of which could be directly transposed to the stern of the *Hummeren*. (Author's collection reproduced by courtesy of Horsens Church, Denmark)

on to design ships for the Swedish navy (an account of his long career there will follow in the next section). He was by all accounts not the easiest of characters to endure, having strong opinions that he was not afraid to voice. Denmark's desire to employ him was certainly due to his reputation as an excellent designer (in the Scanian War the Danes considered the Sheldon-designed Swedish ships superior to their own more lightly built Dutch-style ships). His immediate acceptance resulted from a feeling of indignation following various confrontations with his previous employers.

His arrival in Copenhagen came at a time when Denmark was striving to develop its own indigenous shipbuilding style in an effort to end the continuous debates as to whose designs were the best to emulate. The keel of the 84-gun ship *Printz Frederik* was on the stocks when Sheldon was assigned to complete the vessel, which he naturally did in the English manner. The desire of the Danish admiralty was clearly to educate its nationals in the merits and shortcomings of the ships from other nations in order to improve on their designs. Sheldon's detailed terms of employment stipulated that he must choose a suitable Danish apprentice from the yard, to personally pass on his skills. He was further

required to prepare draughts of all vessels (creating the first record of ships' plans for the Danish navy); any design put forward by Sheldon was first to be approved by the king. In short, he was to be obedient to their commands.

Sheldon's rigid certainty of the merit of his own work soon showed itself to be unbending to the ideas of others. In his next project he was required to work with Admiral Henrik Span (1634-1694) in the rebuilding of *Christianus Quintus*. A votive model of this ship is displayed at the naval church in Holmen. Although constructed in 1904, it was created from the original drawings, to give a good representation of her decorative work, which is purely French in composition and layout of her galleries.

Sheldon insisted on English sheathing methods, leading to heated disagreements with Span, who was himself a competent ship designer but an adherent to Dutch construction methods. Their differing views, or incompatible natures, resulted in an end to their attempted cooperation. Sheldon's stubborn nature was, however, offset by a great talent, still capable of innovative designs – aimed, ironically, at the destruction of his previous employers – in the form of bomb ketches, and also in the ability of his first design to act as landing craft to allow the speedy disembarkation of troops.

With the many years of war at an end and the power of the monarchy established, in Denmark efforts were made to rebuild the economy and confidence of the people. The East India Company was granted a new charter, the arts began to flourish with the building of the Charlottenborg Palace, its decorative forms in the guise of the Dutch-inspired derivative of Italian Baroque. The style also persisted in ship decoration through to the 1680s, as displayed on this model of the *Elephanten* of 1687.

Sheldon's model of *Elephanten*, showing carving to the quarter gallery, gun ports, main channel and frieze work between the rails. (By courtesy of the Danish Naval Museum, Copenhagen)

An elephant forms the central motif of the tafferel held by his chains. The Elephant is the highest Order of the Danish realm, and as such the motif appears on many ships. He is flanked by a composition of palm trees and surmounted by two coloured putti, reflecting the East India Company's influence through the import of exotic goods and imagery (the DAC had its charter renewed when Christian V ascended the throne in 1670). His C5 cypher forms the central cartouche below the elephant. (By courtesy of the Danish Naval Museum, Copenhagen)

His next assignment took the form of a royal yacht armed as a frigate, the *Elephanten* launched in 1687.

A model made by Sheldon in order to gain the king's approval survives, complete with its carvings to the stern and quarter galleries. Tyge Lauritzen Worm was master carver at Holmen when the ship was built, assisted by journeyman carvers. He submitted designs to Sheldon, which were reluctantly accepted, indicating that cooperation between the two was expected, before the model was presented to the king for final approval. From 1703 *Elephanten* served as a station ship guarding the sea area known as the Store Bælt (Great Belt). However, in 1720 while attempting to reach her home port before the onset of winter, she became icebound near Stubbekøbing, where she was crushed by the ice and sank.

Under royal patronage the arts began to flourish. Construction of the Charlottenborg Palace began in 1672 in an area of Copenhagen redeveloped as the King's New Square. Originally known as the Gyldenløve Palace, it was the residence of Ulrik Frederik Gyldenløve, the illegitimate son of Christian V's father, King Frederik III.

Sheldon's model illustrates the full extent of carved work that was lavishly applied to such a prestigious vessel, where its appearance viewed from on board was of equal importance. (By courtesy of the Danish Naval Museum, Copenhagen)

It was in turn inherited by Christian's illegitimate son, Ulrik Christian Gyldenløve (1678-1719).

Ulrik Christian Gyldenløve followed a career in the navy, training as an officer in Holland before returning to Denmark in 1695. He was awarded the Order of the Elephant and in 1697, when just 19 years old, was made admiral of the fleet. Three years later he was in command of the entire Danish navy, with his ships poised to attack the might of the Swedish fleet. Fearing the Sound would fall too heavily under the control of Denmark, England and Holland then joined Sweden, allowing the Swedish army to invade Zealand. After the bombardment of Copenhagen by the Swedes, the balance was in danger of swinging the other way, so the allies withdrew their support, effectively creating a truce that led to the signing of a peace treaty and the withdrawal of Swedish troops.

The Charlottenborg Palace was designed by Lambert van Haven (born 1630). Having studied in Italy, his form of decoration favours Italian Baroque but retains distinctively Dutch elements, creating a style that can also be seen on *Elephanten*. Swags of exotic fruit reminiscent of Quellin's designs drape sumptuously across the counter. Mullions to the lights take the form of caryatid figures similar to those in the Kronborg Castle fireplace illustrated here, although they are of a later date.

Sheldon went on to design a further five vessels, but unfortunately little information survives on the carving of these ships, with the exception of the *Tre Løver* launched in 1689. A model exists of this 70/74-gun ship showing details of the carvings. The stern incorporates a very low tafferel for the period rising only slightly above the stern lights. It is surmounted by a cartouche bearing the cypher of King Christian V supported by two lions *couchant* as they are called in heraldry – that is, sitting to maintain the low profile of the tafferel. The cartouche and other decorations, consisting mainly of scrolling acanthus, are greatly inspired by the Italian Baroque, with little Dutch influence in evidence

His next ship, the 44-gun frigate *Kronan*, was launched in 1690. The ship-carver was instructed to carry out such carved work as Sheldon deemed necessary, implying that he had control over the composition, if not the subject matter, and may explain why the *Tre Løver* carries the style of carving favoured in England. This was followed in 1691 by the 36-gun frigate *Oldenborg*.

The year 1690 was a turning point in the

Detail taken from a fireplace surround in Kronborg Castle, Helsingør, possibly designed by Hans van Steenwinkel who was employed at the castle from 1635 following the completion of Copenhagen's stock exchange. They represent the style of caryatid displayed on the *Elephanten*. Interestingly, the fireplace is situated in the chambers used for an extended period by the heir apparent, Christian IV's son, who would have been king when Sheldon presented the model to him. (Author's collection reproduced by courtesy of the Danish Maritime Museum, Helsingør)

Model of *Tre Løver* (Three Lions) designed by Francis Sheldon in 1689. She proved to be a good sailer and served in the navy until broken up in 1729. (Danish Naval Museum Copenhagen)

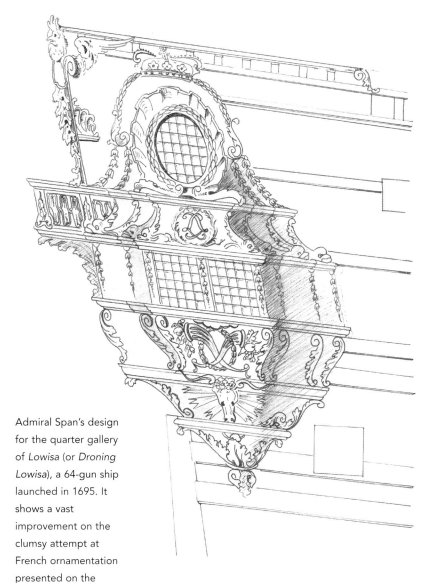

Admiral Span's design for the quarter gallery of *Lowisa* (or *Droning Lowisa*), a 64-gun ship launched in 1695. It shows a vast improvement on the clumsy attempt at French ornamentation presented on the *Dannebroge*, with a greater sense of cohesiveness in the placement and use of the various stock motifs.

Admiral Span appointed the mathematician Ole Judichær (1661-1729) to assist him with his designs, the first ship to be built under the new regime being the *Dannebroge*. This 94-gun ship was launched in 1692, but her career was tragically short-lived. As part of Admiral Gyldenløve's fleet she fought in the Great Northern War (1707-1720). Following an engagement with the Swedish fleet in Køge Bay (1710), her rigging caught fire; an hour later she exploded and was lost together with 600 men.

Having appointed Ole Judichær chief constructor in 1692, the final design of Admiral Span was the 64-gun *Lowisa*, which was launched in 1695. The designs he produced adopted many French fashions, particularly the layout of the stern and quarter galleries. Although decorated with purely French-inspired motifs, the *Dannebroge* in particular lacks the fundamental principles of composition required to create the brilliant interplay of form and vitality present in the French style.

While the Dutch-inspired decorative arts remained popular in mainstream society, French fashions were being introduced through the Danish court's adoption of the example set by Versailles. With Christian V still responsible for the final acceptance of ships' draughts, ornamentation presented in the French style was sure to find favour. These early attempts to embrace a new style, in what was also a novel design system, to some extent capture the enthusiasm of what must have been exciting times.

This aside, the resulting compositions project an experimental air through lack of knowledge. Admiral Span must have been aware of this shortcoming, for in 1693 he sent a party of naval officers to study abroad (among them was the then 15-year-old Gyldenløve). They were accompanied by the Danish artist Hendrich Krock (1671-1738), with the specific brief to make sketches of the ornamentation of French ships. Krock produced over thirty drawings detailing the ornamentation of eleven newly built French ships of war. Gyldenløve later accompanied Krock to Italy to further their knowledge of the Baroque, which became the major influence on Krock's work. He travelled to Italy again in 1703 and on his return to Copenhagen was named painter to the royal court in 1706.

Such assignments abroad were to become an obligatory part of the training for shipbuilders and naval architects at the new naval academy

organisation of shipbuilding for the Danish navy. The admiralty instigated changes intended to ensure that future ships would be constructed without the aid of foreign designers. Admiral Span was appointed overseer of all ship construction in what was to become effectively a nationalised yard. The English building methods employed by Sheldon continued to be a point of contention with Admiral Span, despite their often proven success. Sheldon offered his resignation on the grounds that having reached the age of 78 he wished to return to England. He had made enquiries in England a year earlier with this in mind and in January of 1690 accepted a post to source timber in Wexford for the construction of a new vessel. This was to be his last move. Like so many of his contemporaries, he was actively engaged in his career until the final days of his life. He died at Chatham in 1692, having reached the age of 80.

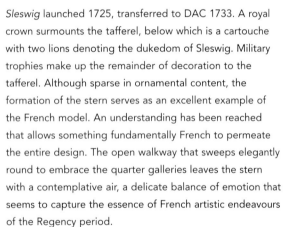

Sleswig launched 1725, transferred to DAC 1733. A royal crown surmounts the tafferel, below which is a cartouche with two lions denoting the dukedom of Sleswig. Military trophies make up the remainder of decoration to the tafferel. Although sparse in ornamental content, the formation of the stern serves as an excellent example of the French model. An understanding has been reached that allows something fundamentally French to permeate the entire design. The open walkway that sweeps elegantly round to embrace the quarter galleries leaves the stern with a contemplative air, a delicate balance of emotion that seems to capture the essence of French artistic endeavours of the Regency period.

Wax maquette of a lion in the British style, here holding the shield of Sleswig. While the stern of the *Sleswig* remained faithful to the French fashion, the figurehead takes the form of a lion, a common motif on English ships of the period, but less popular in France. This was due mainly to the naming policy of their ships, which required more explicit representations to personify a specific quality, and later under Napoleon the nation's adoption of the eagle rather than lion as a national emblem. It is interesting to note that when a country's leader aspires to the status of emperor, he invariably adopts an all-powerful policy of aggression and chooses an eagle, while those who maintain a constitutional monarchy tend to adopt the lion as a national emblem. (By courtesy of the Danish Maritime Museum, Helsingør)

established by Ole Judichær in 1701. Considering his initial employment was that of a mathematician, to be given the position of chief constructor and naval architect should have been sufficient to fill his time, but Judichær also served as an admiral with a seat on the admiralty board and was in charge of the dockyard at Holmen. He now also gave instruction at the academy. In this context, his endeavours to fulfil the additional task of designing ornamentation have to be admired. Having forgone the opportunity to study in France (owing to the outbreak of the Great Northern War), he had instead to rely on the drawings of Krock.

Judichær's resultant compositions inevitably lack the cohesive quality that is only achieved when the principles of a given genre are mastered. Conscious of the commissioners' wish to create thoroughly Danish ships, a number of his designs show a degree of artistic inventiveness as he dutifully incorporates motifs of national identity within his compositions (see colour plate 14).

Tyge Worm's position as master carver was largely self-appointed, helped apparently by a degree of self-importance. He appears to have left work in the hands of journeyman carvers employed at his whim, for in 1685 he received a

Detail from a relief carved panel over the entrance to Kronborg Castle, providing a good example of the composition and style of carving that would have been used on the tafferel of *Sleswig* when launched in 1725. The central cartouche in this example is inscribed with the cypher of King Frederik IV (1699-1730). (Author's collection)

reprimand, instructing him that in future he was to present his workforce to the deputy every Wednesday and Saturday to establish a workload schedule. Further more, Tyge was expected to attend his workshop and carry out his duties with greater zeal. The situation seems not to have improved, or the admiralty were simply seeking to find further justification for the actions they were about to take, for in 1692 he was further reprimanded on the grounds of unsatisfactory supervision within the workshop and the abuse of his position in dealing with his fellows. The position in which he was placed effectively forced him to resign.

The motivation for this may have been their desire to limit the amount of decorative work on ships for practical and possibly financial considerations. The royal chancery issued an order in 1692 to the effect that 'ornaments are no longer to be made so large because of their weight and partly because of the rain and sea causing rot.' It goes on to say that 'ornamentation is to consist of lists of better shape in naval fashion', suggesting a greater attention to practicality of design. The English order of 1703 makes reference to a very similar requirement, where 'lists' are defined as mouldings fabricated in a joiner's works. With the resulting reduction in carvings, the post of master carver was abolished on the argument that carving could be completed by journeyman carvers. Management of the workshop was handed over to the current foreman carver, Peder Michelsen (16??-1712).

The often fragmented appearance of Judichær's designs may be due in part to his adherence to the order on the use of lists. There does, however, appear to be little reduction in the amount of carving. In 1695 Michelsen was promoted to the re-established position of master carver, and so the old order and perceived importance of carving was restored. During his term in office Ole Judichær was able to call upon the artistic skills of Peder Michelsen, who appears to have had the ability to produce sketches, if not the academic learning with regard to the subject matter of ancient mythology. With large civic and royal building programmes under way in the city, the journeyman carpenters would have been valuable employees, not only for their skill, but possible knowledge of foreign fashions. The position of master carver passed from Peder Michelsen to Nils Olsen in 1712, who then held the post until 1721.

The marriage of King Frederik IV in April 1721 to Anna Sophie Reventlow called for a ship to be named in her honour. The king naturally demanded the highest standard of ornamentation in the style of French Baroque. Imagery was to include a double portrait and appropriate mythological iconography to symbolise the qualities of his radiant queen. The daunting responsibility for the task fell on Judichær and his master carver Nils Olsen, who in the same year was succeeded by Anders Bruun.

Aware of their limitations, they prudently sought – or perhaps were given – assistance in creating the compositions by the artist and sculptor Johann Christian Heimbrod (16??-1733). The resultant composition stands as the first truly accomplished representation of French Baroque ornamentation on a Danish ship. Launched in 1722 as the *Dronning Anna Sophia*, the masterful quality of her ornamentation satisfied the requirements of the king, whilst remaining practical in its application, a requirement the loyal Judichær would have deemed necessary to fulfil his obligations to the admiralty.

The less prestigious commissions that followed were completed in a capable manner by Bruun. One example is the *Sleswig*, designed by Ole Judichær in 1725 and refitted as a merchantman in 1733. With her armament reduced to 36 guns, she entered the service of the Danish Asiatic Company and made her first voyage to Macao in the same year, returning to Copenhagen in 1735. Part of the cargo on her second voyage (1736-7) included Chinese furniture for the embellishment of Frederiksborg Slot. This castle, dating from 1560, was enlarged to designs by Hans and Lorenz van Steenwinckel from 1602 to 1620. By the 1720s it had become famous for housing the royal family's art collection, to which was added sculptural work by Heimbrod in the formal Baroque garden. Heimbrod was appointed sculptor to the royal court in 1724, having previously completed many prestigious commissions, including the tomb of Admiral Gyldenløve. He went on to create the carved work for the great hall at Hisholm Castle and the royal palace in Copenhagen.

The success of Judichær's academy was to become the source of his own downfall. His policy of sending aspiring students abroad continued, four of whom were to become important figures in future ship design:

Knud Nielsen Benstrup	(1692-1742)
Lauritz (Lars) Bragenes	(1687-1729)
Nicolay Peter Judichær, son of Ole Judichær	(1705-1748)
Diderik de Thurah	(1704-1788)

In 1723 they were sent to study in France and Britain. On their return they added their voices to the concerns already expressed by Gyldenløve regarding the merit of Ole Judichær's designs – particularly their draught of water, which was something of a compromise to deal with the differing conditions in shallow Danish and deeper Norwegian waters. Furthermore, the debate about British versus French design still wrangled on within a hierarchy of naval commanders vying for positions of power.

In 1727 Johan Anthon Paulsen (1687-1736) was placed in command of the yard at Holmen. His arrival marked a period when the admiralty

was keen to adopt British ship design principles. He played a part in the design of Judichær's next ship, the 80-gun *Sophia Magdalena*, for which Anders Bruun submitted two alternative designs for the decoration. One followed the French style, complete with bottle-shaped quarter galleries and open walkway placed beyond the line of the stern, while the second conformed to British conventions in both decoration and gallery layout.

The drawings of Anders Bruun clearly demonstrate his competence in replicating the ornamentation and gallery layout of a British ship. The stern of *Sophia Magdalena* displays the typical cove line terminating at the fashion pieces, with smaller arches connecting to the quarter pieces. Large sculptural figures decorate the quarter pieces, below which is the only departure from the British convention – the inclusion of a second figure, which rarely appears in this position on a British ship of the 1720s. Generally, figurative work to the quarter pieces of three-decked ships terminated at the upper deck. When an additional figure was added to the middle deck, they terminated at the breast rail and would not extend on to the counter. The style of this figure is also very French.

Bruun's alternative design in the French fashion displays a faithful representation with regard to the general layout of the galleries and provides a reasonable standard of composition; but the demeanour of his subjects have a weighty bearing, lacking the necessary finesse associated with the original French. The prevailing desire for French fashions seemingly overlooked such shortcomings, as the ship was launched in 1727 with this design. The effect on Bruun's reputation was

Frederiksborg Slot, with statue in French Baroque style. (Author's collection)

General layout of Heimbrod's design for the stern of *Printz Fridorich* (1727)

Quarter gallery of *Sophia Magdalena* launched 1727; a sketch by the author giving an impression of the carved work as designed by Anders Bruun. The layout of the galleries agrees very well with English conventions. The authenticity of his subject matter and the style in which it is depicted are considerably better than Heimbrod, who, despite his best endeavours, is unable or unwilling to suppress an innate sense of Frenchness in his style.

to cast him as a poor exponent of the French style, rather than the highly talented carver in the British (Italian Baroque) style. He was to live under the shadow of Heimbrod, who continued to fulfil the desire for French decoration.

Ole Judichær's authority was further undermined when Rasmus Krag (1677-1755), a naval officer who had trained under Judichær, also submitted designs for a 72-gun ship in the British fashion. The returning officers Bragenes and Thura, having studied in Britain, also submitted designs in the British manner, but it was Krag's plans that were approved.

The ornamentation for his ship was created by Heimbrod. The very British depiction of Hercules triumphant with his club decorates the quarter piece, between which the gallery layout follows the British fashion, with balustrading to the open gallery and the use of pilasters, all of which are set in a radiating manner. Beyond this, the decoration is purely an attempt to adapt French ornamentation to a British stern. The compositional make up, subject matter and style of motif all emanate from French Baroque. Krag's ship, the *Printz Friderich*, was launched in December of 1727, at which point Ole Judichær was dismissed.

Decoration to the counter of *Printz Friderich*

consists of scrolling acanthus transmuting into fantastical figures, all of which carries the hallmark of Le Brun's reworking of earlier grotesque designs. The lower counter is decorated in painted drapery with a pelmet of lambrequin, a device frequently used by Bérain. The central cartouche inscribed with the vessel's name was a device introduced by the French and would not have appeared on a British ship, where the convention of placing the ship's name on the stern did not come into effect until 1771. In 1772 the use of a cartouche or compartment was prohibited on the grounds that it 'Frenchified' the king's ships; henceforth the name was painted across the counter of British ships.

The lanterns display an elegance of French design, surmounted by crowns in the style adopted by France and Denmark. A representation of Printz Friderich forms the centrepiece of the tafferel, his power magnified by the inclusion of a baldachin. This form of canopy became a favoured motif of Bérain to highlight the importance of its occupant. He is supported by voluptuous attendants that represent Abundance and Peace, who are in turn supported by trophies depicting military might. Such panoplies are reminiscent of the symbolic style of Le Brun.

During the building of *Printz Friderich* Rasmus Krag's ability came into question and when he submitted the plans for his following ship, they were examined by the returning officers, who considered the design to be unsatisfactory. They succeeded in convincing Paulsen to abandon the project and to undertake, instead, a design by Benstrup.

Following Krag's fall from favour, the post of master constructor was awarded in 1729 to Benstrup. In the same year Bruun was also dismissed and the post of master carver awarded to Heimbrod. The following year saw the launch of Benstrup's 60-gun ship *Tre Løver*. His strict adherence to French construction methods bought him little support from the admiralty, whose officers still favoured British ships; ornamentation was presumably of secondary importance to them. When the British-trained Bragenes proposed designs for a similar sized ship in the British manner, they were eagerly approved. Sadly Bragenes died the same year, but his ship, the *Svanen*, was completed by his colleague Thura, allowing both the *Svanen* and *Tre Løver* to be launched in March of 1730.

Benstrup called on Heimbrod to assist him with the decoration of his ship, which resulted in a superb example of French Baroque ornamentation. The drawings that survive show a design that could have come from the pen of Bérain, and may indeed be so. During his training Benstrup studied at Brest, where he made faithful copies of the decoration to many French ships, possibly directly from the plans of Bérain, as they are complete with his device of showing two alternative compositions on the same elevation. Benstrup's sketches of *Le Mercure* contain many details that have been copied directly onto the stern of *Tre Løver*. Benstrup also studied at the Academie de Beaux Arts in Paris, returning in 1724, providing him with a grounding in the French Baroque that would have steered much of the decision-making in the ornamental design. The connection with *Le Mercure* also explains the somewhat outdated style of decoration, as the French ship was launched in 1696. The figurehead displays the French penchant for a grandiose display, depicting Mars, the Roman god of war, with sword in hand and cape billowing behind.

Heimbrod's maquette, reputedly for the figurehead of *Tre Løver* (1730) depicted as Mars, a motif and decorative style that would not have been out of place in the court of Louis XIV. The ship also adopts French principles in the design of its head, stern and quarter galleries, in a decorative style that embodies the influence of Bérain (although France herself had by now moved on to the Regency style). (By courtesy of the Danish Naval Museum, Copenhagen)

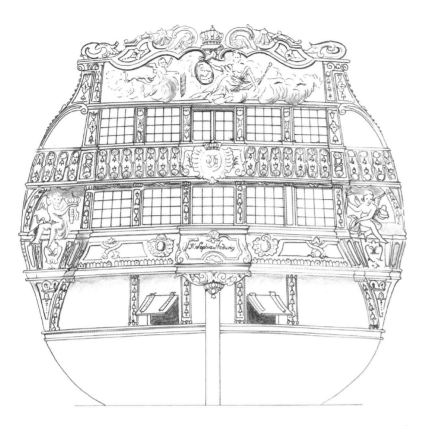

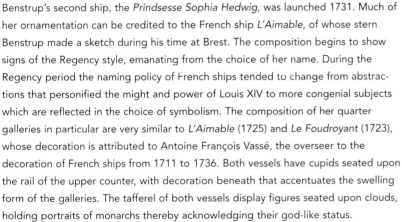

Sketch to indicate the general layout of the stern and quarter galleries to *Prindsesse Sophia Hedwig* of 1731, designed by Knud N Benstrup with ornamentation by Christian Heimbrod. The typical French layout is not dissimilar to *Sleswig* of 1725.

Benstrup's second ship, the *Prindsesse Sophia Hedwig*, was launched 1731. Much of her ornamentation can be credited to the French ship *L'Aimable*, of whose stern Benstrup made a sketch during his time at Brest. The composition begins to show signs of the Regency style, emanating from the choice of her name. During the Regency period the naming policy of French ships tended to change from abstractions that personified the might and power of Louis XIV to more congenial subjects which are reflected in the choice of symbolism. The composition of her quarter galleries in particular are very similar to *L'Aimable* (1725) and *Le Foudroyant* (1723), whose decoration is attributed to Antoine François Vassé, the overseer to the decoration of French ships from 1711 to 1736. Both vessels have cupids seated upon the rail of the upper counter, with decoration beneath that accentuates the swelling form of the galleries. The tafferel of both vessels display figures seated upon clouds, holding portraits of monarchs thereby acknowledging their god-like status.

Heimbrod is also credited with the decorative composition of the *Svanen*, which conforms very well to British conventions, although close inspection of the motifs and demeanour of the figures betrays a feeling of softness and delicacy that is too French to be a British interpretation of the Baroque. The counter depicts a scene, possibly painted, which would accord with British style, consisting of swans and water nymphs frolicking in the water, but with a central cartouche inscribed with the vessel's name – by now a firmly rooted feature in the composition of Danish sterns. The employment of a lion for the figurehead follows the British fashion, but displays the subdued appearance of a faithful pet rather than the ferocious beast depicted on British ships. On the few occasions that lions appear on French ships, their demeanour generally projects an aloof sense of superiority.

With a fleet that now contained models of British and French designs by the old school of Judichær/Krag and the new regime, the time had come for some comparative sea trials. Any expectations of settling the British versus French debate were soon dissipated by the conclusion that each had qualities to commend them. Benstrup's *Tre Løver* was, however, felt to have the best sailing qualities, with the *Svanen* being a steadier gun platform, particularly in heavy weather.

Following the perceived success of his French design, the cooperation between Benstrup and Heimbrod continued with the 60-gun ship *Prindsesse Sophia Hedwig* in 1731. Heimbrod went on producing superb examples of French Baroque ornamentation up to his untimely death in 1733. Benstrup's work, however, fell under the increasingly critical scrutiny of the admiralty, whose officers, while accepting Benstrup's ship to be the better sailer, maintained the view that British designs were the superior ships of war, provoking the question as to which was the preferable quality.

They were provided with ammunition when Benstrup's 90-gun ship *Christianus Sextus* was launched in 1732 and her draught of water proved greater than calculated. In 1734 Benstrup was suspended from his duties while the admiralty investigated complaints about his competence.

Benstrup may have lost favour with the navy but the Danish East India Company (DAC) were keen to engage his services, requesting him to submit plans for a well-armed ship that was still capable of carrying a substantial cargo. His initial draught for a 36-gun ship met with their approval, but lacked decorative details beyond the inclusion of a lion figurehead. This, he explained, was on account of the vessel not having been named, indicating the degree of interaction that existed between the ship's initial design and the decorative scheme. The ship, eventually named *Kongen af Denmark*, was the first to be launched from the company's own yard at Christianshavn in 1735, successfully completing her first voyage to China in 1737. Unfortunately, details of the ornamentation are not known to have been recorded, but it is clear that exchange of labour between the DAC and naval yards would have resulted in a similarity of carved work.

Once more the royal yard found itself without a master constructor or carver. To continue with the construction programme the commander of the navy, F Dannerskiold-Samsø (1703-1770), turned to Diderik de Thurah (1704-1788), the officer who had studied in Britain and gained some success in completing the *Svanen*. The first design to be completed by Thurah was *Fyen*. Launched in 1736, she represents a complete departure from the slavish copies of French or British designs with regard to the outward expression of her ornamentation and gallery formation. She adopted a stern with an elliptical profile, a shape that began to appear on Swedish ships from the 1730s, heralding what would become known as the Baltic Stern.

Despite such innovations, her sailing qualities were disappointing. She was found to be too heavily rigged and alterations were made, but she still heeled to such an extent that the lower gun ports could only be opened in calm weather (not an uncommon situation on British ships, but one which experienced crews coped with). His second ship also failed to live up to expectations, after which his future designs were completed under supervision. Dannerskiold-Samsø must have seen

Stern and quarter galleries of the French *L'Aimable*. This may be Benstrup's original drawing. (Danish Archives, Copenhagen)

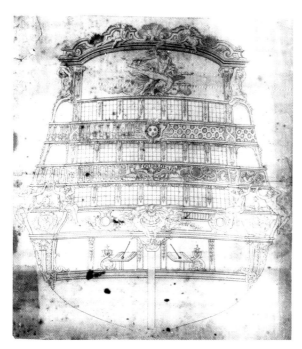
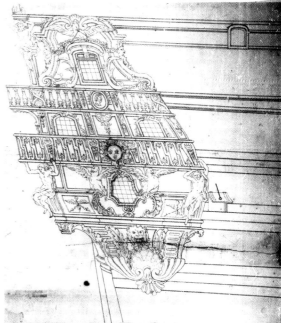

Stern and quarter galleries of the French *Foudroyant*. (Danish Archives, Copenhagen)

some potential in his work, for on his recommendation Thurah was appointed master constructor in 1739 following the dismissal of Benstrup.

The position of master carver was filled by the appointment of Just Wiedewelt (1677-1757). His father, Hans Wiedewelt, was an architect and stone mason who had emigrated to Denmark from the

The DAC company's yard still stands in Strandegade, Copenhagen. The casual passerby would pay little attention to the bollards that protect the entrance of the central archway, which are in fact cannons from a former ship, serving as a reminder of the many vessels that once unloaded their cargo into the surrounding warehouses. A similar building continues to the left of the arch, both displaying much carved stonework, alterations and additions to which make accurate dating unreliable, but still conveying the sense of prestige and wealth that was generated by the Company. (Author's collection)

German town of Schleitz. Just began a five-year apprenticeship in 1692 with the sculptor Thomas Quellin (1661-1709). As son of the famous Artus Quellin II, Thomas had himself emigrated to Denmark to oversee commissions for his father, but soon established an independent reputation with commissions such as the memorial tombs to Ulrik Frederik Gyldenløve and Cort Adeler. Just assisted Thomas on many funeral monuments and, on the completion of his apprenticeship, was accepted into the workshop of Thomas's father in Antwerp.

Having gained a year's experience with Artus Quellin II, he travelled on to study in Paris, returning to Copenhagen in 1707. In the same year Thomas departed for Antwerp, where he died two years later. Just also left Copenhagen to continue his studies in France and Italy, finally returning in 1715 to become sculptor to the Danish royal court. His first commission was a bust of King Frederik V and Queen Louise, followed by an altar for the garrison church and the Copenhagen Castle chapel, establishing a reputation as a fine sculptor in stone and wood. In 1726 he married Birgitte Lauridsdatter; their son Johannes (1731-1802) followed in his father's footsteps, becoming the most famous sculptor of his age in Denmark. Johannes's success unfortunately came to a tragic end in 1802 when he drowned – a suspected suicide bought about by events in later life that left him in a state of abject poverty. These were events from which both parents were spared, by Just's death in 1757 followed by his grief-stricken wife the same year.

Through his extensive studies abroad, Just Wiedewelt gained a good knowledge of the French court style and an understanding of form that enabled him to express new concepts, coupled with the practical ability of applying them to ships. He was the perfect candidate to fulfil the post of master carver, which he accepted in 1734, taking ship ornamentation on Danish ships to a new level of originality and competence. The *Fyen* of 1736 is a good example of his work.

As pointed out above, *Fyen* displays an early example of the so-called Baltic Stern. This elliptical shape first appears on Dutch East Indiamen of the 1720s, but there the similarity ends. Unlike the Dutch form, *Fyen* and her Swedish counterparts incorporate a quarter gallery to the quarterdeck, coming aft to the stern in the British fashion, all of which is open and balustraded. In *Fyen* the stern incorporates columns and balusters, echoing the Palladian concepts popular in England at this time, which may also have inspired the delightful form of the

window to the quarter gallery. Although such comparisons can be made, the integrity of the composition goes beyond the mere assemblage of imitated parts by expressing an ideology in a new and beautifully proportioned form. As such, it epitomises the essence of the Scandinavian character, in creating works that are both functional and beautiful. In *Fyen* Danish ship ornamentation finally comes of age: it no longer resorts to imitation, but confidently expresses innovation in its ornamental style.

Fyen remained in naval service until 1745, when she was sold to the DAC. The reduction in her armament and increased ballast as a merchantman improved her sailing ability considerably. She set sail for Canton in 1746, returning to Copenhagen in 1747, having gained a reputation as a ship in which her crew were proud to serve.

Thurah's younger brother Lauritz de Thurah trained as an architect and contributed to the interior decoration of Prinsens Palace, constructed for Christian VI in 1731. The oriental-inspired interior designed by Lauritz complemented the many items of furniture, porcelain and wall

A model of *Fyen* of 1736 with ornamentation by Just Wiedewelt (see also colour plates 15 and 16). (Author's collection reproduced by courtesy of the Danish Naval Museum, Copenhagen)

hangings imported from China during the period to create the chinoiserie style. The figurehead of *Fyen* is interesting in that it also adopts the chinoiserie style of a tightly curling mane, examples of which can be found on British ships of the same period, reflecting the influence of trade with the East (see also colour plates 17 and 18).

Unfortunately, the elder Thurah's reputation did not fare so well. At the time of his appointment, Dannerskiold-Samsø instigated significant changes within the administration by appointing a construction committee to evaluate the performance of each new ship, noting design development and the vessel's ability under sea trials, to meet its claimed performance. The commissioning committee consisted of:

N P Judichær	(1705-1748)
F Wegersløff	(1702-1763)
A Gerner	(1698-1749)
N J Herbst	(1699-1762)
H R Schumacher	(1707-1750)
F L Norden	(1708-1742)
A Turesen	(???? -1757)

Under their scrutiny, Thurah's designs continued to attract criticism, resulting in the chief overseer to ship construction Anders Turesen undertaking the design of the 60-gun ship *Oldenburg*, launched in 1740. Turesen also engaged the French designer Laurent Barbé (1696-1754), but he too failed to meet the expectations of the committee and was dismissed in 1746.

The *Tre Croner* of 1742 was designed by Barbé with decoration by Wiedewelt which, curiously, shows a return to large figurative ornamentation that quite obscures the fine lines of the Baltic Stern (see colour plate 19). French ships had by this period adopted the Regency style, with minimal use of figurative work. British ships still employed large figures to the quarters, but here they are depicted very much in the French style, particularly the six mermen, sitting on the rail of the upper counter, their twisting tails extending onto the counter. This detail is uncommon on British ships; similarly carved work to the counter had by this period been replaced with painted work. The positioning of the ship's name and placement within a cartouche is also a French custom, along

Decoration submitted by Just Wiedewelt. The fine composition of *Oldenburg*'s figurehead is of lavish proportions compared with the stern, where ornamentation is restricted to applied mouldings. The layout of the rails is unusual in that the main rail terminates before the cat head, with the middle rail carried up to support the cat head itself. The manner in which the main rail reaches the limit of its upward curve before reaching the stem head is more akin to French practice. (By courtesy of the Danish Maritime Museum, Helsingør)

with royal insignia placed centrally on the gallery above. Three arches to the underside of the tafferel, here divided equally, is a Danish adaptation of the British cove, where the springing point of the outer arches would correspond with the fashion pieces.

With the dismissal of Barbé, Thurah remained master shipwright under Turesen, both of whom continued to design ships with decoration by

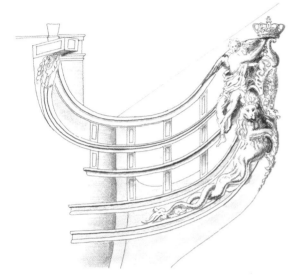

Figurehead to *Dronning Lovisa*, with decoration by Just Wiedewelt encapsulating the flamboyant majesty of French Baroque. In contrast, the decoration and arrangement of the head rails remain in the reserved British style. (Author's collection)

Wiedewelt. Benstrup's last ship, *Dronning Lovisa*, was launched two years after his death in 1744. This 70-gun ship was adorned with the most resplendent decoration by Wiedewelt, overflowing with Baroque exuberance, perfectly embodying the flamboyant nature of the French genre. The quality of decoration under the direction of Wiedewelt had reached an exceptional standard, creating a reputation he was keen to uphold, despite increasing difficulties under an administration keen to cut expenditure in such areas.

With funds no longer available to send aspiring students to study at the art academies of Paris or Copenhagen, it was decided that the naval academy at Holmen should undertake the task, leading to the employment in 1735 of Franz Toxverd, an artist who had trained at the royal academy in Copenhagen. Wiedewelt successfully campaigned to retain the policy of sending the most aspiring students among the naval officers to continue their training abroad, primarily in Britain and France, to study their ship design and construction methods. The training they received from Toxverd ensured they were also competent in the

Architectural decoration to a building in Aalborg, Denmark, built in 1739, displaying many of the decorative motifs found on *Tre Croner*, such as the figure of Hercules and scrollwork to the tafferel. (Author's collection)

Figurehead to *Dronning Lovisa*, with a lion continuing down onto the cheeks of the starboard side of the stem and a Unicorn to the port side. (Author's collection)

Baroque-inspired cartouche from the same period as the *Dronning Lovisa*, Kronborg Castle, Helsingør. (Author's collection)

  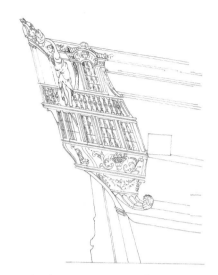

Augusta, launched Deptford 1726   Gerner's draught for *Fyen* 1745   Stanley's ornamentation for *Fyen* 1745

Augusta's quarter gallery presents the typical layout of a British ship of the period, with carved work to the upper and lower finishings; painted work in compositions of panoply decorate the walkway of the quarterdeck; a crude representation of a bird and foliate forms decorate the upper counter.

Gerner in his line drawing for *Fyen* suggests a narrowing of the quarter gallery, but still maintaining the layout of a British stern.

Stanley has taken Gerner's basic layout, but altered the stern to suit the curving form of a Baltic Stern. Solid panelling to the walkway of the quarterdeck has been replaced with balusters of a typically French design; the upper finishing adopts shell forms with narrowing sides reminiscent of the French bottle-shaped galleries, to create a perfect balance with the curving profile of the stern. The repeating use of cornucopia dispensing the fruits of the harvest provides a unifying theme of abundance, with the figurehead being a representation of the goddess Ceres.

art of drawing, to record the changing fashions and application of ship ornamentation.

One such officer was Andreas Gerner (1698-1749). Whilst studying in Britain, Gerner recorded details of the *Augusta*, a 60-gun ship built at Deptford and launched in 1736. She spent her early career stationed in the West Indies before returning to England to serve as a patrol vessel guarding the approaches to the Channel, where she narrowly missed engagement with the *Apollon* during her capture of the *Anglesey*. She may well have been on the slip during Gerner's period in England.

On his return to Denmark in 1739 Gerner sat on the commissioning committee alongside Turesen, and in 1745 submitted designs for a ship to be named *Fyen*, based on the *Augusta*. The 50-gun *Fyen* soon earned a reputation as the best sailing ship in the navy, leading to a further seven ships being built to her lines. Sadly, Gerner completed just one other design, for a small frigate, before his death in 1749.

Although the lines of *Fyen* were remarkably close to those of *Augusta*, the ornamentation, executed by the sculptor Simon Carl Stanley (1703-1761), was decidedly different. Born in Denmark to an English father and Danish mother,

Stanley was apprenticed in 1718 to the Danish sculptor Johan Christian Sturmberg. The wide-ranging talents of Sturmberg suited the equally versatile Stanley with whom he learnt the art of sculpting in stone, and stucco work. Sturmberg's last commission, to execute elaborate stucco work to ceilings of Fredensborg Castle in 1722, was largely completed by Stanley. Sturmberg was a master of the Italian Baroque and a gifted stone carver, completing the marble tombs of King Christian V and Queen Charlotte Amalie, who, like all Danish monarchs, are buried at the cathedral in Roskilde.

After his teacher's death in 1722, Stanley furthered his studies in Germany and Holland, before travelling to Britain in 1727, where he joined Sturmberg's former assistant Pieter Scheemaecker (1691-1781) who had set up a workshop with fellow Dutch sculptor Laurent Delvaux. Stanley was to spend the next twenty years in England, initially as Scheemaecker's assistant before receiving his own commissions, the first of which was for Earl Wilmington, to execute stucco decorations to Compton Place in Sussex in 1728-9. There he met his first wife, a tenant farmer's daughter named Anna Allen, who, sadly, died after only five years of marriage in 1735.

Stanley moved to Westminster, where he established his workshop as a sculptor. Two years later he married Magdalene Lindemann, the daughter of a pastor, with whom he had two sons. The first, Carl Frederick (1738-1813), was to become a famous sculptor in his own right, working in Neoclassical style. His early life must have been an unstable existence as his father continued to pursue commissions beyond the capital. In 1740 he carried out stucco work to Langley Park in Norfolk and in 1742 was employed by the monumental mason Thomas Maynard in Suffolk. His journey southwards continued a year later, to work for the architect Humphrey Smith in Ely, Cambridgeshire. In 1744 he was employed at the Oxford Camera, which was built to house the library of John Radcliffe, who had studied medicine at Oxford. On his death in 1715 he left £40,000 for the library, where stucco work to the ceiling was partially carried out by Stanley, to designs by the architect James Gibbs. From there he went to Kirtlington in Oxfordshire, then in 1746 to Lord William Maynard's estate of Little Easton in Essex.

Andreas Gerner called on Stanley whilst in London to collect a ship in 1743. The two had previously met during Gerner's earlier period of study in England. Aware that the yard at Holmen lacked any aspiring artist to succeed the ageing Wiedewelt, Gerner offered Stanley the opportunity to compose ornamentation for *Fyen*, the success of which led to Stanley being offered a post at Holmen; this he accepted, moving back to Denmark in 1746.

With Gerner's death in 1749, ship design at Holmen was once more in the hands of Turesen and Thurah. Hendrick Krock had died some years earlier (1738), leaving his position as head of the art academy to the sculptor Louis August Le Clerc (1688-1771). Krock's death coincided with a move away from his Baroque-inspired painting and decorative style, to embrace the burgeoning Rococo of which Le Clerc was an adherent. He arrived in Denmark from his native France in 1735 and was immediately employed as a sculptor to the royal court.

Despite his extensive period in Britain, Stanley had acquired a confident grasp of the Rococo, thus providing a welcome opportunity to import new ideas to the compositions of Wiedewelt, who had himself experimented with some small Rococo-inspired motifs, such as a cartouche to carry the name of the 22-gun frigate *Samsøe* designed by Barbé in 1746.

The first collaboration between Stanley and Wiedewelt was for the ornamentation of *Fredericus Quintus*. Designed by Turesen, this 90-gun ship was launched in 1752. Although Baroque compositions dominate the tafferel, the galleries are edged with Rococo-inspired motifs of palms and shells that

The Oxford Camera was built to house the library of John Radcliffe, who studied medicine at Oxford. On his death in 1715 he left £5000 to his college, £6000 for the Radcliffe infirmary, £30,000 for the Radcliffe Observatory and £40,000 for the library, which was designed by the architect James Gibbs. Simon Carl Stanley was commissioned to carry out ornate stucco work to the ceilings, many elements of which are reworked into his designs for the ornamentation of the 50-gun ship *Fyen* of 1745. (Author's collection)

Detail from the stern of *Fredericus Quintus* showing the introduction of Rococo by Stanley and Wiedewelt in 1752. In the cartouche Frederik V is rendered in its Danish rather than Latin form.

twist and turn in their asymmetric path, to frame the leading edge of the quarter galleries, curling onto the stern as they continue to decorate the lower finishing. The two men clearly worked well together, with Stanley injecting new ideas manifest in the vitality of their compositions, the balanced nature of which must surely mirror the empathy that existed between them, creating a fertile ground where such ideas could be developed.

Wiedewelt's Baroque imagery for *Fredericus Quintus* is presented with lively enthusiasm; the sense of power and grandeur it evokes could, in less skilled hands, become belittled by the introduction of Rococo's wayward nature, but here each remains respectful of the other. Interpreting such visual scenes into three-dimensional art would certainly challenge the skill of most carvers, particularly the grandiose figurehead, with its extensive use of clouds. Portraying such weightless objects can easily

Figurehead to *Fredericus Quintus* (1752) displaying the majesty befitting a ship of the line in an imposing composition full of the lively expressiveness associated with Baroque sculpture. The same style of composition appears in Wiedewelt's earlier maquette for *Falster* (1742), shown right. (Author's drawing; image by courtesy of the Danish Maritime Museum, Helsingør)

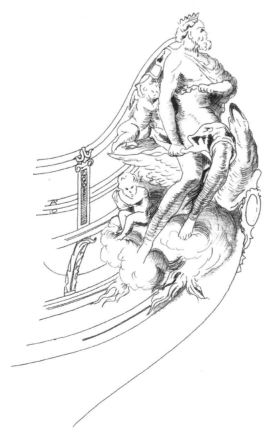

Detail taken from a mirror frame carved by Le Clerc in 1744, demonstrating the inclusion of chinoiserie motifs similar to those found in ship ornamentation. The mirror formed part of the interior decoration of Prinsens Palace, where Diderik Thurah's brother Lauritz also contributed designs. Stanley was well connected with such men and at times involved in the same projects.

The subtle interplay of asymmetry maintains a balance that allows its use to be employed within the strict precepts of Classicism. Where Baroque ornamentation holds the structure, here the ornamentation is supported by it.

Rococo ornamentation to the buildings of Amalienhavn inspired by N H Jardin and S C Stanley. Many aspects of the design can be seen in ship ornamentation, such as the repeating pattern on the parapet (which precedes Rococo), examples of which were used extensively as balustrading to stern and quarter galleries by Puget in the 1690s and later by Bérain. (Author's collection)

In the mid-century Copenhagen underwent a series of major building programmes. An area fronting the river opposite Holmen was set out as Amalienhavn, beyond which an imposing complex of four palaces forms Amalienborg, set at the junction of four wide avenues forming a central octagon. Based on the French system of urban planning, the area, with its strict sense of Classical architecture, was designed by the court architect Nicolaj Eigtved (1701-1754), but after his death much of the exterior decoration to the buildings was completed by the French architect N H Jardin. Le Clerc was also involved with the project, completing such works as Rococo woodcarvings to the great hall of Christian VII's palace. Stanley worked closely with Jardin, designing much of the exterior Rococo ornamentation which bears great similarity to compositions found in Stanley's work for the navy. With such a cast of master craftsmen,

result in clumsy interpretations when presented as a solid object. A recognisable, if less dramatic effect had been achieved in an earlier maquette by Wiedewelt for *Falster* (1742), but it would need the addition of paint to detract from its solidity.

The decoration at Amalienborg provides a valuable record of how the drawings for Stanley's ship ornamentation would have been transformed into three-dimensional work.

The palms and shell-inspired motifs employed to the leading edge of the quarter gallery to *Fredericus Quintus* are interpreted into compositions decorating set panels at Amalienborg. Although asymmetric in their construction, the completed composition still sits comfortably within the geometric confines of Classicism. (Author's collection)

A more modest example of Rococo ornamentation and classical structure, by craftsmen working away from the capital: Frederikshavn, North Jutland, 1762. The simplicity of carving that forms the drapery offers a fine example of how to produce an effective composition with the minimum of costly detail – an all important consideration when working beyond the royal purse. (Author's collection)

Amalienborg stands as the most significant example of Rococo ornamentation in Denmark.

By the time Stanley had completed *Fredericus Quintus* in 1752, he had also undertaken royal

The collaboration between Wiedewelt and Stanley continued to embrace the Rococo genre, which completely dominates the ornamentation of their next ship, *Møen*. Designed by Turesen, the 40-gun ship was launched in 1753. The same pattern of decoration continues onto the stern, while the figurehead takes the form of a crowned lion with head rails in the English fashion, decorated with simple mouldings. (Author's collection)

commissions, such as a group sculpture depicting Venus, Adonis and Cupid for the marble gardens at Frederik V's Fredensborg Castle. In the same year he was appointed professor at the art academy and in 1754 to the newly formed Royal Academy of Fine Arts. Ship decoration was firmly in the hands of a man in touch with – and to some extent instrumental in – the shaping of artistic fashions ashore.

The deaths of both Wiedewelt and Turesen occurred in 1757, and a year later Thurah relinquished his post as chief constructor, to be succeeded by Michael Krabbe (1725-96). Krabbe had studied in Britain, Holland and France, but during his time in office he strongly favoured French construction methods. His cooperation with Stanley, who was appointed master carver in 1757, appears to have been a harmonious one, with his penchant for French-inspired ornamentation perfectly suiting Krabbe's constructional preference.

One of a series of sculptures by Just Wiedewelt's son Johannes, who became one of the most celebrated of Danish sculptors. Carved between 1759 and 1769, the sculptures stand in the park to the summer residence of the royal family. Designed by N H Jardin, the park forms part of the grounds to Fredensborg Palace, where Simon Stanley was also commissioned to provide sculptures to the marble garden. The many military trophies depicted in the composition would be used on ship ornamentation through to the Neoclassical period. (Author's collection)

Stanley's first commission, for the *Dannemark*, consisted predominantly of rocaille-inspired motifs that create a less exuberant form of decor than his joint work with Wiedewelt for *Møen*. Wiedewelt's Baroque influence has now been left firmly behind, with the figurative work introduced by Stanley to the tafferel and quarter pieces adopting a sense of Classical composure, with reclining figures depicting Hercules contained within a series of curved mouldings that frame the narrow tafferel. This 70-gun ship, designed by Barbé, was launched in 1757 and set the style of ornament that Stanley would adopt until his death in 1761.

The yard was now in a position for the first time to appoint a master carver who was the product of their own training programme: Christian Jacobsen Møllerup (1729-17??). During his early career Møllerup gained employment from private yards, carving decorative work for merchantmen. By the time a son was born to him in 1761, he was described on the birth certificate as master sculptor to Amalienborg. Having clearly established a reputation that warranted his employment as master carver, he had already submitted designs to the admiralty before being appointed to the post in 1761.

Krabbe appears to have been an affable character for, as with his predecessor, the partnership was an agreeable one. In his first year Møllerup designed the decorative work for the 70-gun ship *Printz Friderich* and a ship for the DAC, also designed by Krabbe, named *Rigernes Ønske*. The decorative composition for this last may have been designed, or at least strongly influenced, by Stanley, as it follows in his rocaille genre, with shell-inspired motifs that merge into Rococo scrolls, decorating the upper and lower finishings to the quarter galleries in a similar manner to *Møen*. However, the 'painterly quality' of his designs is quite different from that of Stanley, exhibiting a wistfulness that would be extremely difficult to transpose into solid objects; this suggests that much of the ornamentation would either be painted, or that the sketches exist purely to impart a sense of the composition, which Møllerup was capable of carving himself and therefore felt unnecessary to describe in detail.

Similarly, the drawings for *Sophia Magdalena*, launched in 1763, offer little instruction to the carver in how such effects could be realised in three-dimensional form. The wistful nature of Møllerup's composition makes reference to the idea of the *fête champêtre* and the 'pastoral idyll' popularised by François Boucher in the 1750s and

1760s. The theme is taken to its extreme in Møllerup's design for *Norske Løve*, launched in 1765, which bristles with scenes depicting contented country folk. Such ideology reflected the age, as Denmark relaxed in a period of relative peace, at least with its immediate neighbours, allowing the contemplative mind to indulge in such visions of well-being.

Møllerup's maquette for the figurehead of *Printz Friderich* (1761), demonstrating his ability to envisage objects three-dimensionally, despite his apparent inability to impart such information in his drawings. This was, perhaps, a task which he simply felt was superfluous, wishing to place greater emphasis instead on the feeling or emotive expression of the model, when presented to an audience for whom this would be more comprehensible than the technicalities of a working drawing. (By courtesy of the Danish Maritime Museum, Helsingør)

Quarter gallery to *Sophia Magdalena*, designed by Michael Krabbe with decoration by Christian Jacobsen Møllerup, and launched in 1763.

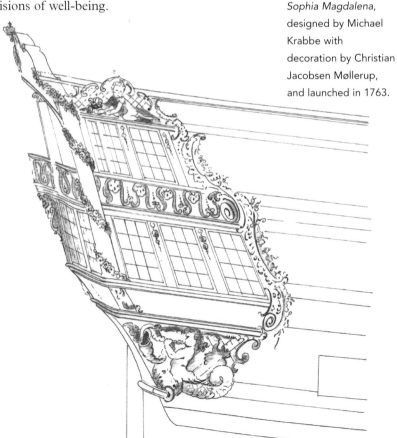

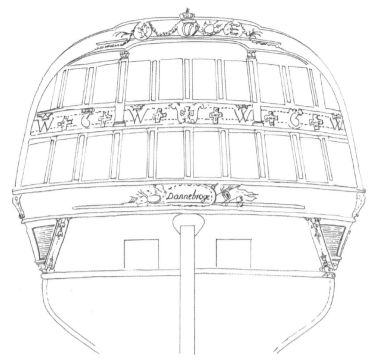

Dannebroge, launched in 1772 to a design by F Krabbe with ornamentation by C J Møllerup. The central shield of the tafferel contains the monogram of King Christian VII. A portrait decorates the shield to the left and the three lions of Denmark to the right, around which is draped a festoon of foliage. The uninspired repeating pattern of cyphers and crosses that decorates the quarter gallery is a reworking of an old standard design. The ship's name within a cartouche, supported by military trophies, decorates the upper counter.

The style adopted by Møllerup continued with his predominantly rocaille-inspired motifs, set amidst the asymmetric curves of Rococo, interspersed with angelic figures and scenes from country life. The addition of such figures helped to restore a sense of scale to the otherwise intricate detail of Møllerup's ornamentation, although the romanticised effect created an unusual softness to the appearance of what was, after all, a man of war.

Danish ships were increasingly built in Norway, where a yard was established at Frederiksværn near Stavern, but the carved works continued to be produced at Holmen, from where they were forwarded to Norway for fixing to the new ship. Krabbe's drawings included draughts with and without ornamentation to allow construction of the ship, and then the subsequent placement of carved work. An example is the *Christiania*, a frigate launched from Frederiksværn in 1772. The plans show a lion figurehead as a removable slip of paper that can be placed over the constructional draught. Other decorations were either painted, produced at Holmen, or consisted of mouldings that could be manufactured in the joiner's shop. Such descriptions reflect the process already underway in Britain and France to reduce the expenditure and, subsequently, the extent of carved work.

Among Krabbe's ambitions was a desire to standardise ship design, an example of which are his draughts for eight bomb vessels. These heavily built ships were designed after a failed assault on Tripoli in 1770 that was intended to curb piracy and the taking of crews into slavery from Danish ships. They were to act as convoy vessels with the additional ability to make their presence felt by shore bombardment if need be. Krabbe appears to have named the vessels at an early stage, as the figurehead for each is depicted on his drawings in a form relevant to the name. For example, *Dragen* has a dragon, *Comet* a star, *Dristigheden* (Boldness) a lion, and *Mandigheden* (Manliness) a horse. The stern of each ship was presented with the outline of the tafferel and quarter pieces for each ship in varying sweeping curves that define the structure, but are devoid of ornamental content. Drawings of British warships were similarly presented from the 1730s, suggesting a system whereby the general layout was established with a theme that could be expanded upon by the carver.

Wax maquettes of the figureheads for *Oresund* (1766) and *Perlen* (1773). Although produced during Møllerup's period in office, they may well be the work of the aspiring Willerup. (By courtesy of the Danish Maritime Museum, Helsingør)

By this time the importance of ornamentation had declined to a token gesture, begrudgingly sanctioned by an admiralty that was increasingly questioning their relevance, or more precisely the expenditure they incurred. The *Dannebroge* provides an example of how abysmal decorative compositions had become in the space of just ten years. The figurehead stands as the only piece of figurative work remaining on the ship, illustrating that this element at least retained a high level of importance, particularly among the men that served on board such ships, and would be an icon that the admiralties of many nations would find hard to dispense with for some time to come. The figurehead on *Dannebroge* depicts a Roman centurion and in its composition still retains a sense of grandeur that would impress many an onlooker, and give its crew a sense of pride in the vessel on which they were to depend.

Møllerup retired in 1785 leaving the position of master carver to be filled by Frederik Christian Willerup (1742-1819). Having already established a reputation as an exceptional carver, Willerup was the natural choice to fill the post. Despite the decline in stern decoration, the tradition of impressive figureheads continued, and indeed flourished in the capable hands of Willerup, who produced an endless array of monumental figures, accompanied by token gestures of ornamentation in Neoclassical style, a format that continued up to his retirement in 1816 when the post of master carver at Holmen was abolished.

Danish Carvers

Holmen, Copenhagen

Overseer / Master Carver		*Held Office*
Ole Judicær	(1661-1729)	1690-1722
J C Heimbrod	(16??-1733)	1729-1733
Just Wiedwelt	(1677-1757)	1733-1757
Simon Carl Stanley	(1703-1761)	1757-1761
C J Møllerup	(1729-17??)	1761-1785
F C Willerup	(1742-1819)	1785-1816

Carvers		
Baltasar Ellertsen		1652-1657
Lauritz Hansen Worm		1657-1694
Tyge Lauritzen Worm		1669-1692
Peder Michelson	(died 1712)	1692-1712
Nils Olsen		1712-1721
Anders Bruun		1721-1729

Norway

Tyge Lauritzen Worm		1669-1674

Sweden

When the Swedish warship *Vasa* was recovered in 1961 from the depths where she sank 333 years earlier, it gave historians the most complete record of naval architecture ever discovered from the 1600s. Apart from the almost intact hull, complete with its contents, over 700 pieces of carved work were also recovered. The historian Hans Soop produced an informative book (see Bibliography) on the findings of his research, cataloguing each item in terms of the material used, location on the ship, decorative style, subject matter and quality of workmanship. By analysing the carving characteristics of each piece, he has been able to identify the individual sculptors responsible for a large number of the pieces. The three main sculptors that worked on the ship were also commissioned to provide work for the church, many examples of which still exist in Stockholm, providing further examples of each craftsman's carving style.

Dutch shipwrights had been working in Sweden since at least 1616, when the crown engaged the services of Paridon van Hoorn and Christian Welshuizen to build ships at the yard in Vestervik. King Gustaf II Adolph had ordered the establishment of well-equipped yards, capable of building a fleet of ships to control his expanding Swedish empire. Ten years later work commenced on the *Vasa*, under the guidance of another Dutch master shipwright named Hendrik Hybertszoon and his brother Arendt. She was to be the flagship of a new fleet.

Hans Soop draws comparisons between the carving style and method of finish with the polychromed woodcarvings to be found in churches of the period. The carvings display the typical Mannerist-Renaissance style in its German and Dutch mode, produced by the many craftsmen travelling to Sweden from those regions. The wealthy merchants' houses of Stockholm offer many examples of the style that would have mirrored the compositions to be found afloat.

The principal carver on the *Vasa* was Martin Redtmer. Originally from Germany, this journeyman carver had by 1618 reached Estonia, from where he presumably travelled to Sweden, for in 1621 he carved sculptures to decorate the organ of the German Church in Stockholm. The organ was sold and moved to Övertorneå Church in 1779, where it can still be admired. The lively fluid style of his work retains many Mannerist and late Renaissance motifs, while the expressiveness of the figurative work begins to move away from the exaggerated grotesques of Mannerism, to embrace the realistic elements of early Baroque. This characteristic helped to identify his work on the *Vasa*. Redtmer settled in Sweden, where he worked until his death in 1655. Almost forty per cent of the sculptures on the *Vasa* have been identified as the work of Redtmer. He was clearly held in high regard at the navy yard, where he was employed for many years. During the last ten years of his life he was entrusted with the task of training the apprentice carvers assigned to the yard.

The second carver, Hans Clausink, was believed to have come from Westphalia, although his name suggests either he or his family were originally from the Netherlands. He is mentioned on the payroll of the yard in 1608 and was therefore well established by the time work commenced on the *Vasa*. Folowing his marriage to Maria Anna Schubert, they had a son named Bengt (1612-1683), who was ennobled in 1650 by Queen Christina, which gives an indication of the wealth and social standing the family of this ship-carver had attained. His last recorded commission was to carve a pulpit for the church at the shipyard

Entrance to a Stockholm residence built in 1640. The delicacy of the figurative work heralds the emergence of Baroque, amidst Mannerist decoration in the exuberant Dutch style. The mixing of earth pigments with wet plaster create a permanent colour wash to the house, in this case a pale red; similar pigments were used in the decoration of polychromed carvings. (Author's collection)

This Atlantis figure formed a bracket to the beakhead of the *Vasa* and represents a Roman emperor such as can be found in the pattern books of de Vries. Many traces of gold leaf and paint pigments were found on the original carving, which is possibly the work of Martin Redtmer. This painted copy was taken from a mould of the original figure, and the quality of the casting still allows the original chisel marks to be seen, clearly demonstrating that no sanding or finishing beyond a chiselled finish was carried out. The speed at which carvers were required to work would not allow such time-consuming operations, which would in any case have been deemed both unnecessary on account of the distance from which the figures would be viewed, and unprofessional in the need for an experienced carver to go over work a second time. (Author's collection)

in 1631, which unfortunately has not survived. In the same year Clausink was succeeded by the master carver Jost Schultz.

The third carver, Johann Thesson, came to Sweden from his native Holland in 1624, along with other Dutch craftsmen, to work on the royal castle known as Tre Kronor in Stockholm. Accounts record that he worked in stone and wood. The standard of workmanship ascribed to them on the *Vasa* clearly demonstrates they were indeed masters of their craft, although the compo-

sitions offer little in the way of artistic innovation, relying on standard examples of the late Renaissance style, where the Classical structure has been overturned by the bizarre elements of Mannerism. The burlesque quality of this can be traced to the Flemish development of the genre, a style that would have formed the basis of Thesson's training.

Cornelis Floris (1514-1575) was a primary innovator of this style. His compositions of heavy metallic strapwork imprisoning naked figures became influential across the Netherlands, and spread to Germany and Scandinavia through the dissemination of pattern books such as *New Inventions for Sepulchral Monuments*, published in 1557. Hans Vredeman de Vries (1526-1604), a student of Floris, developed the theme to include cartouche designs that frame masked figures of a softer, less macabre nature than the, at times, warped visions of Floris. A sepulchral monument for Jesper Kruus (Lord High Treasurer) in Stockholm Cathedral has a surrounding baldaquin of ornately carved columns and entablature believed to be the work of Thesson. The ornamental compositions of strapwork and grotesques framed by cartouche embellishment carry the hallmark of de Vries.

They also contain elements of Auricular compositions, a style of decoration developed by goldsmiths in Utrecht at the beginning of the 1600s that is based around the soft folding forms of the human ear. These organic shapes make a token appearance on the *Vasa*, but only in the form of early attempts to master the style; as such they appear very stiff, lacking comprehension of this innovation, or perhaps purposely restrained to blend unobtrusively with the predominantly Mannerist style. The pattern books of de Vries included many designs for herms similar to those of the *Vasa*, together with Roman figures and panels of military paraphernalia, all of which could serve as models for the ship's decoration.

Description of the Carved Work to *Vasa*

Carving to the tafferel has been cut clear to create filigree work, or *hakkebord* in the Dutch tradition, depicting two griffins holding the royal crown, beneath which is the portrait of a child, possibly representing the king as a young boy. The arcading panel below is supported by eleven figures,

The stern and quarter of *Vasa*, launched at Stockholm in 1628.

alternating male Atlantes and female caryatid forms. The panel at their base is inscribed with the king's initials G.A.R.S. – for Gustavus Adolphus Rex Sueciae (King of Sweden) – with a cherub forming the centrepiece.

The Swedish national coat of arms takes pride of place in the large panel below the tafferel, beneath which five grotesque masks form the mullions to the four arched lights of the upper gallery. The quarter piece figures, which rise from this level up to the tafferel, consist of two knights in contemporary dress, crowned with coronets, above which are two male figures clothed in flowing drapery. All of these have been attributed to the carver Martin Redtmer.

The seven figures below the quarter pieces are a continuation of those on each quarter gallery, presenting a total of twenty-seven figures that portray the warriors of Gideon from the Old Testament, and are possibly the work of Hans Clausink. The four large figures on the stern below them dressed as Roman warriors act as supporters to the coat of arms of the Wasa dynasty. This consists of two cherubs holding a wheatsheaf, and from the drapery behind them falls an abundance

of fruit, signifying the wealth brought to the nation under the prudent leadership of their king. Each cherub holds an olive branch, symbolising the peace he has brought through 'The strength tempered by good intent, that leads to peace and posterity'.

The final panel, which forms the upper counter, has as its centrepiece a figure representing David, who by playing his harp dispelled the evil spirits that were upon him. The two outer figures portray Hercules in different stages of life: the first, as a young man armed only with a club, has the strength and courage to become victorious in the various encounters that befall him; on the starboard quarter, he is seen in old age, having gained the wisdom to enter the world of the immortals. The handling of facial features and style of carving are similar to works known to have been carried out by Redtmer and are therefore attributed to him.

An army of warriors continues at the same level to form the base of the quarter galleries. The mullions to the lights above take the form of pedestals, with masks carved on the front face of the lower section, whilst the sides and upper part are decorated with simple Mannerist scrollwork. The domed turrets have upon their pedestals an assortment of well-carved figures in the form of herms, their bases decorated in a multifarious array of grotesque masks, scroll and leaf work, twisting tails and husk-like repeating patterns: all very Mannerist in artistic style, but well executed. Along the length of the galleries, figures of 'Wild Men' stand precariously on the roof's edge, alternating with obelisk ornamentation of acanthus leaves and swags of drapery of Renaissance origin. Similar in stature to Hercules, Wild Men were in Norse mythology keepers of the ancient forests and wilderness. They appear as supporters on the Danish coat of arms and were assigned to represent Lapland when it became part of Sweden in 1606.

The roof of each gallery is decorated with mermen and mermaids, their twisting tails following the contour of the curving structure, creating a very organic feel to their well-carved forms. They are placed alternately with grotesque masks on the lower gallery, to give a sense of continuity with the pedestal figures below. The shorter form of the obelisks also allows the figures on the roof to be seen more clearly.

Of the carvings found on the *Vasa*, 57 per cent were completed in oak, 26 per cent in lime and 17 per cent in pine. Although lime is an excellent timber for carving, its use for exterior decoration is unusual on account of its poor durability. The large lion figurehead serves to demonstrate this point, where the surface has deteriorated to a far greater extent than the carvings in pine or oak. Fragments of gold leaf suggest the lion was originally completely gilded. The more durable timbers provide a better record of the finished surface, where gold leaf has outlasted painted finishings in its ability to stay attached to both oak and pine. It is estimated that 75 per cent of the carvings were gilded, creating a stunning contrast to the predominantly red background of the hull (colour plate 20).

Analysis of the paint has identified the use of at least four pigments to produce the red paints: the mineral rock cinnabar to create vermilion; iron red produced through the annealing and pulverising of iron ores; orange red, through a complex compound of lead and oxygen; and red ochre. Ochre is a collective name for earth pigments derived from decomposed rock. Ferric hydrated oxide creates a yellow pigment, which when combusted, becomes deeper and eventually red. Yellow was also produced from a lead-tin compound to create pigments ranging from lemon yellow to reddish yellow. Blues, greens, white and black were similarly produced to give vibrant painted effects to the carved work.

On her launch, the *Vasa* was the largest and most magnificent ship of the fleet, but concerns about her stability had already been voiced. During the course of her construction she had been lengthened and an additional gun deck added. Such major alterations to the original design were bound to cause problems. Having taken on ballast and stores, she set sail from Stockholm on 10 August 1628, but at the first gust of wind she heeled alarmingly. Pressure to complete delivery of the ship did not allow time to re-stow her ballast, so she sailed on, but the voyage soon ended in disaster as a further gust caused her to heel to such an extent that water poured in through the open lower gun ports. The assembled crowds watched in horror as she sank whilst still within the confines of Stockholm's harbour.

Stockholm's Riddarhuset, designed by Simon de la Vallée in 1641, represents the introduction of Baroque classicism to Sweden. The abrupt departure from the Dutch Mannerist style was softened by the employment of Dutch architects to provide an element of the emerging Dutch-inspired Baroque, mainly to the interior which was left incomplete following the death of Simon de la Vallée in 1642. (Author's collection)

Despite this national disaster, Dutch shipbuilding methods continued in Swedish shipyards, with the yards of Holland and Zeeland supplying a further thirty-three ships to the Swedish navy by 1645. During this period Holland had a major influence on the economy of Sweden, with many Dutch merchants settling in Stockholm. The financier Louis de Geer assisted Sweden in obtaining loans to finance their wars, and in 1620 took over the management of the crown's arms factories, with the result that they were able not only to supply the needs of the Swedish forces, but also to export a considerable number of surplus weapons. De Geer developed the Swedish iron industry to cope with demand, raising production to the point where iron became Stockholm's chief export commodity. Dealings in other goods, such as timber for masts and spars, hemp, Stockholm tar and wheat from other Baltic nations, were also dominated by the Dutch. Their unparalleled success gave them a near-monopoly of trade in the Baltic.

The Dutch Mannerist-Renaissance style of decoration continued to dominate through the 1630s, but exposure to Baroque Classicism intensified when the Frenchman Simon de la Vallée (*c*1590-1642) became architect to the royal court in 1638. The French-born Vallée studied under his father Marin, who had participated in the building of the Palais du Luxembourg and the Hôtel de Ville in Paris. Simon's most influential work in Sweden was Stockholm's Riddarhuset (House of Nobility); commenced in 1641, it displays the decisive shift towards Baroque Classicism.

Simon de la Vallée was in turn responsible for the early training of his son Jean (1620-1696) and Nicodemus Tessin the elder (1615-1681), both of whom were to have a major influence in the introduction of Baroque architecture to Sweden. Unfortunately, Simon was only able to present the fundamental concept of the building before being stabbed to death by a nobleman in a dispute over the building's design in 1642.

The design for Simon de la Vallée's Riddarhuset is strongly influenced by the formal plan of the Palais du Luxembourg (1624) with its Corinthian pilasters and entablature, between which swags of fruit and husk ornament create a contrast to the rigidity of the Classical forms. Such ornamentation is typical of the early French Baroque, where a strong emphasis is placed on Classical symmetry. Ornamentation to the principal entrance provides an early example of Baroque figurative work, where an attempt has been made in the composure of the figures to overcome the constraints of the surrounding structure.

Jean de la Vallée was responsible for the design of the two-tiered curving roof, which became a prominent feature of Swedish Baroque architecture, known as a 'Säteri'. The exterior was completed during the 1650s, with interior work continuing through to 1674. The introduction of the new style was, not surprisingly, restricted to the aristocracy, while the houses of wealthy merchants (the majority of whom were Dutch) and the ornamentation of churches, continued to be influenced by Dutch and German artisans.

As depicted in the elder van de Velde's work, the ornamentation of the 56-gun *Carolus* launched 1650 and the 34-gun *Fenix* launched 1651 is typical of Dutch-built ships of the period, with carvings that have developed from the late Renaissance style to encompass elements of the fluidity associated with Dutch-inspired Baroque. The Classical elements, which are more akin to architectural development, are as yet unable to take hold, for they ultimately rely on a change to the underlying structure of ship design. Such developments would not be introduced before individual countries moved away from the dominating influence of Dutch naval architecture; by the time they had developed their own style of ship design, French Baroque ornamentation had been embraced and accepted beyond the elite and into mainstream society. The carved work for both ships was executed by Jost Schütz, or Schultz (died 1678). He succeeded Hans Clausink as master carver in 1631 and, in all practical terms, Mårten Redtmer, who was increasingly engaged in artistic commissions beyond the navy yard.

The Dutch shipwright Gert Croon was employed at the navy yard in Stockholm during this period, where his 50-gun ship *Amarant* was launched in 1653. A model of the ship survives and, although heavily restored in the 1890s, it does give a reasonable indication of the ship's ornamentation, which was also executed by Schultz. By 1655 ten journeyman carvers, plus apprentices, were in service to Schultz, who had also accepted commissions beyond the yard at Skeppsgården, for altarpieces, organ decoration and pulpits for Stockholm's church and that of St Jakob, which functioned as the church for the admiralty.

The quality of his work was also considered suitable for the decoration of the royal yachts. A

Quarter gallery of a model of the *Amarant*, launched 1653. (Author's collection by courtesy of the Maritime Museum, Göteborg)

description survives for the *Hörten*, launched in the autumn of 1650 for the coronation of Queen Christina. The yacht was also of typical Dutch design, and carried on her stern the royal coat of arms flanked by two oval windows decorated with wreaths and festoons. These were held by two female figures dressed in blue, with two further figures forming the quarter pieces.

The admiralty since the mid-1650s had been attempting to formulate a set pattern of decoration for the stern of their ships, using the *Vasa* as an example, which many ships had adopted since her launch in 1628. Admiral Clerck in a description of the *Draken* launched in October 1655 notes:

> That the crown's coat of arms, measuring four and three quarter yards high, was to be carved in the large hackebrädet [the tafferel] and under this on the panel, two paintings of dragons to symbolise the ship's name. The name would thus occupy the larger space or field, and the national coat of arms in the smaller space above.

The king's advice was sought when the *Victoria* was nearing completion in 1658 as to whether the crown's or some other coat of arms should be carried on the stern. His reply was quite specific:

> That the crown's arms be carved on the hackebrädet and the name on the panel beneath accompanied by a carving of the queen's

[Victoria's] arms of Holstein Schlesvig, so the name clearly relates to this symbol.

The carved works to *Draken* were also carried out by Jost Schultz and follow the same pattern of placement as the carvings on *Carolus* and *Fenix*. This format effectively distinguished Swedish ships from the Dutch, who tended to place symbolism relating to the ship's home port on the panel below the tafferel.

Stern of the *Amarant*, launched at Stockholm in 1653, with carved work by Jost Schultz. When the carving is compared to ships being built in Holland during the same period, there is very little difference regarding subject matter, style of decoration or density of composition. The figurehead of a lion is uncrowned, a feature that also appears on Dutch ships of the period. *Amarant* took part in many sea battles, capturing the Danish *Lolland* in 1677. The ship was finally broken up in 1688.

The products exported from the Baltic region were vital to the navies of both the Netherlands and England, whose interest in the area therefore extended to ensuring political stability. Holland not only supplied ships, but also troops to aid Sweden's expansion (as did Scotland: by 1630 12,000 Scots were serving in the Swedish army). Amsterdam merchants extended credit to increase trade, effectively acting as bankers to the Swedish economy. The potential leverage this created would inevitably produce an undercurrent of concern in England.

As pointed out in the Netherlands chapter, the backbone of the Dutch merchant fleet were the fluyts. The extreme tumblehome of their hulls was of great benefit in the Baltic trade, where it was accentuated still further to take advantage of the toll regulations on vessels entering the Baltic through the Öresund Sound where the charge was calculated on the area of the weather deck. Control of the Sound was crucial to the balance of power within the Baltic states, so trading nations took a keen interest in this narrow channel that separates Denmark and Sweden, to ensure a favourable toll could be maintained.

When Sweden took control of the Sound in 1658, the Netherlands felt their hold on the economy was under threat and responded by sending 75 ships and 4000 troops to aid the Danes. The bloody battle that followed led to a Dutch victory, albeit with the loss of Admiral de With and Vice-Admiral Floriszoon. Unfortunately, the Dutch stopped twenty English ships as they attempted to pass through the Sound, causing diplomatic complications with a country that needed little encouragement to enter the affray.

The Swedish Commissioner in London, Sir Johan Barkman Leijonbergh, had been relaying information to the Swedish king on the performance of English ships compared to those of other lands. Through his well-placed contacts, he was able to survey ships at Chatham, particularly noting the performance of the *Sovereign*, *Naseby* and *Resolution*. During the recent war with Holland, they had proved to be superior in both their firepower and sailing qualities. At Leijonbergh's request, Richard Cromwell sent a fleet of 40 ships to Öresund under the command of Sir George Ayscue, who sailed aboard the flagship *Naseby* in August of 1658.

The fleet maintained a presence in the Sound, with Ayscue acting as naval adviser to the King Charles X Gustaf of Sweden, who was greatly impressed by the *Naseby*. When winter weather would not allow the fleet to remain any longer, it was sent home under the command of Ayscue's vice-admiral, Goodsonn. The fleet returned the following year under General Montague and remained until the political unrest in England required its return. Cromwell's commonwealth regime was about to collapse; within a year the monarchy was restored and the *Naseby* set sail for Holland to bring the exiled king back to England as Charles II.

However, in the interim a request had been made to Cromwell that resulted in an agreement for English shipwrights to work for the Swedish navy. The dominance of Dutch shipbuilding in

Kronborg Castle, Helsingør looks out across the Öresund Sound from the Danish side to the shore of Sweden. Famous as the setting for Shakespeare's Hamlet, and the site of many bloody conflicts, the castle now houses the collections of the Danish Maritime Museum. (Author's collection)

Sweden was about to turn. In the autumn of 1659 the designer of the *Naseby*, Francis Sheldon (1612-1692), together with his assistant from the Chatham yard Robert Turner (160?-1686), arrived in Sweden to be employed at the Van Velden shipyard in Göteborg. Sheldon was given full authority over all shipbuilding at the yard, and with this position came a substantial salary and a farm close to the yard in Hissingen. All of this must have ruffled the feathers of the established Dutch workforce.

King Charles Gustaf's shipbuilding programme required the setting up of new yards, so a third shipwright, Thomas Day, who had been a foreman at Deptford, was sent to the new yard at Bodekull, initially to source timber with the yard inspector Ebbe Simonsson and to set up a new yard at Bodön. Day had previously worked in Denmark, and the Swedish admiralty, possibly drawing on his

experience there, set him the task of building vessels capable of landing troops in a proposed invasion of Denmark. Admiral Daniel Strussflycht had spent some time discussing the designs of the vessels with Day, particularly regarding the technicalities of getting cavalry horses on and off ships. Described as like a small frigate, the vessel became known as a Struss. In a report to the admiralty, Strussflycht noted that Day had three Struss ready and rigged, adding that the strongly built vessels sailed well. He held Day in high regard, praising his ability as a shipwright. Unfortunately no mention is made of any decorative work they may have carried.

Sheldon's first commission at the Van Velden yard was the 22-gun frigate *Postiljonen* (Post boy). A model of the ship survives, which, it is assumed, was part of a collection he bought with him from England. Although some motifs, such as the Roman-clad soldiers forming the quarter pieces are similar to those displayed on the *Naseby*, the style of carving is predominantly Dutch. The curiously uncrowned lion that forms the figurehead would accord with Cromwell's commonwealth regime but not the Swedish monarchy. The style in which the lion is portrayed is also typical of Dutch ships of the period, which also tended to be uncrowned. With the ship's launch recorded as the same year that Sheldon arrived in Sweden, it is more likely that he acted as overseer to its completion.

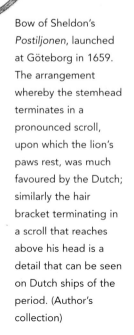

Bow of Sheldon's *Postiljonen*, launched at Göteborg in 1659. The arrangement whereby the stemhead terminates in a pronounced scroll, upon which the lion's paws rest, was much favoured by the Dutch; similarly the hair bracket terminating in a scroll that reaches above his head is a detail that can be seen on Dutch ships of the period. (Author's collection)

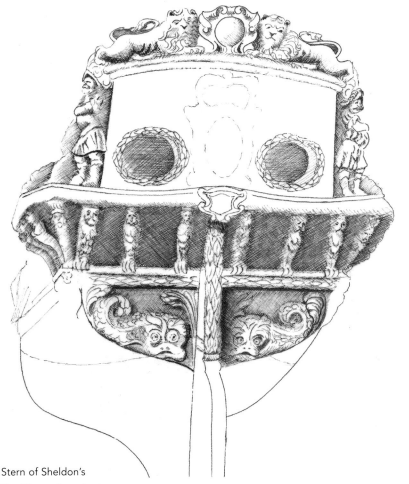

Stern of Sheldon's
Postiljonen, launched
at Göteborg in 1659.
The drawing is a repre-
sentation of Sheldon's
original model, on
which traces of painted
work can be seen on
the panel below the
tafferel. This conforms
to Admiral Clerck's
description of
decoration to the
Draken, where symbols
pertaining to the
vessel's name were
also painted rather
than carved in this
location. (Author's
collection)

On 26 June 1659 the keel was laid for Sheldon's 78-gun ship *Riksäpplet* (Orb of the Realm), which is thought to have been based on the *Naseby*. He met with fierce opposition from the Dutch shipwrights, who complained that he was unfamiliar with the needs of ships for the Baltic; he also insisted on seasoned oak and not the green oak favoured by the Dutch. In every respect, they set out to oppose his changes, and were determined not to adopt any English shipbuilding methods. The Dutch-born Lieutenant-Admiral at Göteborg, Henrik Sjöhielm, ascribed their lack of motivation to the failings of Sheldon. In his report to Admiral Strussflycht in Stockholm, he noted that 'They spend a third of their time standing idly about not knowing what to do.' He further commented that Sheldon 'spent much of his time on going into town to conduct his own private affairs, or on inventions that were of no use to the crown.' Such a state of affairs was in part due to the admiralty's inability to pay Sheldon's salary, effectively forcing him to seek other means of income with the help of contacts back home.

Sheldon's former position as master shipwright

at Chatham brought him into contact with Samuel Pepys, who, as a prominent member of London society, was already well acquainted with the Swedish commissioner Leijonbergh. Pepys records in his diary that they enjoyed twenty-six years of happy friendship, despite on one occasion coming close to confronting each other in a duel, an event that was only stopped by the intervention of the king. This may have been on account of Pepys's privateering enterprises. In 1666 he begged the loan of a vessel from the king, with a commission to prey on Dutch merchantmen. Having been granted the use of the vessel *Flying Greyhound*, a crew was engaged. The captain, a former pirate named Hogg, extended the brief by taking two Swedish ships, which caused some anxiety with the subsequent substantiation before the prize court. Leijonbergh protested on behalf of his countrymen, but a bribe from Pepys eventually settled the matter. There may have been other con-siderations, as Captain Hogg, who Pepys described as 'that veriest rogue, the most observable embezzler that ever was known', whilst having command of the *Flying Greyhound* undertook a little piracy on his own account. Leijonbergh later married the widow of Pepys's privateering partner Sir William Batten.

The entrepreneurial Pepys also had a vested interest in the importation of masts and timber from Sweden and placed contracts with the timber importer Sir William Warren to supply the navy. Sheldon was in an ideal position to source timber for Warren, and did so often in order to help finance his shipbuilding projects, when his remu-neration from the Swedish authorities fell deeply into arrears.

The year after Sheldon arrived in Sweden, the export of timber boards rose to 16,200 dozen, and the export of masts and spars went up by 300 per cent to 900 masts and 1800 spars. In 1664 Pepys signed a further contract for Warren to supply masts that he described as 'the biggest that was ever made in the navy' (for which Warren handed him a bag containing £100). Sheldon was to supply the masts, and travelled to the deep forests in the northern Swedish provinces of Värmland and Dalsland. In the ice and snow of winter, the trees were sledged to Lake Vänern, where with the coming of spring they were floated downstream to Göteborg for export. Such trips would combine sourcing timber for the Göteborg yard itself, where shortages of materials added to the frustrations of an unwilling workforce.

Despite Sjöhielm's remonstrations, Strussflycht often came to the defence of Sheldon, on one occasion instructing Sjöhielm to 'keep the Englishman in good humour and allow him to build the ship as he wished'. This may have been in part to cover his own back, as he also advised Sjöhielm that he should not cause any obstruction that could ultimately bring blame upon the admiralty for interference in the outcome of the project. Instruction was, however, given with respect to the carving, although once more the diplomacy of Strussflycht allowed Sheldon's sensitivities to be taken into consideration. Unfortunately, the identity of the carver is not known, but on 27 November 1660 Strussflycht wrote in a letter to the admiralty stating that 'Decoration to *Riksäpplet* shall be executed after the ship model which Francis Sheldon has conveyed from England' (the model now known as *Ö3* in the Stockholm Maritime Museum), although there was some disagreement between Sheldon and Strussflycht over the placing of the carvings, which did not conform to the set pattern that the admiralty wished to enforce. Sheldon argued that there was insufficient room for the national coat of arms to be placed on the stern together with the ship's emblem and name, so he proposed that the arms should be placed on the ship's side. The admiralty responded by ordering the arms to be placed on the stern. Strussflycht, by way of offering an insight into the image desired by the admiralty, remembered that the previous ship named *Äpplet* had as its symbol a gilded orb surmounted by a small cross.

Sheldon's abrupt manner is understandable when consideration is given to his situation. Having been invited to a foreign land for his supposed expertise, and having met nothing but obstruction from a workforce that should have supported him, his only option if his reputation were to be retained was constantly to make a stand in order to maintain his authority. Sheldon insisted that a master carver should be engaged who could carve in the English fashion. Strussflycht continues in his letter: 'that he [Sheldon] went to town [Göteborg] but could find no suitable carvers. Those that had started the work informed him that they could not continue in portraying those on the model without the guidance of a master carver.' Strussflycht continues: 'If such a carver could not be found in Göteborg, then Sheldon would bring one from England,' and gave as an example that carving to the *London* was completed at a cost of £250.

The ship eventually slid down the ways in March of 1661, to allow the laying down of Sheldon's next ship and the completion of *Äpplet's* rigging and decoration. In 1675 Sweden was once more at war with Denmark, over the annexation by Sweden of the southern Danish provinces of Skåna and Blekinge. *Riksäpplet* formed part of the Swedish fleet that engaged with the combined forces of the Dutch and Danish off the island of Öland in 1676. She survived the battle, but on her return to Stockholm she was wrecked in a storm whilst anchored off Dalarö.

When diving was carried out on the wreck in 1953, some of the carvings were recovered, including a section from an orb which was indeed surmounted with a small cross, a curving border of pearls and well-preserved sections from the head of a cherub. The carving is clearly from the hand of a skilled carver, with fine, well-proportioned detail. In 1956 divers recovered an intact, though

Carvings recovered from the wreck of Sheldon's *Riks Äpplet* of 1661. (Author's collection)

much worn, winged cupid carved in pine, measuring some two feet in length, together with a complete and well-preserved carving of a small stylised dolphin. The carving style is certainly different from that depicted on the model of *Postiljonen*, the less flamboyant nature of the dolphin suggesting that it may be the hand of an English carver.

In 1662 Sheldon's assistant Robert Turner was given the responsibility to oversee the building of the 86-gun ship *Svärdet* (Sword), which was to be constructed in Stockholm. The design came in for sharp criticism from Sheldon, who considered the ship would not answer well to the helm as the stern was too wide, advising that the hull should be tapered for a further six feet. Paintings of the ship show the ship afloat, with a decidedly English-shaped stern which is wide for the period; the layout of carvings comply with the admiralty's set pattern, with the ship's name symbolised by two 'lions *rampant*' holding between them a sword with the point downwards. The carvings may have been executed by Jost Schultz, who was master carver at Stockholm, and were much praised, being held as an example to set the standard of craftmanship for future ornamentation.

In the same year the first of Thomas Day's ships, the 64-gun *Saturnus*, was launched from the yard at Bodekull, followed in 1664 by the 88-gun *Nyckeln* (The Key), which on 12 August set sail for Stockholm. It was noted in a report of the voyage that the woodcarvers followed in order to complete their work. The resolute attitude of the admiralty to have 'the most beautiful of ornamentation' prompted them, apparently at a late date, to engage the services of Sheldon 'to produce with all speed drawings for the decorative work to the galleries and stern in the latest and most graceful English manner.' When completed these were to be sent to the admiralty for their assessment and earliest approval.

The decorative work to Sheldon's *Riksäpplet* and Turner's *Svärdet* were painted in the English manner of the Commonwealth period, with gilded carvings on a black ground, while Day's *Nyckeln* adopted colours representative of the Swedish flag, with gilded carvings on a blue ground. Day had employed English carpenters at his yard and thus avoided the confrontations experienced by Sheldon, allowing the construction to be completed in the English manner. *Nyckeln* proved to be a well-balanced ship that gained the reputation of being the fastest in the fleet, much to the consternation of the Dutch, who strongly criticised the ship on her

arrival in Stockholm. A description of her carved work survives, which begins:

> The crown's coat of arms being placed on the tafferel, below which a large and well-proportioned key to symbolise the ship's name was carved together with an imposing lion, both gilded on a blue ground. The figurehead of a lion similarly gilded. The interior of her cabin was richly furnished in hardwood panelling and upon the floor were laid black and white wooden blocks.

The admiralty had its opponents – critics of what they perceived as 'adornments that were as unnecessary as feathers upon a ladies hat'. As in England, stricken by the costly business of war, the purse strings of Sweden's navy were continually being tightened. An order was issued that 'There would be no more handouts to woodcarvers, who were making their ships look like those of Copenhagen.' Ships already under construction were allowed to be completed as planned, but when *Solen* was built (1669) costs were ordered to be kept in check: both floors and panelling were to be pine, the bulkheads only to be painted and the floors scraped; her carved work was to be painted gold and black, similar to *Äpplet*'s, with the crown's arms the same. The figurehead seemingly escaped any curtailment and was allowed to be gilded.

Sheldon continued to labour under the scrutiny of the authorities, for his ongoing private dealings ventured beyond the export of masts and other materials to the contract building of ships for his own clients within the navy yard. This he contested was out of necessity because of the continued late or unpaid wages owed to him. The workforce within the yard was in a similar position and no doubt welcomed the ready cash in working directly for Sheldon.

In 1663 he was summoned before the admiralty in Stockholm, who, keen to keep him within their employ, presented a proposal to replace the now aged flagship *Kronan*. This at last was Sheldon's chance to build a three-decked ship, which at 170 feet was to be the largest yet built in Sweden. Work commenced under his supervision during the autumn of 1663 to cut timber in the province of Halland. It was important that sufficient was felled through the winter so the spring flood would carry them down to the coast for shipment to Stockholm. When wages were still unforthcoming, Sheldon refused to work until the admiralty settled what was owing to both him and Turner. The commencement of the project by Turner in Stockholm was in part financed with funds from Sheldon's continued private dealings.

Agreement was finally reached on 13 April 1664 and the search for timber was resumed, with Sheldon overseeing the felling of trees in the provinces of Värmland and Dalsland. Construction work continued under Turner's guidance, but at an incredibly slow pace owing to the shortage of money and craftsmen, who moved from one yard to another in search of work that paid. In May of 1665 Sheldon was ordered by the admiralty to make his way to Stockholm 'the sooner the better' to direct the work. This he refused to do until outstanding wages had been paid. The admiralty's desire to see the ship's designer take control prompted them to settle the account; timber began to arrive at the yard, but Sheldon did not. He did, however, arrange for the supply of other materials, including the import from England of 1000 tons of coal, to ensure the continued production of the extensive forge work.

Unshaken by the admiralty's growing annoyance at his dalliance, Sheldon continued to ignore their demands that he come immediately to Stockholm, and continued with his work in Göteborg. Finally, in January of 1666, he presented himself at Skeppsholmen to take charge of the work. Further carpenters were brought in from the yard at Bodekull in the summer of 1667, followed by thirty craftsmen to start roughing out the decorative work. Jost Schultz was the master carver at the yard, and presumably acted as overseer to the work, but another carver, Hans Jacobsson, is recorded as having 'completed a blaze of work to the master cabin'. Jacobsson worked intensively through the summer of 1668, during which time he lived on board the ship, where he was given strict instructions to guard against the risk of fire from the lighted lanterns.

Proof of his labours were discovered in the 1980s, when pieces of carving from the cabin were brought up from the wreck of the ship. They display Mannerist motifs in well-carved compositions. Decorative work from the galleries were also retrieved, including a well-preserved carving of a warrior in Roman attire; this popular motif can be seen on the *Vasa* and many of Sheldon's ships. *Kronan*'s example is particularly fine, the imposing presence of the figure demonstrating how the carver has progressed from the Mannerist style to embrace the lively expressiveness that typifies the Baroque idiom.

The *Stora*, or Great, *Kronan* was finally launched on 31 July 1668, but because of the continued lack of funds she was not rigged and ready for service until 1672; with an armament of 126 guns, she was the most heavily armed warship of the period. Despite Sheldon's foresight in engaging Anthony Deane to calculate her displacement and centre of gravity, she sat lower in the water than expected, requiring the removal of ballast, which consequently altered her stability and required the closing of her lowest gun ports when going about. This situation was not uncommon on heavily armed English ships, such as the *Prince*; designed by Phineas Pett and launched in 1670, she suffered from the same miscalculation. Despite this setback, the *Prince*, manned with an experienced, well-trained crew, was still able to be manoeuvred confidently, although Deane expressed frustration at the apparent inability to calculate a ship's displacement accurately, which in the worst cases resulted in the ship being 'girdled' (adding a belt timbers around the waterline) to increase breadth and hence stability.

Sheldon, therefore, dismissed criticism regarding her handling and once more sought remuneration for his efforts, claiming that he faced total ruin through the debts he had incurred. When payments for his services were still not forthcoming, and with his family close to starvation, the disgruntled Sheldon returned to England.

With the two ships built within a few years of each other the temptation to compare their decorative style is irresistible. With the *Kronan* we are fortunate in having a few samples of the original carving, which still embody many Mannerist motifs, while the figurative work shows a move towards the Classical composure associated with early Baroque. The model of the *Prince* (illustrated in the British chapter) displays a greater shift towards embracing the precepts of Baroque art. The abundance of richly scrolling vegetal forms reflects a greater adherence to its Italian origins than *Kronan*'s northern adaptation. It is perhaps unfair to draw comparisons regarding the general composition with so little of the *Kronan* surviving, but one gets the sense that the *Prince* displays greater innovation in the composition and expressiveness of the decorative forms.

Three unsigned drawings, but with notes by Sheldon, exist and have long been connected with the *Kronan*. Although they carry the seal of the

Opposite: The example from the *Vasa* is attributed to the German-born Martin Redtmer (far left). The dress and demeanour of the warrior from Sheldon's *Naseby* is markedly different from the three carved in Sweden (centre left). *Postiljonen*, carved at the yard in Göteborg, is probably the work of a Dutch carver (centre right). The example from *Kronan* may have been carved by Jost Schultz (far right). The quality of carving from the two Stockholm-built ships far surpasses the other two. The best craftsmen would naturally be drawn to the capital, where the cultural and spiritual elite would demand the highest standards.

| 1628 *Vasa* | 1655 *Naseby* | 1659 *Postiljonen* | 1665-1672 *Kronan* |

Warriors decorating the entrance to a Stockholm residence of 1643. (Author's collection)

fleet command, they are clearly French, displaying all the hallmarks of Bérain, and therefore of a later date. The small number of carvings recovered from the wreck are therefore the only record of her decorative design, but are sufficient to establish the style of the period, which has yet to show any influence from France.

Sheldon's hasty retreat to England was viewed by the Swedish authorities as deserting his post. His claims, they felt, were exaggerated, having gained considerable wealth from his private dealings, but the fact remained that a large proportion of his annual salary was still owed to him. He left with his wife Ipsa Smitt and their young daughter, leaving behind his two sons, Frans Johan, born Göteborg on 29 June 1660, and Charles, born Göteborg on 29 September 1665. Frans appears to have been apprenticed to the admiralty, the familiar faces of Day and Turner no doubt providing some support to the child. Charles was in all probability put into the care of a military school.

Thomas Day completed his last ship, the 62-gun *Venus*, in 1667. He was by then an old man and wished to spend his remaining years back home. The proposed replacement for Day was

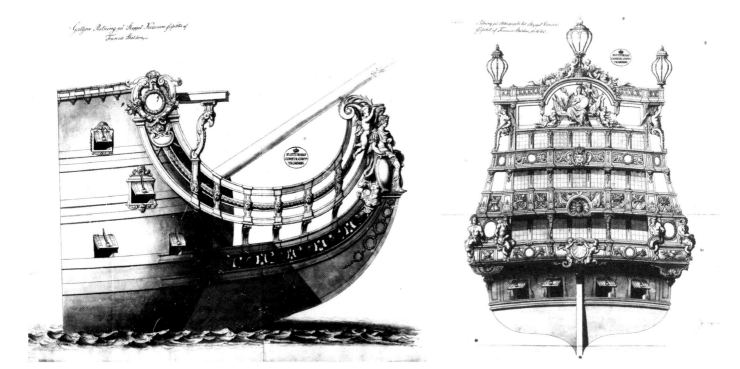

Gunar Olofsson Root, who had worked under Sheldon at Göteborg and was also known to Turner, who considered him to be well-qualified for the post, and so on 21 June 1669 Day prepared to set sail. The cargo of the ship which took him home consisted of pine planks, which he had secured in lieu of outstanding salary, on the understanding that he could sell them for his own profit upon arrival in England.

In 1674 Sweden, allied to France, joined in their war against Holland, culminating in the Battle of Öland, where the Swedish fleet encountered the joint forces of the Dutch and Danish navies on 30 May 1676. Among the Swedish fleet was Turner's 86-gun *Svärdet*, Day's 88-gun *Nykeln*, Sheldon's flagship the 126-gun *Stora Kronan*, and his earlier ship, the 84-gun *Äpplet*.

In an early stage of the battle Admiral Uggla, commanding the van from the *Svärdet*, fired a shot which the fleet took as a signal to alter course towards the enemy. This apparently unplanned alteration was perceived by the commanders of the other ships to be a mistake, but Admiral Bär in the *Nyckeln* had already acted upon the order and altered course, leaving Admiral Creutz in the *Kronan* to follow suit. This action was questioned by officers on board, who protested that before doing so they should reduce sail on account of the strong wind, and run in the lee guns. Their demands were met with indifference by Creutz, who was no seaman. As the ship came about, the sailors were unable to haul the heavy guns inboard

along the now upward slope of the deck. With the guns still protruding through her open ports, the ship continued to heel until their muzzles disappeared beneath the incoming sea. Fire broke out below which soon spread to her magazine, causing the already sinking ship to explode. Within a few minutes 800 of the 842 men onboard had lost their lives. The *Svärdet*, set ablaze by a fireship, was also lost during the engagement. *Äpplet* survived the battle, but was wrecked on her return to Stockholm. *Nykeln* also survived but was then lost in action in 1679.

The destruction of so many of Sweden's ships required a further rebuilding programme, providing opportunities for employment which may have been the reason for Sheldon to attempt a return. There must also have been the desire to see his sons, now aged 12 and 17. In the summer of 1677 he wrote to King Charles XI requesting that he might be of service. Turner, who in recognition of his skill had been appointed master shipwright at Skeppsholmen, made it clear that should Sheldon return, he would not work under or indeed alongside him. With Sweden still at war with Denmark, the king wrote from his field camp at Norrvidinge, stating that Sheldon had offered his services, and that he, the king, had graciously accepted, acknowledging the experience and scientific knowledge that Sheldon had to offer. The king, however, was under no allusion as to Sheldon's fiery temperament, and advised that, with this in mind, his colleagues

Bow and stern decoration officially catalogued as belonging to the *Kronan*. Although attributed to Sheldon, it is extremely doubtful that the drawings are by his hand. They show the stern and figurehead of a French ship of similar size to the *Kronan*, possibly to provide an alternative to the English style of ornamentation that was eventually chosen. References to the French monarchy on the stern of the ship have been replaced with the Three Crowns of Sweden. (Swedish War Archives, Stockholm)

should remain calm and clear in their dealings with him.

The admiralty neatly avoided any confrontation by putting Sheldon in charge of their new yard at Riga, in the Swedish-held territory of Latvia. With the navy constantly in need of new supplies, this former commercial yard offered the perfect solution. The plentiful supplies of timber and a workforce from the local yard gave Sheldon all the resources to be of use to the admiralty, whilst keeping him at a distance where he would not be an annoyance to them.

He was afforded some respite from his isolation when his son Frans Johan, having assisted Day and lately Turner in Stockholm, received a three-year posting to Riga to train under his father. Sheldon appears unusually happy in his work at this time, expressing his eagerness to start building with the plentiful supply of good strong oaks. On 23 October 1682 he wrote informing the admiralty that his first ship, the 56-gun *Wachtmeister*, was ready, but his jubilant tone soon turned to one of frustration as payment of his wages once more fell into arrears. Again he sought alternative forms of income and bought a quarter share in the ship *Maria*, trading in salt. This led to the first of many disputes between him and the quartermaster Frans Lou.

By the summer of 1683 Sheldon's son requested that he be given his certificate to build ships. He no longer wished to follow in his father's

Charles XI carved by Hendrik Schultz for the *Carolus XI*, 1677. The ship was renamed *Sverige* in 1683, at which time the carving was removed, and is now on display at the Stockholm Maritime Museum. (Author's collection)

footsteps, or work under the Dutch shipwright at the yard. In an attempt to escape from the yard, he went into hiding to divert the guards, who were under the impression he was making for Stockholm. As they searched departing ships Lou confronted his father, demanding to know his whereabouts and reminding Sheldon that they were both in the service of the king and could not come and go as they pleased. Sheldon replied that it was no concern of Lou's, and his son was right to leave rather than be held here as a slave to the crown. Confronted by such insubordination, Lou threatened Sheldon with arrest and forbade him from leaving the yard. Sheldon then refused to work and was put under arrest. He was transported first to Karlskrona and then to Kalmar, where he was imprisoned for eight months. Frans Johan was moved to the new yard at Karlskrona.

Whilst the dramatic events of Sheldon's life continued to unfold, Turner had completed the 22-gun *Delfin*. This little ship proved to be extremely fast and manoeuvrable. As such she was used extensively for covert operations, with a marked departure from the usual format for stern carvings, intended to make her provenance and purpose hard to determine. Turner then embarked upon the building of his next major ship at Skeppsholmen, the 80-gun *Carolus XI*. Her launch in 1678 coincided with the death of Jost Schultz and the position of Stockholm's master carver being awarded to his son Hendrik (1650-1701).

After some years studying in England, Hendrik returned to Sweden in 1674 following the death in that year of his brother Nicolaus (Clas), who had also been employed as woodcarver to the admiralty. Hendrik is recorded as having been employed as woodcarver from 1677, together with Nicolaus Enander and Clas Swant. A carving from the stern of the ship survives and has been credited to Hendrik. It is a representation of King Charles XI on horseback. The remarkable attention to detail provides the finishing touches to what is undoubtedly a masterpiece of carving. The imposing portrait of the king is reputed to be a good likeness, captured in a well-balanced, naturalistic composition. It summons up the enthusiasm of the Baroque age, portraying the subject with a vibrancy and confidence that no longer holds on to the precepts of Mannerism.

Nicolaus Enander's mother married the accomplished Swedish woodcarver Johan Werner following the death of his first wife. Nicolaus was therefore brought up within an established family of woodcarvers, working predominantly for the church. The altarpiece in Nyköping Church was carved by him and presented to the church in 1674. It contains figurative and decorative work, both of which are in the Mannerist style, quite different from that of *Carolus XI*, so if Enander assisted with decorative work on the ship, the change of style must have been quite a challenge.

The *Carolus* horse, unfortunately, provides only a glimpse at what must have been an extraordinary advance in the decoration of Swedish ships. The only other information comes from a report to the admiralty describing the interior of its two principal cabins:

> The small was for dining, from which doors led out on deck. They were painted light grey and had on either side a galley covered in copper. The galleries were with three windows, isolated from the cabin with a door. In the cabin stood a stove with picture work. Beside this a bed with some embellishment. The remaining furniture consisting of a dozen chairs, wardrobes for the admiral's belongings and table with carved feet and embellishments, covered in leather. The great cabin was divided into five compartments, the whole having thirty-six windows.

The development in Hendrik Schultz's understanding of the Baroque coincides with a wider proliferation of the style ashore. Following the death of Simon de la Vallée in 1642, Nicodemus Tessin the elder was appointed court architect in 1649, shortly after which he embarked upon a tour of Italy, France and the Netherlands. Each country clearly left a lasting impression, as influences from each were used in the design of various palaces on his return. The crowning of Charles XI's queen, Hedvig Eleonora, in 1654 led to his greatest achievement, Drottningholm Palace (literally 'Queen's Islet').

Commenced in 1662, it was inspired by the chateau of Vaux-le-Vicomte. This innovative palace was designed by the French court architect Louis Le Vau in 1656, with lavish interiors by Le Brun. By the time of Tessin's death in 1681, Drottningholm was filled with examples of all the French, Italian and Dutch fashions the queen could desire. Such a vast body of artistic endeavours would clearly influence the work of aspiring craftsmen, eager to emulate the new fashions.

In contrast to the lavish ornamentation of a large warship, Turner's next vessel, the 36-gun *Stenbock*, would have been modest in comparison. *Stenbock* was launched from the Skeppsholmen yard in 1679, from where she sailed to Kalmar transporting gunpowder. She later served an uneventful career as a guard ship based at Göteborg. In 1714 she formed part of the Swedish naval force in Norway and in 1716 was captured by the Norwegians during the Battle of Dynekien. The badly damaged ship was put into service as a gun lighter, but sank the same year. In 1932 remains of the ship were brought ashore, but they caught fire in 1952. Some remnants of the ship remain, and are on display in the old town of Fredrikstad in Norway, together with a model constructed from information gathered from the wreck. The carvings displayed on the

Stenbock, designed by Robert Turner and launched at Stockholm in 1679. The carvings displayed here do not relate to compositions of that era and probably represent those of a subsequent rebuild. Although balusters were used on French ships around 1670, they do not appear on English or Swedish ships until the turn of the century, by which time the stern above the gallery no longer appeared as narrow as the construction shown here. Similarly the inwardly curving tiled roof to the quarter gallery is of a later date. The figurehead is of a lion wearing the Swedish crown. (Author's collection)

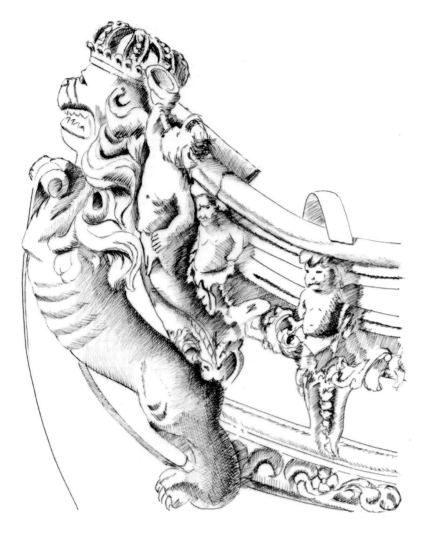

Victoria, designed by Frans Johan Sheldon, launched at Karlskrona in June 1690.
This very successful ship was finally sunk at the Battle of Köge Bay, 24 September 1710.

recently deported from Riga but apparently able to avoid the imprisoned state of his father by convincing the authorities of his desire to serve the crown. Frans proved to be a diligent student, assisting Turner with the 68-gun *Blekinge*, launched in 1682, followed by the 84-gun *Göta Rike* 1684. Turner's last ship, the 70-gun *Karlskrona*, launched 1686, was completed by Frans Sheldon. Turner was by then an old man, and struggling to continue with his work. He had retired to his cottage near the old yard in Lindholmen, where admiralty representatives travelled to his sick bed seeking advice regarding the rebuilding of *Victoria*: 'Sink it as a block ship and build a new one' was his response, reminding them that he had been patching up the old vessel for the last fifteen years and could do no more.

Turner died on 13 April 1686, leaving Frans Sheldon and Gunnar Roth as candidates to fulfil the post. The admiralty expressed their concern in having to deal with another Sheldon, but it was noted that, unlike his father, Frans was obedient and his temperament was docile in comparison. He had spent his life within Swedish shipyards, having learnt much from his father and Turner. He also attended the Swedish church and had taken a Swedish wife. After due consideration, the 26-year-old Frans was appointed master shipwright at the navy's prestigious new yard.

The admiralty were not to be disappointed. With the launch of his first ship, the new 80-gun *Victoria*, in June 1690, Frans proved his worth. Admiral Wachtmeister recorded in a letter to the king: 'The ship has proved to be very capable and good. Her construction surpasses mostly all other ships in the fleet.' Hendrik Schultz joined the yard at Karlskrona in 1686 and may have been responsible for her decorative work. A model exists, complete with very fine carving to the head, but unfortunately none of the stern carvings have survived. The figurehead is of a lion, very much in the English fashion, but wearing a Swedish crown. Carved work to the head timbers are ornamented with putti, the foremost of which rises up beside the lion, blowing a conch shell. The very fine detail and poise of the composition provides a competent example of Baroque ornament.

model are from a later date than the ship's launch and probably relate to a rebuild dating from around 1700.

After *Stenbock*, Turner built his last ship to be launched from Skeppsholmen, the 70-gun *Drottning Hedvig Eleonora*. The wars with Denmark had proved that Stockholm, in the north of the country, was too far from the likely theatre of war. Consequently a new base was established in the recently acquired southern province of Blekinge. In 1680 Turner, accompanied by the admiralty's advisor Eric Ehrenskiöd, went to the established yard at Kalmar, to audit the removal of stores and labour needed to assist with the construction of the complete new town and yard of Karlskrona. Hendrik Schultz also moved to Kalmar, where he was employed on the 70-gun *Drottning Ulrika Eleonora*, designed by the master shipwright at the yard, Gunnar Roth. In the autumn of 1681 Turner moved to Karlskrona, where he was joined by his wife Elisabet and son Ringo.

The following year he was joined by his old apprentice, Sheldon's aspiring son Frans Johan,

Frans Sheldon's success continued with his second ship, the 80-gun *Drottning Ulrika Eleonora*, launched on 13 May 1692. A report to the admiralty stated she was the most imposing ship to have yet come from the yard at Karlskrona, while the 56-gun *Pommern*, launched in October of the same year, was considered to be his masterpiece.

However, on 15 December 1692, after a sudden illness, the 32-year-old Frans died. The shock of his untimely death was a cause of great sorrow to all. When news reached the king, he proclaimed that Sweden had lost its greatest shipwright, who had so much more to give. What provision was made for his wife and son, is not known. Frans' younger brother Charles was still on the payroll as a soldier in the Swedish army in 1689, but shortly after that date appears to have transferred to the navy to train as a shipwright at his own expense. He was apprenticed to Gunnar Roth, but seems to have spent some time in England training under Jonas Shish at Deptford. Roth recommended him in 1691 to the post of shipwright at the Hovjaktvarvet in Stockholm (yard of the king's yachts). Following his brother's death, the 28-year-old Charles was appointed his successor by King Charles XI. He therefore joined his brother's bereaved family, to take up the post of master shipwright to the navy's fleet at Karlskrona.

⟿ Charles Sheldon ⟿

His first ship, the 56-gun *Södermanland*, was launched in 1693, followed by the 100-gun *Konung Karl* in October of 1694, to plans which were essentially the work of his brother Frans. *Konung Karl* stands as a turning point in Swedish ship decoration, reflecting the acceptance on shore of the French Baroque.

Nicodemus Tessin's son, also named Nicodemus (1654-1728), embarked upon a tour of Italy in 1673-4 with the German woodcarver Buchard Precht (1651-1738), where they studied under Gian Lorenzo Bernini and Carlo Fontana. Buchard Precht came from a family of carvers; his older brother Christian was born around 1635 in the German town of Oldenburg, and in 1650 the family moved to Bremen, where Christian trained as a woodcarver and sculptor. During this period he travelled to the Netherlands, returning to Germany around 1660. In 1663, having married Agnetha Rige, he set up his workshop in Hamburg. His earliest known work was as a ship-carver, completing ornamentation to *Leopoldus Primus* and *Wapen von Hamburg*, both launched in 1668 as 54-gun convoy ships. A carving from the stern of *Leopoldus* survives, depicting the Holy Roman Emperor Leopold I. The figure, which stands 8 feet tall, is reasonably expressive, if somewhat stiffly carved. Buchard was working in his brother's workshop at this time, and may well have had a part in executing this early work. Christian continued to work in Hamburg, having been commissioned in 1674 to provide the altar for the Church of St Cosmae et Damiani in the town of Stade, which displays workmanship of an entirely different order, the figurative work demonstrating a far greater sense of movement and grace.

Buchard, having returned from his European tour the same year, remained in Stockholm, where he was appointed as sculptor to the crown. His brother continued to work both for the church and for shipyards. In 1686 he completed the carvings for *Wapen von Hamburg III*. In 1688 he completed the altar and pulpit for St Pancras Church in Neuenfelde. *Leopoldus Primus* underwent a refit in 1689, during which Christian carried out repairs to her carved work. During 1691-2 he completed carvings to the ship *Admiral von Hamburg*, followed by carvings to the organ of St James Church, Hamburg in 1692-4. This was probably his last commission, as he died at some time between 1694 and 1695.

Tessin the younger made a further European tour during 1677-8, in the company of his stepbrother Abraham Wynantz (1644-1709), visiting England and France. Abraham's father had died before his birth; his mother married Tessin's father in 1653 and so the two had grown up together almost from birth. In France they were able to study Charles Le Brun's interior decoration as it developed at Versailles, the transition of his work to that of Jean Bérain, and the work of sculptors such as François Girardon (1628-1715) and Jean Lépautre (1618-1682).

On their return they worked extensively on their father's projects and on his death in 1681, Tessin the younger was appointed court architect. His first commission was to modernise the northern part of the royal castle in Stockholm. He made a further trip to Italy and France, no doubt clarifying in his mind aspects of the design, gathering further information and making contacts. Among these was Daniel Cronström, a Swedish ambassador in Paris, who was to prove invaluable in future negotiations with manufacturers and artists required by Tessin to work at the castle, which was completed in 1695. The exterior was inspired by Bernini's design for the Louvre, but with a more sombre mood that befitted its northern climes, while much of the interior was inspired predominantly by the fashions of

Above: Compardel's painting based on Jean Bérain's drawings for the decoration of *Konung Karl*. The format of the painting follows a common convention of ship portraiture, where the subject is shown from a number of different angles, so every aspect of the ship is represented. This suggests the purpose of the painting is to illustrate the proposed features of a design, or record the actual appearance of a new ship. (By courtesy of the Maritime Museum, Stockholm)

Right: The projecting walkways to the stern were at this period essentially a French fashion, but their termination with the quarter piece retains figurative work rather than the open junction seen on French ships. This detail, combined with the shape of the tafferel, allows the stern to maintain the outline appearance of an English ship, but Bérain has adapted his distinctly French ornamentation within these constraints. The use of open balusters to the quarter gallery first appear in the designs of Colbert and Puget during the 1660s but was generally confined to French ships until the turn of the century. *Konung Karl* was therefore the first ship outside of France to adopt this detail. (By courtesy of the Maritime Museum, Stockholm)

Versailles, with the work undertaken by French craftsmen.

At the time of Tessin's visits to France, Bérain held the post of overseer to the master carvers of the French navy, where his designs fulfilled the request of his predecessor Le Brun to reduce the amount of figurative work by implementing other forms of decoration, such as interlacing foliage and bandwork panels. The formula he came to perfect created a balance of artistic expression and functionality that was well suited to the ornamentation of ships.

Tessin appears to have held a similar position to that of Bérain within the Swedish navy. His desire to implement decorative work to the same high standard as that within the royal court, prompted him to write to Cronström, asking him to approach Bérain with a view to designing the decorative work for Charles Sheldon's latest ship *Konung Karl*. Bérain submitted pen and ink drawings depicting the stern, quarter galleries and figurehead. These were transposed to a painting by

This detail from Compardel's painting shows the format of Bérain's design, adapted to suit the shape of an English stern. The low central lantern obscuring the tafferel has necessitated the coat of arms being duplicated, rather than a single central design, but carvings that are believed to come from the ship show an alternative solution, where the shield is split between the two lions. Tessin, in a later drawing, adjusted the pose of the quarter piece figures, directing their outer arms inboard to a less vulnerable position. (By courtesy of the Maritime Museum, Stockholm)

the French artist Etienne Compardel, where, to meet Tessin's requirements, colour was added. Compardel had studied with Gérard Dou, who in turn had been a pupil of Rembrandt from 1628 to 1631. Gérard Dou was the leader of what was known as the Precise School in Leiden. In 1670 Compardel entered the art academy of St Luke, specialising as a miniaturist painter. His talents were therefore well suited to impart intricate detail, providing the carvers with a clear picture of the desired effect.

Tessin's original intention was to have the ship transferred from Karlskrona to Stockholm, where the decorative work could be completed under his personal supervision. The plan was for carving to be carried out by the French sculptor René Chauveau (1663-1722), who had been working at the castle for the past year. Chauveau was the son of the famous wood engraver François Chauveau. He initially trained under Philippe Caffieri (master carver at Dunkirk) and thus had experience with ship decoration. He then worked at Versailles under the sculptor François Girardon. The naturalistic style of his figurative work, which imparts great depth of emotive expression, was to greatly influence the work of Chauveau. Girardon had also been employed as a carver to the French navy, working from the yard at Toulon.

When the scheme to move the ship proved impracticable, Tessin's stepbrother Abraham Wjnantz (ennobled as Svansköld in 1692) was appointed ornamental designer to the admiralty and sent to Karlskrona to oversee the work, which was undertaken by Hendrik Schultz. The terms of his contract, which he signed on 4 September 1696, stated that the total sum of 2000 riksdalers was to be paid in three instalments, the first to be paid at the time of signing. With a contract period of one year, such a sum would allow for seven journeymen carvers to assist Hendrik on the project.

Bérain continued to receive commissions from Tessin, a notable example of which is the ceremonial coach for King Charles XI. Cronström was once more kept busy, as all the component parts of the coach were produced in Paris, then transported to Stockholm, where they were reassembled. The coach still survives, offering an insight into the detail that would have been found on the stern of *Konung Karl*. The superb craftsmanship displays the brilliance of Bérain's artistic ability. Motifs that would normally serve to exemplify the glory of Louis XIV have been

Royal Palace (Stockholm Castle), east entrance. (Author's collection)

replaced with those of the Swedish crown: the North Star replaces the symbol of the Sun King; allegorical figures signifying justice and prudence sit beside the Swedish lion; tapestries to the interior are richly decorated with Bérain's distinctive format of bandwork panels – here the foliate forms are considerably lighter than the examples of Le Brun, but regain a sense of richness when expressed as three-dimensional carvings to the exterior of the coach.

While Tessin continued to immerse himself in

Two small details from Bérain's coach for the King of Sweden, 1696. Cronström engaged Maillard the elder, the finest coachbuilder in Paris, to design the body of the coach, to which Bérain added his ornamentation; alternatively, he may have approved that of the builders, such as these designs which were the work the sculptor I Doluiar, who presumably then executed the work. The coach was then disassembled and transported to Sweden.

Precht's design for panelling to the pulpit of Stockholm Cathedral, 1698-1702. The density and vigorous nature of the foliage is akin to the work of Le Brun, which he characteristically worked within set panels of bandwork, but with greater virtuosity and fullness, typical of the style that developed in northern Germany and into Scandinavia.

Watercolour designs for decoration to the ceiling of the master cabin of *Enigheten*, Charles Sheldon's three-decked 94-gun ship launched from Karlskrona in June 1696. The style shown here reflects the work of carvers from Precht's homeland of northern Germany, further developed by his studies in Italy and the earlier exponents of French Baroque. (Author's collection by courtesy of the Maritime Museum, Stockholm)

the evolving artistic achievements of French Baroque, Buchard Precht, perhaps already influenced by the style prevalent in his native Germany, was drawn more to the earlier work of Le Brun, where the richness of composition was more akin to their Italian origins. During their tour of Italy and France it was clearly examples of this style that inspired him the most. His work within Stockholm Cathedral shows a clear affinity with the work of Bérain's predecessor Le Brun, in set panels that could with ease be transcribed to the stern of a ship.

Konung Karl proved to be a successful, well-built vessel, serving as flagship to Admiral Wachtmeister during the Great Northern War (1700-1721), following which she was the first ship to use Karlskrona's dry dock – built by Charles Sheldon in 1724 – where she underwent a refit. She outlived the reigns of both Charles XI and Charles XII and was not broken up until 1771.

Little information remains on Charles's subsequent ships, with the exception of *Enigheten*, a 94-gun ship launched in 1696. She too enjoyed a long and successful career before being broken up, also in 1771. A series of watercolour sketches show proposed decoration to her master cabin. The artist is unknown, but the style shows a return to the more luxuriant quality associated with the work of Precht.

Such grandiose embellishment to the interior of the ship implies that an equally extravagant degree of ornamentation would have been exhibited on her stern. The return to a form of scrolling acanthus whose density is more akin to Italian examples suggests that the ship, designed by Charles Sheldon to English principles, was also ornamented more in line with English fashions than the prevailing French. Decorative work consisting purely of scrolling acanthus would have been unthinkable in France, particularly by this late date. The artist Jean Lépautre, who was an early exponent of the style and to which Precht was a strong adherent, had died in 1682, by which time Jean Bérain's considerably lighter form of acanthus, set within compositions that combined a variety of other motifs, had come to dominate the ornamental fashions at Versailles.

Precht-inspired compositions were replicated beyond the wealthy churches of the capital by journeyman painters and carvers, many examples of which can be seen throughout Sweden, Norway and Denmark in both domestic and secular settings. This being the poor man's access to art, it was soon replicated in a painted form on the walls and ceilings of even the most humble of dwellings. As a form of folk art it was used at every opportunity, decorating furniture and household articles.

The vigorous style of foliage used for the interior of *Enigheten* appears again on the plans of a 72-gun ship designed by Charles Sheldon dated 1702, by which time such compositions consisting purely of scrolling acanthus had developed into a unique Scandinavian style. Tessin openly opposed the use of such decoration, but clearly failed to stem its popularity.

An unusual feature on English ships during the reign of Queen Anne (1702-1714) was a deepening of the head, necessitating the introduction of a fourth head rail. This can be seen in his 1702 design, so Charles must have been aware of the latest developments in English ship design and decorative fashions. However, one unfortunate consequence of the deeper head was to produce a disproportionally long figure, often resulting in the adoption of composite figures rather than the single lion.

The organ of Vor Frelsers Church, Copenhagen: acanthus compositions carved by Christian Nerger, 1696-1698. (Author's collection)

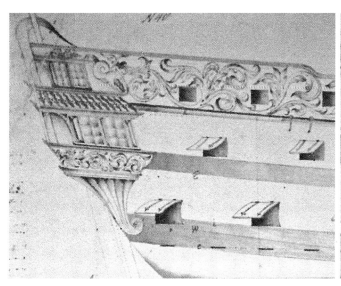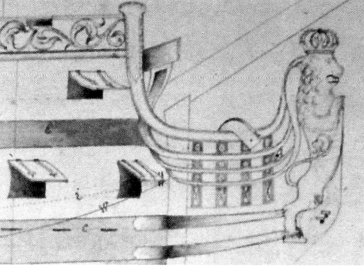

Quarter gallery and head to Charles Sheldon's *Enigheten* of 1702. The disproportionately long lion is a result of the deep head, requiring the addition of a fourth rail. This unusual detail first appears on English ships during the reign of Queen Anne (1702-1714). (Author's collection by courtesy of the Maritime Museum, Stockholm)

Sheldon's marriage to Eva Maria Mesterton produced nineteen children, of whom only three daughters and two sons survived. The youngest, Gilbert, was born in 1710 and would become Charles's successor. Later correspondence between Gilbert and the admiralty gives an insight into the working conditions of the carver Hendrik Schultz and his successor Jacob Waldau (1671-1743). On the 19 March 1747 Gilbert Sheldon sought to give an explanation to the admiralty regarding what they perceived as the unauthorised employment of ship's carpenters by the carvers. He gave examples from legal records to shed light on the procedures adopted by the figurehead carvers of the past, detailing their business operations and methods of remuneration, in order to defend the current practice.

Among these was a contract was drawn up on 11 November 1689 with the carver Hendrik Schultz (possibly for Frans Sheldon's *Victoria*), with rates and conditions regarding periods of payment agreed. A woodcarver working for the admiralty at this time would expect to earn 600 dalers per annum, with three to four journeyman carvers as his staff, who received 200 dalers per annum each. A price was negotiated, and payment was made accordingly by the piece. By comparison, the result of a further contract drawn up with Schultz on 15 August 1698 shows that earnings had reduced to 400 dalers, with a staff of only two journeymen carvers.

By 1715-16 the normal payment had dropped to 200 dalers per annum, with no payments made to journeyman carvers. At this time all woodcarving was in pine or lime cut flat (this presumably means the carving was either flat relief, or carved from separate sections), but

the method then changed to the English manner of using oak or pine laminated together to form a solid block, 'which falls hard on the carver'! Sheldon explained that the now deceased carver Jacob Waldau had used this method for the *Drottning Ulrika Eleonora*'s decorative work, which was why he had received a one-third increase in payment, as agreed in the admiralty's resolution of 16 March 1721. After this time all proposed carved work continued by this method. Waldau's income for 1722 still remained at 200 dalers, indicating the lack of work following the end of the war, with pricing fixed by the piece to keep a tight check on expenditure.

Sheldon went on to observe that following the introduction of this method it had always been the custom for the woodcarver to receive assistance from the carpenters, to rough out and then join up the sections to form the block. What earnings they shared, he considered, was their business. Sheldon further notes that in former years the woodcarver's place of work was not situated on the crown's land but often at his own home, which necessitated the much-needed carpenters leaving the yard to work daily at the carver's workplace. This situation was rectified in 1736 by the building of a woodcarver's shop at the yard, which was later referred to as the woodcarving school.

COLOUR PLATES

Plate 11: The identity of this model of an 80-gun two-decker is fixed by an inscription on the poop deck rail which reads 'Ye Boyne built by Mr. Harding.' Fisher Harding was the master shipwright at Deptford at the time of the ship's launch in 1692. It is common to find the name of a shipwright attached to a ship model, but it is not clear if the shipwright is the modelmaker as well as the designer of the ship. (National Maritime Museum F3860-006)

Plate 12: This model of the *Yarmouth* launched from Deptford Dockyard in 1745. Her carved work conforms to the Admiralty order of 1703 in restricting carved work to the tafferel and quarters on the stern, and to the upper and lower finishings of the quarter galleries. The model presents a superb composition, making full use of the restricted area available (*see page 130*). (National Maritime Museum F5797-004)

Plate 13: The 100-gun First Rate *Royal George* was launched from the Woolwich yard in 1756, with carved work by Thomas Burrough (*see page 134*). (National Maritime Museum D4082-007)

Plate 14: Ole Judichær's design for the stern of the 90-gun ship *Elephanten* launched in 1703. The French-inspired design has been augmented with homegrown Danish motifs. The use of lists create set panels of decoration, the uppermost of which adopts the use of painted work to create a decorative frieze. Colour has been added to only one side in order to demonstrate the design's dependence on the medium, without which the intricacy of the design is hard to comprehend. For the designer of carved work, it serves to demonstrate the importance of scale in relation to the distance from which the piece is to be viewed (*see page 150*). (Author's collection)

Plate 15: On the *Fyen* of 1736 sweeping curves dominate the composition of stern and quarter galleries, which incorporate a Palladian style window (*see page 158*). (Author's collection reproduced by courtesy of the Danish Naval Museum, Copenhagen)

Plate 16: The windows of *Fyen*'s quarterdeck follow the elliptical shape of the stern and are complemented by those of the quarter gallery. The reduction in carving resulting from the narrowing of the tafferel is balanced by the inclusion of relief carved panels to the counter. Their composition of relief carved figures, or lightly scrolling acanthus, returns to the simplicity of Classical form, but without losing the sense of movement and emotive power that embodies the essence of Baroque grandeur. This Wiedewelt has achieved, not by imitating the highly emotional French, but by creating in his design the perfect balance of Classical structure and applied decoration, with a confidence that allows the Scandinavian nature to be expressed in its own right, manifesting the natural laws of harmonic perfection (*see page 158*). (Author's collection reproduced by courtesy of the Danish Naval Museum, Copenhagen)

Plate 17, 18: Wiedewelt produced maquettes of his figureheads, many of which survive, providing a valuable record of his work (*see page 158*). The illustration shows his maquette for *Fyen*, here compared with the figure as depicted on the model of the ship now in the collection of the Danish Naval Museum, Copenhagen. (Author's collection reproduced by courtesy of the Danish Naval Museum, Copenhagen)

Plate 19: The *Tre Croner* of 1742 designed by Barbé with decoration by Wiedewelt (*see page 159*). (Image reproduced by courtesy of the Danish Naval Museum Copenhagen)

Plate 20: Casts have been taken from many of the original carvings from the Swedish warship *Vasa* of 1628, such as the Wasa coat of arms from the stern of the ship, which have been finished in colours that represent their original appearance. The blue cartouche is interesting in that the timber has been saved from an earlier carving. On its reverse side there is the outline of a lion, partially roughed out. The Wasa arms are believed to be the work of the Dutch carver Johann Thesson (*see page 172*). (Author's collection reproduced by courtesy of the Wasa Museum, Stockholm)

Plate 21: Seen in this model, the unique arrangement of *Enigheten*'s tafferel creates a simple elegance that sets her apart from other ships of the period (*see page 197*). (By courtesy of the Maritime Museum, Stockholm)

Plate 22: Chapman's 74-gun ship *Gustaf IV Adolph*, launched 1790 (*see page 207*). (Author's collection by courtesy of the Maritime Museum, Stockholm)

Plate 23: The replica Swedish East India ship *Götheborg* with decorative work designed and carved by the author.

PLATE 11

PLATE 12

PLATE 13

ROYAL GEORGE

PLATE 14

PLATE 15

PLATE 16

PLATE 17

PLATE 18

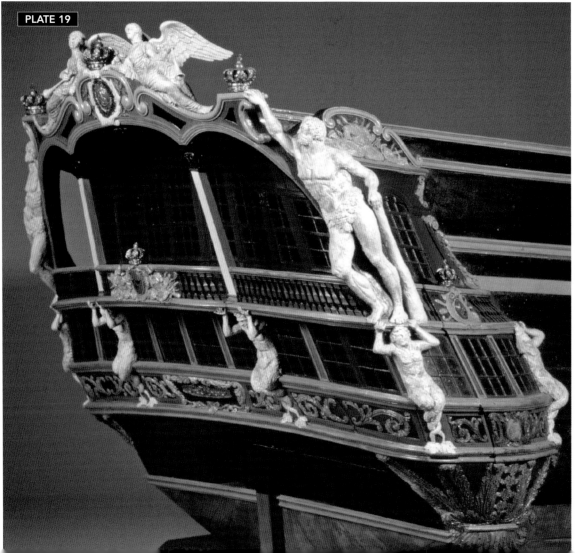

PLATE 19

PLATE 20

PLATE 21

PLATE 22

PLATE 23

Charles Sheldon's drawing showing the decorative composition for his 70-gun ship of 1703, *Nord Stjärnan*. (Author's collection by courtesy of the Maritime Museum, Stockholm)

stern. *Bremen*, by comparison, sports a balustraded walkway presenting a sense of stoic solidity in its Classical form, lacking the flourishes of French finesse.

Nord Stjärnan remained in active service up until 1715, when she was captured by the Danes whilst on guard duty south of the Öresund Sound. She served in the Danish navy as the *Nordstiernen* until 1785, having benefited from an extensive refit during 1746-7.

Waldau appears to come in for some criticism over his work on Charles Sheldon's 86-gun *Drottning Ulrika Eleonora*, launched in 1719. In a letter of 1720, Admiral Sparre wrote about the decoration that he considered the overall design of Sheldon's composition to be an inspired masterpiece, but its quality had been let down in the carvings. He records his reservations regarding the ability of the carvers, noting that a Triton, which had been suggested as the figurehead:

> appeared thick and deformed. The proportions of the figure being hard to make use of and therefore a lion would be preferred, thereby giving prominence to the English ship, which in design is very well formed, although it doth come exceedingly costly, but this is necessary to meet the requirement of a beautiful appearance.

Following the death of Hendrik Schultz in 1701 the position of master carver went to his stepson Jacob Waldau. His acceptance of the post coincided with the outbreak of the Great Northern War (1700-1721) and subsequent heightened activity at the yard. Charles Sheldon's 70-gun ship *Nord Stjärnan* (North Star) was launched in 1703, followed by *Prins Karl Fredrik* in 1704 and *Bremen* in 1706. Similar in design, both *Nord Stjärnan* and *Bremen* display decorative compositions that are a mixture of English and French styles.

The figurehead of *Bremen* is depicted as a lion in the English mode, *rampant*, crowned with curling mane. *Nord Stjärnan*'s figurehead depicts a merman or triton holding the North Star. The head rails of both vessels terminate behind the cathead as on French ships, while the remaining head arrangement subscribes to the English fashion. There are elements of the quarter galleries to *Nord Stjärnan* that maintain a French feel, particularly the bottle shape and elegant nature of the ornamentation, but fitted to a distinctly English

A contemporary model of *Nord Stjärnan* survives; although crudely constructed, it does offer an insight into the shape of the stern, which is typical of an English ship of the period in both layout and decorative composition. (Author's collection by courtesy of the Maritime Museum, Stockholm)

Sparre insisted that the woodcarver Jacob Waldau make adjustments to the work of other craftsmen as they became ready, and that Waldau himself add the finer details. The previously quoted letter from Gilbert Sheldon shows that Waldau had been instructed to work partly in oak, which he pointed out 'falls hard on the carver'. Although he was given a third increase in payment to compensate for this, his wages were still very low. Carvers worked to a fixed price, being paid by the piece, reflecting the lack of money during the war, which was also reflected in the lower number of assistant carvers employed at the yard. Criticism of the work's quality should perhaps be viewed in this context. Possibly as a result, the sizes of the carvings were documented, probably in order to fix a price: the lion stood 16 feet high and 6 feet wide (deep); the stern had five independent carvings, of which two had a length of 6 feet with a width of 3 feet, decorated with palm branches and leaf work.

As the war dragged on, finances dwindled and shipbuilding declined, leaving a period of little enthusiasm for innovation or thought towards artistic endeavours. Charles XII was killed in battle, effectively marking the end of Sweden's Baltic empire and an era in which the monarch ruled supreme. By the end of the war in 1721 the government had severely reduced the power of the monarchy in an effort to rebuild the economy. It looked to Britain as a model for its political ideology, and greater trade between the two countries led to the import of British goods, particularly furniture and the accompanying decorative arts which, being less flamboyant than the French, found a natural empathy with the similarly reserved nature of the Swedish people. This was particularly the case among the expanding merchant class on the west coast, where Göteborg grew as a trading centre, with the town displaying many examples of English-inspired architecture.

The period also saw the opening of new yards in Stockholm to cater for this burgeoning merchant trade and to replace the many merchant ships lost during the war. The Terra Nova yard had been purchased in 1716 by one Abraham Gill, who appointed William Mackett master shipwright. The first record of a ship built by him at the yard was the *Fredericus Rex*, launched in 1725; she was sold to the newly formed Swedish East India Company to become their first ship in 1731.

Another shipwright connected with this period is William Smith (1670-1733). Little is known of this remarkable man, yet he received honours that surpass even those of the renowned F H Chapman. Born in Stockholm around 1680, he spent some time serving as a shipwright in Stralsund, a port in the Swedish-held territory of Pomerania, but apart from this, where he gained his knowledge is unknown. He came to Karlskrona penniless in 1704, gaining employment as a shipwright at the yard. He proved to be a remarkably talented man: 1711 saw the launch of a ship to his own design, a 30-gun frigate named *Vita Örn* that Admiral Sparre hailed as very beautiful, perfect, and very well built. She proved to be an exceptionally fast, easily handled vessel, for which Smith was awarded a medal. She famously sank the Danish frigate *Blå Hager* in 1712 but was finally captured by the Danes in 1715, to become the command of Peter Wessel, later the famous Vice Admiral Tordenskiold. He also considered her swift and very seaworthy. A painting of the ship shows her with a lion figurehead wearing a British-style crown; the stern and quarter galleries are richly decorated in Baroque compositions with the Swedish coat of arms forming the centre piece of the tafferel.

By 1715 Smith had risen to the position of master shipwright, on the same pay as Charles Sheldon. Sparre wrote to the admiralty in 1720, following the launch of his next ship the *Svarta Örn*, that Smith had built two incomparable frigates and encouragement should be given to further his work. The state commissioners wrote to the king requesting that not less than 2000 dalers be awarded to him in recognition of his talent and diligence, and to encourage his further education. To this end, in 1723 he established a private yard in Stockholm, securing a contract to supply the navy. He was joined in the venture by an influential entrepreneur named Hans Lenman, who had already financed the building of ships at the Stora Stad yard.

Smith and Lenman disagreed from the start, and relations only got worse. Lenman insisted that the admiralty remove him on the grounds of his inexperience and suggested a replacement. Smith remained, but this open hostility led to vengeful and vindictive behaviour from Lenman, who was famed for his use of satire and took every opportunity to injure Smith's reputation. His colleagues who found themselves similarly wronged asked the king for gracious protection against such insinuations and reproach.

Amidst such antagonism Smith produced two

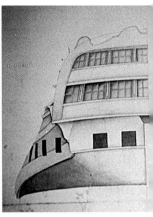

William Smith's 60-gun *Friheten*, launched from Djurgårds yard, Stockholm in 1725. Although the drawing is devoid of any ornamental detail, it is clear from the layout that the composition would have conformed to the British precepts of the period. The ship gained a reputation for being well balanced and strongly built. (Krigsarkivet, Stockholm)

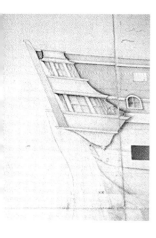

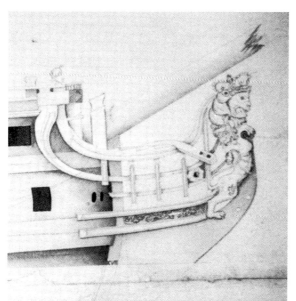

ships, the 60-gun *Friheten*, launched in 1725, followed by the 40-gun *Freden*. The perfection he demanded in the building of his ships led to disaffection in the attitude of some workers. On one occasion he observed a man swinging an axe into the air, coming down taking off too much timber. He scolded him, saying such careless work ruined the accuracy of the entire frame and advised him that the precision required could only be achieved by taking smaller cuts. This was not possible with such a tool, responded the man; yes, declared Smith, it was quite possible, and with skill you could remove whatever you wished: 1/16th of an inch, 1/32nd even. The timberman argued that such accuracy would take too long; then the frame will be ruined and another must be made, replied Smith. Such incidents only fuelled the sarcastic wit of Lenman, who protested to the navy that skilled men, having worked for twenty years in building naval and merchant ships, now had to be taught by Smith how to hold an axe!

Smith's drawing of the lion figurehead for *Friheten* bears an uncanny resemblance to a carving held at Stockholm Maritime Museum from the same period. Adorned with an English style of crown, the facial expression, position of paws and hind legs, and the style of curling mane are all identical.

The carving is reputed to be from a Swedish East Indiaman, but standing at only 8 feet tall (2.4m) it would only be in proportion to a ship of, say, up to 100 feet in length. A 60-gun ship would be in the region of 140 feet, requiring a figurehead of some 10 feet (3m) in height. (Author's collection by courtesy of the Maritime Museum, Stockholm)

Lion figurehead dating from 1720-1740. This well-preserved figure held at Stockholm Maritime Museum provides a good example of the ship-carver's art of the period. (Author's collection by courtesy of the Maritime Museum, Stockholm)

Thus was introduced a general unease at the yard. In the autumn of 1732 Smith complained of illness, which he claimed was brought about by the pressures of work. On 15 January 1733 he died, leaving behind his wife Anna Beata Kohl and their children in great poverty and misery. The shipwright Daniel Fries trained with Smith in Karlskrona, designing a galley under Smith's direction that he submitted for approval to the yard at Västervik. Unfortunately, his lack of previous experience led to the commission going to another designer. He subsequently moved to Stockholm with Smith, remaining a loyal servant until his master's death. Fries later married one of his daughters, and another married the yard commissioner Olof Rahm, which may have helped Smith's widow. Fries remained in Stockholm, working at the Djurgård yard where he built the 60-gun ship *Fredericus Rex* in 1742, the 64-gun *Konung Adolph Friedrich* designed by Gilbert Sheldon but built by Fries in 1744, and the 72-gun *Drottning Lovisa Ulrica* in 1745, after which there is no further mention of his name.

At the time of Smith's death the admiralty were proposing a method of standardising ship types and the extent to which the master shipwrights would be governed by detailed regulations issued by the admiralty. It was decided that models from the most successful ships should be made, to record their lines and form of construction for future reference. The three chosen were Karl Falk's 40-gun *Drottningholm* of 1731, Charles Sheldon's 70-gun *Enigheten* of 1732, and William Smith's 60-gun *Friheten* of 1725. The intention was for the constructor of each ship to build a model, and so Karl Falk was to build *Drottningholm*, Gilbert Sheldon to build *Enigheten*, and Daniel Fries to build the model of his now deceased father-in-law William Smith's *Friheten*.

Stern detail from Gilbert Sheldon's exam paper of 1732 depicting a 50-gun ship. The gallery layout is remarkably similar to *Enigheten*, particularly the continuous line of lights and the painted acanthus frieze, the main alteration being the adoption of balusters to the galleries of the quarterdeck. Because of his ill health, the completion of Charles's project was taken on by his son Gilbert, suggesting that he was responsible for the design of the ornamentation, which he based on this proposal for a smaller ship. (By courtesy of the Maritime Museum, Stockholm)

The tail and mane display elements of chinoiserie in the tightness of the curls, which double back in a manner typical of lions depicted in Chinese art. Such influence in figureheads is generally seen around the 1730s. (Author's collection by courtesy of the Maritime Museum, Stockholm)

Charles Sheldon clearly had the greatest respect for Smith, requesting him to examine the papers of his aspiring son Gilbert, who had studied at the university in Lund and at the yard in Karlskrona. Shortly before his death Smith took his place on the board of examiners with Admirals Wachtmeister and Rajalin, who awarded Gilbert his papers as master shipwright.

The model of the *Enigheten*, which is now in the maritime museum in Stockholm, is complete in all its decorative detail. Although the general layout of the galleries conforms to the British convention in having an open gallery to the quarterdeck with a closed gallery below, the arrangement of the tafferel is quite different. On a British ship it would terminate with the roof of the quarter gallery to allow quarter-piece figures to carry on down to the base of the lower lights. The Danes had by this time adopted the Baltic Stern, where the horseshoe shape consisting of figurative work to the quarters would also terminate at this point or extend lower in the French fashion. This unique arrangement creates a continuous line of lights, as they sweep gracefully round to form the quarter galleries. Painted decoration to the upper counter conforms to the British convention, and is particularly appropriate in this instance, where the line of lights

forms a natural completion to the carved work.

The lighter effect of painted work accentuates the elegant curving form, here decorated in a simple band of acanthus, the construction of which draws inspiration from the Scandinavian development of folk art rather than the contemporary French or Italian conventions. By discarding the orthodox approach of setting a continuous thread that rises and falls in an alternating sequence of scrolls, this somewhat wayward form avoids repetition, creating an unpretentious freedom, expressed as variations on a theme, where the essence of Classicism is glimpsed through a spontaneous arrangement of inventive detail. A central cartouche houses the F.R.S. initials of the reigning king, Fredericus Rex Sueciae (Svea being the Norse name for Sweden and Suecia the Latin).

The balustrading also resembles examples found in the folk art tradition, seen in various designs to decorate everything from the verandas of imposing manor houses down to the simple porches of farming communities. The fretwork nature of the design creates an effective form of decoration that could be cheaply reproduced. Ornamentation to brackets, bargeboards, and window surrounds adopted the same technique to

Model of the *Enigheten* of 1732 (see also colour plate 21). (Author's collection by courtesy of the Maritime Museum, Stockholm)

bring a wealth of ornament to the buildings of towns and farms, with local variations evolving to give styles unique to each region.

The tafferel strays from the set format previously adhered to, at least in a formal sense. The central motif of the royal arms has been replaced by a female figure representing Svea, the personification of Sweden, which in Norse mythology was ruled by kings descended from Freya, the goddess of love. Svea holds in her right hand a heart, symbol of love and unity (*Enigheten* being the Swedish for unity).

On her port side is a seated figure, possibly a representation of the nereid Amphitrite. She holds a shield depicting a lion *passant* on a blue and gold ground. Beyond this is a stylised dolphin, the mythical beast that delivered Amphitrite to her husband Neptune, represented by a crowned figure sitting to the starboard side of Svea. He holds a shield with the three crowns of Sweden. Neptune was devoured on the day of his birth by his father, but restored to life, an event that may be alluded to by a bird beyond Neptune that resembles a phoenix. Two standing figures form the quarter pieces, below which are two further nereids, their fishy tails shown twisting upwards behind them.

Gilbert's father Charles was responsible for the initial design of *Enigheten*; although not launched until 1732, the keel was laid in 1728. Charles was facing increasing hostility from the admiralty, who commented that, unlike his brother Frans, Charles had inherited their father's temperament, the obstinate nature of which was no doubt fuelled by the weariness of old age and the petty attitude of his colleagues. Admiral Rajalin complained that (the now 67-year-old) Charles was becoming difficult to deal with, and he maintained that repairs to the vessel *Snaren Sven* in 1732 were not properly supervised by Charles, resulting in her developing a severe leak on being re-floated. Thomas von Rajalin, who held the post of equipment master at Karlskrona, also reprimanded Charles for removing a stove from an admiralty building for use in his own home.

It was suggested that Gilbert take over responsibility for his father's work. The resident master carver, Johan Waldau, who had also been criticised for failing to maintain the standard of carved work, now came under the direction of Gilbert. One must therefore assume that this new team were responsible for the ornamentation of *Enigheten*. Being a well-educated man, Gilbert was certainly capable of conceiving the mythologically based composition for the stern, with Waldau being responsible for at least the overseeing and final detailing of the work.

The admiralty clearly placed great confidence in the aspirations of Gilbert, for on the completion of *Enigheten* he was given leave to spend three years abroad at the crown's expense to further his studies. He wished to occupy his time in Britain but fearing that the name of Sheldon was well known in the navy yards there, he was given two passports: one in the name of Gilbert Kalsson, without mentioning his profession, and one with the correct information. After spending some time visiting Denmark, he arrived in England in October 1734. By May of 1735 he was employed at the royal dockyard in Deptford, where he spent the remainder of his time. Returning home in June of 1737, he was granted the position of assistant master shipwright working under Karl Falk.

His father was by this time a sick man; he suffered a fall at the yard and had to be taken home on a stretcher, after which he was no longer able to

Gilbert Sheldon's exam drawing showing the lion figurehead compared with the completed model of *Enigheten*. The latter differs in that a shield is placed behind the lion, effectively shortening the apparent excessive length of the rails and acting as a *cagouille* in the French manner, to widen the flare of the rails. The main rail shows notched stops to hold the bumpkin at preset positions. The gap between the lion's head and the bowsprit is unusually large, even for a British ship, which had a larger clearance than that of the French. The gap has been rectified on the rigged model, bringing it very close, as in the French fashion. (Author's collection by courtesy of the Maritime Museum, Stockholm)

travel to the yard. There was now no alternative but for Gilbert to oversee his father's work, while Charles willingly shared what knowledge he had acquired with all who sought it, before passing away on 6 August 1739. The last drawing to carry his signature was in 1738 for the 24-gun frigate *Castor*, completed by his son and launched together with the 32-gun frigate *Fama* in 1739.

During his forty years in office at Karlskrona, Charles Sheldon had built over 25 ships of the line, and around 32 frigates, plus numerous bomb vessels, galleys and other smaller craft. He also designed Karlskrona's dry dock, blasted out of the rock at Lindholmen. Mårten Triewald (1691-1747), who is best known for his 'air and fire machines', designed the pumps, the ingenuity of which Charles was able to witness on its completion in 1724, when it was pumped dry for repair works to be undertaken to his ship *Konung Karl* of 1694. The irritating foibles of an old man are of little consequence when one considers the enormous diligence and distinguished service he had given through the years.

Before leaving for Britain, Gilbert must have had some input into the design of the 60-gun ship *Finland*, which was built by Karl Falk and launched in 1735. In a letter to the admiralty Gilbert Sheldon described in detail the ornamentation of the stern. Unfortunately, the accompanying drawing has not survived, which makes the description difficult to envisage in places, but it provides an insight into the magnitude of the lavish composition, and the meaning attributed to many of the motifs. It is also significant in illustrating the authority he was given to create the designs:

> In the centre of the hackbrädet [tafferel] is placed Sweden's coat of arms painted in the appropriate colours. On either side is a bear, his front paws holding the vapen [arms] while his hind legs trample a cannon. On the starboard side is placed a lion, also Friheten [Freedom] holding in her right hand a spear and wreath, while the left rests on a bear who sits between her knees.

Sheldon then describes a small scene where a figure blows a trumpet while holding a palm, on what he describes as the *hörnposten* [quarter piece], signifying a proclamation of peace, while the right supports a pillar which stands upon a disc carved with the arms of Northern Finland, having a bear in two fields, with a sword in one arm and a star in front and behind. The description continues: the afore-mentioned pillar stood on a plate with the arms of Northern Finland and under that was carved the arms of Tavastland, which is a lynx with three stars over.

On the port side of the tafferel is Hercules with bearskin and club in hand. With reference to another figure, Sheldon notes that the corresponding image represents 'Factum Laudabile', or praiseworthy work and deeds depicted as a radiant figure, with spear in his right hand which pierces the head of a serpent, the second hand holding an open book; his left foot standing on a skull and in this picture is again a sign which is Stora Finland's arms [the arms of the country as a whole] carved, being a lion with sword held in its front paws; around the lion the ground is laden with roses. Another scene refers to Southern Finland's arms with two flags level with a helm over which was a crown. A reference to painting notes that the whole work was to be gilded, whilst the lion figurehead was to be painted only in yellow colour.

The ship was built in Stockholm, with funding and possible subsidies from the admiralty, by the entrepreneur Hans Lenman. At the time of the ship's launch, Waldau was still master carver at Karlskrona, but at 64 years of age and only eight years before his death, it is unlikely that health, or commitments at the yard, would have made it possible for him to travel to Stockholm. It is likely, therefore, that another carver completed the work, where the fashions of high society in the capital were making themselves felt in ornamentation beyond the court.

Work on the palace in Stockholm, which had ceased during the war, recommenced in 1728, the same year that Tessin the younger died, leaving his son Carl Gustav to oversee the work. The exterior was completed to his father's design, whilst the interior was entrusted to new court architect Carl Hårleman (1700-1753). Carl Gustav himself was not without influence. He was a great admirer of the artist François Boucher. Following the death of Louis XIV in 1715, the French court became less formal, which is reflected in the Regency style. By the 1720s this in turn was evolving into the chinoiserie and Rococo of which Boucher was a keen exponent. With the death in 1715 of Queen Hedvig Eleonora, responsibility for Drottningholm was left to her daughter Ulrika Eleonora. Her choice of furnishings would also come to reflect the emergence of chinoiserie. It was under Hårleman's direction with his work at the palace that the Regency, and particularly the Rococo, influences were introduced, together with Jean Eric Rehn

(1717-1793) who was responsible for furniture and textiles, created the less extreme Swedish variant of the style, which began to be accepted by society during the 1750s.

The formation of the Swedish East India Company (SOIC) in 1731 with their imports from the East also fuelled the desire for exotic goods. Furthermore, the expansion in trade required an increase in the number of shipyards in the capital to supply the company's ships, one of which, the *Götheborg*, was launched from the Terra Nova yard in 1738 to a design by the British shipwright employed at the yard, William Mackett. In 1994 the keel was laid of a replica of this ship, for which the author was commissioned initially to carry out the historical research and later to carve the decorative work. A full description of this project appears in Part III of this book.

Documentation on Swedish ships from this period is scarce, but from research gathered for the *Götheborg* it was clear that ships (particularly those built in Stockholm) were adopting ornamentation influenced by the French Baroque. Examples such as Charles Sheldon's *Fama* (drawn in 1738) suggest that by this date compositions were reflecting the lighter Regency feel. The general trend is that fashions established ashore take some

ten to fifteen years before being adopted on ships. Although Rococo ornament was also making a tentative appearance, it would have no real impact in ship ornamentation until the 1760s, with the intervening period evolving from the Baroque to the Regency, with designs inspired by Karl Hårleman, who in 1748 came into contact with the admiralty directly by submitting ornamental designs for the brigantine *Prins Gustaf*, constructed by Daniel Fries.

The year 1748 also saw the arrival in Stockholm of one Fredrik Henrik Chapman. His father, an officer in the British navy, was married to Susan Colson, the daughter of a London shipwright. In 1716 Chapman senior had joined the Swedish navy and by 1720 was the captain of the Nya Varvet (The New Yard) in Göteborg, where their son Fredrik was born. Within such an environment, the boy soon developed a keen interest in the working and sailing of ships. At the age of 10 he was given a drawing of what was reputed to be a very fast ship, the Ostend privateer *Neptunus*. From this drawing he made a body plan, which so impressed his father that instruction was given to the shipwrights to take the project to the next stage, of laying out the full-size frames. The accuracy of his son's drawing was sufficient to

Karl Hårleman's proposed design for the stern of the brigantine *Prins Gustaf*, built as a cadet ship at Stockholm in 1748 by Daniel Fries. A second proposal was submitted by the painter Lorentz Gottman in pure Rococo style but this appears to have been considered too extreme at the time. (Author's collection by courtesy of the Maritime Museum, Stockholm)

allow the building of a ship. At 15 he went to sea but returned to his love of shipbuilding to work as a ship's carpenter in London between the years 1741 and 1744. Returning to Göteborg, he established a small yard to carry out repairs to vessels of the SOIC and build smaller vessels for private investors. With a growing interest in the sciences, and a desire to understand the technical advancement of ship design, he moved to Stockholm in 1748 to study mathematics.

This period of study was followed by a tour of the Royal Navy dockyards at Woolwich, Chatham and Deptford, where he observed British shipbuilding methods and the launching of ships. The authorities naturally became interested in the

Gilbert Sheldon's cursory attempt at Rococo ornament proposed for the frigate *Jarramas* of 1754. (Author's collection)

purpose of his activities, and arrested him on suspicion of attempting to engage English shipwrights to work abroad. His detailed notes were confiscated while he was placed under house arrest. This was of little concern to Chapman, who had absorbed what information was needed to further his own knowledge and was capable of reproducing his drawings from memory. On his release he travelled to the Netherlands, where the predominant building methods that relied on non-scientific methods were of little interest to him. In 1755 he arrived in France where he stayed for six months to observe the building of the 60-gun ship

Célèbre at Brest. He clearly had an astounding capacity to absorb what was before him, observing not only their construction technique, but also the artistic composition of their ornamentation.

His ability to comprehend three-dimensional form is further illustrated by the remarkable drawings he produced to illustrate the stability of his ships. He could rotate the hull through 360 degrees, noting its visual aspect with an accuracy that we now marvel at when constructed by computer animation. To transpose to paper what was clearly seen in his mind justifies his description as a man of extraordinary vision. Both Britain and France offered Chapman favourable terms of employment to tempt him into their service, but in 1757 he returned to Sweden, having accepted the appointment as assistant shipwright at Karlskrona. His appointment met with some opposition from the supporters of Sheldon, who saw his scientific approach to shipbuilding as undermining the experience of Sheldon.

The position of master carver at the yard had been appointed to Niklas Ekekrantz (1712-1772) following the death of Jacob Waldau in 1742. Ekekrantz benefited from the ability to work from a purpose-built carver's shop, which was first established at the yard in 1736, thereby eliminating the need for carvers and carpenters to work off-site. Born in Karlskrona, Niklas served his apprenticeship as a painter and woodcarver in the commune of Skåna, where he received his master's papers as burgher of Kristianstad in 1737. In doing so, his qualifications were not recognised by the guilds dominating artistic circles. He therefore continued to work in the local area, where he carved the pulpits in Oderljunga and Perstorp's churches and a facade to the gallery of Degerberga Church.

During this period woodcarvers employed by the church were strongly influenced by the work of Buchard Precht, and a number of sculptors formed a group in the Skåne town of Ystad to study with Precht. One of his most famous pupils was Mathias Stenberger, who received his national papers in Ystad in 1724; a good example of his work can be seen in Löderup Church. Niklas Ekekrantz was for a time a pupil of Stenberger, providing him with a grounding in the Italian Baroque. In 1742 he moved back to Karlskrona, where Sheldon commissioned him to carve a font cover for the newly built Fredrick Church, designed by Tessin the younger; Charles Sheldon's son Gilbert was to be baptised there on the day of its consecration in

1744. Ekekrantz was later commissioned (1764) to execute carved work to the organ.

In contrast to the ornamentation of Stockholm ships, the designs illustrated on Gilbert Sheldon's drawings show a leaning towards the style of decoration seen on British ships of the period. In a design for the *Jarramas* dated 1754, Sheldon attempts to embrace Rococo with a bizarre composition of nonsensical sproutings that displays not only a total lack of understanding, but probably a contempt for the genre. The 62-gun *Prinsessan Sophia Albertina* (drawn in 1759 but not launched until 1764) returns to a standard set of motifs, stiffly arranged in a manner that lacks the fluidity of French-inspired designs, but retains a sense of dignity and poise more suited to a man of war. The figurehead is more adventurous, adopting a lion in a pose more associated with French ships by holding a shield before him, while an infant rides on his back, the wings of whom stretch down to form the hair bracket.

The carving to *Prinsessan Sophia Albertina* was completed by Ekekrantz, along with the eventual plan for *Jarramas* which included a crowned lion for the figurehead and central shield to the stern. The quality of his work apparently gathered little praise from the yard's director Gustaf Halldin, or the overseer master shipwright Harold Sohlberg, who came to Karlskrona for the purpose of constructing two ships designed by Chapman. The first was the 70-gun *Konung Adolf Fredrik*, launched in 1768. Chapman resented the admiralty's decision that the ship be built by Sohlberg, which was the first to be designed using his scientific principles.

Chapman's drawings included the ship's ornamentation, which embraced rocaille motifs and balustrading of chinoiserie-style latticework. An alternative design was submitted by Jean Eric Rehn, the flamboyant nature of which exposes his training as an artist. The imagery is portrayed as a dramatic painting, and may have been intended as such, as it gives no indication as to how it could possibly be transposed to three-dimensional sculpture, whereas Chapman's alternative could easily be executed using his drawing. If Rehn's was the chosen design, my sympathies would rest with Ekekrantz in the unenviable task of realising the suggested motifs. In a letter to the admiralty dated 1771 Sohlberg put forward his reasons for the need to find a skilled and scholarly woodcarver at the yard. He was clearly not impressed with the work of Ekekrantz, opining that 'if the carving is of a lion, it should not look like a dog. If a figure is to

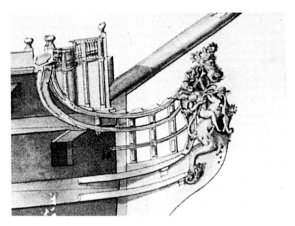

Gilbert Sheldon's drawings for the 62-gun *Prinsessan Sophia Albertina* displayed conventional ornamentation to the stern and quarter galleries, but the figurehead incorporated elements of French-inspired design. Note the wings of the infant forming the hair bracket. (By courtesy of the Maritime Museum, Stockholm)

Rococo ornament from the Royal Castle, Stockholm, produced during the time when the carvers G J Fast, Adrien Masreliez and Johan Törnström were employed there. The composition incorporates the royal insignia, which also appears on ship ornamentation. The three crowns represent the three kingdoms of the Swedish empire and the North Star symbol the king of Sweden. (Author's collection)

represent Mars or Jupiter, it should not appear like some unrecognisable spectre.' In his view, all future drawings must be produced with text describing the composition.

If a replacement carver were to be found, the most likely place would be Stockholm, where work on the castle continued to attract craftsman from abroad, including Adrien Masreliez, who came to Sweden from his native Grenoble in 1748. Masreliez had worked with Rehn on the palace of Chantilly near Paris and gained employment through him at the Drottningholm Palace and the Royal Castle in Stockholm, where the carver Gustaf Johan Fast was also employed. Both were well versed in the French decorative arts, including the now fashionable Rococo. By the 1760s both naval and merchant ships built in Stockholm displayed Rococo ornamentation: the frigate *Enigheten* does so with measured poise, whilst the SOIC provided their ship *Lovisa Ulrika* with a more lavish display. Both ships were originally designed by Harold Sohlberg and built at the Djurgård yard in Stockholm. The *Lovisa Ulrika* was commenced as a warship in 1757 but, owing to lack of funds, was sold to the SOIC and completed as an East Indiaman in 1763. She made four trips to Canton before being sold back to the navy in 1783.

The Djurgård yard also employed Fredrik Chapman, who in 1760 was assigned to General Augustin Ehrensvärd (1710-1772) with the brief to develop an inshore fleet that was to defend the Swedish territories of Pomerania and Finland. A major fortification was under construction on the island of Svea (modern Helsinki) to protect Swedish-held Finland from Russian attack. The rocky islands that formed the skerries around the southern coast of Finland formed a natural defence, leaving only the main channels to be protected from the larger warships. To counter this Tsar Peter the Great established a galley fleet on the lines of those used by Mediterranean powers like the French and Venetians. These shallow-draught, cheaply-built vessels could outmanoeuvre the large men of war in combat or seek shelter among the skerries when threatened.

Chapman was to develop a Swedish fleet to counter this force. The 'Skerry Frigates' he developed were to come under the command of the army, and have the ability to transport troops. These larger vessels offered greater firepower than the galleys, along with better seakeeping ability. They developed a particular design of stern, which required a substantial revision to ornamental composition.

Chapman sketched designs for the figureheads to decorate the first four of his 'Turunmaa' type frigates built at Karlskrona in 1774 for the inshore fleet, depicting the sons of the legendary Viking King Ragnur Lodbrok, who sought to expand the Viking kingdom in the 800s. His sons Björn Ironside, Ivar the Boneless and Sigur Seer of Wind, continued his regime, besieging Paris in 885. The mythological dragon Ragvall decorated the fourth vessel.

Harold Sohlberg's 24-gun *Enigheten*, launched from the Djurgård yard at Stockholm in 1764, displaying Rococo-inspired ornament in the subdued Swedish style. (Author's collection by courtesy of the Maritime Museum, Stockholm)

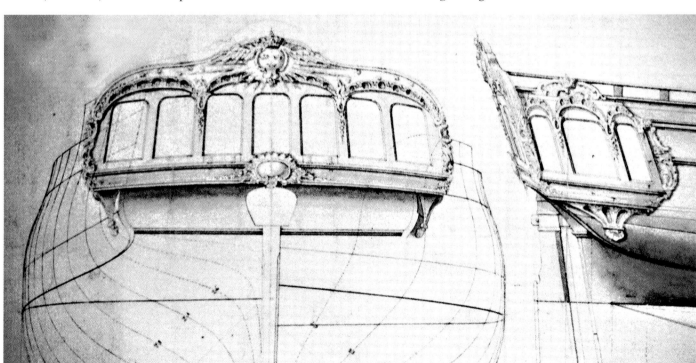

Following the success of these vessels, a further six were built at Sveaborg in 1788. The sculptor Johan Sergel (1740-1814) was employed to make wax maquettes for their figureheads, all depicting various animals. A close friend of Chapman, Johan was the son of the German artists Christopher and Elizabeth Sergel, who had emigrated to Sweden shortly before his birth. Johan had studied extensively in Paris, Rome and Naples; returning to work in Sweden, he specialised in portrait sculpture and in 1779 was made sculptor to the royal court. Association with the artist and his circle of friends would have provided Chapman with enthusiastic company, eager to keep abreast of news in the art world. He was therefore able to design ornamentation himself for his vessels that justly portrayed the fashions of the day and perfectly suited the design of his ships. Chapman reflected upon this himself, commenting in 1799 that:

> The decoration should express its purpose in a manner that retains a beautiful contour and sense of well-being in the ordinance of the stern. Furthermore, the weight and proportion of the carvings should present a profile equally suited to the quarter galleries, that its profile is not at the cost of disrupting the flow of carvings from the quarter galleries to the stern.

He developed compositions that were lightly decorated in Rococo-inspired designs, which still held elements of the grandeur of the earlier Baroque that would soon develop into the structured simplicity of the Gustavian style.

The island of Svea stands as a monumental legacy to the achievements of Augustin Ehrensvärd. A leader of men with great ambition, he became supreme commander of the Swedish armed forces and was responsible for constructing the defences of Finland against the Russians. His residence and the impressive fortified town of Sveaborg, which was to become his final resting place, remain intact on the island, where models and paintings of Chapman's inshore fleet can be viewed.

Ehrensvärd's son Carl August (1745-1800) settled on a career in the navy, although more naturally inclined to the arts. He studied under the leading landscape artist Elias Martin at Sveaborg in 1763-1765, followed in 1766 by a tour of France with Henrik af Trolle, the supreme admiral at Karlskrona. It was during this time that Carl made detailed studies of the ornamentation on French ships, a number of which have already been illustrated in the French section of this book. His drawings provided the admiralty with a valuable insight into the development of French decoration, which added to the work carried out by Chapman on a similar trip to Brest some ten years earlier. Carl August Ehrensvärd went on to become fleet admiral at Karlskrona in 1784 where he became a

One of the massive dry docks constructed at the fortress island of Svea in Finland to build and maintain the inshore fleet. Constructed in 1751, the dock is still in working order today. (Author's collection)

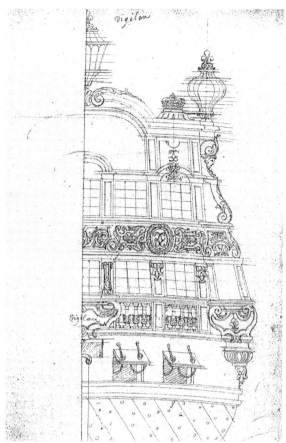

Ehrensvärd's drawing of *Agréable*, launched at Brest in 1670. (By courtesy of the Göteborg Maritime Museum: SMG 31072)

'Vigilan' as drawn by Ehrensvärd in 1766. The style of orna- mentation suggests the ship may be *Entreprenant*, launched from Rochefort in 1672 but renamed *Vigilant* in 1673. Another possibility is the *Dauphin*, launched at Toulon in 1662 and similarly renamed in 1678. Ehrensvärd's drawings do not always accurately document the appearance of the ship as launched, suggesting that he was either gathering ornamental details from a number of ships and simply relating them to a period, or recording later changes to their ornamentation. (By courtesy of the Göteborg Maritime Museum: SMG 31071)

great admirer and patron of the next sculptor to be appointed at the yard, Johan Törnström (1744-1828).

In 1769 Törnström was apprenticed to G J Fast at his workshop in Västra Kyrkogatan, Stockholm. He soon proved to be an exceptionally talented sculptor and assisted Fast with his work at the Royal Castle. By 1775 Törnström was employed in the workshop of Adrien Masreliez, again employed on royal commissions with Masreliez and Fast. In 1775 Törnström was employed at the Djurgård shipyard, carving the ornamental work for Chapman's ships. Masreliez was also commis- sioned to carry out carved work to numerous ships and royal barges constructed at the yard. Chapman had some years earlier been transferred to Karlskrona, which led to the management of the Djurgård yard being purchased by a consortium. Chapman resigned from his government service at Djurgård, allowing him to accept the post, but remained in their pay as the nominal head of the yard to supply drawings.

The position regarding the quality of carved work at Karlskrona had still not been resolved. With the death of Ekekrantz in 1772 it was agreed that painters and woodcarvers must in future be trained in the appropriate academies, where the level of their skill could be approved. However, the modest payments offered to carvers enticed no suitable applicants, so the journeyman carver Olof Bergren was appointed. It is not known how long he was employed, nor anything of the quality of his work, but he may have carved the figurehead to Chapman's *Konung Gustaf III* of 1777. Chapman produced detailed drawings of the figurehead showing the king in the dress of a Roman emperor. The king, who subsequently sat for the sculpture, visited the yard to see the figurehead attached to

In 1787 Chapman was asked to design two pleasure craft for the king's water garden at the Haga Palace. *Valfisiken* and *Vildsvinet* (whose figurehead is shown here) were built at the Hovjaktvarvet in Stockholm, with carved work by Törnström. They were inspired by the Venetian gondolas used for pageants on the Grand Canal, a theme which similarly gave rise to Caffieri being commissioned to build gondolas for Versailles. (Author's collection)

Surviving figureheads: left *Galathé* (1788); right background *Göteborg*, ex-*Minerva* (1783); right foreground *Fäderneslandet* (1785). (Author's collection reproduced by courtesy of the Karlskrona Maritime Museum)

Chapman's 74-gun ship *Gustaf IV Adolph*, launched 1790 (see also colour plate 22). (Author's collection by courtesy of the Maritime Museum, Stockholm)

Ehrensvärd, in his capacity as painter and art historian, provided Törnström with his initial drawings. The immense size of the figures required blocks of wood to be assembled by the ships' carpenters, ready for roughing out by Törnström's apprentices. The stern carvings to the ships were completed by the carver Peter Sundberg.

In addition to his work at the yard, Törnström undertook many commissions from private clients and sculptural work for municipal and royal projects. He completed little more than two figureheads a year, sometimes less, for which a wax maquette was first produced. When Chapman complained that the simple task of constructing a wax maquette from his drawings should not take so long, Törnström rolled the wax into a ball and suggested that if that was the case, perhaps he would like to try. The ball was returned.

With Törnström's move to Karlskrona, decoration to ships at the Djurgård yard was undertaken by Per Ljung (1743-1819), who had served his apprenticeship in the workshop of his father Johan, assisting him from the age of 10 on commissions such as a new pulpit and font for the Santa Clara Church in Stockholm. Per followed his own course of study and soon gained the respect of noted artists such as Rehn, who by the 1770s had established the Neoclassical mode of ornament known as the Gustavian style. Per was employed by Rehn in 1772 to carry out ornamental work at Tullgarn Palace, which was being modernised in the Gustavian style. The sons of Adrien Masreliez, Louis Adrien and Jean Baptiste, were also employed at Tullgarn. Per worked on vessels built at Djurgård to Chapman's designs such as the royal yacht *Amphion*, which was decorated in the Gustavian style. Per became one of the most skillful and frequently commissioned ornamental sculptors of the Gustavian age, which provided the last vestiges of great ornamentation to Swedish ships. Törnström continued carving his monumental figures, and finally retired at the age of 80. He died three years later in 1828.

the ship bearing his name. He said of the artwork: 'Do I really look like that? It is the personification of a blockhead, not the countenance of a brilliant monarch!' In high astonishment he exclaimed 'Shall I forever be represented thus?' He reiterated the earlier decree, adding his own authority to the instruction. Being well acquainted with Carl August Ehrensvärd from their time at Sveaborg, Chapman recommended Törnström, despite the fact that he had not been trained at the royal academy. His recommendation was endorsed by Masreliez, and in 1781 Törnström was appointed master carver at the yard.

The shipbuilding programme instigated by Gustaf III consisted of ships of the line that were to be named after 'manly virtues', and frigates after females from Classical mythology. Carl

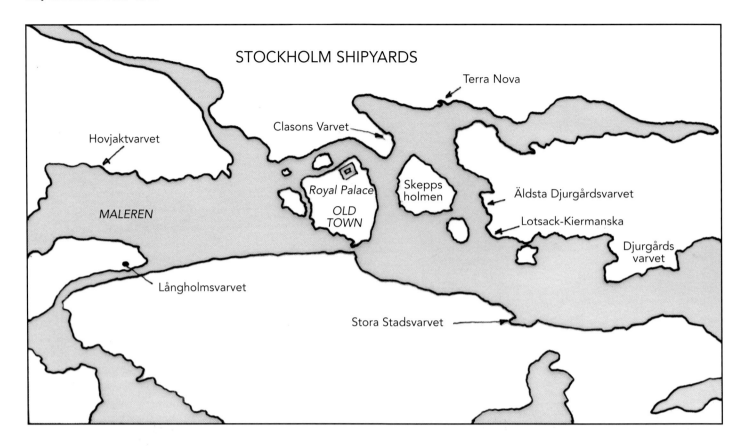

Stockholm's shipyards

Stora Stadsvarvet

Established 1687; remained an important yard up until 1694 when others became more prominent. Constructed ships for the navy, then from 1739 the yard concentrated on merchant ships, including at least six for SOIC.

Äldsta Djurgårdsvarvet

Old yard at Djurgård; *Vasa* constructed there.

Lotsack-Kiermanska (Djurgårdsvarvet)

Established by E Lotsack in the area known as Djurgården in 1735; on Lotsakäsk's death, around 1752, the yard was taken over by G Kierman and continued up to 1850 constructing merchant and naval ships.

Terra Nova varvet

First registered in 1625, it was purchased in 1716 by Abraham Grill who sold the yard in 1782; it was then taken over by the crown in 1819 and was active until 1875.

Clasons varvet

Established in 1725 by Johan Clason, who sold the yard in 1787; continued in operation until 1819; constructed merchant and naval ships.

Skutskeppare or Långholmsvarvet

Established in 1740 as a repair yard and survived until 1956 when it was producing barges and lighters.

Skeppsholmen

Established as a naval base in 1638 but declined as a shipbuilding facility following the relocation to Karlskrona.

Hovjaktvarvet

Established in 1685, where it it was the primary location for the navy's fleet until the move to Karlskrona. It then accommodated the royal yachts. It was finally dissolved in 1850.

William Smith - Norra Skeppsvarv

Shipwright to the crown, established a private yard in 1723.

SWEDISH CARVERS

Äldsta Djurgårdsvarvet

Hans von der Borg		1606-1608
Hans Clausink	(15??-1638?)	1608-1631
Martin Redtmer	(1575?-1655)	1625-1655
Johann Thesson		1625
Gert [surname unknown]		1626
Petter [surname unknown]		1626
Marcus Leden		1626

Djurgårdsvarvet

Johan Burchard		1765
C P Gerdes		1773-1775
Adrien Masreliez	(1717-1808)	1779-1789
Johan Törnström	(1744-1828)	1779-1789
Per Ljung	(1743-1819	1770-1800

Skeppsholmen

Jost Schultz father of Hendrik	(died 1678)	1631-1678
Nicolaus Schultz	(died 1674)	
Hans Jacobsson		1668
Hendrik Schultz stepfather to Waldau	(1650-1701)	1677-1679
Nicolaus Enander		1677
Clas Swant		1677

Stora Stadsvarvet

C P Gerdes

Kalmar

Hendrik Schultz		1683-1686
Peter Hagman		1770

Karlskrona

Hendrik Schultz		1683-1701
Johann Jacob Waldau	(1671-1743)	1701-1742
Niklas Ekekrantz	(1712-1772)	1742-1771
Olof Bergren		
Johan Törnstöm		1781-1825
Peter Sundberg	1785-1800	
L Nordin		
Henrik Nerpin		
Carl Sundwall		

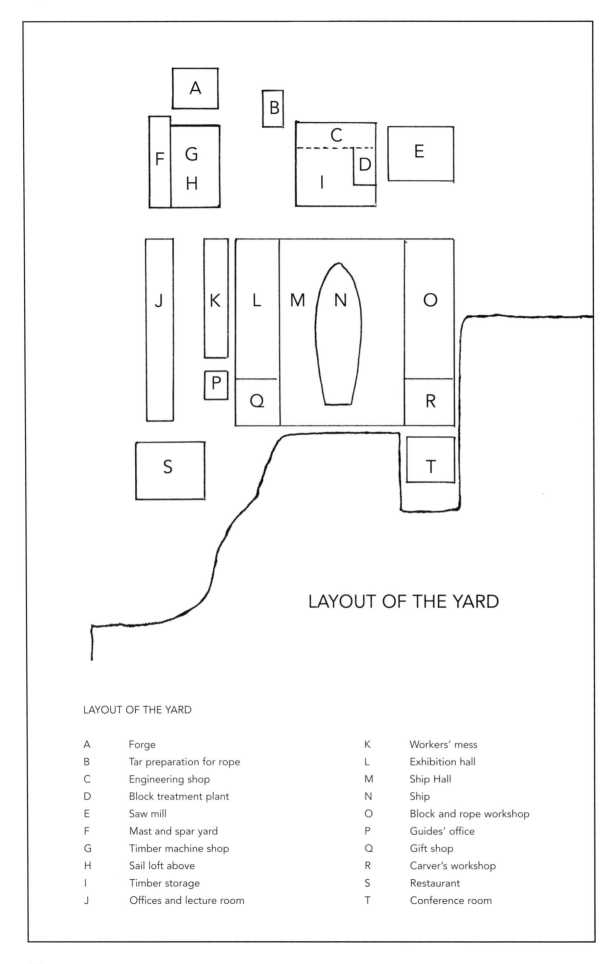

LAYOUT OF THE YARD

LAYOUT OF THE YARD

A	Forge	K	Workers' mess
B	Tar preparation for rope	L	Exhibition hall
C	Engineering shop	M	Ship Hall
D	Block treatment plant	N	Ship
E	Saw mill	O	Block and rope workshop
F	Mast and spar yard	P	Guides' office
G	Timber machine shop	Q	Gift shop
H	Sail loft above	R	Carver's workshop
I	Timber storage	S	Restaurant
J	Offices and lecture room	T	Conference room

PART III
~ The *Götheborg* Project ~

Triewald's diving bell of
1720.

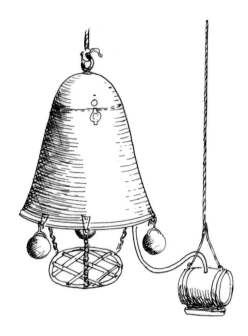

The *Götheborg* was launched in 1738 from the Terra Nova yard in Stockholm, and after two successful voyages to Canton she set out for her third on 14 March 1743. A delay of six months due to bad weather meant that she finally arrived at Canton in the summer of 1744. After lengthy negotiations she eventually secured a cargo consisting of Tutanego, China ware, tea, silks, galingale (an aromatic root), mother of pearl, rattan and pepper. Leaving Canton in January 1745, the ship arrived at the approaches to Göteborg on 12 September where she took on a pilot from his station at the island of Vinga. The ship then ran aground and sank on the well-charted Hunnebåden underwater rock.

Why the *Götheborg* should run aground in good weather on such a well-known hazard remains a mystery, although there are, of course, many theories. With a round trip to China taking two years or more, ships were only expected to last the rigours of three voyages, by which time they had earned their keep. The un-coppered hulls of early ships were attacked by teredo worm and the cost of repairs outweighed that of building a new ship. So was there some form of insurance fraud? There was no loss of life, and most of the crew's personal belongings were salvaged (items that would not have been covered by insurance and replaced at the owner's expense).

Three days after the incident salvage work commenced using diving bells. Sweden was regarded as one of the world leaders in salvage expertise and had been using diving bells since the mid-1600s during salvage attempts on the *Vasa*. By the time salvage operations were under way on the *Götheborg*, the engineer Mårten Triewald had designed his improved bell – constructed of elm, with iron fittings and covered with lead, it housed two divers who sat on a bench as the bell was lowered. On reaching the wreck, ropes were attached to objects such as the valuable cannons or smaller objects placed into baskets to be pulled to the surface. To allow the bell to stay down longer, barrels of air were lowered, as new air entered the bell, a valve in the upper section of the bell was opened to expel the consumed air.

Over the next two years a third of the cargo was recovered, together with valuable items from the ship such as her guns and items of rigging. Despite the loss of the ship and a year's delay on the voyage, the company still showed a profit of 14.5 per cent. In the mid-1800s a large quantity of wood was recovered from the wreck and used to make exclusive furniture, then in 1906-7 a third operation headed by James Keiller recovered more of the cargo, including large amounts of porcelain still intact. Many pieces were sold to private collectors with some now housed in Göteborg's Stad Museet.

In 1984 members of the Swedish Underwater Archaeological Society conducted an extensive survey of the wreck, recovering sections of timber and parts of the rigging such as blocks, fragments of rope and sails. Tutanego bars, galingale and mother of pearl were also found, awakening fresh interest in this link with the past.

The idea of building a replica ship was aired and preliminary investigations undertaken. With a growing public interest in the project, the Friends of the Götheborg III Society was formed to raise funds. This in turn led to a foundation being

established in 1993 and was registered as The Swedish East India Company. The local authority offered land due for redevelopment and so the Terra Nova yard and the SOIC were reborn.

When the keel was laid in the winter of 1994 all that remained of the Eriksberg shipyard was the concrete slipway and the massive crane which, now empty of its operating cable, serves only as a monument to a yard that once created so many fine ships. Founded in 1873, it led a life of continuous expansion until by 1978 its workforce exceeded 5000 employees; but a year later the yard closed, as Taiwan became the world's dominant shipbuilding nation.

A large hangar was constructed over the slipway to house the ship, followed by a number of buildings to accommodate the various trades. Many of the buildings were donated, and erected by volunteers who continued to provide support to the project. There was also the essential task of gathering fragments of information from plans that have survived from similar ships, preserved artefacts from museums, essays on shipbuilding and its associated skills – a search that would continue as ever more details would be needed to

unravel the workings of a sailing ship that had not seen the light of day for 250 years. The infrastructure needed to support such a project is immense. Drawings have to be produced not only to build from, but also to comply with the requirements of Norske Veritas, who provide the certification needed to allow the ship to sail unaided around the world with trainees and passengers.

To meet their regulations, the replica ship needed the installation of engines, generators, desalination plant, fire alarms and and fire fighting equipment, and a mass of electronics, all requiring specialist engineers. Progress of the work and tests on components also need to meet with their approval. The workforce require changing rooms, dining areas, toilets, showers, protective clothing and visitors want guided tours, exhibitions, gift shop, restaurant, activities for school parties, and hospitality for sponsors. Staff are needed to meet the daily needs of raising funds, accounting, corresponding, purchasing, employing staff, checking health and safety, and so on. For those pioneering souls who laid the keel on that simple slipway, the joy of building a ship must at times have been horribly lost in an administrative nightmare.

The Ship Hall of the Terra Nova yard sits next to the former Eriksberg gantry crane. (Author's collection)

Sawmill

Over 1000 oak trees went through here, sourced from Sweden and Denmark, for planking to the hull, which is cut from 9-inch deep timbers measuring between 4 and 6 inches thick. Oak was also used for the deck beams, brackets, rails, etc, and internal lining to the hull. The frames were laminated from over 50 kilometres of pine. Originally oak would have been used, grown specifically for the purpose, but now it is no longer available in the quantity required. With temperatures approaching -20°C in winter, work continued on the hull for nine years.

Ropewalk

The ship required 40 tons of rope, the majority of which was made at Älvängen, home of the former Carlmarks rope factory where their ropewalk has been preserved as a museum. With the requirements of our ship, the ropewalk was back in business, producing all the larger section rope for both standing and running rigging, all of which is in hemp. The rope was then sent to the yard to be pre-stretched, weather-proofed with Stockholm tar and crafted into the various components of the rig, which is totally authentic to the period of the original ship.

Many of the smaller ropes were made entirely by hand as well as specialist ropes such as the one shown above which was made from elk hide – because it does not stretch, it was used to connect the wheel to the tiller.

Machine shop

Initially used to mould and laminate the frames, here the planks were then shaped prior to steaming. Heavy lifting gear is needed to handle such large timbers; a typical oak plank can be seen passing through a thicknesser, being guided by three people with the weight supported by overhead travelling hoist, while a fourth person is preparing lifting gear to support the plank as it emerges from the machine. Similar lifting gear exists to manoeuvre timbers of this weight in and out of the steam box and for positioning onto the hull. Timber for the carvings was prepared and laminated into the various blocks here before being transferred to the more conducive environment of the carver's workshop. The machine shop was finally used to make all the joinery work for fitting out, such as doors, partitions, bunks, furniture, gun carriages, window frames, balustrades, etc.

Sail loft

Above the machine shop was the sail loft. The ship's standard rig carries 1200 square metres of sail; a further 250 square metres can be added in light winds. Made from traditional materials, the sails were all sewn by hand.

Masts and spars

The main and fore lower masts are built up from interlocking sections, bound below decks by iron hoops manufactured in the forge, and above decks by rope called wooldings. Other masts and spars are solid in section, although the longer yards – which measure up to 80 feet in length – are formed from two timbers which are spliced and also bound with iron hoops. The task of masting and rigging commenced after the launch of the ship in 2003, assembling the mass of components that had been prepared during the preceding nine years.

The forge

A ship of this size needs an unbelievable quantity of fixings, brackets and sundry ironwork for the hull and rig. The forge was set up to help train blacksmiths and over the course of the project has smelted over 50 tons of iron to hand-forge these items, which include over 50,000 nails and 10,000 bolts.

Rudder pintles stand in front of the first timber section to form the rudder.

Rig workshop

Many blocks were recovered from the wreck, providing a record of the various shapes, sizes and methods of construction. They were all constructed in one piece from a solid block of elm, used in preference to oak on account of its lighter weight which, with over 700 blocks in the rig and a further 250 carried as spares, is a serious consideration. They have all been hand carved to faithfully replicate the originals, with pulleys turned from lignum vitae.

All the rope required dressing with Stockholm tar before being worked into the many component parts of the rig. Everything and everyone became permeated with the smell of tar. When in town you could soon tell who was employed at the Terra Nova yard.

The vast hangar providing cover to the ship was erected largely by volunteers, allowing work to continue through the winter months. It also housed a visitor centre and various workshops.

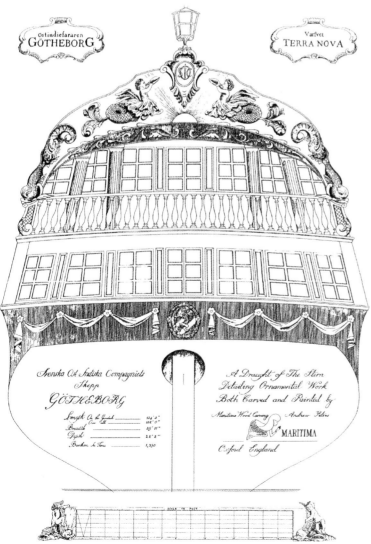

The carved work

I first saw the *Götheborg* project in 1998, by which time most of the frames were in place. At that time I was working in Sweden with the woodcarver Ingemar Johansson, carving the figurehead for the Swedish sail training ship *Gunilla*. Originally built in 1939, the vessel had in later years been converted to a motor coaster, but now restored to sail, she required a figurehead. The original had been preserved in the town of Oskarsham where she was built, and by taking measurements and drawings of this we were able to carve a faithful replica for the ship.

As very little detail had been discovered regarding the ornamentation of the original *Götheborg*, my services were called upon to carry out the historical research for this part of the project, and eventually to design and carve the sculptures. I was given three months to carry out research in the maritime museums of Scandinavia, to get a feel for the style of carving and subject matter that might have adorned such a ship.

Having presented the findings of my research, a preliminary sketch was produced, which, with some alterations along the way, was generally adhered to. With many British shipwrights working in both the naval and merchant yards of Sweden at the time of the ship's launch, the general layout of the stern conforms to British conventions, but tending towards an elliptical stern. The decorative composition is more strongly influenced by the

French Baroque, which in the form displayed on ships is of a more reserved nature than the original French. A cove line forms the demarcation between carved and painted work to the tafferel, with further painted work to the counter, the only carving to which is a shield bearing the arms of Göteborg. It was later decided that turned balusters would be replaced with flat, cut to a pattern commonly used in the architecture of the period and similarly used on *Enigheten* of 1732.

With the exception of the catheads, all carved work was completed in pine, sourced from the north of Sweden, where the slow growth of the trees provides a denser material due to the lesser amount of soft summer growth. The carvings on the original ship would also have been carved in pine, which in the environment of salt water would, if well maintained, last for the expected lifespan of the ship. The original carvings would also have been laminated, as I have discovered through many years dismantling and restoring original carved work for museums. The main difference between the construction of the original and the new carvings is the use of modern glues and smaller sectioned laminates to obtain better quality wood.

The first carving to be completed for the ship was the city arms of Göteborg. The heraldic emblem of a two-tailed lion set within a wreath of laurel leaves was replicated from a 1738 example and formed the centrepiece of the upper counter.

Göteborg shield.

SOIC shield.

A monogram of the Swedish East India Company set within a cartouche forms the centrepiece of the tafferel. The design is in fact from a later period, but it was decided to use it for the emblem as it has become such a well-known symbol of the SOIC. Coming originally from a design by Fredrik af Chapman, the only alteration is the inclusion of the three crowns, being the coin of the realm and therefore a symbol of trade, but a play on the three royal crowns that represent the national emblem of Sweden as displayed on the lion's shield.

To the starboard side of the SOIC shield sits the nereid Amphitrite. As the daughters of the gods Nereus and Doris, the nereids personify the waves of the sea. Their son Triton is depicted on the port side; by blowing on his conch shell, he had the power to raise wind from a calm, or quell a storm. Each figure measures over 6 feet in length (2.1m), displaying the sense of movement and theatricality associated with Baroque figurative work. The SOIC shield is often displayed against the rays of the sun, which on the stern of the ship, were to be shown as painted work, the gilded rays radiating behind the two figures, who appear as supporters to the shield, raising a fanfare to the company, amidst the dawning of a new age of prosperity.

The nereid Amphitrite.

At the turn of the tafferel are two C-shaped scrolls, an early arrival of the coming Rococo and rocaille. The undulating foliage on the scrolls takes the form of seaweed moved by water. Sitting at the point where the tafferel turns into the quarter piece, the scrolls form the transition from the flat of the tafferel, to the fully three-dimensional dolphins and will also link with the upper finishing of the quarter gallery (temporarily fixed to the ship's side). The quarter galleries could not be completed before the ship's maiden voyage because of issues relating to the ship's certification, so a scrolled plinth that was originally planned to sit beneath the dolphin, creating a link with the galleries, was unfortunately also omitted, leaving an awkward detail which hopefully will be resolved in time.

Some of the carved work prior to fixing,

Upper finishing to the quarter gallery.

Cockerel to the quarter gallery lower finishing.

Detail of dolphin.

The design of the upper finishing was inspired by the work of Daniel Marot, whose use of infilling panels with scale work provided the perfect composition to form the roof to the quarter gallery. Palms form the foliate work to the central shield, while curling acanthus decorates the end scrolls that eventually link with the dolphins' tails.

The only carving recovered from the wreck of the original ship was a small section of a cockerel which formed the lower finishing to the quarter galleries. Completion of the design required me to research the breeds of cockerel common in Sweden during the 1730s, but eventually I discovered a match whose head and tail fitted the body and legs of the original.

Dolphins have long been associated with the role of guide and companion to sailors. As such, those on the *Götheborg* stand at the vantage point of the quarter piece, where they can survey the sea around them. There are many legends where dolphins have saved shipwrecked mariners, or those lost at sea have themselves become dolphins. In Greek mythology they are the attendants of Poseidon; when he sought to marry the nereid

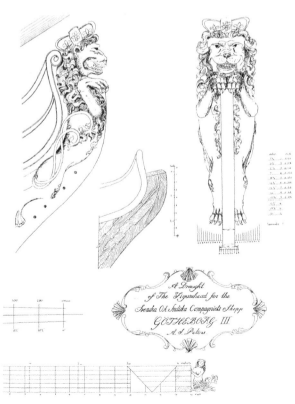

LION FIGUREHEADS

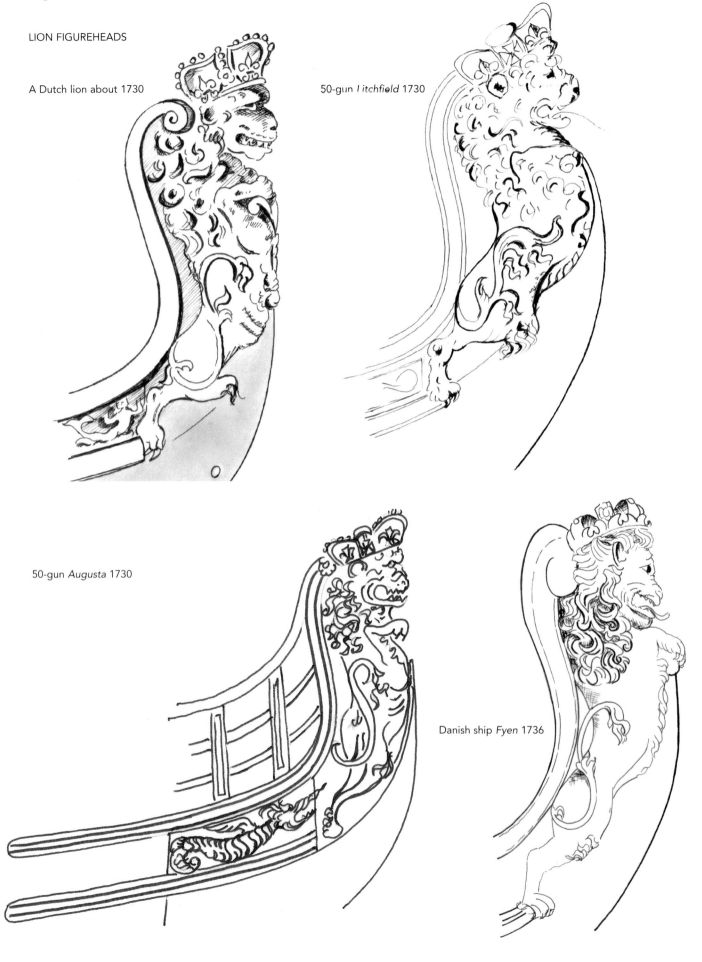

A Dutch lion about 1730

50-gun *Litchfield* 1730

50-gun *Augusta* 1730

Danish ship *Fyen* 1736

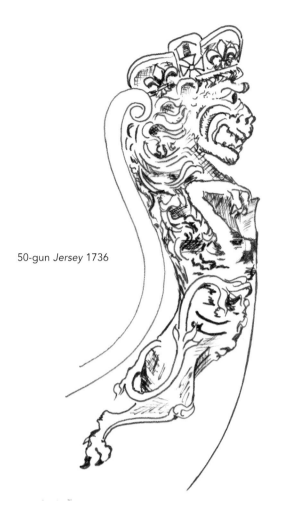

50-gun *Jersey* 1736

Swedish *Lovisa Ulrika* 1757

Amphitrite, she was delivered to him on a dolphin. In Baroque art they are depicted as these highly stylised mythical creatures, whose flexible form could be adapted to suit many applications.

Research suggested that the figurehead would almost certainly have been a lion. During the period when the ship was built, trade with the East influenced ornamentation with Chinese motifs that became known as chinoiserie. On lion figureheads this was manifest in the manes taking on tight curls that double back in a final flourish. The lion was also given the two tails associated with the heraldic lion of Göteborg. The accompanying drawing gives information necessary to calculate the laminating process and orientation of the laminates to the stem head, which tapers in its section.

The shape of the lion is largely dictated by the proportions of the ship's stem head, with the body shape expanding or contracting to suit its width and length, so that the feet spring from the lower cheek rail. During the 1730s the panel between the cheeks often held a composition influenced by chinoiserie, with motifs such as oriental-inspired

dragons, as shown on the *Augusta* of 1736. The majority of Swedish lions followed the English pattern in being crowned, tight curled and with a definite growl. Their tails invariably curl onto the body to form an S-shape, rather than trailing behind the lion where it would become vulnerable. In contrast, the stem head of French ships with the introduction of a *cagouille* often provided space for the tail to sit off the body.

A sequence of profiles was established from the initial drawing and scaled up to provide templates for each laminate. A cutting list to make efficient use of timber was prepared for each laminate, in order to work out the running length of planks which were then glued alongside each other to create one laminate. These were then cut to the profile from the master drawing before gluing to the previous laminate to form the block ready for carving. Laminates for the centre section of the lion can be seen in the foreground while one complete side is starting to be built up behind it.

With a total length of 14 feet (4.2m) the sections of lion dwarfed the previously large carvings. At the commencement of carving, each half weighed one and a half tons, which required specialist lifting equipment to be installed in the workshop in order to manoeuvre the pieces during carving. All of this was completed totally by hand in the traditional manner. The final design of the lion resulted from the study of numerous examples from the period, which were adapted to suit the

space available on the ship, with due consideration given to the gammoning (lacing) to the bowsprit and attachment points of standing rigging which needed to be accommodated on the stem, the top of which took the centre section of the lion, tapered to the same section. The simple task of moving each section to check their alignment with each other would involve half a day's work, followed by climbing a ladder in order to get sufficiently above the sculpture to view it from a true perspective.

The figurehead was fitted in two halves, and bolts were passed through the figure, securing it to the stem of the vessel. The paint was made on site, according to a recipe from the 1730s consisting of linseed oil, turpentine, and natural pigments such as white lead, zinc and yellow ochre. Repainting of the carvings would have come under the remit of general maintenance taken on by the crew. Gilded work on the *Götheborg* was soon painted over during the course of her maiden voyage in order to keep the carvings protected, a practice that must have been followed on the original ship, bringing into question how often gilded work would have been renewed on a ship after her launch.

Masting and rigging commenced straight after the launch of the ship in 2003, followed by ballasting, internal fitting out, cannons being mounted on the gun deck, the fixing of the carvings and final painting of the hull. On 2 October 2005 the King of Sweden, who as a keen follower of the project and whose wife had christened the ship, returned to Göteborg as the ship prepared to set sail on her maiden voyage to China. Thousands of people had been gathering since the early hours to line the banks of the Göta river or taking to the water in a flotilla of boats. Many would have visited the yard, filled with fascination at the skills displayed before them. All had journeyed here to be a part of this momentous day. Such recognition for the workers, now forever imbued with the scent of Stockholm tar, made for the most emotional of occasions: a day that none would forget as the ship they created sailed past the town with crowds cheering in admiration of their achievements. As the ship approached the yard where she was born, a few familiar faces gave their last farewell from the now empty slipway. For them the passing ship was the culmination of eleven years' work; for those on board, the big adventure had just begun.

An historic moment, as the Swedish East Indiaman enters the former docks of the English East India Company in London, during her return journey to Sweden from China, a voyage that retraced the trading route of the original ship.

Bibliography

France

Published sources
Association des Amis des Musées de La Marine Association, *Le Chébec* (Paris 1954)
Ballu, J, *La Fayette's Liberty Ship* (EU 2011)
Belec, F, *Musée de la Marine* (Paris 1994)
Boudriot, J, *History of the French Frigate* (Rotherfield 1993)
Boudriot, J & Berti, H, *Modèles Historiques* (Nice 1997)
Carr Laughton, L G, *Old Ship Figureheads and Sterns* (London 1925)
Gardiner, R, *The First Frigates* (London 1992)
Haudrère, P & Le Bouëdec, G, *Les Compagnies des Indes* (Rennes 1999)
Hughes, P, *Eighteenth Century France and the East* (London 1981)
Le Drian, J Y, *Musée de la Compagnie Des Indes* (Lorient 1990)
Lescallier, D, *Vocabulaire des Termes de Marine* (Paris 1783)
Lyon, D, *Sailing Navy List, 1688-1860* (London 1993)
Morgat, A, *L'Arsenal de Rochefort* (Rochefort 2008)
Mourot, M & Béland, M, *Les Génies de la Mer* (Quebec 2001)
Pierre, J, *Les Constructions Navales à Rochefort* (Paris 2003)

Further information gathered from:
Chamber of Commerce, La Rochelle
Göteborg Sjöfartsmuseet Archives
Musée National de la Marine, Brest
Musée National de la Marine, Paris
Musée National de la Marine, Port-Louis
Musée National de la Marine, Rochefort
Musée du Rochefort

The Netherlands

Published sources
Blake, R, *Anthony van Dyck* (Chicago 1999)
Blok, P J, Mulhuysen, P C, et al, *Nieuw Nederlandsch Biografisch Woordenboek* (Leiden 1911)
Bruijn, J R, *The Dutch Navy of the Seventeenth and Eighteenth Centuries* (Columbia, South Carolina 1993)
Cordingly, D, *The Art of the Van de Veldes* (London 1979)
Davis, R, *English Merchant Shipping and Anglo-Dutch Rivalry* (London 1975)
Garwronski, J H G, *The VOC ship Amsterdam* (Amsterdam 1987)
Goosens, E J, *The Palace of Amsterdam* (Amsterdam 2010)
Hoving, A, *The Ships of Abel Tasman* (Amsterdam 2000)
Hoving, A, *William Rex* (Amsterdam 2005)
Howard, F, *Sailing Ships of War* (London 1979)
Jacobs, E M, *Dutch East Indiaman Amsterdam* (Amsterdam 1997)
Jacobs, E M, *In Pursuit of Pepper and Tea* (Amsterdam 1991
Lemmers, A, *Van werf tot facilitair complex (Kattenburg)* (Den Haag 2011)

Schokkenbroek, J C A & Zonnevylle-Heyning, C E, *Kunst op het water* (Amsterdam 1995)
Spits, E & Daalder, R, *Schepen van de Gouden Eeuw* (Amsterdam 2005)
Stevens, H, *The Art of Technology* (Amsterdam 1995)
Various, *Amsterdam Scheepvaart Museum catalogue* (Amsterdam 1969)

Further information gathered from:
Scheepvaartmuseum, Amsterdam
City Archives, Amsterdam
City Hall, Amsterdam
Zuiderzeemuseum, Enkhuizen
Old Church, Amsterdam
Maritiem Museum, Rotterdam
Söndre Harritslev Church, Denmark
St Laurens Church, Rotterdam

Great Britain

Published sources
Anderson, R C, *Catalogue of Ship-Models (Greenwich)* (London 1952)
Barnard B, *Building Britain's Wooden Walls* (London 1997)
Beard, G, *The Works of Grinling Gibbons* (London 1989)
Beard, G, *The Works of Robert Adam* (London 1992)
Blake, R, *Anthony van Dyck* (Chicago 1999)
Bowen, F C, *Carrack to Clipper* (London 1927)
Bryant, A, *Samuel Pepys: The Man in the Making* (Cambridge 1939)
Bryant, A, *Samuel Pepys: The Years of Peril* (Cambridge 1935)
Burns, K V, *Plymouth's Ships of War* Basildon 1972)
Carr Laughton, L G, *Old Ship Figureheads and Sterns* (London 1925)
Christie's, *Juste-Aurèle Meissonnier* (London 1977)
Clark, K, *Subjects and Symbols in Art* (Cambridge 1974)
Cockett, F B, *Peter Monomy and his Circle* (Woodbridge 1988)
Ede, M, *Art and Society under William and Mary* (London 1979)
Fleming, J & Honour, H, *Dictionary of Decorative Arts* (London 1977)
Franklin, J, *Navy Board Ship Models* (London 1989)
Gardiner, R, *The First Frigates* (London 1992)
Green, J R, *A Short History of the English People* (London 1898)
Grimal, P, *Dictionary of Classical Mythology* (London 1985)
Historical Soc, *Chatham Figurehead Carvers* (Chatham 2011)
Historical Soc, *The Prince of 1670* (Chatham 2007)
Howard, F, *Sailing Ships of War* (London 1979)
Jackson, A, *Period Styles* (London 2002)
Keble, E, *Chats on Naval Prints* (London 1926)
Kenyon, L, *State Barges of the Stationers Company* (London 1972)
Kitson, M, *The Age of Baroque* (London 1966)
Knighton, C S, *Samuel Pepys: The Later Diaries* (London 2006)
Laird Clowes, G S, *Sailing Ships: Their History and Development*, 2 vols (London 1937)
Laird Clowes, W, *The Royal Navy*, Vols II & III (London 1996
Lambert, A, *War at Sea in the Age of Sail* (reprinted London 2000)
Lavery, B & Stephens, S, *Ship Models* (London 1995)
Lenman, B, *The Jacobite Cause* (Glasgow 1986)
Lewis, P & Darley, G, *Dictionary of Ornament* (London 1986)
Lyon, D, *Sailing Navy List, 1688-1860* (London 1993)

Montagu, Lord, *Buckler's Hard* (Stockport 1963)

Norton, P, *State Barges* (London 1972)

Osborne, H, *The Oxford Companion to Art* (Oxford 1979)

Palmer, K N, *Ceremonial Barges of the River Thames* (London 1997)

Sutton, J, *Lords of the East* (London 1981)

Thomas, P N, *British Figurehead and Ship Carvers* (Wolverhampton 1995)

Thornton, P, *Form and Decoration* (London 1988)

Toman, R, *Baroque Architecture, Sculpture and Painting* (Cologne 1998)

US Naval Academy Museum, *Henry Huddleston Rogers Collection of Ship Models* (Annapolis, Maryland 1971)

Various, *National Maritime Museum Catalogue 1937* (London 1937)

Winfield, R, *The 50-Gun Ship* (London 1997)

Denmark

Published sources

Berg, H C & Erichsen, J, *Danske Orlogsskibe 1690-1860* (Copenhagen 1980)

Bøggild, H & Dames, W, *Skibsudsmykninger* (Rønne 1978)

Brick, C F, *Dansk Biografisk Lexicon* (Copenhagen 1898)

Carr Laughton, L G, *Old Ship Figureheads and Sterns* (London 1925)

Clemmensen, T & Mackeprang, M, *Kina og Danmark* Copenhagen 1980)

Holck, P, *Historiske Modelsamling paa Holmen* (Copenhagen 1939)

Jørgensen, S, *Søhistorisk Billedbog (Kronborg)* (Copenhagen 1967)

Larsen, K, *Den Danske Kinafart* (Copenhagen 1932)

Lisberg-Jensen, O, *The Royal Danish Naval Museum* (Copenhagen 1994)

Poulsen, H, *Danish Figureheads* (Copenhagen 1977)

Søfartsmuseet Helsingør, *1974: Årborg* Copenhagen 1974)

Søfartsmuseet Helsingør, *1975: Årborg* (Copenhagen 1975)

Søfartsmuseet Helsingør, *1992: Årborg* (Copenhagen 1992)

Søfartsmuseet Helsingør, *1998: Årborg* (Copenhagen 1998)

Søfartsmuseet Helsingør, *2003: Årborg* (Copenhagen 2003)

Steensen, S, *Orlogsmuseet, No 6* (Copenhagen 1961)

Further information gathered from:
Altona, Germany
Amalienborg, Copenhagen
Assens Museum.
Helsinør Cathedral
Federiksborg Slot, Hillerød
Fredensborg Palace
Frederiksberg Palace
Frelsers Church, Copenhagen
Glückstad, Germany
Handels-og Søfartsmuseet, Helsingør
Holby Church
Holmen's Church, Copenhagen
Kronborg Slot, Helsingør
Orlogsmuseet, Copenhagen
Roskilde Cathedral

Sweden

Published sources
Abrahamson, A, *Aktuelt (Marinmusei Karlskrona)* (Karlskrona 1967)
Albe, G, *Statens Sjöhistoriska Museum* (Stockholm 1960)
Alm, G & Millhagen, R, *Drottningholm Slott* (Stockholm 2004)
Almqvist, H, *Unda Maris 1971-1972 (Göteborg)* (Kungsbacka 1972)
Chapman, F af, *Architectura Navalis Mercatoria* (Stockholm 1768)
Fahlborg, B, *Handelflottans Historia 1660-1675* (Gothenburg 1933)
Fajersson, M & Soop, H, *Vasa Bekänner färg* (Stockholm 1999)
Färnström, M, *Johan Törnström* (Karlskrona 1994)
Hägg, J, *Svenska Sjötåg* (Stockholm 1908)
Hallberg, P & Koninckx, C, *A Passage to China* (Gothenburg 1994)
Halldin, G, *Sjöhistorisk Museet Catalogue No 9* (Stockholm 1953)
Harris, D G, *F H Chapman: The First Naval Architect and his Work* (London 1989)
Hermansson, R, *The Great East India Adventure* (Gothenburg 2004)
Hofberg, H, *Svensk Biografisk Lexicon* (Stockholm 1917)
Hovstadius, B, *A Swedish Legacy* (Stockholm 1998)
Johansson, Bengt, *Golden Age of the China Trade* (Hong Kong 1992)
Johansson, Björn, *Regalskeppet Kronan* (Höganäs 1985)
Lindqvist, H, *The Swedish East India Saga* (Gothenburg 2002)
Lundgren, K, *Sheldon, Day and Turner* (Oland. 2000.
Norberg, E, *Karlskrona Varvets Historia* (Karlskrona 1993)
Ogg, D, *Europe in the Seventeenth Century* (London 1925)
Salmon, P, *Britain and the Baltic* (Sunderland 2003)
Sjöfartsmuseum Stockholm, *Sjöhistorisk Årsbok 1955-1956* (Stockholm 1956)
Sjöfartsmuseum Stockholm, *Sjöhistorisk Årsbok 1959-1960* (Stockholm 1960)
Sjöfartsmuseum Stockholm, *Sjöhistorisk Årsbok 1969-1970* (Stockholm 1970)
Sjöfartsmuseum Stockholm, *Sjöhistorisk Årsbok 1979-1980* (Stockholm 1980)
Sjöfartsmuseum Stockholm, *Sjöhistorisk Årsbok 1985-1986* (Stockholm 1986)
Sjöfartsmuseum Stockholm, *Sjöhistorisk Årsbok 1988-1989* (Stockholm 1989)
Sjöfartsmuseum Stockholm, *Sjöhistorisk Årsbok 1990-1991* (Stockholm 1991)
Soop, H, *The Power and the Glory* (Uddevalla 1992)
Tydén-Jorden, A, *Kröningsvagnen* (Stockholm 1985)
Various, *Svensk Uppsalgsbok* (Stockholm 1955)
Various, *Svenska Flottans Historia*, Vols I-III (Malmö 1942)
Weibull, J, *Swedish History* (London 1993)

Information also gathered from:
Frederick Church, Karlskrona
Gothenburg Cathedral
Krigsarkivet, Stockholm
Marinmuseum, Karlskrona
National Museum, Stockholm
Royal Castle, Stockholm
Sjöfartsmuseet, Gothenburg
Sjöhistoriska Museet, Stockholm
Stad Museet, Gothenburg
Stockholm Cathedral

General Index

References to illustrations are given in *italic*

Nationalities are denoted by the following abbreviations: (Aus) Austrian; (Eng) English; (F) French; (Dk) Danish; (G) German; (GB) British; (NL) Dutch; (O) Ostend; (P) Portuguese; (Scot) Scottish; (Sw) Swedish.

Aalborg 160
Académie des Beaux Arts 38, 55, 154
Adam, Balthasar 142
Adam, Edward 142
Adam, Henry 142
Adam, Robert 134, 135, 138
Adelere, Admiral Cort 21, 144, 145, 157
Adelere, Captain Silvert 21
Albemarle, Duke of 102
Algiers 30
Allen, Anna 161
Allen, Anthony 140
Allen, Lewis 140
Altona 21
Älvängen *214*
Amalienborg 164–166
Amalienhavn 164
Amboyna 17
Amsterdam 16, 66, 68, 72, 78, 82, 83, 86, 104
Amsterdam City Hall 67, 68, 71, 83, 88, 89, 91
Amsterdam Oude Kerke 83
Amsterdam yard, Kattenburg 90, 92
Anderson, J R 142
Anne, Queen (GB) 114, 117, 121–123, 134, 190, 191
Anson, Lord George 130
Antoinette, Marie 52
Antwerp 65, 66, 87, 157
Apeldorn 82
Asiatische Compagnie 18
Athens 134
Aubenton, François-Ambroise d' 59
Augère, René d' 44, 63
Augsberg 75
Austrian East India Co 29
Ayscue, Sir George 175

Badminton House 133
Bailey, John 142
Balfour, David 144
Ballin, Claude 1 40
Banda Islands 17
Banquibazar 29, 30
Baptiste, Jean 207
Bär, Admiral 182
Barbé, Laurent 159–160, 162 166, *192 plate 19*
Barfleur, Battle of 111
Barkman, Sir Johan 175

Barnards 131, 139
Barnstaple 30
Bartholomew Hospital 112
Batavia 16, 34, 74, 81
Batten, Sir William 17
Batton & Glover 131, 142
Beachy Head, Battle of 111
Beaufort, Duke and Duchess of 133
Beke, Jan Baptist van der 87, 88, 93
Belle Isle 134
Bengal 29
Bengal, Nawab of 29, 30
Benstrup, Knud Nielsen 152, 154–156, 160
Bentham, Charles 83–86, 90, 93, 129
Berain, Jean 45–48, 57, 63, 72, 73, 77, 87, 164, 181, 186–190
Berchem, Nicolaes 77
Bergren, Olof 205, 209
Bernini, Gian Lorenzo 38, 43, 68, 75, 186
Black Sea 13
Blackwall 19, 143, 121
Bleklinge 178, 185
Blitterswijk, J H van 93
Blommendal, Jan 82, 87
Blondel, François 54, 55
Bodekull 176, 179, 180
Bodön 176
Bogemaker, Anthony 82, 93
Bokenham, William 111
Bombay 19
Bonaparte, King Louis (NL) 91
Bonaparte, Napoleon *see* Napoleon
Booy 93
Borg, Hans von der 209
Bos, Cornelis 65
Boucher, François 52, 166, 199
Bourbon, House of 27
Bourguignon, Victor 56, 57, 63
Bragenes, L 152–154
Brakel, Admiral van 82
Bremen 186
Bremerholm yard 144, 145
Brest 26, 39, 42, 49, 50, 53, 55–61, 154, 155, 201, 204, 205,
Bristol 113, 138
Brixham 72
Bronsdon & Wells 34, 35, 131
Brotherhood of Holy Trinity 31
Brun, Félix 63, 64
Brussels 65
Bruun, Anders 151–154, 168
Buckler's Hard 19
Buirette, Claude 44, 63
Buirette, Claude-Ambroise 44, 63
Buirette, Thomas 44
Burchard, Johan 209
Burlington House 126

Burlington, Lord Richard 125, 126
Burrell, William 19, 141
Burrough, Thomas 130, 131, 134, 137, 141, *192 plate 13*
Butey, Suzanne 45
Byng, Admiral Sir George 121, 134

Cadiz 15, 31, 32, 33
Caffieri, Charles-Marie 45, 59, 63
Caffieri, Charles Philippe 45, 49, 53–55, 57 58, 59, 63
Caffieri, Philippe 44, 45, 49, 63, 188
Caffieri, François 45, 49, 50, 51, 53, 63, 206
Caffieri, Philippe (cousin) 59
Calcutta 19
Calraet, Michiel van 82, 93
Calraet, Pieter Jan van 82
Calraet, Abraham 82
Campbell, Colin 29, 30, 32, 33, 34
Campen, Jacob van 67, 68, 88
Canton 17, 21, 22, 23, 26, 27, 33, 34, 158, 203, 211
Cape Finistère 130
Cape of Good Hope 15, 16, 18, 22, 32,
Cape Passaro 121
Cape St Vincent 134
Cape York 16
Caravaque, François 63
Caravaque, Jean 63
Cardinaal, Hendrik 93
Carl X Gustaf, King (Sw) 175
Carlmark ropeworks 214
Carolina, Princess (NL) 87
Caron, François 25
Carraway, Jeremiah 141
Cartagena 128
Carter, John 141
Caspian Sea 13
Castlemaine, Countess of 110
Cavendish, Captain Thomas 16
Chambers, William 133
Chandernagore 26, 30
Chantilly palace 202
Chapman, Fredrik af 14, 35, 41, 194, 200–207, 219
Charles I, King (GB) 95, 96, 98, 100, 144
Charles II, King (GB) 39, 66, 72, 99, 102–105, 108, 110, 115–117, 120
Charles VI, King (Aus) 29, 30
Charles XI, King (Sw) 46, 182–184, 186, 189
Charles XII, King (Sw) 31, 189, 194
Charlotte Amalia, Queen (Dk) 161
Charlottenborg palace 1, 47, 148
Chatham 60, 83, 98, 103, 107, 108, 111, 113, 131, 134, 137, 149, 175, 200
Chatham Chest 119
Chauveau, François 188

Chauveau, René 188
Chelsea Hospital 119
Chevillard, sr 60
Chichley, Abigail 137, 138, 141, 142
Chichley, Elizabeth 136, 137, 141, 142
Chichley, Richard 131, 134, 137, 141, 142
Chippendale, Thomas 132, 133
Christian IV, King (Dk) 19, 143
Christian V, King (Dk) 144, 147, 149, 161
Christian VI, King (Dk) 158
Christian VII, King (Dk) 164, 167
Christiana 144
Christianshavn 22, 156
Christina, Queen (Sw) 169, 174
Christmas, Garret (Gerrard) 98, 106, 141, 142
Christmas, Henry 142
Christmas, James 142
Christmas, John 64 plate 8, 97, 98, 141
Christmas, Mathias 64 plate 8, 97, 98, 100, 141
Christmas, William 142
Clausink, Bengt 169
Clausink, Hans 169–171, 173, 209
Clayden House 134
Clerck, Admiral 174, 177
Clive, Robert 27
Cliveden House 38
Cobbé, André 29
Cochin, Nicholas 54, 55
Cocques, Anna Maria 71
Colbert, de Seinelay 44, 46, 187
Colbert, Jean-Baptiste 25, 39, 40, 44, 45, 50, 56
Collet, Jacques-Étienne 55, 58, 63
Collet, Yves-Étienne 55, 56, 63
Colson, Susan 200
Compagnie d'Occident 26
Compagnie d'Orient 25
Compagnie de la Chine 25, 26
Compagnie des Indes 25, 26, 27
Compagnie des Indes Orientales de Madagascar 25
Compagnie du Sénégal 26
Compagnie Meilleraye 25
Compagnie Perpétuelle des Indes 26
Compagnie Royal de la Chine 26
Compardel, Etienne 187, 188
Compton Place 161
Confrerie Pictura 82
Constantinople 13, 14
Copenhagen 19, 22, 30, 71, 148, 149, 152, 157, 158, 164
Copenhagen Castle 157
Copenhagen Royal Palace 152
Copenhagen Stock Exchange 143, 148
Cord, Richard 142
Cork 111
Corsevoix, Antoine 46
Cortona, Pietro da 38, 43, 75
Coulomb, Jacques-Luc 55
Coward, Thomas 140
Crappé, Roland 19
Creutz, Admiral Lorentz 257, 282
Croisac 60
Cromwell, Oliver 98, 100–103, 175
Cronström, Daniel 186, 187, 188
Croon, Gert 173
Cuddalore 130

DAC 19, 21, 22, 23, 30, 147, 150, 152 156, 158

Dalerö 178
Dalsland 177, 180
Dannermarnagore 21, 29
Dannerskiold-Samsø, F 156, 159
Dartmouth 81
Dartmouth, Lord Admiral 111
Davidson, Thomas 141
Davis, Thomas 83–85, 93, 129
Day, Thomas 176, 179, 181–83
Deane, Anthony 102, 106, 107, 180
Degerberga Church 201
Delfshaven 78
Delft 16
Delizy, Nicolas 61, 63, 64
Delvaux, Laurent 161
Deptford 18, 19, 38, 98, 105, 110, 121, 129–131, 139, 161, 176, 198, 200
Dickerson, Frederick 140
Dickerson, James 140
Dickerson, Samuel 140
Dickerson, William 140
Dieppe 39
Djurgård shipyard 196, 203–205, 207,
Dokkum 66
Doluiar, I 188
Dominique 130
Dordrecht 79, 82
Dou, Gérard 188
Douwe, Franciscus Carolus 73, 79, 93
Douwe, François jr 73, 80, 81, 87, 93
Douwe, François sr 73, 76, 77, 82, 93
Douwe, Johannes Hubertus 88
Douwe, Micheal van 73
Douwe, Willem van, jr 79, 80, 81, 87 93
Douwe, William van, sr 71, 73, 76, 93
Dowglass, Captain 104
Drake, Francis 14, 15, 119
Drapers' Company 105, 106, 125
Drottningholm palace 184, 202,
Dunkirk 39, 45, 49, 53, 188
Dupin, Charles 64
Dupleix, Joseph François 26
Duquesne, Admiral 44
Duquesnoy, François 68
Dyck, Anthony van 96, 97, 100
Dynekien, Battle of 184

Edgar, King 97
Edinburgh 29
Eekhout, J B 91
Eertvelt, Andries van 14
Ehrenskiöd, Eric 185
Ehrensvärd, Augustin 203, 204
Ehrensvärd, Carl August 45, 48, 57, 58, 204, 205, 207,
Eigtved, Nicolaj 164
Ekekrantz, Niklas 201, 202, 205, 209
Elizabeth I, Queen (Eng) 15
Ellerstsen, Baltasar 144, 145, 168
Elton (captain) 47
Ely 162
Enander, Nicolaus 183, 184, 209
Enkhuizen 66, 78, 91, 94
Epping Forest 102
Eriksberg 212
Eriksberg shipyard 305
Euston, Henry Earl of 110

Falk, Karl 196, 198, 199
Faouédic, La 25
Fast, Gustaf Johan 202, 204
Fishmongers' Company 125
Fitch, Ralph 15
Fitzroy, Henry Duke of 110
Fletcher, John 98, 141
Fletcher, Mathew 98, 113, 141, 142
Fletcher, Thomas 98, 100, 103, 107, 111, 113
Floris, Cornelis 170
Floriszoon, Vice-Admiral 175
Fontana, Carlo 186
Forbin, Claude Chevalier de 111
Forest of Dean 102
Fort, Alexander 106
Four Days' Battle 103
Fredensborg Palace 161, 165,
Frederick I, King (Sw) 33
Frederik III, King (Dk) 20, 143, 147
Frederik IV, King (Dk) 151
Frederik V, King (Dk) 157, 164
Frederiksborg slot 152
Frederikshald 144
Frederikshavn 165
Frederiksnagar 19, 22
Frederiksværn 165, 167
Fredrik Church 201
Fredrikstad 184
Fremantle, Thomas 59
Friends of Götheborg society 305
Fries, Daniel 196, 200
Friesland 66, 84

Geer, Louis de 173
Gellée, Claude 77
Gendt, Willem van 91
Genoa 43
George I, King (GB) 121, 123, 134
George II, King (GB) 130, 134
George III, King (GB) 136, 139
George IV, King (GB) 139
Gerdes, C P 209
German Church, Stockholm 169
Gerner, Andreas 159–162
Gert 209
Geslain, Blaise 57
Ghent, Willem W van 93
Ghent, Willem-Joseph van 68, 103
Gheselle, Joseph de 30
Gibbons, Grinling 71, 105, 106, 110, 115, 117, 125, 128, 140, 141
Gibbs, James 162
Gibraltar 19, 111, 134
Gilbert, Antoine 42, 63, 64
Gill, Abraham 194
Girardon, François 186, 64
Glavimans, P 91
Glückstad 21, 144, 145
Goddard 141
Goodsonn, Vice-Admiral 175
Goodwin Sands 107
Goosman, Gerrit 93
Gothenburg / Göteborg 30, 31, 32, 33, 34, 176, 178, 180–182, 184, 194, 200
Gottman, Lorent 200
Gouda 81
Grafton, Henry, Duke of 110, 111
Great Yarmouth 129

Greenwich 60, 98, 106, 119
Greenwich Hospital 119
Grenada 130
Grenoble 202
Groen, Hermanus van 93
Groignard, Antoine 57, 58
Groucé, Jean Jourdan de 26
Gught, Jean-Joseph van der 87
Guichen, de 58
Guidici, Jan 91
Guild of Coopers 73
Guild of St Luke 66, 73, 82, 188
Guild of Winemakers 73
Gustaf II Adolph, King (Sw) 169
Gustaf III Adolph, King (Sw) 205, 299
Gyldenløve Palace 147
Gyldenløve, Ulryk C 147, 149, 152
Gyldenløve, Ulryk F 147, 157

Haarlem 77
Haberdashers' Company 125
Habsburg dynasty 29
Hagman, Peter 209
Hague City Hall 82
Hall, John 125
Halland 179
Halldin, Gustaf 202
Hamburg 21, 30, 145, 186
Hampton Court 72, 115, 119,
Harding, Fisher *192 plate 11*
Hårleman Carl 199, 200
Harlingen 66, 84
Harwich 98, 106, 131
Hastings Bay 85
Hatfield House 97
Haven, Lambert van 148
Hawke, Edward Rear Admiral 55, 134
Hawkins, Captain William 17
Hawksmoor, Nicholas 119
Hedvig Eleonora, Queen (Sw) 184, 199
Heeren XVII 78, 85
Heimbrod, Johann C 151–155, 168
Helby, Joseph 141
Helligands Church 68, 69
Hellyer, Edward 140
Helsingør *175*
Helsinki 203
Herbst, N J 159
Herculaneum 54, 134
Herring, Richard 142
Het Loo Palace 72, 82
Heywood, Thomas 96, 97, 101
Hilhouse of Bristol 138
Hindelopen *64 plate 3*
Hisholm Castle 152
Hissingen 176
Hog, Captain 177
Holmen 144–147, 150, 152, 160, 162, 164, 167, 168
Holstein Slesvig 21, 174
Holy Roman Empire 29
Honourable East India Company 14, 17, 27, 29, 35, 123
Hong Kong 18
Hoogstraaten, Akida van 73
Hoorn 66, 78
Hoorn, Paridon van 169
Horsen Church *146*

Hôtel d'Assy 50
Hôtel de Toulouse 50
Hôtel de Ville, Paris 173
Houghton Hall 126
Hovjaktvarvet 186, 206
Hubac, Louis 63
Hugli river 19, 21, 26, 29
Hume, Alexander 29
Hunnebåden 211
Hunt, Abraham 142
Huppe, Aemilius 82
Huppe, Samuel 82
Hybertszoon, Arendt 169
Hybertszoon, Hendrik 169

Île Bourbon 25, 26, 27
Île d'Aix 134
Île de France 26, 27
Indes Orientales 25, 26
Ipswich 19, 174
Ireland, William 106
Isaacson, Richard 101
Isle of Wight 107
Ive, Samuel 140

Jacobsson, Hans 180, 209
Jakarta 16
James I, King (GB) 17, 95, 105
James II, King (GB) 72, 98, 111, 116, 117, 120
James VI, King (Scot) 105
Jamestown 16
Jardin, N H 164, 165
Java 19
Jedda 17
Jehangir, Emperor 17
Jerusalem 14
Jones, Inigo 95, 96, 105, 124
Jones, Robert 141
Jonquière, Admiral 130
Jonson, Ben 96
Jourdan de Groucé, Jean 26
Judichær, Nicolay P 152, 159
Judichær, Ole 149–155, 168, *192 plate 14*
Kalmar 183, 184, 185
Kalsson, Gilbert 198
Karl XI, King (Sw) *see* Charles XI
Karl XII, King (Sw) *see* Charles XII
Karlskrona 183, 185–189, 194, 196–198, 201, 202, 203, 205–207
Keast, Nathaniel 141
Keerbergen, Johannes 91, 92, 93
Keiller, James 211
Kempenfelt, Admiral 134
Kent, William 106, 124–126, 129
Kentish Knock, Battle of 71
Kew Gardens 133
Keyser, Thoms de 70
Kinsale 47
Kirtlington 162
Klingenberg, Poul 21
Köge Bay, Battle of 144, 149, 185
Kohl, Anna Beata 196
Kolding, Peder Jensen 145, 146
Kongsbakke, Eskild 20
König, Hindrich 31, 32
Korsør, Povl Hansen 20
Krabbe, Michael 165–167
Krag, Rasmus 153–155

Kristianstad 201
Krock, Hendrich 149–150, 162
Kronborg Castle *148*, 151, 160, *175*
Kruus, Jesper 170

La Bourdonnais, B F M de 26
La Faouédic 25
La Fayette, General 60
La Rochelle 44
Lancaster, James 15
Lange, Jean 56, 64
Langley Park 162
Lantore 17
Launay, de (goldsmith) 40
Lauridsdatter, Birgitte 157
Lavasseur, Pierre-Noel 63
Lavasseur, René 45
Law, John 26
Le Brun, Charles 38, 40, 41, 43, 44, 45, 46, 47, 63, 72 75, 104, 184–89
Le Clerc, Louis August 162, 164
Le Havre 39, 45
Le Lorrain, Louis-Joseph 59
Le Nôtre 38
Le Vau, Louis 38, 184
Leadman, John 103, 110, 122, 141
Leden, Marcus 209
Leeward islands 55
Legeret, Jean 63
Legge, George 110
Leiden 68, 188
Leijonbergh Barkman, Sir Johan 175, 177
Lely, Peter *64 plate 8*
Lenman, Hans 194, 195, 199
Leopold I, Holy Roman Emperor 186
Lépautre, Jean 186, 190
Lescallier, Daniel 59, 63
Lewis, Allen 107, 122
Leyel, William 20
Lightfoot, Luke 134
Lindemann, Magdalene 162
Lindholmen 185, 198
Lindsay, Thomas 144
Linnell, John 133
Linnell, William 133
Lisbon 14
Little Easton 162
Ljung, Johan 207, 209
Ljung, Per 207, 209
Lock, Mathias 131, 133
Löderup Church 201
Loftus, John 106
London 104, 105, 200
Longueneux, Romaut 64
Lorient 25, 26, 134
Lorrain, Claude 77
Lou, Frans 183
Louis XIII, King (Fr) 38
Louis XIV, King (Fr) 25, 38, 39, 41, 48, 72, 73 77, 116, 188, 199
Louis XV, King (Fr) 49, 52, 54
Louis XVI, King (Fr) 52
Louisbourg 47, 54,
Louisbourg, Battle of 60
Louise, Queen (Dk) 157
Louvre 8, 186
Lowestoft 103
Lowndes, William 106

Lubet, Pierre-Philippe 59, 60
Luijpen, Pieter F 93
Lund, University 197
Luny, Thomas 17

Macao 152
Mackett, William 33, 34, 194, 199
Madagascar 25
Madras 27
Madrid 77
Magellan Straits 15, 16
Mahé de la Bourdonnais *see* La Bourdonnais
Maillard, the elder 188
Malacca 16
Malaga, Battle of 77
Maintenon, Madame de 40
Maritima 11
Marot, Daniel 72, 73, 79, 80, 82, 87, 106, 125,
   134, 223
Marot, Jean 72
Marseilles 40, 41, 42, 43
Martin, Elias 204
Martinique 58
Mary, Queen (GB) 106, 120
Mascarene 25
Masefield, John 11
Masreliez, Adrien 202, 204, 205, 207, 209
Masreliez, Jean Baptiste 207
Masreliez, Louis Adrien 207
Mast, Cornelis 92, 93
Masulipatnam 19
Mathias, Jean 41, 63
Mattingly, Cuthbert 128, 140
Mattingly, William 128, 140
Maucard, Jean-Ange 64
Mauritius 26, 27
Mauritshuis, Amsterdam 67
May, John 83, 90, 93
May, William 90, 93
Maynard, Lord William 162
Maynard, Thomas 162
Mayne, Jonathon 106
Maystre, Balthasar 89, 90, 91, 93
Maystre, Evert 91, 92, 93
Mazarin, Cardinal 39
Mechelen 68
Medici, Cosimo III de' 106
Medway 103
Meer, van der 86
Meknes 31
Mesié, Pierre-Jacques 27
Messonnier, Juste-Aurèle 52, 30
Mesterton, Eva Maria 191
Michelangelo 43
Michelsen, Peder 151, 168
Middelburg 66, 78
Miklagård 13
Mission Française de Chine 25, 26
Mississippi Bubble 26
Moerman, Cornelis 73, 93
Moerman, Gretel 74
Moerman, Jan W 74
Moerman, Maartje 4
Moerman, Willem 74
Møllerup, C J 166–168
Monamy, Peter 114
Mondon, Jean 50, *53*
Montague (Lord Sandwich) 102, 175

Morley, John 141
Moscow 31

Nantes 26
Naples 77, 83, 203
Napoleon Bonaparte, Emperor 17, 23, 34, 91
Nelson, Admiral Lord 59, 137, 138,
Nerger, Christian 190
Nerpin, Henrik 209
Neuenfelde 186
Nicholls, Maynard 128, 140
Nile, Battle of 138
Nooms, Reinier 76
Norden, F L 159
Nordin, L 209
Norrvidinge 182
Norske Veritas 305
Nürnberg 75
Nya Varvet shipyard 200
Nyholm yard 144
Nyköping Church 184

Oderljunga Church 201
Öland 178, 182
Oldenburg 186
Olérys, Jean-Baptiste 63
Ollivier, Blaise 58
Olsen, Nils 151, 168
Oostenburg 72
Oostende Company 21, 29, 31, 32, 34
Oppenard, Gilles-Marie 50
Öresund sound 69, 102, 175, 193
Orientales de Madagascar 25
Orléans, Duc d' 49
Orvilliers, Count d' 59
Orwell river 131
Oskarsham 219
Oslo 144
Ostend 29
Övertorneå Church 169
Oxford Camera *162*

Paestum 134
Palais du Luxembourg 173
Palladio, Andrea 95, 124, 125, 127, *192 plate 15*
Papegaaij, Jacob 93
Parenteau, Jean-Joseph 63
Paris 50, 59, 157, 186, 203
Parks, Captain 104
Paulsen, Johan Anthon 152, 154
Pavey, Kingston 140
Payne, John 96
Peace of Westphalia 29
Peking 26
Pepys, Samuel 98, 101, 102, 106, 107, 110, 111
   177
Perstorp Church 201
Pessart, Behrendt 19, 20
Peter the Great, Tsar 203
Petit, Paul 125
Pett, Peter *64 plate 8*, 96, 98
Pett, Phineas *64 plate 8*, 96, 102, 106–108, 180
Petter 209
Philip II, King (Sp) 15
Phillips (lieutenant) 47
Phillips, Henry 106, 140
Pic, Augustin 56
Pierce, Thomas 140

Pippin, John 140
Pirenne, Henri 13
Plymouth 127, 128, 139
Poll, Christina van der 73
Pomerania 31, 194, 203
Pompadour, Madame de 52, 56
Pompeii 54, 134
Pondicherry 25, 26, 27, 130
Port Louis (Île de France) 26
Port Louis 25, 44
Portsmouth 83, 107, 121, 134
Precht, Buchard 186, 189, 190, 201
Precht, Christian 186
Puerto Rico 15
Puget, Pierre 40, 43, 50, 64, 76, 104, 187
Pulo Ron 17
Pyrenees, Peace of 29

Quebec 44
Queens Harbour, Cork 111
Queens House 95
Quellin, Arnold 71, 106,
Quellin, Artus 67–68, 71, 73, 75, 83, 89
Quellin, Artus II 71, 157
Quellin, Thomas 71, 157
Quenington, Gloucester 119
Quiberon Bay 134

Radcliffe, John 162
Rahm, Olof 196
Rajalin, Admiral Thomas von 197, 198
Réunion 27
Read, Phillip 140
Red House, Bristol *113*
Redtmer, Mårtin 169–171, 173, 209
Rehn, Jean Eric 199, 202, 203, 207
Rembrandt, Harmensz van Rijn 70, 188
Renard, Nicolas 63
Renault de Beavallon, Françoise 45
Reventlow, Anna Sophie 151
Reynolds, Robert 106, 140
Rheen, Jan van 78, 93
Richards, James 106, 125, 126, 140
Riddarhus 172, 173
Riga 183, 185
Rige, Agnetha 186
Robbins, James 144
Rochefort 39, 44, 47, 56, 58, 59, 60, 61, 134, 205
Rodney, Admiral Sir George 58, 130
Roe, Sir Thomas 17
Rogers, Henry Huddleston, models collection
   110–113, 118, 135
Rome 38, 44, 65, 68, 75, 203
Rood, Jan 91
Root, Gunar Olofsson 182
Rosenburg 74, 76
Roskilde 161
Roth, Gunnar 185, 186
Rotherhithe 111
Rotterdam 66, 73, 78
Rubens, Sir Peter 96
Ruyter, Michiel de *64 plate 4*, 68, 69, 103

SOIC 29, 30, 31, 32, 199, 200, 203, 212
Sahlgren, Niclas 31, 32
Sailmaker, Isaac 114
St Cosmae 186
St Elena 15, 16, 17

Saint-Florent 59
St Jakob Church 173
St James Church 186
St James' Day Fight 103
St Katherine's Dock 86
St Laurens Church, Rotterdam 82, 87
St Malo 26, 39
St Pancras Church 186
San Domingo 55
San Fiorenzo 59
Santa Clara Church 205
Sartine, Gabriel de 59
Savage, Edward 141
Savage, William 136–138, 141, 142
Sawyer, Lewis 140
Scheemaker, Pieter 161
Scheveningen, Battle of 71
Schleitz 157
Schonamille, François de 30
Schor, Paul 75
Schrijver, Cornelis 77, 83, 84
Schrijver, Philip 77, 83
Schubert, Maria Anna 169
Schultz, Hendrik 183–185, 191, 193, 209
Schultz, Jost (Schütz) 173, 174, 179, 180, 183, 209
Schultz, Nicolaus (Clas) 183, 209
Schumacher, H R 159
Schut, Pieter H 70
Scorf Estuary 25
Serampore 19, 21, 23,
Sergel, Johan 203
Sheerness 88, 98, 103, 131, 137
Sheldon, Charles 181, 186, 187, 189, 190, 191 193, 197–200
Sheldon, Francis 97, 98, 102, 145–149, 176–180, 182, 183
Sheldon, Frans Johan 181, 183–186, 198
Sheldon, Gilbert 191, 193, 196–198, 199, 200
Sheldonian theatre 105
Sheraton, Thomas 138
Shish, Jonas 186
Shish, Thomas 110, 121, 186
Simonsson, Ebbe 176
Sinclair, Daniel 144
Sjöhielm, Henrik 177, 178
Skåna 178, 201
Skeppsgården 173
Skeppsholmen 180–185
Slegt, Gerbrand 83, 93
Slesvig-Holstein 21, 174
Smith, Humphrey 162
Smith, Imossi & Co 19
Smith, Robert 121, 140
Smith, W H 19
Smith, William 194–197, 140
Smitt, Ipsa 181
Société Dilettanti 134
Société Jourdan 26
Sohlberg, Harold 202, 203
Sole Bay, Battle of 108
Söndre Harritslev *64 plate 3*
Soop, Hans 169
South Sea Bubble 29
Span, Admiral Henrik 146, 149, *149,*
Spanish Armada 119
Sparre, Admiral 193, 194,
Spence, Robert 100

Spendelow, Peter 30
Spithead 111, 134
Stade 186
Stanley, Carl Frederick 162, 168
Stanley, Simon Carl 161–166
Stapert, S J 93
Start Point 81
Stavern 167
Steenwinkel, Hans van 143, 148, 152
Steenwinkel, Laurens 152
Stenburger, Mathias 201
Stockholm 66, 76, 185, 186, 188, 194 , 200
Stockholm Castle 170, 186, 188, 199, 202, 204
Stockholm Cathedral 170, 189
Stockholm Riddarhuset *172*
Stora Stad shipyard 194
Storck, Abraham *64 plate 4,* 5
Store Bælt 147
Stralsund 194
Strandegade *157*
Strussflycht, Admiral Daniel 176–178
Stuart, James 134
Stubbeköbing 147
Sturmberg, Johan Christian 161
Sunda 33
Sundberg, Peter 207, 209
Surat 17, 29
Svansköld, Abraham 188
Svea 203, *204*
Sveaborg 203–205
Swant, Clas 183, 209
Sweers, Isaac Admiral 83
Swerus, J 93

Table Bay 15, 16
Tangiers 31, 111
Tanjore 19, 20
Tanjore, Nayak of 19
Terra Nova shipyard 194, 199, 211, *212–223*
Tessin, Carl Gustav 199
Tessin, Nicodemus jr 186–190, 199, 200, 201
Tessin, Nicodemus sr 184, 186,
Texel 85
Thesson, Johann 170, 172, *192 plate 20,* 209
Thomas, William 119
Thurah, Diderik de 152, 153, 156–160, 162 164, 165
Thurah, Lauritz de 158, 164
Tordenskiold, Admiral 194
Törnström, Johan 202, 204, 205, 207, 209
Toro, Bernard 64
Toulon 39, 40, 42, 43, 50, 56, 59, 61, 83, 129
Toxverd, Franz 160
Trægaard, Hans 19
Trafalgar, Battle of 35
Tranquebar 19, *20,* 21, 22, 23, 30, 144
Tre Kronor Castle 169
Treaty of Nijmegen 38
Treaty of Nystad 31
Treaty of the Pyrenees 25
Trèves Hall (Hague) 82
Triewald, Mårten 198, 211
Trinidad 15
Tripoli 167
Trolle, Henrik af 204
Tromp, Maerten Admiral *64 plate 5,* 71
Tullgarn Palace 207
Turesen, A 159, 160, 162, 165

Turner, Elisabet 185
Turner, Ringo 185
Turner, Robert 176, 179–184, 185
Turreau, Pierre 63
Tuscany, Duke of 106

US Naval Academy 110
Uggla, Admiral 182
Urban II, Pope 14
Ushant, Battle of 58
Utrecht 82, 170

VOC 16, 18, 19, 31, 70, 72, 74, 78–81, 83 84, 86, 90, 105
Vallée, Jean 173
Vallée, Marin 173
Vallée, Simon de la 172, 173, 184
Vambourg, Louis-Adolphe 63
Van Dyck, Anthony 96, 97, 100
Van Velden shipyard 176
Vanbrugh, John 119
Vänern Lake 177
Värmland 177, 180
Vassé, Antoine 49, 50–53, 54, 56, 63, 64, 155
Västervik 196
Vaux-le-Vicomte (chateau) 184
Velde, van de, Willem, jr 72, 107
Velde, van de, Willem, sr 39, 71, 72, 100, 101, 105, 144, 173
Velius, T 69
Venice 26
Verhulst, Rombout 68, 82, 83, 93
Vermeer, Marijte 74
Vernon, Sir Edward 128
Versailles 38, 39, 40, 43, 45, 47, 50, 149, 186 187, 206
Verschuier, Lieve 76, 93
Verschuier, Pieter C 76, 93
Veyrier, Christopher 64
Vicars, Sebastian 141
Vienna, Congress of 27
Vigo Bay, Battle of 111
Villiers, Barbara 110
Vinga 211
Vis, Dingeman van der 93
Visscher, Claes J 70
Visser, Solomon de 87, 93
Vlaming, P 90
Vlieger, Simon de 72
Vlissingen 66, 73
Vor Frelsers Church *190*
Vriend, Adriaen de 73
Vries, Hans Vredeman de 170

Wachtmeister, Admiral 185.189, 197
Wade, Joseph 141
Waerdeniers, Emmerentia 73
Waghenaer L J 14
Waldau, Jacob 191, 193, 194, 199, 201, 209
Walker, Richard 141
Walpole, Sir Robert 126
Ware, Isaac 126, 127, 134
Warren, Sir William 102, 177
Wars:
  American Independence 27, 34, 60
  Anglo-Dutch, 1st 70
  Anglo-Dutch, 2nd 104
  Anglo-Dutch, 3rd 104

Austrian Succession 54
Great Northern 21, 31, 149, 150, 189, 193
Scanian 144, 146
Seven Years 54
Spanish Succession 29, 77
Thirty Years 19, 29, 31, 143
Waterloo 17
Waterperry House 125
Wegersløff, F 159
Welshuizen, Christian 169
Werner, Johan 183
Wessel, Peter 194
Westminster 162
Westphalia 169
Westphalia, Peace of 29
Wexford 149
Whitehall 98, 106
Whitfield, George 141
Wiedewelt, Hans 157
Wiedewelt, Johannes 157, 165
Wiedewelt, Just 157–166, 168, *192 plates 16–18*
Willerup, F C 167, 168, 168
William & Mary, King & Queen (GB) 72, 113–118, 123
William III, of Orange, King (GB) 38, 72, 73, 83, 91, 106, 111, 119
Williams, George 137, 141, 142
Williams, Robert Price 142
Wilmington, Earl 161
Windsor Castle 106
Wismar 31
With, Corneliszoon de 175
Witt, Cornelis de 103
Witt, Jacob de 79
Woolwich 96, 98, 100, 103, 106, 110, 121 134, 139, 200
Worm, Lauritz Hansen 144, 145, 168
Worm, Tyge Lauritzen 145, 147, 150, 151, 168
Wren, Sir Christopher 105, 106, 117, 119, 120
Wrotham Park 134
Wyatt, James 142
Wymhurst, Joseph 113, 141
Wynantz, Abraham 186

York, Duke of 103, 108
Yorktown 60
Ystad 201

Zwijndregt, Leendert 87, 88, 90, 91
Zwijndregt, Paulus van 78, 80, 81, 86–88, 91
Zwijndregt, Pieter 87, 91

INDEX OF SHIPS
Italic entries denote illustrations

Ship lists

Danish East India Co 23–24
French East India Co 27–28
Swedish East India Co 35–36

Abraham's Offerhande (NL) *64 plate 3*
Actif (F) 60
Admiral von Hamburg (G) 186
Agamemnon (GB) 59
Agatha (Dk) 23

Agréable (F) *205*
Aimable (F) *155, 156*
Amarant (Sw) 173–*174*
Amphion (Sw) 207
Amphitrite (O) 26
Amphytrite (F) 45
Amsterdam (NL) 16, 85, 86
Anglesey (GB) 47, 161
Antelope (GB) 101
Antoinette (Dk) 23
Äpplet (Sw) 178, 182
Apollo (O/Sw) 30, 34
Apollon (F) 47, *48*, 161
Argos (F) *43*
Arniston (GB) 131
Assuré (F) *49*
Arveprinsessen (Dk) 22
Augusta (GB) 47, 161, *224*, 226

Babet (F) 61
Bellona (GB) 88
Berschermer (NL) *91*
Blå Hager (Dk) 194
Blandford (GB) 124
Blekinge (Sw) 185
Boekenrode (NL) *84*, 85
Boot (NL) *81*, 82
Boyne (GB) *192 plate 11*
Brederode (NL) *71*
Bremen (Sw) 193
Briel (NL) 76, 77
Brillant (F) *48, 49*
Britannia (GB) 111, *112–115*, 119
Buckingham (GB) 134
Ça Ira (F) 58
Cambridge (GB) 130
Captain (GB) *120–122*
Carolus (Sw) 173, 174
Carolus XI (Sw) *183*, 184
Charles VI (O) 29
Castor (Sw) 198
Célèbre (F) 201
Christiana (Dk) 167
Christianshavn (Dk) 23
Christianus Quintus (Dk) 146
Christianus Sextus (Dk) 156
Cleopâtre (F) 61
Comercie (NL) 92
Comet (Dk) 167
Commonwealth (GB) 98
Concorde (F) 60
Concordia (O) 30
Coronation (GB) 101
Cromhout (NL) 22
Couronne (F) 53, 57, *58*
Dam (NL) 74
Damiaten (NL) 84
Dannebroge (Dk) 149, *167*, 168
Dannemark (Dk) 165
Dauphin (F) *58, 205*
Dauphin Royal (F) 56, 58
Delfin (Sw) 183
Den Flyvende Ulv (Sw) 144
Desire (GB) 16
Diadème (F) 58
Dordrecht (NL) 87
Dover (GB) 55
Dragen (Dk) 167

Draken (Sw) 174, 177
Drapers' Company barge (GB) 106, 125
Dristigheden (Dk) 167
Droning Lowisa (Dk) 148, *149*
Droning Lovisa (Dk) *160*
Dronning Anna Sophia (Dk) 151
Drott Hedvig Eleonora (Sw) 185
Drottningholm (Sw) 196
Drottning Lovisa Ulrica (Sw) 196
Drottning Ulrika Eleonora (Sw) 34, 185, 191, 193
Dunkirk (GB) 78
Duyfken (NL) *16*

Edward Bonaventure 15
Elephanten (Dk) *147, 192 plate 14*, 187–189, 195, 224
Eendracht (NL) 76, 103
Enigheten (Sw) *189*, 190, *191, 192 plate 21, 196–198, 203*
Entreprenant (F) *205*

Fäderneslandet (Sw) *206*
Færø (Dk) 21
Falster (Dk) 164
Fama (Sw) 198, 200
Favorite (F) *40*
Fenix (Sw) 173, 174
Finland (Sw) 199
Fishmongers' Company barge (GB) 106
Flying Greyhound (GB) 177
Fredericus Rex (Sw) 194, 196
Fredericus Rex Sueciae (Sw) 33, 34, 194
Fredericu Quintus (Dk) 162, *163, 164*, 165,
Freden (Sw) 195
Friheten (Sw) *194, 195*, 196
Foudroyant (F) *50, 52*, 56, 155, 157
Fyen (Dk) 156, *158–162, 192 plates 15–18*, 224

Galathé (Sw) *206*
Gelderland (NL) *77*
Gloire (F) *51*
Göta Rike (Sw) 185
Göteborg (Sw) *206*
Götheborg (Sw) 33, 34, 161, *192 plate 23*, 199, 200, 211, *219*, 223, *227–229*
Gouda (NL) 76
Gouden Leeuw (NL) *64 plate 5*
Graaf Floris (NL) *70*
Grafton (GB) 109, *110*, 111
Grand Réale (F) 41
Guirlande (F) 55
Gunilla (Sw) 219
Gustaf Adolph IV (Sw) *192 plate 22, 207*

Haberdashers' barge (GB) 125
Hampton Court (GB) 98
Hannibal (Dk) *144*
Heathcote (GB/Sw) 34
Henry (GB) 101
Hercules (NL) 91
Hermes (GB) 104
Hermione (F) 60, 61, *62, 64 plate 1–2*
Hertogh van Lorreyman (O) 30, 33
Hollandia 1595 (NL) *14*, 16,
Hollandia 1665 (NL) *69*
Hörten (Sw) 174
Hummeren (Dk) *145*, 146

Inconstant (GB) 59
Intrepide (F) 58
Ipswich (GB) *37*
Isis (GB) 129

Jarramas (Sw) *201*
Java (GB) *18*, 19
Jersey (GB) *127–129, 225*
Johanna Francisca (NL) 91
Jonge Jacob (NL) *78*, 79
Josias van Aspen (O) 30

Karlskrona (Sw) 185
Katherine (GB) 108
Kent (GB) 111
Keyserinne Elisabeth (O) 31
Kongen af Danmark (Dk) 22, 156
Konung Adolf Fredrik (Sw) 202
Konung Adolph Friedrich (Sw) 196
Konung Gustaf III (Sw) 205
Konung Karl (Sw) 186, *187*, 188, 189, 199
Kronan (Dk) 148
Kronan (Sw) 179–181, *182*
Kronprinsessen (Dk) 22

Laurier (F) 43
Leopard (GB) 129
Leopoldus Primus (G) 186
Lion (GB) 101
Litchfield (GB) *224*
Livery Company barge (GB) 106
Lolland (Dk) 174
London (GB) 101, 108, 178,
Lord Mayor's barge (GB) 106
Louisa Augusta (Dk) 22
Lovisa Ulrika (Sw) 203, 225
Lowisa (Dk) 148, *149*
Loyal London (GB) 104
Lutine (F) 61
Maas (N) *80*, 72, 76
Madame (F) *43*
Magicienne (F) *61*
Mandigheden (Dk) 167
Maria (Sw) 183
Mary yacht (GB) 104, *105*
Mary (GB) 107
Mars, 36 guns (NL) 90
Mars, 60 guns (NL) *90*
Mathias (GB) 104
Mauritius (NL) *14*, 16,
Merchant Royal (GB) 15
Mercure (F) 154
Minerva (GB) *135*, 136
Minerva (Sw) *206*
Møen (Dk) *165*, 166
Monarque (F) *55*
Monmouth (GB) 84
Montague (GB) 98

Naseby (GB) *99*, 100, *101*, 102, 103, 106, 108,
    110, 111, 145, 175–177, *181*
Neptune (GB) 104, 121, 122
Neptune (F) 44
Neptunus (O) 200
Néréide (F) 50–*51*
Nord Stjärnan (Sw) *193*
Norden (Dk) 23
Nordstiernen (Dk) 193

Norfolk (GB) 104
Norge (Dk) 22
Norske Løve (Dk) 166
Northumberland (GB) *17*
Nykeln (Sw) 179, 182
Nymphe (F) 61

Old James (GB) 104
Oldenborg (Dk) 148, *159*
Oresund (Dk) *167*
Ossory (GB) 121, 122
Overijssel (NL) *14*

Paris (F) *44*
Penelope (GB) 15
Perlen (Dk) *167*
Pieter Paulus (NL) 91, *92*
Pléiade (F) 56
Pommern (Sw) 185
Postiljonen (Sw) *176, 178,* 179, *181*
Prince (GB) 107, *108,* 109, 112, 180
Prince Edward (GB) 90
Prince Frederick barge (GB) 106, *125*
Prince George (GB) 136
Prince Karl Fredrik (Sw) 193
Prince of Orange (GB) 92
Prince van Orange (NL) *64 plate 7*
Princess Carolina (NL) *88,* 89
Princess Caroline (GB) 88
Prindsesse Sophia Hedwig (Dk) *155*
Prins Friso (NL) 84
Prins Gustaf (Sw) *200*
Prinsessan Sophia Albertina (Sw) 201, *202*
Printz Frederik (Dk) 146
Printz Friderich (Dk) *153,166*
Provincie van Utrecht (NL) 84

Queen Mary shallop (GB) 106

Réale (F) 41
Renommée (F) *54,* 55
Renown (GB) 55
Requin (F) *42*
Resolution (GB) 106, *107,* 175
Riksäpplet (Sw) 177–179
Rigernes Ønske (Dk) 166
Rotterdam (NL) *64 plate 6, 77, 80, 87*
Royal Charles (GB) 100–104, 110, 111
Royal George (GB) *192 plate 13,* 134
Royal Louis (F) 44
Royal Oak (GB) *37,* 104
Royal Thérèse (F) *44,* 50
Royal William (GB) 108
Rynhurse (NL) 81

St Andrew (GB) 108, 111
St Esprit (F) 128
St George (GB) *64 plate 10*
St Michael (GB) *64 plate 9,* 108, 109
Samsøe (Dk) 162
San Felipe (P) 15
Sans Pareil (F) 59, 61
Saturnus (Sw) 179
Schiedam (NL) 87
Sérieux (F) 56, 59
Slesvig (Dk) 22, *150–152,* 155
Snaren Sven (Sw) 198
Södermanland (Sw) 186

Soleil Royal (F) 46, 47, *52*
Solen (Sw) 179
Somerset (GB) *10, 131*–133
Sophia Amalia (Dk) 144
Sophia Hedwig (Dk) 155
Sophia Magdalena (Dk) 152, *153, 166*
Souverain (F) 44
Sovereign (GB) 98, 100, 111, 175
Sovereign of the Seas (GB) *64 plate 8, 96,* 101,
    111
Staaten Generaal (NL) 91
Stadhoder jacht (NL) 82
Staten jacht (NL) 79
Stenbock (Sw) *84,* 185
Sterling Castle (GB) 137
Suecia (Sw) 30, 34
Superbe (F) 60
Svanen (Dk) 144, 154–156
Svärdet (Sw) 179, 182
Svarta Örn (Sw) 194
Sverige (Sw) 183
Swiftsure (GB) 134

Terra Nova (Sw) 33
Tre Croner (Dk) 159, *192 plate 19*
Tre Cronor (Sw) 30, 34
Tre Løver (Dk) 144, *148, 154,* 155, 159
Triton (GB) *139*
Trusty (GB) *138*

Unity (GB) 104
Utrecht (NL) 91

Valfisken (Sw) *206*
Valiant (GB) 104
Vasa (Sw) *67, 76,* 169, *170, 171, 181, 192 plate
    20, 211*
Vengeur (F) *59*
Venus (Sw) 181
Victoria (Sw) 174, *185,* 186, 191
Victory (GB) 54, *137*
Vigilan (F) *205*
Vigilant (F) 130, 205
Vigilante (F) 55
Vildsvinet (Sw) *206*
Vita Örn (Sw) 194
Vriesland (N) 14

Wachmeister (Sw) 183
Wageningen (NL) 83
Wapen von Hamburg (G) 186
Washington (NL) 92
Willem V (NL) 88
William Rex (NL) 73, *74,* 75, 79
Woolwich (GB) 106

Yarmouth (GB) 129, *130,* 131, *192 plate 12,* 170,
    202

Zeven Provinciën (NL) *64 plate 4*